The Last Muslim Intellectual

Edinburgh Historical Studies of Iran and the Persian World

Published in association with Elahé Omidyar Mir-Djalali, Founder and Chair, Roshan Cultural Heritage Institute

R✲SHAN
CULTURAL HERITAGE
INSTITUTE

Series General Editor: Stephanie Cronin, Elahé Omidyar Mir-Djalali Research Fellow, University of Oxford

Series Advisory Board: Professor Janet Afary (UC Santa Barbara), Professor Abbas Amanat (Yale University), Professor Touraj Atabaki (International Institute of Social History), Dr Joanna de Groot (University of York), Professor Vanessa Martin (Royal Holloway, University of London), Professor Rudi Matthee (University of Delaware) and Professor Cyrus Schayegh (The Graduate Institute, Geneva)

Covering the history of Iran and the Persian world from the medieval period to the present, this series aims to become the pre-eminent place for publication in this field. As well as its core concern with Iran, it extends its concerns to encompass a much wider and more loosely defined cultural and linguistic world, to include Afghanistan, the Caucasus, Central Asia, Xinjiang and northern India. Books in the series present a range of conceptual and methodological approaches, looking not only at states, dynasties and elites, but at subalterns, minorities and everyday life.

Published and forthcoming titles

Religion, Orientalism and Modernity: The Case of the Babis and Baha'is in Iran
Geoffrey Nash

Remapping Persian Literary History, 1700–1900
Kevin L. Schwartz

Muslim-Christian Polemics in Safavid Iran
Alberto Tiburcio

The Last Muslim Intellectual: The Life and Legacy of Jalal Al-e Ahmad
Hamid Dabashi

edinburghuniversitypress.com/series/ehsipw

The Last Muslim Intellectual

The Life and Legacy of Jalal Al-e Ahmad

Hamid Dabashi

EDINBURGH
University Press

Edinburgh University Press is one of the leading university presses in the UK. We publish academic books and journals in our selected subject areas across the humanities and social sciences, combining cutting-edge scholarship with high editorial and production values to produce academic works of lasting importance. For more information visit our website: edinburghuniversitypress.com

Edinburgh University Press Ltd
The Tun – Holyrood Road
12 (2f) Jackson's Entry
Edinburgh EH8 8PJ

First published in hardback by Edinburgh University Press 2021

Typeset in 11/15 Adobe Garamond by
Servis Filmsetting Ltd, Stockport, Cheshire

A CIP record for this book is available from the British Library

ISBN 978 1 4744 7928 8 (hardback)
ISBN 978 1 4744 7929 5 (paperback)
ISBN 978 1 4744 7930 1 (webready PDF)
ISBN 978 1 4744 7931 8 (epub)

Published with the support of the University of Edinburgh Scholarly Publishing Initiatives Fund.

Contents

Figures

Acknowledgements

I shared the idea of this book with Edinburgh University Press after an initial consultation with my dear friend Adham Saouli, Senior Lecturer at the University of St Andrews, to whom I am grateful for having facilitated my initial contacts. Nicola Ramsey, Head of Editorial at Edinburgh University Press, soon took charge of the idea and in her capable hands the book proposal was accepted and I began working. Three anonymous reviewers offered constructive suggestions for which I am thankful. Stephanie Cronin, Elahé Omidyar Mir-Djalali Research Fellow at St Antony's College, University of Oxford had just assumed responsibility for a series for the press under the general heading of *Edinburgh Historical Studies of Iran and the Persian World*. I was delighted she graciously accepted my book in her series.

My dear friend Mahmoud Omidsalar as always has been a chief source for finding me obscure books from Iranian libraries and elsewhere. Without Omidsalar I'd be like that proverbial cat with half of my whiskers lost! In Tehran my old friend Ali Dehbashi was exceptionally generous with his time and resources. I am grateful for his help locating old pictures of Al-e Ahmad and kindly giving me permission to use his archive.

My research assistant Laila Hisham Fouad is my eyes and my mind in the winding labyrinth of Columbia University libraries – and a wizard with finding pdf copies of obscure books and articles. I would not be able to write without her diligent work. My distinguished colleague Peter Magierski, Middle East and Islamic Studies Librarian at Columbia University Libraries, has always been generous with his time and guidance. I am honoured by his friendship and blessed with his exquisite professionalism. The final shape of the book is indebted to the exceptional work of George MacBeth as the copy-editor to whom Edinburgh University Press had entrusted my prose. I am as finicky and possessive of my prose as any other critical thinker humouring himself that the world is awaiting his revelations. Two pages into George MacBeth's edits I breathed a sigh of relief I was in gentle and caring hands. I thank him for his exceptional gift of grace to allow me my signature prose and yet making sure my phrasings behave.

I thank all these good and godsent friends and colleagues who have given generously from their time and attention to enable me to write this book on Jalal Al-e Ahmad.

For my friends

Amir Naderi, Nicky Nodjoumi, Shirin Neshat, Shoja Azari, Susan Deyhim

And in memory of Ardeshir Mohassess (1938–2008) and Manouchehr Yektai (1921–2019)

The Last of 'the Mohicans'

Familiar Faces in a Foreign Land

We are not like the people south of the Twins and we are not like the people north of the Twins. In the Citadel, we lead different lives for different reasons. We are this world's memory, Samwell Tarly. Without us, men would be little better than dogs. Don't remember any meal but the last, can't see forward to any but the next. And every time you leave the house and shut the door, they howl like you're gone forever.

Archmaester Ebrose (to Samwell Tarly), *Game of Thrones* – Season 7 Episode 1: 'Dragonstone' (7×01)

Introduction:
'The Last Muslim Intellectual'

I thought if I were to deliver a paper in this conference, I'd say
that the first anthropologists were following Alexander the Great,
then following Christianity and then Islam. In other words,
anthropologists have always camped with world conquerors. Alexander
was the best among them, and [the age of] machine the worst. In other
words, what is called 'anthropology' or 'ethnography' etc. have all been
there because world conquerors needed to know the people they were
going to rule.[1]

Jalal Al-e Ahmad, *Safar-nameh-ye Rus*
(*The Russian Travelogue*) (1964)

He lived a very short life. His biography is well known and documented.
He came from a learned Shiʻa family, but soon dispensed with any
form of formal higher education, seminarian or secular. He read and travelled widely, wrote vociferously, married one of the towering literary masters
of his time and died childless at the prime age of forty-six having squeezed
every ounce of energy from his weak, fragile and agitated bones. Today we
do not remember him as a mortal human being, for he has been turned into
an allegory of himself, a metaphor for our time, emblematic of something
larger than himself. A poet once referred to him as the man who was 'the
summary of himself'. That poet later denied his poem was meant for whom
we all thought he meant it. He was stretching the truth. He, on the other
hand, independent of anyone else's devotion or damnation, was true – bone,
blood, courage, conviction, anger, love, hope, despair and then a prose he
commanded and drove, sharpened and used as a swordsman would his
sword.

Remembrance of Things Past

How does one write about such a towering intellectual figure without either lionising or demonising him? I was born and raised to Al-e Ahmad's prose, came to political maturity with his politics and when, one fine day at college in Tehran in the early 1970s, a leading intellectual of my youth wrote something critical of him I could not sleep for days. My mind had been turned upside down. Today, long after my college years in Tehran, I have neither nostalgia for Al-e Ahmad nor regret for my youthful fascinations with him, neither adulation for his myth nor an ahistorical condemnation of his reality. I went through Al-e Ahmad as they say all healthy sons go with their mortal fathers. When they are young, they think their father is the greatest man who ever was. When they grow older and enter their teenage years, they wonder how an idiot like that could be their father, and a few years into their own adulthood they discover their father is just a man like any other man. Al-e Ahmad though was not a man like any other man – nor was he a father to any son or daughter. Not being able to father any child was a major trauma of his and his wife Simin Daneshvar's lives. Thirty years after I first put pen to paper and wrote on Al-e Ahmad and other formative forces of the Iranian revolution of 1977–9, some forty years after that revolution and now close to half a century after I left my homeland for good and left all my youthful credulities behind, I had an urge to go back to Al-e Ahmad and rethink him through. This book is the fulfilment of that urge. First, I missed reading him, and when I began to reread him, I discovered why I had missed reading him. I did not miss the substance of his writings, which I knew quite well, but the soul of his musings that still roamed in the chambers of my memories; not the subjects of his contentions, which I knew by heart, but the music of his prose that still echoed in my mind. I knew there was something in Al-e Ahmad I had left behind when I last read him cover to cover. I wrote this book to share that discovery. To be sure, I am not the only Iranian of my generation or even younger who has been preoccupied by Jalal Al-e Ahmad. Over the last forty years, and in fact even earlier and soon after his death, Al-e Ahmad (1923–69) has been the subject of a plethora of articles and essays on his life and thoughts, particularly in Persian and especially in his own homeland. Everyone seems to be either drawn to or repelled by him. The ruling regime in Iran loves him for all the wrong reasons. The new cadre of neoliberal detractors of the Islamic Republic hates him for even more false reasons. Most these shorter or longer essays therefore fall into two major categories, extremely laudatory and panegyric, or else unfairly critical, damning and dismissive. His admirers adore him, whilst his political enemies despise him and hold him responsible for the atrocities of the Islamic Republic – ignoring the fact that he died decades before Khomeini returned to Iran to launch his tyranny. He has therefore become something of an Oedipal figure – as if without simultaneously loving and killing him his admirers or detractors cannot be born as adults. That psychopathology seems to dwell in the hidden labyrinths of all postcolonial nationhood.

Figure I.1 Jalal Al-e Ahmad, Tehran, c. 1957. (Photo courtesy of Ali Dehbashi, from the *Bokhara Magazine* archive) Who took this picture, what was the reason, occasion, purpose? Most of Al-e Ahmad's pictures were obviously taken by his close friends and family. Though on most occasions we do not know who these photographers are, what remains constant is how Al-e Ahmad commands attention, and how entirely self-absorbed he is in these photographs. His gaze is at once specific and far-reaching, detailed and universal, as the camera probes to discover something behind the placid face. There is a powerful element of nostalgia in these mostly black-and-white photographs when we look at them today, at once reminiscent of bygone ages and yet visually conscious and expectant of things to come.

There is a paradoxical blessing to be found therefore in staying far away from that pathology, and reading Al-e Ahmad in his own healthy and robust Persian and writing of him in a liberated and expansive English. This linguistic dissonance opens up liberating horizons for a healthy dose of critical thinking that disallows undue parental deference and thus keeps misplaced Oedipal instincts at bay. Almost all of Al-e Ahmad's major critical essays and some of his literary works have been translated into English and other European languages by competent scholars, to which learned introductions have been added. That has given Al-e Ahmad a distant but solid place to breathe normally outside his own home and habitat. It is not accidental that to this day the single most comprehensive study of all of Al-e Ahmad's output remains my own chapter on him in my *Theology of Discontent* (1993), which I wrote in the larger context of the ideological foregrounding of the Iranian revolution of 1977–9. But the fever of that revolutionary moment has long since disappeared, and we are now all sobered up from the intoxicating magic potion of its delusions – and its despairs.

Reclaiming the Past for the Future

This book on Al-e Ahmad you now hold in your hands is not just about what happened before that revolution, but in fact far more urgently about what lay ahead for the Muslim world long after that 'Islamic' revolution had transpired. After the Iranian revolution of 1977–9 came the devastating Iran–Iraq war of the 1980s, then the two successive US invasions of Iraq in the 1990s and 2000s, the Afghanistan invasion in 2001, the Green Movement of 2008–10 in Iran, and then the Arab Spring of 2010–12, then the rise of the criminal gang of ISIS, followed by the mayhem in Syria and the Saudi genocide in Yemen. By returning to Al-e Ahmad I want to come steadily forward to this moment we now live and make some sense of it via the reconfiguration of a towering figure I would here submit as 'the last Muslim intellectual', of now an entirely bygone age. After he and his world were gone, another world was fast upon us, in which a Muslim as a worldly human being could never claim the world the way he did.

In what sense have we lost the world of Al-e Ahmad? There is an excellent volume in Persian on Al-e Ahmad, Hassan Mirza'i's *Jalal-e Ahl-e Qalam* (*The Glory of Writers*, 2013), which I consider the last vestige of that bygone age, a straightforward intellectual biography consisting of two parts, one his birth and upbringing and then a close examination of his most important work. There are also several edited memorial volumes that consist of various essays on aspects of Al-e Ahmad's life and career. All these excellent works are archival, nostalgic and almost melancholic, foregrounding the anger and rancour of those who denounce Al-e Ahmad for the failings of the Islamic Republic, which he never saw nor even anticipated. Dwelling in worlds not in persona, what I intend to do in this book is of an entirely different character. Here I wish to provide a critical reappraisal of Al-e Ahmad's life and legacy, his critical thoughts and literary output, all in the context of our own contemporary post-Islamist moment: a moment that is in dire need of retrieving the intellectual heritage that made thinkers like Al-e Ahmad possible. If we are to fathom a new organicity for the figure of the intellectual in a post-Islamist world we must remember how other, older, forms of organicity once worked. I write this book therefore for a new generation of critical thinking and scholarship that will have to come to terms with a much more balanced understanding of the calm before the storm of Islamism of the last half a century in both the Muslim world and beyond. That Islamism has now entirely exhausted itself. What lies ahead is contingent on a retrieval and rethinking of what came before, of the world Al-e Ahmad personified.

The task at hand is therefore to denativise Jalal Al-e Ahmad and place him in the company of the other leading critical thinkers of his time beyond the Iranian borders. Decades before Talal Asad and Edward Said, Jalal Al-e Ahmad wrote critically of anthropology and ethnography. Léopold Sédar Senghor, Aimé Césaire and Frantz Fanon were his contemporaries and he thought along the same lines as they did. Something is amiss about our current understanding of the global scene of critical anticolonial thinking. Al-e Ahmad is reasonably well known, and yet he does not figure in the global mapping of postcolonial thinking. I do not just write this book to set that record straight, however. I wish to do something far more important. I wish to rediscover what is this figure of 'the last Muslim Intellectual' that now needs to be reconfigured. I will therefore turn to examine not just *what* Al-e Ahmad wrote but *how* he wrote what he did. The spirit of his age dwells in the *manner* of his thinking and not just in its *matter*. I am after his critical lyricism – the powerful prose he unleashed into the politics of his time – dwelling in his impatient mind, his staccato phrasings, his quick wit, his rushed rumination. Al-e Ahmad wrote as if he had seen something past and something coming, and he had to alert others before it was too late. He always thought he was too late.

Where in the World?

But what is the world in which we live today and into which we are now going to rethink this 'last Muslim intellectual?' My primary reason for going back to Al-e Ahmad is to move forward to think of a post-Islamist moral and intellectual agency for a world he could not anticipate. Rethinking a towering intellectual of a bygone age in the age of social media and the internet, however, raises its own daunting questions. The active operation of a transnational public sphere is definitive for the rise and legacy of a public intellectual. But is the transnational public sphere and its degenerative commercialisation, as Habermas has diagnosed it, ready or caring enough to encounter such a bygone age? The question, again as Habermas put it, is not where or who the intellectuals of this digital age *are*, so much as who will *read* these intellectuals, where their readership lies and whether that symbiotic relationship between intellectual and his or her readership will continue to matter? Before we know the presence or absence of a public intellectual we need to ask where and what is the public that would be able to enable and behold such an intellectual. What this public has lost, and with such a loss has also forgotten, is the virtue of reading: the patience of cover-to-cover reading, reading not just to quote a passage from here or there, but reading to recap the truth and spontaneity, the wit and moral wherewithal of a thinking human being.

Towards the end of his Russian travelogue, in which he gives us an account of an anthropological conference he attended in Moscow, Al-e Ahmad provides a list of the previous conferences and where they were held, and then he notes how in 1940 and 1942 there were no conferences, at which point he adds, 'because when you don't know people you can kill them more easily, and if you were to know them you would not kill them'.[2] One is apt to miss such moments of sudden truth if one does not have the patience and perseverance of reading page after page of a rather prosaic and trite reportage of what he did and what he heard and what he said in the course of a huge conference the likes of which we have attended numerous times. If one was to read him for the substance of what he says there is a lot to be discarded. But if one reads him to see how his mind works, for the musicality of his prose and politics rather than its mere particulars, then he will become a conduit of a healthy passage into the world he both inhabited and personified.

What has survived his own age and reached us intact, in other words, is the tonality of Al-e Ahmad's thinking, the rhythm of his prose punctuating his politics, which will ring true even in the age of the internet, when we should listen and read less for the substance of what he said and more for the music of how he said it. Al-e Ahmad's prose must be read, I propose, as the melodious echo of his time, the surface surety of what he thought and how he wrote the world, a penmanship staged and performed pitch-perfectly against the melodious musings of two seminal events of his generation: one evident in the sphere of iconoclastic poetry, and the other in the musical lyricism of the Constructional period (1906–11). Nima Yushij's revolutionary trans-formation of Persian prosody and the liberatory songs, *tasnif,* of the same period were the melodic foregrounding upon which Al-e Ahmad's signature prose emerged and thrived. His writing was an event, not just in terms of what he wrote but in *how* he wrote, in cacophonous tunes syncopated with the urgency of his time, with the beats in his prose displacing the obvi-ous with the hidden, the mundane with the revelatory. His prose resonated with a revolutionary poetics, in Nimaic poetry and lyrical songs, that in two complementary ways enabled a manner of being that took its clues from the paramount urgencies of his time. More than anything else I have written this book to discover and lay bare the punctual urgency of that prose. An entire world was unfolding on that prose. We are all, men and women born just before or just after the Anglo-American treachery of 1953, the products of that prose. We think in that Persian prose even when we write in English, or perhaps particularly when we write in the reclaimed language of our colonial conquerors.

Notes

1. See Jalal Al-e Ahmad, *Safar-nameh-ye Rus (The Russian Travelogue)* (Tehran: Ferdows Publications, 1343/1963, 1368/1989): 29. All translations from the original works of Al-e Ahmad in this book are mine. There are some excellent

translations of his work available in English. But for the purpose of this book, as indeed in all my previous works, I rather do my own translations from the original Persian. Al-e Ahmad has his own unique signature prose, and I prefer to supply the translations myself.

2. Ibid, 277.

I

Remembrance of Things Past

I have no clue what to do with this concept of 'the intellectual'. And even worse with the intellectuals themselves! What to do with this term, and what it means in the Persian language, and with it the fate of the Persian-speaking world, have been stuck since the Constitutional Revolution [of 1906–11]. It has no clear conceptual boundaries, nor indeed any precise characteristics, nor is its past known . . . or its future – so, what in the world is this 'intellectual?' Who is this 'intellectual?' Who is an intellectual? Where and upon what hierarchy does he or she sit?[1]

Jalal Al-e Ahmad, *Dar Khedmat va Khiyanat-e Roshanfekran*
(*On the Services and Treasons of Intellectuals*) (1964–8)

In this chapter I wish to map out the historical and theoretical landscape upon which I intend to construct this book on Jalal Al-e Ahmad, whom I am proposing be read as 'the last Muslim intellectual'. To do so I would like to begin with the last time I had an urgent occasion to write on Al-e Ahmad. Detailing the particular time of that occasion and why I then turned to Al-e Ahmad is the best means of describing why I have now returned to this seminal figure in the history of the Iranian encounter with *colonial modernity*. Al-e Ahmad was, and to this day remains, the epitome of that colonial modernity in which our historical fate has been cast. The *colonialism* of that modernity he expended his entire intellectual energy dissecting, confronting, criticising and seeking to dismantle, and the fact that this very phenomenon of colonialism was the conduit of our *modernity*, mapped out his lifelong preoccupation, and remains the primary reason why we need to reconsider his short life and enduring legacy.

Forty Years of Punishment

More than forty years ago, the Iranian revolution of 1977–9 turned my homeland upside down. At the time of the revolution I was a doctoral student in the department of Sociology at the University of Pennsylvania in Philadelphia, in the United States. Like millions of other Iranians, I was of course sucked into the events taking place in my homeland and the best that I thought I could do was to write my doctoral dissertation on the cataclysmic event. The American Hostage Crisis of 1979–81 that soon followed the Islamist takeover of the revolution put an immediate end to that wish. Our student visas in the US were summarily cancelled by President Jimmy Carter's administration, and we were unable to travel to Iran, or anywhere else for that matter, without jeopardising the chance of coming back to finish our doctoral work. Perforce I changed the subject of my dissertation, and wrote instead on the charismatic authority of Prophet Muhammad centuries earlier, in a not-so-subtle way transforming the character of Ayatollah Khomeini back into history and trying to figure out how the central issue of authority works in an Islamic context.[2] In a significant and enduring way whatever else I have pursued in my scholarship over the last forty years in effect constitute varied attempts at answering that simple and haunting question – with Max Weber and Philip Rieff (under whom I wrote my doctoral thesis) casting their enduring gaze upon what I write. The Iranian revolution of 1977–9 thus remains the touchstone of my entire academic career.

The idea of writing on the Iranian revolution remained with me, and so I spent the next decade after Khomeini's takeover of the revolution and the consolidation of an 'Islamic Republic' thoroughly documenting, analysing and theorising the Islamist component of the revolution at its ideological foregrounding. Picture me sitting in solitude on some distant floor of the Widener Library in Harvard where I had a year of postdoctoral fellowship, reading like a little termite through obscure journals published in Qom. The place was so sombre and somnambular that I would be startled if anyone would for a bizarre reason step onto that floor. At the time there was a Chinese restaurant right across from Widener and next to Harvard Book Store that was my haven and reprieve from that godforsaken floor and the august presence of Ayatollah Khomeini and his revolutionary gatherings a couple of decades earlier in Qom. I am forever grateful to Roy Mottahedeh for arranging that crucial postdoctoral year at Harvard for me. It was indeed a bizarre place on that floor of the main Harvard library to read and write and think and wonder about how an 'Islamic' revolution had happened in my homeland.

The result was my book *Theology of Discontent: The Ideological Foundations of the Islamic Revolution in Iran* (1993).[3] In this book I examined the ideas of eight seminal thinkers who in one way or another were important in the ideological makeup of the 'Islamic Ideology'. The first figure I included in that book was Jalal Al-e Amad (1923–69), about whose works I wrote a detailed chapter, given how foundational they were for the rise of the kind of critical thinking that ultimately culminated in a constellation of works and thoughts that informed the ideological potency of the revolution's Islamic component and then its Islamist takeover. In a subsequent Introduction I wrote for a second printing of that book, I made a point to stress how there was no inevitability behind the authors I was examining necessarily having resulted in an Islamist claim on that revolution, but that certainly there was a crescendo of thinking that had paved the way towards Ayatollah Khomeini's absolutist Islamist claim on that seminal revolution. None of the thinkers I had examined, least of all Jalal Al-e Ahmad, were entirely on the same page even with each other let alone with Ayatollah Khomeini and his political parlance. But there was a synergy among all the thinkers examined in my *Theology of Discontent* that was gathering momentum, measuring political power and gradually mapping out a triumphalist tone. None of these thinkers had anticipated the Islamic revolution, not even Ayatollah Khomeini himself, as I had made a point to document, and yet in retrospect we could now see how they were pointing towards a potential outcome.

Jalal Al-e Ahmad became a seminal figure in my configuration of how the Islamic component of the revolutionary ideologies had gathered force and momentum, but there was quite a serious distance between Jalal Al-e Ahmad and Ali Shari'ati, the second figure I examined, or between Ali Shari'ati and any number of other thinkers I had carefully examined in that book – both in moral imagination and political purpose. No one of them necessarily led to the other, there was no trajectory, teleology, or inevitability, but a constellation of thinkers who had surfaced over a period of close to half a century and willingly or unwittingly pointed in a direction. In all my subsequent work on Iran, perhaps most particularly in my *Iran: A People Interrupted* (2008), I mapped out in more detail the varieties and dexterities of other ideological forces – anticolonial nationalism and Third World socialism in particular – that had framed the dialogical making of the Islamic ideology. In this larger context, I had occasion to emphasise the dialogical disposition of all the ideological formations leading to the Iranian revolution before its Islamist takeover had begun to cannibalise them for its own survival. The greater the distance we had from the events of 1977–9, the clearer we could see every strand of ideological formation in its more expansive hermeneutic circle. Yes Al-e Ahmad still belonged to the constellation in which I had originally placed him, but so could any number of them be placed in any number of other gatherings.

My thinking about the very first critical thinker I had included in my book on the ideological foregrounding of the Iranian revolution, Jalal Al-e Ahmad, continued apace and gradually became far more detailed precisely in the dialogical and contrapuntal manner in which I had once read him, long before the Islamist takeover had turned them into solitary, sectarian, mutually exclusive and tribal bifurcations that had by now categorically distorted the very texture and disposition of the Iranian moral imagination and political thinking. The Islamic Republic was triumphant, its leading intellectual cadre was triumphalist, and they could do and write and read whatever they wished into the political forestructure of their Republic. At this point once again, and for an entirely different set of reasons, the figure of Jalal Al-e Ahmad resurfaced prominently and I knew I needed to revisit him in even more detail to capture the spirit of an age that is today almost entirely lost and forgotten and yet which, paradoxically or otherwise, we most desperately need to actively retrieve and reimagine. At this point I have neither nostalgic urges nor teleological reasons for returning to Al-e Ahmad. Some forty years of scholarship after the Iranian revolution of 1977–9, my concern is the futurity of that past that now needs a historical retrieval. The present perfect of the Islamic Republic as a *fait accompli* demands a retrieval of the imperfect past of the Islamic ideology that had not yet promised it. I was looking after that un-promised realm of multiple possibilities. We need to go back to that moment, and no other towering figure comes even close to Al-e Ahmad in typifying the age that framed his flamboyant musings.

Here I wish to demonstrate how Jalal Al-e Ahmad was the single most important public intellectual of his time. But that claim in and of itself is entirely useless unless I explain why or indeed whether this claim would matter more than half a century after his passing. Calling him the most significant intellectual of his time is not to agree with all he said and did, or to ignore the uses and abuses to which his name, thought and legacy was posthumously put by a triumphalist Islamic Republic. Considering him the most important public intellectual of his time does not mean there were no other figures who were more learned, more erudite, or more provocative in their thoughts. To consider him a towering figure of his time is rather to show how his character and culture were in remarkable harmony with the spirit of his age. The nature of that harmony is what compels me to write this book – because today we have lost that harmony and the political culture of the Muslim world has degenerated into a pathological sectarianism. In that lost harmony I detect an unsurpassed dialectical engagement with the spirit of Al-e Ahmad's time, and in that harmony I also detect a moment in the history of Iranian and Islamic anticolonial modernity when *identity* and *alterity* were in unsurpassed dialogical engagement with one another. I write this book neither to praise nor to fault Al-e Ahmad – but instead to detect the enduring resonances of that pluralistic harmony. I write this book to navigate and map out the spirit of an age Al-e Ahmad best personified and which we have ever since lost. I write this book neither to mourn nor to bemoan that loss. Instead I intend to argue that the moral imagination of our post-Islamism is rooted in the pre-Islamist momentum of a worldliness that Al-e Ahmad best represented.

On 9 November 1948, Al-e Ahmad wrote a short letter to the publisher to whom he was submitting his Persian translation of Dostoyevsky's *The Gambler* (1866), in which he explains that his friend Ibrahim Golestan (a leading literary figure of this time) had suggested he submit this book to the publisher, and then on the margin of the letter he writes that the publisher had agreed to pay him 1500 Riyals (about US$20.00 with the rate of that time) and ten copies of the book.[4] He was twenty-five years old at this time, and at the epicentre of the intellectual effervescence in his homeland, and his very livelihood depended on that centrality. What was a leading Muslim intellectual of his time doing translating Dostoyevsky into Persian?

His literary curiosity, restive soul, ambition, comparative literary drive, moral imagination and tireless work placed him right where the world was taking place. We need to retrieve and excavate that location.

Historical Impatience

It is impossible to exaggerate the significance of a patient historiography in retrieving the historical impatience at the roots of the possibilities and particularities of a Muslim intellectual set in a cosmopolitan worldliness, when the thinker remains a Muslim in a serious and significant way and yet engaged with the differing world around him or her. Everything we read and everything we understand today about 'the Muslim world' informs us against such a patience. The post-9/11 world has become a chimeric truth unto itself. The speed and avalanche of events since the Iranian revolution of 1977–9 have made this proposition however both an urgent and yet a very difficult task. Our critical consciousness is assaulted by too much information and too little thinking. The faster and the heavier the speed and volume of useless information the slower and more meditative must become the pace of our critical thinking, all of it predicated on a judiciously patient precision with history – particularly the history of our vanishing presence. The actual life and the enduring legacy of Al-e Ahmad, I propose, serve as a perfect conduit for retrieving the quintessence of that vanishing presence.

Al-e Ahmad was a unique Muslim intellectual engaged in full, healthy and robust conversation with all the non-Islamic factors and forces that had come to animate the Iranian society of his time. As he began to face and alter those forces, those forces in turn altered and defined him. Those forces, rooted in the Constitutional Revolution of 1906–11, effectively culminated in distinguishing Al-e Ahmad as the single most influential public intellectual of his time. He was known neither as a literary figure nor as a poet, a film-maker, or any other subcategory except as a *public intellectual* that defined and occupied that space. As a result, his work constitutes a unique com-mentary on a lost transnational public sphere; one that had given ample room for his character and courage to grow and thrive. He wrote about anything and everything – and powerfully so. He had a vision of the world, which he carried up his sleeves and delivered in his work. That vision was far subtler in the Persian poetry of his time, far more implicit in fiction, far more palpable in cinema and other visual and performing arts. But in his signature prose they were all there – ready, articulated, staged and widely read. As such he was the culmination of a constellation of cosmopolitan forces that had come before him and began systematically and consistently to dwindle after him. Capturing the spirit of his time is to capture the moment when Al-e Ahmad was made possible and with him the possibility of a *homo Iranicus*, or a *homo Islamicus* – an Iranian Muslim in happy harmony and diligent conversation with the world. After him no one else ever could do or did as he did or speak the language he had mastered and made proverbial. The concerted efforts of the ruling Islamist regime in Iran to celebrate him is in fact an attempt to co-opt his memory to lend legitimacy to their state, an endeavour in which his 'secular' critics are equally complicit. If he were alive today, he would lead the principled opposition against the Islamic Republic. Everything we know of Al-e Ahmad speaks to that truth.

The course of the Iranian revolution of 1977–9 was the historic rendez-vous of that cultivated language of global consciousness in the making of which Al-e Ahmad had a major role to play. More than forty years after that revolution, we can now look back at that momentous occasion and, through a fresh look at a seminal Iranian intellectual of the mid-twentieth century, recapture the world that revolution both staged and yet paradoxically ended in order to regain a better grasp of the sectarian world to which it gave birth. It is an extraordinary thought to think of the world of Al-e Ahmad just before the revolution and then compare it with the world the Islamic Republic, which succeeded the monarchy, ushered in and enabled. The question of where that world originated from and then disappeared into is neither nostalgic nor ahistorical, neither in celebration nor in condemnation of either the monarchy that collapsed or the Islamic Republic that succeeded it. The question is far more serious, and far more potent in its historical implications. The question is to measure the timbre of a time, which in the span of a single century, the twentieth century, saw a vision to full fruition before bringing it to a violent closure. Jalal Al-e Ahmad stood at the equatorial dividing line of those two worlds.

Jalal Al-e-Ahmad lived a short but fruitful life and left an indelible mark on our living history. He was a revolutionary activist, a powerful essayist, a widely read novelist and short-story writer, a literary critic of enormous power and influence, an amateur sociologist and anthropologist, an ethnographer of deeply caring curiosity, and putting all of these together we still come short of what he meant and what he did for his contemporaries. His piercing and powerful essay, *Gharbzadegi* (*Westoxication*) (1962), in which he severely criticised the systematic acculturation of his homeland in dominant colonial terms, both economic and cultural, became the iconic emblem of an entire generation. He was our Frantz Fanon, Aimé Césaire, Léopold Sédar Senghor, C. L. R. James and Edward Said all in one. Our time was expecting him, and he delivered – and it is precisely within the framework of that expectation that we must place and always (re)consider him.

From an early attraction to Ahmad Kasravi, Al-e Ahmad was eventually
Born in Tehran into a learned and devout Shi'a family, Al-e Ahmad's ancestral roots in the Taliban district of Mazandaran linked him to the lush and beautiful shores of the Caspian Sea. In Tehran he had the early child-hood life of an impoverished clerical family, and began working as a child in the bazaar while studying at both a seminary and a prominent school called Dar al-Funun. He was sent to Najaf to undertake seminary studies in 1944, but the idea did not appeal to him and he quickly returned home to Iran. Iran was now in the snare of World War II, extraordinary ideas and political activism were in the air and the prospect of a commitment to clerical studies was not particularly appealing to him. A notable anti-clerical agitator, Ahmad Kasravi (1890–1946), had a considerable appeal among the youth at this moment. The young Al-e Ahmad was one of those enthralled by his ideas. After high school he obtained a Master's degree in education from a Teachers College, and enrolled in a PhD programme but never finished his graduate work or wrote a doctoral dissertation. Systemic and patient graduate work did not suit him well.

From an early attraction to Ahmad Kasravi, Al-e Ahmad was eventually drawn to the most progressive political organisation of his time, the Tudeh Party, but soon he discovered its servile relationship to the Soviet Union, which resulted in his joining a few other like-minded members and leaving the party. His restless soul and agitated intellect were ill-suited for disciplined political membership and commitment. He navigated through and within the contours of the world that embraced his homeland. Al-e-Ahmad travelled far and wide in search of himself more than anything else, as when, following an invitation by the late Professor of Iranian Studies Richard Nelson Frye

(1920–2014), he attended a summer seminar at Harvard University in 1965, as part of a programme initiated by (of all people) Henry Kissinger for supporting promising 'Third World' intellectuals. What figures like Al-e Ahmad were thinking and doing and saying was evidently entirely unbeknownst to Kissinger and those who had agreed to fund these seminars at Harvard. They must have thought they were co-opting these intellectuals. Little did they know. What mattered for Al-e Ahmad was moving – always moving – from his attraction to Moscow to his sojourn in the United States, and in between his journeys to Mecca for his Hajj pilgrimage and then through Europe, and among them all his controversial trip to Israel. He devoured the world and was impatient to read it back for his prose, for his homeland, for his point of origin and reference. He travelled inside his homeland, he travelled beyond it and above all he traversed through the ideological genres of his time without a single-minded commitment to any one of them. That, precisely, made him the public intellectual that he was and markedly distinguished him from the committed ideologues who came before and after him. His pen was his measure of truth. He referred to himself as '*in qalam* (this pen)!'

Beyond and yet through such vicissitude, eventually Al-e Ahmad found his calling in his writings – novels, essays, travelogues, letters and ethnographic monographs – in which he mastered a unique and powerful Persian prose. This prose was not accidental but definitive to his towering presence in the most significant literary and artistic movements of his time. Al-e-Ahmad supported Nima Yushij's ground-breaking innovations in Persian poetry and was integral to popularising the latter's iconoclastic innovations amongst his generation. Precisely for such reasons, and there are plenty of such reasons, it is crucial to keep in mind in what particularly compelling ways Al-e Ahmad was and remained a cosmopolitan Muslim but never an Islamist. Although Al-e Ahmad's ideas were integral to the ideological foregrounding of the Iranian revolution of 1977–9, as indeed I have argued in detail in my *Theology of Discontent*, he never wished for any 'Islamic Republic', and he would have opposed the tyranny that Khomeini established from day one. That he was critical of liberal, what he called *Gharbzadeh* ('Westoxicated'), intellectuals, does not mean he would have supported the tyranny of an Islamic Republic. His views will have to be read dialogically, contrapuntally, against the grain of the time.

Revisiting the seminal figure of Al-e Ahmad is crucial today, for the Islamist takeover in Iran during the 1977–9 revolution ushered in about half a century of militant sectarianism throughout the Muslim world. The Islamic Republic did exactly the opposite of what the Iranian revolution of 1977–9 had intended – to open up the horizons of political visions for the widening possibilities of being a Muslim in the world – the subject of my book *Being a Muslim in the World* (2012).[5] The colossal calamity of this Islamist sectarianism was surpassed only by the cosmopolitan worldliness and progressive politics of when Islam stood in a healthy and robust relationship to other worldly forces demanding attention of the Muslim world – a subject I have already addressed in my *Islamic Liberation Theology* (2008).[6] The brutal takeover of power in Iran by militant Islamists placed Shi'i Islam in hostile contestation with the other fanatical Islamists of the Salafis, the Jihadis, the Wahhabis that Saudi Arabia financed, sustained and unleashed on the Muslim world. In the neighbourhood of the settler colonial Zionism, Islamist sectarianism created the catalytic condition for all these triumphalist ideologies to systematically destroy the facts, phenomena and institutions of a postcolonial worldliness that was the result of decades of struggle against European colonialism. Jalal Al-e Ahmad was the paramount example of a Muslim intellectual, the last Muslim intellectual, whose healthy and robust Islam never degenerated into fanatical Islamism.

What happened in Iran after Al-e Ahmad, and what distorted his legacy, was not accidental but in fact definitive to the colonial and postcolonial dynamics of European legacy in the region. Today political Islamism, militant Zionism and Christian imperialism have come together to cover up and dismantle the memories of that pluralist worldliness. These three complementary ideological fanaticisms are chiefly responsible for the sustained bifurcation manufactured today between Islam and Judaism – all of them handmade by European colonialism, all of them invested in denying and dismissing the legacies of the Judeo-Islamic tradition. Militant Islamism, triumphalist Zionism and Christian imperialism are the triangulated foregrounding of fear and fanaticism that have wreaked havoc in our world and systematically and consistently distorted the clarity of our historical visions. Reactionary Wahhabism in Saudi Arabia, vindictive militant Shi'ism in Iran and racist Zionism in Israel are today the identical ideological by-products of European colonialism. In opposition to European colonialism, militant Islamism (in both its Sunni and Shi'a versions), stripped Islamic intellectual history of its factual pluralistic and cosmopolitan character, reducing it to a singular site of militant resistance to European colonialism.

In the same vein, Zionism, extending the racist logic of European colonialism into the heart of the Arab world, stripped Judaism of its equally worldly moral imagination to conquer Palestine and place it in the service of a neocolonial project. Today more than ever it is imperative to retrieve the memory of the cosmopolitan worldliness of Al-e Ahmad, for fanatical Islamism, settler colonial Zionism and imperial evangelicalism are chiefly responsible for this manufactured rift between Judaism and Islam against the historical grain of their proximities. And precisely for that reason, any legitimate criticism of Zionism as a racist colonial project that spills over into a bigoted attack on Judaism and Jews is falling fast into the Zionist trap. Of course, what has historically exacerbated the mutual impacts of Islamism and Zionism is the course of Christian imperialism, now best represented in the malignancies of the likes of Steve Bannon, whom the world first noticed as an ally and advisor of Donald Trump. His brand of evangelical imperialism actively presides over and exacerbates both militant Islamism and fanatical Zionism. Steve Bannon, Abu Bakr al-Baghdadi and Naftali Bennett are all cut from the same cloth. Against this backdrop retrieving the cosmopolitan worldliness of Al-e Ahmad's generation is not a mere act of political archaeology. The project, as I best see it through this reconsideration of the life and legacy of Al-e Ahmad, is a cut deeply towards a post-Islamist and post-Zionist theology of liberation.

There was a rhyme and reason to the historical impatience evident in Al-e Ahmad's thinking and writing. Legible in both are the lost cosmopolitan culture that gave birth and agency to Al-e Ahmad and his generation of Muslims, those who were called 'Third World intellectuals'. This opens up a whole different vista for retrieving a world that now seems impossible even to imagine. It is crucial today to recall how, from its very inception, Islam has been historically definitive for multiple and successive world empires in which (from the Umayyads and the Abbasids to the Safavids and the Ottomans) Zoroastrian, Jewish and Christian communities have lived, worked and defined themselves alongside one another. There could not have possibly

Figure 1.1 Jalal Al-e Ahmad with a group of students in Tehran, 1967. (Photo courtesy of Ali Dehbashi, from the *Bokhara Magazine* archive) Wherever he went Al-e Ahmad was always the centre of attention. His name and reputation towards the end of his short life was nationwide. People wanted to see him and to be seen with him, and he basked in their attention. They were reading him, and they were now listening to him, and they were putting the face and the figure to the name. The time was not saturated with visual registers of daily encounters yet – the way the age of smartphone and selfies have now enabled. It took a person with the luxury of having a camera, buying the negative, taking the picture, having it developed and then one or a few pictures made to be kept for posterity. The very idea of a 'public intellectual' is being performed and photographed here.

been any equality between the ruling elite of the powerful Muslim empires and these small minorities in their domains. However, that in these dynastic and imperial Muslim contexts there was a Judeo-Islamic philosophical tradition unrivalled anywhere else in the world is a testimony to the presence of a potent intellectual culture among Muslim and Jewish philosophers responding to the mighty heritage of Greek philosophical tradition they shared. The fates of both Judaism and Islam have been pitted against each other in the context of European colonial conquests in Arab lands, giving almost simultaneous birth to militant Zionism and triumphalist Islamism – one as a colonial and the other as an anticolonial project of violent state-formation. Militant Islamism and bellicose Zionism are therefore coterminous with the

Christian imperialism that frames them both. All these three triumphalist ideologies are today's morally bankrupt projects. My objective in retrieving the cosmopolitan disposition of Al-e Ahmad's generation is then to reclaim the world at the cusp of a healthy and robust encounter with European imperialism without degenerating into its mirror image.

The World of a Worldly Intellectual

Al-e Ahmad had a moral and imaginative claim on the world – the whole world. The cosmopolitan forces that informed that world formed Al-e Ahmad's generation of Muslim intellectuals. He was in principled contestation with those opposing forces, not in fanatical hatred of them. He was critical of colonial modernity; he was not antimodern. The legacy of the Constitutional Revolution of 1906–11 that had come after a century of travel accounts informed Al-e Ahmad's travels in and out of his homeland. He had a claim on the world he saw. He harboured no animus against it. When Reza Shah's tyranny began in the mid-1920s it was already too late to reverse the course of history – the cosmopolitan forces that had informed the Constitutional Revolution had by then entered the very fabric of the political culture that Al-e Ahmad would soon inherit. At this point no political party could have represented that culture in its rich diversities, however the varied institutions and discourses of literary and artistic creativity most certainly did. The world that Persian travellers of the nineteenth century brought home had gathered during the Constitutional Revolution when the Iranian bourgeoisie recast their homeland on a global capitalist blueprint. The period of 1911–24, from the success of the Constitutional Revolution to the rise of Reza Shah, was replete with even more revolutionary potential in the North, South, East and West of the country. Reza Shah received the full support of the British, expanding their commercial and economic interests in Iran to defeat all the revolutionary or separatist movements from North to South, which included the revolutionary Jangali in the North and the reactionary Sheikh Khaz'al in the South. As Reza Shah's decidedly tyrannical regime took full control of the country and pacified all the separatist uprisings, the groundwork was laid for the next phase of a liberation cosmopolitanism. The quintessence of these movements was ultimately sublated in the prose and poetry of the constitutional period and then unfolded in the fiction of

Sadegh Hedayat (1903–51) and poetry of Nima Yushij (1897–1960) – both of whom are seminal literary and poetic figures who loomed toweringly over Jalal Al-e Ahmad.

Sadegh Hedayat's and Nima Yushij's literary and poetic imagination soared from where Reza Shah's tyranny had landed. They brought the cosmopolitan worldliness of the constitutional period home to a literary prose and a poetic imagination that were decidedly Iranian, pointedly worldly, real, existential, aware of the European modernity and yet not beholden to it, but in fact conscious of its own particular pride of place in the world. The Constitutional Revolution of 1906–11 was the threshold of Iran's entry into colonial modernity. The old regime of the Qajar dynasty (1789–1926) was waning and the anticolonial modernity of the emerging nation waxing at one and the same time. The twilight of the Qajar dynasty after the Constitutional period, the span of some fifteen years between 1911 and 1926, is when the postcolonial nation was fully formed, but the Pahlavi state had not yet succeeded it. In the period of 1926–41, Reza Shah ruled Iran with an iron fist. He also laid out the infrastructure of a sovereign postcolonial state, while still fully in the claws of the British and the Russian imperial powers. He also severely curtailed the power of the clergy and brought Qom, Tehran and Mashhad seminarians under full bureaucratic control of his state. The minor clerical uprising in Mashhad against his social reforms gave the earliest signals of the Shi'a establishment's rising alacrity to their social and political power. Iran was now becoming increasingly open to regional and global configurations of power as a sovereign state. Al-e Ahmad is born here, amidst this crosscurrent of colonial powers and postcolonial national consciousness. His brief attraction to Ahmad Kasravi was among the earliest signs of his political restlessness.

The following decade of 1941–53 saw the abdication of Reza Shah, and the establishment of the Tudeh Party, together usher in a major epistemic shift in Iranian political culture. This is when Al-e Ahmad was a young student and, increasingly active in political and literary scenes, he finally joined the Tudeh Party. This is the most prolific period of Al-e Ahmad's life. Three active political forces are now playing at full throttle. The militant Islamism of Ayatollah Khomeini and Fada'ian-e Islam is now taking shape, the anti-colonial nationalism of Mohammad Mossaddegh and his National Front or

Jebheh-ye Melli is in full swing, and perhaps the most potent of them all, the Third World socialism of the Tudeh Party is now solidly consolidated and widely popular. Even though Al-e Ahmad had joined the Tudeh Party, his prose and politics were in fact shaped by all three of these forces simultaneously. It is imperative to remember that each one of these political forces and metanarratives were in and of themselves formed amidst a transnational public sphere that included Iran but was not limited to Iran. Militant Islamism was rooted in a transnational pan-Islamism that extended from North Africa to the Indian subcontinent, as anticolonial nationalism was equally spread across Asian, African and Latin American anticolonial movements, while the Tudeh Party Third World Socialism was *a fortiori* a global movement without borders. Al-e Ahmad was born and raised and came to political and creative consciousness and fruition all in this multifaceted environment. When we read him all these forces are simultaneously present and evident in his prose.

The next phase in the unfolding worldliness of Al-e Ahmad's moral imagination would be during the crucial decade of 1953–63. This period of his unfolding saga begins with the nationalisation of the oil industry in the early 1950s that came to a crushing collapse with the CIA–MI6 coup of 1953 and culminated in the failed June 1963 uprising led by Ayatollah Khomeini. This is the period of Al-e Ahmad's mature thoughts and public presence. This is the time when he writes and publishes his seminal essay *Gharbzadegi* (*Westoxication*) (1962), which have to be placed next to the seminal texts of Frantz Fanon, Aimé Césaire, Jose Marti and so on to be understood best. *Gharbzadegi* is the summation of Al-e Ahmad's mature thinking, an essay that assumed its towering significance precisely because it was a crystal-clear outcome of a cosmopolitan worldliness innate to the Iranian political culture. The text has been systematically abused in subsequent readings by both its admirers and detractors precisely because it was read according to a single-sited Islamism that was farthest removed from the mindset of its author when he wrote it. Important as it is, *Gharbzadegi* becomes even more alive when placed next to other pieces of Al-e Ahmad's work from this period, particularly his travelogues in Iran and around the world.

The next episode of Iranian history engulfing Al-e Ahmadi's life, the period between 1963–71, begins with the June 1963 uprising of Ayatollah Khomeini, which Al-e Ahmad witnessed, and ends with the Siahkal uprising, which he did not. Again, today it is important to see the June 1963 uprising the way Al-e Ahmad saw it with his open-ended cosmopolitan perspective, and not simply as a precursor to the Iranian revolution of 1977–9, which the militant Islamists took over and Al-e Ahmad neither anticipated nor was alive to see and judge. The June 1963 uprising spoke to the Islamic components of Al-e Ahmad's multifaceted thinking. The Siahkal guerrilla uprising of 1971 spoke to the militant Marxism underlying his political thoughts. There is no reason to doubt he would have celebrated the Siahkal uprising, though he was no longer alive by that time for us to know for sure.

The immediate phase after the passing of Al-e Ahmad in 1969, the crucial years of 1971–7, was the height of two guerrilla movements in Iran – one was Marxist and the other Islamist, both advancing the socialist and the Islamist phases of the previous generations to more committed, single-sited and violent terms. The militant Islamists of the Khomeini brand went underground after the June 1963 uprising, while Khomeini himself would spend his exile first in Turkey and then in Iraq, and then in the Neauphle-le-Château suburb of Paris, before his triumphant return to Iran. But the cultural scene had by now completely taken over, as film, fiction, poetry, theatre and other forms of visual and performing arts now dominated and defined the scene. This is the golden age of Iranian cultural cosmopolitanism of unsurpassed power and range. Iran would never see anything like this again. This is the context in which Al-e Ahmad's legacy began to form for the posterity, before the Islamic Republic began to cast its shadow on him. He was no longer alive to be part of the 1971–7 period but, if he were, he would have been a towering intellectual figure moving it forward in radical and principled ways.

We will have one final crescendo of cosmopolitan politics, 1977–9, that culminated in the 'Ten Nights of Goethe' – as Khomeini and his lieutenants stationed themselves in Neauphle-le-Château and took over the revolution, taking full advantage of the revolutionary momentum to claim its leadership, as they also took full advantage of the Marxist left, the militant Islamists and the anticolonial nationalists who began to command the streets and topple the Pahlavi dynasty. Before that momentous event, however, it is important to recall the series of 'Ten Nights' of lectures and poetry recitation held between 10 and 19 October 1977 at the German Cultural Institute in Tehran. This event marks the last monumental event marking the zenith of

Iranian intellectual scene before the Islamist takeover. Here is what happened during those ten historic nights:

> The 'Ten Nights' (*dah šab*), as they came to be known, took place at the German Cultural Institute on Pahlavi Avenue, the premises of the Goethe Institute having been deemed too small for the expected audience. However, on the first night, so many showed up that even this venue proved inadequate, and the crowd spilled over into neighboring streets, where loudspeakers were set up to broadcast the proceedings. Up to ten thousand attended the first few nights, but then it started to rain, and the numbers went down to about three thousand . . . Weather conditions did not dampen the crowd's enthusiasm, however, and over fifty writers, poets, playwrights, critics, and translators aroused the listeners 'to a peak of emotional communion unprecedented in Iranian cultural history' as they spoke of censorship, freedom of thought, the responsibilities of intellectuals, inequality, and oppression, thus turning a literary event into a political one. Even though armed personnel carriers surrounded the area, no violence occurred . . . and the Ten Nights became the first in a series of mass protest meetings that culminated in the Revolution of 1979.[7]

If Al-e Ahmad were alive, he would have been a fifty-four-year-old doyen of Iranian intellectuals and among the first to speak.

The 'Ten Nights' event of 1977 was the last public occasion when we can actually imagine Jalal Al-e Ahmad being part of the destiny of his homeland. After that Iran drastically changed its face and fanatical sectarianism took over as state policy. The 1979–89 period was the decade of Ayatollah Khomeini's charismatic terror, of the US Hostage Crisis, of the Iran–Iraq war, of the Salman Rushdie Affair, which all led to the brutal consolidation of power, mass executions, cultural revolutions and university purges – under which terrorising conditions we witnessed the rise of the so-called *Roshanfekran Dini* ('religious intellectuals') siding with the ruling tyranny and thinking their foundational ideology. Under the intellectual tutelage of these 'religious intellectuals', the period of 1989–2001 saw the further consolidation of power inside Iran by the active spreading of the Islamist militancy to the regional domains, and the rise of rivalries between Iran and Saudi Arabia exacerbating the sectarian divide the Islamic Republic had inaugurated, as the

US/Israeli agitation of this sectarian divide intensified particularly in Iraq and Afghanistan. The US invasion of Afghanistan in 2001 and of Iraq in 2003 in the aftermath of the events of 9/11 ushered in a period of conquest and chaos that lasted until 2008. Afghanistan and Iraq collapsed in the aftermath of the US-led invasion, which in turn gave more power to the Islamic Republic in the region, as external events took over the domestic issues. When in 2008 the Green Movement and then the Arab Spring happened, the world heard the latest cry for cosmopolitan worldliness and democratic freedom in the region. However, both movements were brutally suppressed, as the rise of the murderous Islamic State (IS) in Iraq and Syria shifted the attention to counterrevolutionary mobilisations led by both Saudi Arabia and Iran.

By 2015 the Iranian Nuclear Deal had restored some domestic hope in Iran, but by 2018 President Donald Trump had dashed that hope and Iran and the US were again on the verge of active military confrontations. By now the memory of who and what and why was Jalal Al-e Ahmad appeared to be completely lost – as was the memory of the cosmopolitan worldliness that had once given birth to him. The active hostilities between Iran and Saudi Arabia had now shifted the geopolitics of the region to both their advantages in fomenting sectarian hostilities concealing their common abuse of tyrannical power.

The Last Organic Muslim Intellectual

Al-e Ahmad was the last organic Muslim intellectual, rooted in layers of Muslim learning and yet openly defiant of all of them at one and the same time. He stood on the edge between his parents' generation of scholastic learning on the one side, and the widening horizons of worldly exposures to the larger postcolonial world on the other. The generation before him was still deeply entrenched in scholastic learnings, whilst that which came after him went either wayward into the Islamist disposition of Ali Shari'ati and Abdolkarim Soroush or else the fanaticism of the militant secularists. What later generations of critics faulted in Al-e Ahmad as contradictory were in fact palpitating signs of a robust critical mind in action. He was the contemporary and a kindred soul of Fanon, Césaire and Senghor, whilst still a decidedly Muslim critical thinker. It is therefore as Muslim intellectual that we will have to place him next to his peers.

What Al-e Ahmad shared with his Asian, African and Latin American peers was of course the coloniality of their conditions. In *The Last Intellectuals: American Culture in the Age of Academe* (2000), Russell Jacoby chronicles 'the disappearance' of public intellectuals in the US, for which he holds academic careerism and suburbanisation chiefly responsible. On the postcolonial edges of the self-same late capitalist developments, Al-e Ahmad would be the counterpart of such American figures as Irving Howe, Daniel Bell and John Kenneth Galbraith. But the urgency and the immediacy that moved critical thinkers like Al-e Ahmad, Fanon, Césaire and Senghor were of an entirely different character. The generation of Irving Howe, Hannah Arendt, Theodor Adorno, Hebert Marcuse and Max Horkheimer was mainly comprised of German Jewish intellectuals who had escaped the horrors of Nazi Germany. But what Nazism had done in Europe, Europe had for long done to the rest of the world, as Césaire was quick to note. The 'disappearance' of American intellectuals as a result had an added momentum from these mostly German (but also Russian and Polish) Jewish émigrés giving way to another generation that was perfectly at home in American liberal democracy and its contradictions. Subtract the influx of these European Jewish intellectuals into the US, and you have to face the fact that the US is a profoundly anti-intellectual environment because their public sphere is always already, as Adorno had noted, seriously compromised by the violent commercialisation of the public sphere. Both the academic careerism and the suburbanisation of what had passed for an 'American intellectuals' were in fact manifestations of this commercially compromised public sphere. The only exemption to that commercialisation is of course the Harlem Renaissance in which the history of African slavery gave birth to a radical parapublic sphere with its own organic intellectuals like W. E. B. Du Bois, James Baldwin, Langston Hughes, Richard Wright and Malcolm X. The same is true with the generations of Al-e Ahmad, Fanon and their peers. So, the history of African slavery, the predicament of global coloniality and the victims of the Nazi Germany were the only types of seriously radical intellectuals that would call for a comparative understanding. The predicament of Al-e Ahmad and his kindred souls of organic intellectuals was the fragile disposition of the public sphere that was always at the mercy of the tyrannical postcolonial state. Commercialisation at the centre of capitalist modernity, and tyranny at its postcolonial edges, were the main culprits of enabling and disabling organic intellectuals.

In this context, my main thesis in this book is as follows: with the systematic destruction of all its alterities, the Islamic Republic upon the fortieth anniversary of its violent takeover following a multifaceted revolution paradoxically ceased to be Islamic, and Muslims ceased to be Muslims, for by now the ruling state had conquered and compromised the entirety of the public sphere. One in which a Muslim could be a Muslim in the world, or *a fortiori* give birth to any worldly intellectual. Al-eAhmad was the very last Muslim intellectual who had a claim on that public sphere at the height of the Pahlavi regime. After him the Islamic Republic manufactured one-dimensional Muslims ruling against one-dimensional seculars – and the false and falsifying binary has exacerbated both sides of its divide. With the systematic destruction of all its viable and equally legitimate alterities, the Islamic Republic ceased to be Islamic, its Muslims ceased to be worldly Muslims and its intellectuals, like Abdolkarim Soroush, became state employees and the purveyors of its ideological nomenclature. Al-e Ahmad was the last Muslim intellectual whose Islam was rooted, tested and dialogical along with other contestants. After the establishment of an 'Islamic' republic, Muslims qua Muslims all became one-dimensional juridical subjects. My task in this book is to retrieve what is left of Al-e Ahmad's legacy from a pre-Islamist liberation theology to think it through a post-Islamist liberation theology that will have to succeed the calamities of this or any other 'Islamic Republic'.

For forty years the ruling Islamic Republic systematically destroyed a vitally cosmopolitan culture that had been in the making for about two centuries before Khomeini returned to Iran in February 1979 to establish his juridically articulated Islamic Republic. The rich and fertile roots of that cosmopolitan worldliness went deeper and deeper into the soil, as film, fiction, poetry, theatre, the visual and performing arts all transcended beyond the one-dimensional fanaticism of the ruling Islamic Republic. The more the ruling Islamic Republic spread itself thinly sideways into the geopolitics of the region the more the alienated culture it had brutalised went inside and turned dormant into the soul of the people. That bifurcation today defies the alienated soul of a nation whose ruling state can never earn the dignity of representing that nation.

The spirit of that bygone age, once manifested in the defiant and eloquent voice of Jalal Al-e Ahmad, was thus lost. In that voice, Islam, Iran and the world were in dialogical and contrapuntal conversation with each other. Today, for Muslims to be delivered from this flat, one-dimensional atrophy Islam will have to be recast in its larger global context and farthest removed from the calamitous conditions of the ruling clerics in Iran or their Sunni counterparts in Saudi Arabia – or any other Muslim-majority country. Islam will have no future in Iran or any other Islamic Republic. Ayatollah Khomeini and all his clerical and non-clerical successors spent and wasted Islam on their Islamic Republic. The future of Islam lies neither in Iran nor in its arch-nemesis Saudi Arabia. Islam is to be found somewhere between Iran and Saudi Arabia and then from there somewhere between Egypt and Turkey. Islam is nowhere in particular. As an amorphous reality and a collective consciousness, Islam is somewhere in between, already somewhere else. Masses of millions of refugees, immigrants and exiles have taken Islam with themselves somewhere else. The most volatile, the most real, location of Islam is on a boat floating desperately somewhere in the Mediterranean Sea. 'Islam' will have to be redefined from there, on that sinking boat, with desperate Muslims and non-Muslims about to be drowned. The ruling Islamic Republic in Iran or Saudi Arabi or any other 'Islamic' state has nothing to say about that sinking boat. Al-e Ahmad would have swum to save its passengers, or else raised hell until those who could did.

Islam has always been dialogical in its distant and near history. The Qur'an is a dialogical text in conversation with the Bible. The Medinan and Meccan verses of the Muslim Holy Scripture have a contrapuntal interface, one destabilising and the other stabilising the social order. Islamic law is in conversation with Jewish Law, Islamic theology and philosophy with Greek, Iranian and Indian philosophies, Islamic mysticism with Buddhism. The more recent history of Islam has emerged in adversarial contestation with European colonial modernity, which gave us militant Islamism that ultimately culminated in the spectacular finale of 9/11 – violence for utter visual spectatorship. Islam in Iran ended when it ended all its real and worldly alterities. Today, in the age of what the distinguished sociologist Asef Bayat has aptly called 'post-Islamism', Islam needs a post-Islamist liberation theology, a liberation of both itself and of Muslims. I have already argued how this militant Islamism was coterminous with Zionism and evangelical triumphalism, and thus the liberation of Islam, Judaism and Christianity from their political abuses cannot happen except as a joint liberation of Islam, Judaism and Christianity in a post-Islamist, post-Zionist and post-evangelical triumphalism. Who would be the intellectual of Al-e Ahmad's stature and significance today? That intellectual would be rooted in an organicity beyond the reach of any single postcolonial nation-state. She or he would be a Muslim of an entirely different gestation, thinking and writing not for any nation but for the nations spread in between. Think of Camp Zaatari, think of the millions of Syrians who have left their homeland in search of somewhere else that already does not want them. Egyptians in the Persian Gulf coasts, Iranians in California, Palestinians in the UK, Turks in Germany, etc. That Muslim intellectual will think and read and write rooted in a whole different sense of selfhood, otherness and organicity.

The central paradox of an Islam that can only thrive in contestatory dialectic in a worldly context and can never be totally triumphant is doubly true of Shi'ism and therefore doubly jeopardises the legitimacy of the triumphalist claims of the Islamic Republic on Islam.[8] Al-e Ahmad therefore becomes not just the last Muslim intellectual but in fact the last Shi'a Muslim intellectual. Two major figures appear after Al-e Ahmad that require attention as Muslim intellectuals and whose comparison tests the truth of calling Al-e Ahmad the 'last' of any such figures that could have been possible before the Islamist takeover of the Iranian political culture. One is Ali Shari'ati (1933–77) and the other Abdolkarim Soroush (born 1945). They both pale in comparison with Al-e Ahmad for the simple reason that they both, to differing degrees, abandoned the cosmopolitan worldliness of the world Al-e Ahmad personified and the dialogical creativity that sustains such a world, and instead plunged deeply into becoming what was later called a 'religious intellectual'. Al-e Ahmad never made any such claims to being a 'religious intellectual' – and precisely for that reason he was the last Muslim intellectual in the healthy and robust worldly context that makes Islam what it has always been: a dialogical proposition.

Immediately after Al-e Ahmad, and yet still before the 1977–9 revolution, Ali Shari'ati pushed his ideas further and further away from Al-e Ahmad's cosmopolitan and contrapuntal context and began thinking in an almost exclusively Islamist frame of reference. His years of education in his native Khurasan and then in Paris had made him entirely alien to the cosmopolitan context of Al-e Ahmad's Tehran. I offer two pieces of evidence here. We can confidently say that Al-e Ahmad was in the same league as Césaire, C. L. R. James, Léopold Sédar Senghor, Frantz Fanon, Edward Said and Gayatri Chakravorty Spivak – and yet it is hard to say the same about Ali Shari'ati. In their brief correspondence, Fanon in fact took issue with Shari'ati's Islamist single-sidedness. In a prophetic passage in his letter to Shari'ati, Fanon wrote:

> Je pense que ranimer l'esprit sectaire et religieux entraverait d'avantage cette unification nécessaire – déjà difficile à atteindre – et éloigne cette nation encore inexistante et qui au mieux, est une « nation en devenir », de son avenir idéal, pour la rapprocher de son passé ! [. . .] Cependant ton interprétation de la renaissance de l'esprit religieux et tes efforts pour mobiliser cette grande puissance – qui à l'heure actuelle est en proie aux conflits internes ou atteinte de paralysie – dans un but d'émancipation d'une grande partie de l'humanité menacée par l'aliénation et la dépersonnalisation et dont le retour à l'islam apparaît comme un repli sur soi, sera le chemin que tu as pris [. . .]. Quant à moi, bien que ma voie se sépare, voir s'oppose à la tienne – je suis persuadé que nos chemins se croiseront finalement vers cette destination où l'homme vit bien.[9]

> I think that rekindling the sectarian and religious spirit would further hinder this necessary unification, which is already difficult to achieve – and distance this still non-existent nation, which is at best a 'nation in the making', from its ideal future, by bringing it closer to this past! . . . However, your interpretation of the rebirth of the religious spirit and your efforts to mobilise this great power – which at the present time is in the grip of internal conflicts or suffering from paralysis – for the purpose of emancipation of a great part of humanity threatened by alienation and self-estrangement, and whose return to Islam appears as a turning towards oneself, will be the path you have taken . . . As for me, although my way is different and evidently opposed to yours, I am convinced that our paths will eventually cross towards this destination where humanity lives a better life.

The second piece of evidence is the fact that Shari'ati was almost entirely divorced from the literary and artistic context of his time and had next to nothing serious to say about film, fiction, poetry or drama, whereas the critical judgement of Al-e Ahmad was definitive to those scenes. It is impossible even to imagine Shari'ati writing anything meaningful about the poetry of Nima Yushij or the fiction of Sadegh Hedayat, or anything remotely related to that entire universe. To be sure, the project of Shari'ati had its own logic and rhetoric, about which I have written extensively and admiringly, but the anticipated consequence of that project was a radical alienation of an Islamist worldview away from the world of Al-e Ahmad. In this regard, if Al-e Ahmad was the last Muslim intellectual it is not accidental that Shari'ati is considered the first 'religious intellectual'.

This compromising situation becomes even more exacerbated with Abdolkarim Soroush after the violent takeover of the Iranian revolution of 1977–9, with which Soroush actively sided and proactively collaborated. He was in fact aiding and abetting the militant takeover of the higher education and cultural coup that accompanied it. With Soroush the degeneration of the cosmopolitan worldliness in which Al-e Ahmad had thrived plunged ever so deeper into outright religious fanaticism, whereby the very alphabet of Iranian intellectual diction was violently twisted towards the justification of an Islamist takeover. Despite his absolutist Islamism, Ali Shari'ati was still in vocal or passive conversation with other non-Islamist critical thinkers. He disregarded them but they were at least his interlocutors. His voice was therefore dialogical. Not so with Abdolkarim Soroush, who was and remains top-to-toe Islamist in the vey timbre of his thinking. Before the ruling elite used and abused him and then expelled him from their system, Soroush was singularly responsible for the violent degeneration of Iranian intellectual cosmopolitan, pluralistic, dialogical and contrapuntal culture into a delusional Islamist fanaticism – self-contained, insular, hermetically sealed. The very idea of a 'religious intellectual', forever associated with his name, was the epitome of this blindfolded fanaticism that at its roots was the manifestation of a *ressentiment* against the secular fanaticism of the other *agent provocateurs* like Aramesh Dostdar who published a pamphlet in Paris he belligerently called *Imtena'-e Tafakkor dar Farhang Dini* (*The Impossibility of Thinking in Religious Culture*) (1991). Between Abdolkarim Soroush and Aramesh

Dostdar, a fanatical Islamist and a fanatical secular fundamentalist, the two sides of the same coin, what was lost was the robust critical space that Al-e Ahmad had once personified.

The final acid test of this comparative assessment of Islamist ideologues like Abdolkarim Soroush in contrast to Al-e Ahmad is the fact that these 'religious intellectuals' had nowhere near the literary panache of Al-e Ahmad, nor his command of a powerful and electrified Persian prose, for which short-coming Soroush over-compensates with an outdated neo-classism. Soroush commands and flaunts a cliché-ridden stylised prose, affected and artificially mimicking an archaic classicism that is antiquarian, and thus effectively marks his Islamist obscurantism.

That brings us more specifically to Al-e Ahmad's own signature prose that is proverbial and the subject of much admiration and reflection, without precise theoretical insight as to why it was, and why it remains, so effective in defining an entire generation. Al-e Ahmad's prose, I propose, worked through a systematic act of 'defamiliarisation', or *ostranenie* as the Russian formalist Victor Shklovsky would term it in his seminal essay 'Theory of Prose' (1917). I will have many occasions in this book to discuss in more detail this aspect of Al-e Ahmad's prose, definitive to his enduring legacy. In his prose the form of the familiar narrative becomes unfamiliar, the ordinary strange, the common twisted. Al-e Ahmad's prose was often called 'telegraphic' or 'impatient'. This is a truism, and not sufficient. In 'Art as Device' (1917), Shklovsky considered artistic prose as a device to make the familiar unfamiliar, the ordinary strange.[10] In Al-e Ahmad's prose the spasmatic speed of his temper and time found an almost idiomatic expression. An entire generation sought but failed to match his prose – without realising why they were so attracted to that prose. The bold brevity of that prose had a long and illustrious history. The entire gamut of Persian prose was at the disposal of Al-e Ahmad to master his own unique prose. Classical Persian prose had reached its apogee in Naser Khosrow (1004–88) and Sa'di (c. 1213–91), the two master prose stylists Al-e Ahmad most consciously admired. The prose of historians like Abu al-Fadl Bayhaqi (died 1077) also had much to offer Al-e Ahmad. Much of such admirable source material, however, was deeply buried under the heap of affected official prose of court chroniclers. The active simplification of Persian prose began early in the nineteenth century with the rise of travel narrative that faced the world afresh.

All such references and many more are necessary but not sufficient for understanding how Al-e Ahmad's prose, reflecting through his literary character a contemporary political culture, works. Viktor Shklovsky's *Theory of Prose* poses certain enduring questions about the nature of fact and fiction in the making of prose. He understood the way prose does not imitate but alters reality. Working through the works of Cervantes, Tolstoy, Sterne and Dickens, Shklovsky radically changed our perception of the changing encounter between form and truth. In the case of Al-e Ahmad's prose, that formal alteration of reality was purposeful and political. In Al-e Ahmad's fusion of prose and politics, we are witness to a unique encounter with the alienating forces of colonial modernity. Al-e Ahmad's prose did not just reflect that sense of alienation. It confronted and subverted it, and thus made moral and political agency possible.

To understand the working of that paradox between prose and politics in mid-twentieth-century Iran, we must remember that the very idea of a 'Muslim intellectual' is an inherently paradoxical proposition, and it is precisely in that paradox that the truth and power of this proposition lies. We do not have 'Muslim intellectuals' in the history of Islamic civilisation scattered over multiple empires until the time of European colonialism. We have Muslim philosophers, mystics, jurists, poets, literary stylists, artists and so forth – but not 'intellectuals' as we understand such an appellation today, for that idea is coterminous with the formation of a postcolonial public sphere, upon which a critical thinker could become a 'public intellectual'. In other words, the formation of the figure of the public intellectual is coterminous with the period of decline and defeat in Muslim societies. As an amorphous reality, Islam has always been a dialogical proposition. Inherently and intuitively, in both internal and external terms, Islam has always been conversational with the world embracing it. It has thrived at moments of moral, intellectual and political challenge, and conversely something in its soul dies the moment its triumphalist legalism is exclusively transcendent. Islamic law is the most retrograde, the most reactionary and the most recalcitrant trace of its imperial legacy. It thrives at controlling the Muslim body as the singular site of an empire it has now lost. The dialogical character of Islam throughout history has always made it worldly, relevant, pertinent to the material realities that enable and energise it. In and of it itself,

Islam is always dialogical and contrapuntal, for the Islamic political culture is always performed in heteroglossia. Al-e Ahmad was the singular example of that dialogical imagination and disposition. At the receiving end of the European project of colonial modernity, the colonial site of parapublic sphere has always remained perforce contestatory, defiant, rebellious, self-asserting, over-manly and of course masculinist. The world is thus turned upside down for a Muslim intellectual, the negation of itself, everything first must be put last, as Fanon once put it, everything last must be put first. That is the fear and the anxiety, the hope and the despair, that define the person and the persona of a 'Muslim intellectual'.

Notes

1. Jalal Al-e Ahmad, *Dar Khedmat va Khiyanat-e Roshanfekran* (*On the Services and Treasons of Intellectuals*) (Tehran: Khwarizmi Publications, 1343–47/1964–8): 11–12.
2. I subsequently published my doctoral dissertation as my very first book, *Authority in Islam: From the Rise of Muhammad to the Establishment of the Umayyads* (New Brunswick, NJ: Transaction, 1989).
3. See Hamid Dabashi, *Theology of Discontent: The Ideological Foundations of the Islamic Revolution in Iran* (New Brunswick, NJ: Transaction, 2005). Originally published by New York University Press in 1993.
4. See Ali Dehbashi (ed.), *Nameh-ha-ye Jalal Al-e Ahmad* (*The Letters of Jalal Al-e Ahmad*) (Tehran: Bozorgmehr Publishers, 1368/1989): 27.
5. See Hamid Dabashi, *Being a Muslim in the World* (New York: Palgrave, 2012).
6. See Hamid Dabashi, *Islamic Liberation Theology: Resisting the Empire* (London: Routledge, 2008).
7. See 'Goethe Institute', *Encyclopedia Iranica*. Available online here: http://www.iranicaonline.org/articles/goethe-institute.
8. I have explored this central paradox of Islam and Shi'ism in my *Shi'ism: A Religion of Protest* (Cambridge, MA: Harvard University Press, 2012). This paradox is particularly operative in a country like Iran where Shi'ism is a majority religion with a minority complex.
9. See Frantz Fanon, *Écrits sur l'aliénation et la liberté*, collected, introduced and translated by J. Khalfa and R. Young (Paris: La Découverte, 2015): 542. For a cogent reading of the exchange between Shari'ati and Fanon regarding religion see: Sara Shari'ati, 'Fanon, Shari'ati et la question de la religion: cinquante ans après'

(*Dans Politique africaine*, vol. 3, no. 1143, 2016): 59–72. Available online here: https://www.cairn.info/article.php?ID_ARTICLE=POLAF_143_0059#no4.

10. See Viktor Shklovsky, 'Art as Device', translated and introduced by Alexandra Berlina, *Poetics Today* (vol. 36, no. 3, September 2015). Available online here: https://warwick.ac.uk/fac/arts/english/currentstudents/undergraduate/modules/fulllist/first/en122/lecturelist2017-18/art_as_device_2015.pdf.

2

'Something of an Autobiography'

I was born and raised in a Shi'i Muslim clerical family. My father, my
older brother, and one of my brothers-in-law died as high-ranking Shi'a
clerics. Right now, one of my nephews and another brother-in-law are
also clerics. And that is just the beginning of our love affair. The rest of my
family are entirely devout Muslims, with a few exceptions.[1]

Jalal Al-e Ahmad, *Masalan Sharh-e Ahval*
(*Something of an Autobiography*) (1967)

In this chapter I wish to place the short but exceptionally rich and important
life of Jalal Al-e Ahmad (1923–69) in the context of the most vital events
of his deeply consequential life. Born during the waning years of the Qajar
dynasty (1789–1925) and dead at the age of forty-six, soon after the June
1963 uprising of Ayatollah Khomeini against Mohammad Reza Shah, Al-e
Ahmad lived an enduringly influential life, leaving his indelible mark on the
fate of his homeland. His intellectual and political career began at a very
young age in his late teens, and he died of a sudden stroke at the prime of his
literary and intellectual productivities. In two of his own short treatises, *Yek
Chah-o-Do-Chaleh* (*One Dug Well and Two Pits*) (1964) and *Masalan Sharh-e
Ahval* (*Something of an Autobiography*) (1967), he offered us invaluable autobiographical sketches that help us to understand his political disposition and
social consciousness. In these two inimitable narratives we read through the
very soul of his prose and politics.

The Qajar dynasty collapsed and the Pahlavis came to power, and
endured major challenges to its authority during Al-e Ahmad's lifetime.
During his short life, Iran was occupied by the Allied Forces in the course of
World War II and the ruling monarch, Reza Shah, was forced to abdicate in

1941 in favour of his young son Mohammad Reza Shah. The Tudeh Party, perhaps the most significant political organisation in Iranian history, arose during Al-e Ahmad's youth and he joined it with full force and left it in deep disappointment. He was alive and politically active during the tumultuous years of Mohammad Mossaddegh's nationalisation of the Iranian oil indus- try. He was a leading intellectual of his time when the CIA coup of 1953 took place, and he lived to see the most serious challenges to the Shah's monarchy when first the Tudeh Party in the 1940s, then Mossaddegh in the 1950s, and finally Ayatollah Khomeini in the 1960s led major challenges against the Pahlavi monarch. A socialist, an anticolonial nationalist and a towering Muslim intellectual marked the major signposts of his life. He was, in short, the summation of all the major moral and intellectual forces that defined the political destiny of his homeland.

The Bare Facts of a Lifetime

The bare facts of Jalal Al-e Ahmad's life are simple and well known – but what they mean to us today decades after his passing is an entirely different issue. The simplicity of those bare facts remains embedded in an unfolding history that turned the fate of Iran as a nation upside down. Al-e Ahmad was just one particularly poignant critical thinker who happened to be at the right place at the right time when the destiny of a nation was being radically altered. Those bare facts of Al-e Ahmad's life are rich in texture of the long century he defined for his homeland.

Seyyed Hossein, aka Jalal al-Din, Sadat Al-Ahmad was born on the 11th of Azar 1302 on the Iranian calendar, which is 3 December 1923 in the Gregorian calendar, in the Pachenar neighbourhood in southern Tehran.[2] His grandfather Seyyed Mohammad Taleqani had studied in Qom and Najaf and become prominent in the Shi'a clergy. His father Seyyed Ahmad Hosseini Owrazani Taleqani had also studied Islamic law in Tehran and succeeded his father as a leading religious authority in the neighbourhood. Al-e Ahmad's father Seyyed Ahmad had married Amineh Begum Islambulchi, the niece of a celebrated Shi'i author, Sheikh Aqa Bozorg Tehrani, and the couple had twelve children together, of whom eight had survived, and of which Seyyed Jalal, later to be known as Jalal Al-e Ahmad, was the sixth child.[3] He was thus born to the loving care of a big, moderately well-to-do, and prominent family.

The Iran of the 1920s, when Al-e Ahmad was born, experienced a succession of fateful changes that placed it at the heart of global affairs. The country had just experienced the Constitutional Revolution of 1906–11, whereby the absolutist monarchy of the Qajars was curtailed. Soon after that Reza Khan Pahlavi had taken control of the military in 1921, and by 1926, when Al-e Ahmad was just three years old, the military commander had declared himself the king, overthrown the Qajar dynasty and established his own Pahlavi monarchy. In these circumstances, three towering figures defined the political and cultural scene of Al-e Ahmad's early childhood: Reza Shah (1878–1944) in politics, Nima Yushij (1897–1960) in his revolutionary poetry and Sadegh Hedayat (1903–51) in his pathbreaking works of fiction. These three figures will have to be placed next to each other for a better picture of Al-e Ahmad's early childhood and later youth to emerge. The habitual political history of nations is entirely meaningless if bereft of the literary, poetic and cultural context in which those measures of brute power are assayed. We cannot read the politics of nations outside the hermeneutic circle of their cultural creativities.

In the realm of politics, Reza Shah was chiefly responsible for facilitating the British colonial interests in Iran in exchange for their support to establish his new monarchy subservient to European political interests. His ascendency had radically modified the power and authority of the Shi'i clergy into whose ranks Al-e Ahmad was born. At the same time, however, Nima Yushij was busy dismantling the very structural foundations of Persian prosody, liberating it from the stifling tyranny of classical poetry. Nima's poetry was revolutionary in both form and substance and it would have a profound impact on Al-e Ahmad's generation for decades to come. Meanwhile Sadegh Hedayat was writing the very first ground-breaking works of Persian fiction, surpassing all the earlier experiments that had started late in the previous century. The publication of Nima Yushij's pioneering first volume of poetry *Qesseh-ye Rang-e Parideh* (*The Story of the Pale Complexion*) (1921), followed by *Faryad-ha* (*Cries*) (1926), had announced the first resounding bells of the revolution he would introduce in the entire gamut of Persian poetry with powerful social echoes. At the same time Sadegh Hedayat had published a collection of his short stories, *Zendeh Begur* (*Buried Alive*) (1930), followed by *Seh Qatreh Khun* (*Three Drops of Blood*) (1932) and ultimately his masterpiece *Buf-e Kur* (*The Blind Owl*) (1936). Scarcely anyone but a handful of highly erudite literati took notice of these events. Al-e Ahmad would soon grow up to give them the widest public attention they would ever receive in their own homeland. Among other things, Al-e Ahmad would become a pioneering literary critic of his time whose visionary essays would make sense of the poetry of Nima and the fiction of Hedayat and link them to the politics of the ruling regimes of power.

After his elementary education, Al-e Ahmad's father did not allow him to study in the official ('secular') schools and instead sent him to a preparatory school to prepare him to go to a seminary upon graduation. His father also forced the young Al-e Ahmad into child labour at the Tehran bazaar in these early teenage years.[4] This was normal for his class and family background, as the connection between the mosque and the bazaar was quite tightly woven and needed to be cultivated from a very young age. Al-e Ahmad's father was grooming him to succeed him as a member of the Shi'i clergy. Unbeknownst to his father, however, Al-e Ahmad registered at the official regular high school of Dar al-Funun where he would receive an entirely different education through the official state curriculum. This is a clear indication that the parental influence on his young mind was already weakening at a very young age and he was being drawn towards the epicentre of his nation's destiny. While in high school, Al-e Ahmad was drawn to the anti-Shi'a thoughts of the social reformist Ahmad Kasravi (1890–1946) and other critical thinkers like Mohammad Mas'ud (1901–48). He was obviously reading far more diversely than his father had hoped or perhaps even imagined. In 1943, almost twenty years old, Al-e Ahmad graduates from high school, goes to Najaf to consider following his Shi'i scholastic education to fulfil his father's wish, but does not last there for more than a few months and returns to his native Tehran and enrols in a teachers' training college to receive a bachelor's degree in Persian literature. While in college he becomes politically active and starts translating critical tracts on Shi'ism from Arabic into Persian.

As Al-e Ahmad graduates from high school, abandons the idea of pursuing a scholastic career in Najaf and enters college to study literature, Iran is in the grip of World War II, the Allies have occupied the country and in 1941 forced the pro-Axis Reza Shah to abdicate in favour of his young son Mohammad Reza Shah. During the same year that Reza Shah abdicated, the Tudeh Party of Iran was established and gave an institutional basis to a vastly popular political party with a strong subservient relationship to the Soviet Union. The origins of leftist socialist sentiments and aspirations were of course much deeper in Iran and went all the way back to the early 1900s and the prevalent socialist sentiments of Iranian communities in Central Asia under the influence of Russian socialism. The Communist Party of Iran was actively formed and joined the Third International in 1919. Mirza Kuchak Khan Jangali's (1880–1921) revolutionary uprising in Gilan had strong socialist traits that were still present in the 1940s when the Tudeh Party was formed. Abu al-Qasem Lahuti (1887–1957) was a powerful Persian poet with strong Marxist convictions and was still widely popular during Al-e Ahmad's youth. The Tudeh Party was not the first or the last socialist political party in Iran, but certainly the most successful in attracting the courage and convictions of varied social classes to its ranks.

In 1944 Al-e Ahmad joined the Tudeh Party, just a couple of years before he graduated from college in 1946 and started teaching at Tehran high schools. Though he rose high in the echelons of the party, particularly in its official publications' domains, his commitment to disciplined party politics was quite thin and soon in 1947 he left the Tudeh Party, along with a number of like-minded members such as Khalil Maleki (1901–69), a leading socialist intellectual who was one of the founders of the party but had now grown disillusioned with it.[5] They established a new socialist political party but Moscow launched a vicious attack against them and they soon disbanded. Al-e Ahmad's next political move was towards anticolonial nationalism when he again became politically active during the nationalisation of the Iranian oil industry in the 1950s under Mohammad Mossaddegh's leadership. In April 1951, the Iranian parliament had voted to nationalise the oil industry, which was controlled by the British-owned Anglo-Iranian Oil Company. The entire British colonial apparatus was set in motion and Iran was subjected to an embargo and a blockade, which resulted in stoppage of oil export and severe damage to the national economy. Soon the British and the US would conspire against the leader of the anticolonial uprising, Mohammad Mossaddegh, and overthrow his government through a military coup, bringing the exiled monarch back to power.[6] Al-e Ahmad remained vocally pro-Mossaddegh and was briefly arrested and released after the CIA–MI6 coup of 1953. Three years before the coup, Al-e Ahmad had married Simin Daneshvar in 1950. This marriage was a deeply consequential event for the rest of Al-e Ahmad's life and career.

Throughout his political activities Al-e Ahmad was mostly in charge of the literary and intellectual aspects of the movements he joined. After each political failure he repeatedly turned to travels and writings and what they call 'ethnography' – though he had fundamental qualms about the manner in which Eurocentric ethnography was undertaken, and we are in fact better off reading them as extensions of his travelogues, with a certain penchant for 'ethnographic' accounts. The products of this period of his work soon after the coup of 1953 were works such as *Owrazan* (*Owrazan*) (1954), a detailed study of the village of that name in Bala Taleqan rural district, followed by *Tat-Neshin-h ye Blok-e Zahra* (*The Tati Residence of Blok-e Zahra*) (1958), which reads more like a travelogue to the provincial town of Buin-Zahra though with detailed ethnographic reportage, and finally *Jazireh Kharg: Dorr-e Yatim-e Khalij* (*The Kharg Island: The Big Pearl of the Gulf*) (1960), again a kind of ethnographic travelogue to the island of Kharg in the Persian Gulf.[7] Some of these studies were published with Moassesseh Tahqiqat-e Ijtima'i (Institute for Social Research of Tehran University), though he soon abandoned collaborations with them because he disagreed with their blind-folded and slavish Eurocentrism.

Al-e Ahmad's political interests and interludes were increasingly inter-rupted by longer periods of preoccupations with reading, writing, translating, corresponding with friends and comrades, and above all an insatiable thirst for travel. In 1962 he became the chief editor of *Keyhan-e Mah*, of which only two issues were published before it was banned. He and the Shah's security apparatus played an incessant tug of war. In the same year, the Ministry of Culture sent him to Europe to study European textbooks, in 1964 he performed his Hajj pilgrimage, in the summer of the same year he attended an ethnography conference in Moscow and then during the summer of the following year in 1965 he went to Boston to attend a seminar at Harvard – initiated by Henry Kissinger of all people! On his way back from his European trip, early in 1963, he also made a short trip to historic Palestine, where his wife Simin Daneshvar also joined him from Iran, both officially invited by the Israeli foreign ministry. All of these travels resulted in writing his widely popular travelogues.

Meanwhile, the political developments of his homeland were unfolding apace. In January 1963 the Shah initiated his so-called 'White Revolution', which included a programme of land reform and other manners of state-sponsored 'modernisation'. None of these initiatives had helped diminish the force of the rising opposition to his reign in the aftermath of the 1953 coup to topple Mossaddegh or the 1963 uprising led by Khomeini. Quite the contrary. The forces of Third World socialism and anticolonial nationalism were now yielding to militant Islamism – and all of them informing Al-e Ahmad's politics and prose. The Shah's notorious secret police SAVAK was chasing after any sign of dissent. In June 1963, Ayatollah Khomeini staged his first putsch against the Pahlavi regime. He was unsuccessful. Shah had him arrested and exiled first to Turkey and then to Najaf. Al-e Ahmad was drawn to Khomeini and wrote his famous tract *On the Services and Treasons of Intellectuals* (written in 1964, published in 1968) at this time. But still his heart was with the works of Nima Yushij, Sadegh Hedayat, with his friend and comrade Gholamhossein Saedi, and with the younger generation of intellectuals like Samad Behrangi (1939–67). His wife Simin Daneshvar was by now a towering literary figure in her own right. In 1967–8 Al-e Ahmad was instrumental in the establishment of the Kanun-e Nevisandegan-e Iran, a professional association for writers. The world was his oyster, but he had little time left before he would rush to meet his creator.

The Death of a Muslim Intellectual

Al-e Ahmad died at about 4 p.m. on Tuesday, 18 Shahrivar 1348/9 September 1969 of a heart attack in Asalem, Gilan. His conspiratorially minded younger brother Shams Al-e Ahmad (1929–2010) began spreading a false rumour that he had been killed by the SAVAK. His wife Simin Daneshvar denied any such conspiracy. This does not mean either the SAVAK or the security and intelligence apparatus of the Islamic Republic that succeeded it were not capable of murder. There is plenty of evidence to that effect but not in this particular case. Al-e Ahmad himself was not entirely immune to such conspiracy theories, as was evident in his reaction to the death of the leading children's author Samad Behrangi: when Gholamhossein Saedi informed him he instantly decided it was not, as it indeed was, death by drowning in a river, but a murder by the Shah's secret police. The pathology was endemic.[8]

Al-e Ahmad's death was most probably from natural causes and as his wife testifies likely due to his excessive smoking and drinking. But the conspiracy theory of his having been killed by the Shah's secret police, which his avidly pro-Islamic Republic brother initiated and which many were ready to accept, was the premise of another more serious 'character assassination' of Al-e Ahmad's legacy by the Islamists who took over the Iranian revolution, a task then conversely corroborated, aided and abetted by his 'secular' opponents. The death of Al-e Ahmad at the young age of forty-six thus became the premise of the ruling theocracy stripping him of the rich complexities of his character and claiming it all for itself, and the mortal enemies of that Islamic Republic beginning to disparage Al-e Ahmad's legacy in opposition to that manufactured legacy. The Islamic Republic began naming literary prizes and highways in his name, or issuing stamps in his honour, while the enemies of the Islamic Republic resumed their abusive reading of Al-e Ahmad's work. They were the two sides of the same abusive coin. The dead body of Al-e Ahmad thus became the battleground between two adversaries, with little to no interest on either side in discovering what Al-e Ahmad's lifelong achievements and his enduring legacy actually entailed.

Al-e Ahmad's short life will only make sense if it is placed in the context of the long century that embraced it. That century begins with the Constitutional Revolution of 1906–11, and comes to a global reconfiguration of the nascent nation-state emerging from its old imperial memories during World War I (1914–18), when the Anglo-Russian occupation of Iran brought to a culmination a century of European colonial interests in the region. The occasion of the Constitutional Revolution and the subsequent occupation of Iran by the Russian and the British forces intensified the anticolonial sentiments rife in the nation. Separatist movements that plagued the beginning of the Pahlavi dynasty were occasions both to imagine what alternative social formations were possible and what dangers threatened the very territorial integrity of the homeland. In the poetry of Nima Yushij and the fiction of Sadegh Hedayat, chief among a whole generation of poets and novelists emerging, all these events assume most compelling poetic and literary registers – and would later deeply engage Jalal Al-e Ahmad as a literary theorist.

The moral and intellectual character of Jalal Al-e Ahmad was formed during and soon after the occupation of Iran during World War II – and for us to get near the totality of that character we must always place him in the frame of that history. During the Allied occupation of Iran once again the country faced the fear of disintegration until the emergence of the Tudeh Party in the 1940s and then the rise of Mohammad Mossaddegh in the 1950s gave rise to a much more hopeful prospect for political progress. However, the Tudeh Party's political subservience to USSR, which resulted in Al-e Ahmad and others leaving it, had itself become a source of anxiety over the disintegration of the country. At this time the rise of anticolonial nationalism around the globe, and the Third World socialism in Asia, Africa and Latin America, were far stronger sentiments than the militant Islamism that would soon emerge in the figure of Ayatollah Khomeini in the 1960s. The CIA–MI6 coup of 1953 put an end to all that pluralism. The June 1963 Khomeini uprising, which Al-e Ahmad witnessed and endorsed, was the first post-coup occasion to express all these pent-up frustrations. The results of all these experiences were evident in the polyvocal public sphere and dialogical reasoning of that sphere – from domestic to regional to global, when the ruling monarch's arrogance, the US support, and the public resentment they had created had resulted in a volatile condition. Al-e Ahmad's prose and politics were both the result of, and contributor to, the formation of that dialogical reasoning.

There is a slim volume put together by Al-e Ahmad's immediate friends and colleagues just after he passed away and that evidence will show us the way he was actively remembered long before he was appropriated by the Islamic Republic and maligned by its nemesis.[9] In this volume we read how Khosrow Mallah for example praises Al-e Ahmad for having joined 'the eternity', and for his 'love for the authentic culture of Iran'.[10] Mostafa Rahimi, a leading critical thinker contemporary of Al-e Ahmad's, remembers him for having inaugurated the art of writing Persian essays and for his gift as an essayist. He effectively credits Al-e Ahmad with the gift for creating the art of writing essays in Persian.[11] Iraj Afshar, a leading scholar, praises Al-e Ahmad for among other reasons his travels – and for his flair in writing travelogues.[12] Afshar himself was an avid traveller. Ismail Khoi, a major poet, singles out Al-e Ahmad's daring imagination to defend and theorise the provocative poetry of Nima Yushij in exceptionally hostile circumstances.[13] What we encounter here is the leading Iranian intellectuals of the time praising Al-e Ahmad for the art in which the eulogists themselves were widely known and admired. Mehrdad Rahsepar praises Al-e Ahmad for helping young writers;[14] Kazem Sadat Eshkevari turns to Al-e Ahmad's *Owrazan* and admires his gift for writing 'ethnography';[15] Mansur Taraji shares a memory from a day that Al-e Ahmad had come to his class to teach and asked them to reflect on the question of why they were alive;[16] Gholamreza Emami writes of his handsome demeanour.[17] They are all still in mourning, and they remember their friend fondly.

There is no doubt that a strong hagiographical force is at work in this small volume. But still the issue is in what terms these friends and comrades of Al-e Ahmad are praising their fallen friend. Many people in this small volume would later become avid critics of the Islamic Republic, and rightly so. Javad Mojabi described what he called Al-e Ahmad's 'rushed prose'.[18] M. Azad traces Al-e Ahmad's prose to the simplicity of the people he had met in his journeys around the country.[19] A leading painter, Hannibal Alkhas, wrote of their friendship and of his ability to make Al-e Ahmad laugh.[20] Ibrahim Danai also described Al-e Ahmad's physique and physiognomy.[21] The volume then concludes with Al-e Ahmad's short last will and testament in which he asks his wife, his brother Shams and two friends to form his estate, and to dedicate the proceedings of his publications to the poor members of his family for their education, after which he adds, 'after all these [books] my entire possession is my body, which should go to the nearest autopsy hall [at a medical school] near where I die.'[22] Hagiographical though these obituaries are, they all pay tribute to a towering intellectual for his multifaceted gifts as an essayist, a critical thinker, a literary critic, an 'ethnographer', a master prose stylist, a caring teacher, a moral measure of truth. They might be exaggerating the proportions of that measure, as all post-mortem accounts do, but still they are the precise barometer of what terms of endearments governed the spirit of their age. There is no indication of Al-e Ahmad being praised or condemned as 'religious' or 'areligious'. That he was a Muslim, a worldly Muslim, a cosmopolitan thinker, a deeply cultivated and learned intellectual were all taken for granted.

Soon after the Islamic Republic was erected on the ruins of the open-ended hopes of the 1979 revolution, the ruling echelons of the new regime, led by his younger brother Shams who was now a devotee of Ayatollah Khomeini, began appropriating Al-e Ahmad's legacy, naming highways and prizes after him and using and abusing his work, not as integral to the revolutionary disposition of his age as I did in my own *Theology of Discontent* (1993), but rather as anticipating and wishing for an Islamic Republic. Nothing could possibly be farther from the truth. Al-e Ahmad was a Muslim critical thinker. He was not an Islamist fanatic. But there was nothing to stop the ideologues of the Islamic Republic from doing as they pleased, and they remain in power and can recast the entire history of a multifaceted homeland as a manufactured memory that serves their purposes best. What they are doing with Al-e Ahmad's legacy is not that different from the Shah's security and intelligence apparatus which too wrote whatever they wanted about Al-e Ahmad, including a report that said he was in touch with American intelligence and 'does not have much of a career and goes wherever is to his financial benefit'.[23] To counterbalance the image projected of Al-e Ahmad in the Islamic Republic it is therefore instructive to look at the collected archive of the documents the Shah's secret police, the notorious SAVAK, had put together about Al-e Ahmad. Here we see how yet another image of Al-e Ahmad emerges, if we were to take these reports at their face values. Similarly, Al-e Ahmad's brother Shams Al-e Ahmad reports Ayatollah Khomeini had told him how the leader of the Islamic Revolution knew their father and grandfather and had met with Al-e Ahmad for about fifteen minutes, and when they met Khomeini he was reading *Gharbzadegi*, and then he says 'May he Rest in Peace'.[24] Based on such perfectly haphazard evidence, the ruling Islamic regime claims him, thus giving reasons to those who oppose this regime reviling Al-e Ahmad for sins he never committed.

There is however an alternative narrative, another story, neither the SAVAK's nor the Islamic Republic's, a story rooted in the fact and fury of an age and of a homeland for which Al-e Ahmad had become definitive. Al-e Ahmad's life has to be placed historically where it was and not pushed forward to what the Islamic Republic made it out to be years after he had passed away. Al-e Ahmad was a direct product of *Adabiyat-e Mashruteh* (the 'literature of the constitutional period'). For about half a century before and after that momentous occasion Persian prose and poetry went through historic changes when encounters with European colonial modernity had occasioned drastic changes in Iranian collective consciousness. Critical thinkers like Mirza Fath Ali Akhondzadeh (1812–78), Mirza Aqa Khan Kermani

(1854–97) or Mirza Abd al-Rahim Talebof Tabrizi (1834–1911) were the pioneers of critical thinking when they realised their homeland was caught in the snare of European colonial designs, as was much of the rest of the world. It was at this time that Persian prose was simplified, printing machines were introduced, newspapers emerged, a multifaceted public sphere was mapped out and therefore the very idea of a 'nation' was discovered and articulated. The revolutionary prose of this generation eventually gave way to the poetry of such towering figures as Aref Qazvini (1882–1934), Farrokhi Yazdi (1889–1939), Iraj Mirza (1874–1926) and Mirzadeh Eshqi (1893–1924). Al-e Ahmad hailed from this period that culminated in the 1920s and the 1930s; the period of his birth and early education. He cannot be ahistorically assimilated forward to a revolution he did not witness and an Islamic Republic he would have most certainly opposed once its tyrannical fangs were out. He must be rooted in the other direction, in the crucial decades just before he was born and then extended into his own lifetime. Such framing is not a mere theoretical speculation. He has left us enough biographical sketches for us to be able to read them closely, to allow them to breathe in an air outside the contorted limitations of a ruling regime in desperate need of legitimacy. Al-e Ahmad was no saint. He committed monumental acts of folly, to some of which he confessed publicly, all of them reasons to remember him as a human, all-too-human, a flawed but totally real character.

The Politics of Memory

We are fortunate to have a couple of autobiographical sketches from Al-e Ahmad's own pen that can considerably help us to come to terms with his critical consciousness, particularly with the form and the rhetoric of his self-narration. Chief among these narratives is the short autobiographical account he has called *Masalan Sharh-e Ahval* (*Something of an Autobiography*) (1967), where in a typically sarcastic tone he tells us how he was born after seven sisters, of whom three had died. He then tells us how he enjoyed a comfortable and luxurious life of a clerical family. He writes about how his father forced him to quit school after elementary education and sent him off to work in the Tehran bazaar hoping to turn him into a cleric. He did all sorts of odd jobs but also registered at Dar al-Funun high school, a decision he makes a point of telling us he hid from his father. He says he graduated from high school in

1943 right in the middle of World War II. By the end of the war in 1947 he had obtained has master's degree from the teacher's college. By now he was wearing an 'American suit', as he puts it, and a tie and had become a member of the Tudeh Party. At this point he translated religious tracts from Arabic and people in the bazaar would buy and burn them so no one could read them. He chronicles his advancements through the party apparatus until he left the organisation in 1947. He left the party with a number of like-minded independent socialists and they tried to form another socialist party, and when that failed he turned to translations. He speaks lovingly of his marriage to Simin Daneshvar. He shares with us how his wife reads his writing before he publishes it. He then joined Mossaddegh's National Front movement but was again disappointed and left that movement as well. After each political defeat he tells us he turned to translations and writing fiction, or reflecting on poetry and art. Then he tells us he began writing ethnographic pieces, but the organisation with which he was collaborating was too Eurocentric and so he abandoned them altogether but continued his project of travelling and writing. He sums up this period of his life this way:

> And thus it was that that young little religious boy running away from his family and surviving the chaos of the war and of those turgid political games, eventually came to figure out the real contradictions at the roots of Iranian society against what is called 'progress' and 'development' but in fact is following Europe and the US in political and economic matters, pushing the country toward colonisation and turning it into a mere consumer of corporate products, and all of that so unconsciously, and all of these were the impetus behind the writing of *Gharbzadegi* in 1962.[25]

Al-e Ahmad then tells us the publication of his *Gharbzadegi* (*Westoxication*) was a turning point in his intellectual life, but because of censorship he was unable to publish it unmolested. He then turned to travelling to Mecca for his Hajj pilgrimage, to Europe, to the USSR and to the US. At the writing of this text he tells us he is still working on his book on the intellectuals which he began writing in 1964.

The first thing that strikes us when we read Al-e Ahmad's short autobiography is its title, *Masalan Sharh-e Ahval* (*Something of an Autobiography*)! What sort of a title is that? What sort of an autobiography would that be when its very author calls it 'something of . . .', which I choose here for '*masalan*'. The word '*masalan*' in Persian and Arabic is peculiar. Etymologically it simply means 'for example', but here rhetorically it means 'as if', 'something of an', 'if I were to write an autobiography', 'if you insist', etc. – all rhetorical devices embedded in the word that imply '. . . well you see I am not much of a person to write an autobiography, but if I were to write one it would look something like this'. So there is a strong sense of self-deprecation already embedded in the title, as in 'I am not sure I am entitled to write an autobiography but here you are anyway'. The term thus places the person and persona of the autobiographer in a vicarious position, somewhat humble, but yet self-asserting, with '*shekasteh-nafsi*', as we say in Persian, with humility, but the self-same phrase means someone who has reached a certain degree of self-consciousness and subjectivity, of playfulness and confident frivolity. As in much else of what he writes, Al-e Ahmad here performs his prose, in this case the prose of his life and adventures.

The next issue that emerges from reading this short autobiography is the form it assumes – the pattern it repeats. What we notice in Al-e Ahmad's personal recollection of his life, which he wrote just two years before his passing, is how after each political experiment and trauma he turns to writing or travelling – for writing and travelling and his wife and home are evidently therapeutic for him – or so he projects them to be. First, he tells us about his birth and upbringing in what he decidedly terms a '*khanevadeh mazhabi*' ('religious family') – and then immediately he tells us aspects of his family background are evident in some of his stories. He then tells us about his working and studying at the same time until 1943 when he graduated, and here he marks the tension between his being a 'religious boy' and entering the war-torn world. This creative tension culminates in the 1946–7 period when he received his college degree, started teaching, altogether abandoned his family and began wearing 'an American suit and a tie', a clear indication of having left his clergy home behind. He was by now a member of the Tudeh Party, having been drawn to Ahmad Kasravi towards the final years of his high school. The same way that he graduated from high school and went to college, he graduated from Kasravi and went to the Tudeh Party, which he joined in 1945. But in between Kasravi and the Tudeh Party he translates a politically charged tract on Shi'ism from Arabic to Persian and is pleased to see it sold out but then he laughs at himself that in fact the merchants in the bazaar had purchased the whole edition and burnt it to prevent the youth being corrupted in their faith. The formal theatricality of the prose dominates and determines the contours of the autobiography.

He then tells us how he and his few friends, led by Khalil Maleki, a leading socialist intellectual and political leader, left the Tudeh Party and established another socialist party which was sabotaged by the Soviet Union so he left and turned to writing and to marrying Simin Daneshvar, of whom he is very proud and shares with the public how everything he writes she first reads. This is before his next political move, which is to join the Mossaddegh anticolonial struggle, and when that does not go anywhere, he starts translating and travelling around the country and writing his monographs. At the end of this period comes the writing of his seminal book *Gharbzadegi*, and when the Shah's secret police starts harassing him he opts to travel abroad to Europe, then to Mecca, to the Soviet Union and the US. Then the June 1963 uprising led by Ayatollah Khomeini happens, to which he is obviously attracted, and when that too fails, he turns to writing his book on the intellectuals. Central to his life therefore remains his preoccupation, bordering with obsession, with writing, for writing is where he finds not just his vocation, but in fact the very site of his subjection – where he become a subject, an agent, a person and persona. It is not accidental that he refers to himself as '*in qalam*' ('this pen').

In his essay, 'Autobiography as De-facement', Paul de Man challenges the assumption that 'autobiography seems to depend on actual and potentially verifiable events in a less ambivalent way than fiction does' and that it 'seems to belong to a simpler mode of referentiality, of representation and of diegesis'.[26] He then proposes we should instead read autobiography as a 'figure of reading', that projects the illusion of reference. As de Man puts it:

> Are we so certain that autobiography depends on reference, as a photograph depends on its subject or a (realistic) picture on its model? We assume that life produces the autobiography as an act produces its consequences, but can we not suggest, with equal justice, that the autobiographical project may itself produce and determine the life and that whatever the writer does is in fact governed by the technical demands of self-portraiture and thus determined, in all its aspects, by the resources of his medium.[27]

Figure 2.1 Jalal Al-e Ahmad and Simin Daneshvar, second and third from left in sunglasses, picnicking in the company of a few close friends, Shiraz, Noruz Holidays, 1967. (Photo courtesy of Ali Dehbashi, from the *Bokhara Magazine* archive) Jalal Al-e Ahmad and Simin Daneshvar were the Jean-Paul Sartre and Simone de Beauvoir of their time, a learned and cultivated couple whose marriage was a matter of public consciousness. Here as elsewhere their presence was the epicentre of any gathering. Notice they are the only ones with their backs against two comforting trees. This picture is very typical of similar outings by millions of other Iranian families at this time of the Noruz Holidays: the relaxed gathering, the casual looks, with the photographer fully aware of the significance of the moment defining the picture. Only the three friends sitting to the left of Simin Daneshvar are conscious of the camera. The young man sitting in the middle with short sleeves, white shirt, loosened tie and sunglasses is Hassan Shahpari, who decades later was my PhD classmate at the University of Pennsylvania Sociology Department.

His proposal is that the distinction between fiction and autobiography 'is not an either/or polarity but that it is undecidable'. In Al-e Ahmad's case this is far more than undecidable. It is perfectly evident that his turn to autobiographical accounts can be seen as acts of public performance. He is staging himself, and this staging is integral to his public persona, to his ability to speak in the voice of a public intellectual. Such autobiographical accounts do indeed depend upon actual and verifiable events, but they are also from the pen of a writer of fiction, meaning they are rhetorical performances. De Man is correct that 'the autobiographical project may itself produce and determine the life'. Of course, it does. But I would even go further to suggest that such evident references to the actual events add momentum and spontaneity to the fictive power of the autobiography as self-performance. Without that self-performance, the autobiographer does not claim and stage the space that enables and names him a public intellectual.

The Narrative Imperative

Let us now turn to Al-e Ahmad's other autobiographical text, *Yek Chah-o-Do-Chaleh* (*A Dug Well and Two Pits*) (1964) and see what he is up to in this crucial narrative he felt obliged to write just a few short years before his untimely death. He begins this text by first sharing with his readers how since 1944, when he was in his twenties, he has been writing, and he writes this in June 1964 – twenty years later. He tells us his father made a living out of speaking God's words (meaning the Qur'an) but his own commitment is to the words of humans.[28] One of the shrewdest and most endearing turns of phrases he uses in this case is to separate his own person from his writing persona whom he always refers to as *'in qalam'* ('this pen'), or *'saheb-e in qalam'* (the person who holds this pen'). He tells us that 'this pen' has secretly told him that despite his claim to intelligence he has made a number of blunders in his life and he wants to share them with us. The text as a result is a sort of his confessional to mistakes he has made in his life. He is writing them down, sharing them with the public, by way of seeking absolution, not from us, his readers, but from his 'pen', 'this pen'.

In the 'Chah' ('Dug Well') section of these public confessions, namely the major mistake he thinks he has committed in his life, Al-e Ahmad tells us of his episode with a certain Homayoun San'ati-zadeh, and the misstep he had taken of having collaborated with an entrepreneur because there was some financial benefit in it for him and now he regrets it and wishes to publicly confess. Again, here we see him narratively splitting himself between his person and this pen and this pen is always pure and principled while he himself can be fooled and even occasionally comprised. Who was this Homayoun San'ati-zadeh (1925–2009), we might wonder, and why would Al-e Ahmad be wary of having had any dealing with him? San'ati-zadeh was a businessman who traded in paper and who had learned his trade in the Tehran bazaar. After the CIA coup of 1953 San'ati-zadeh became a representative of Franklin Publications in Iran, while owning his own Pars Paper Factory, and the Offset Printing House. Al-e Ahmad and his wife Simin Daneshvar briefly worked with this person doing some translations for a fee and then he regretted it. At issue here is the autonomy and the independence of a public intellectual and how he becomes compromised by working with shady characters. Al-e Ahmad's internal dialogue between himself and his pen continues apace expressing this anxiety:

> How many times the person who holds this pen and I had constant quarrels. My position was why did you have to experience what you had already experienced, and he was telling me, 'there you go, you wanted to have mass publications in 20,000 copies? Well, there you have it!'[29]

This public confession of guilt is meant to exonerate the sanctity of the pen not the fallibility of the pen holder.

Let's look closer at this Franklin publishing business and see what they were up to and why Al-e Ahmad felt the need to be so publicly repentant about having worked with them. It is important that we look at the issue from the distance of more than half a century and from a US source lest we might join Al-e Ahmad's 'secular' liberal critics in claiming that he was paranoid or, as they say in Iran, *'Emrika-setiz'* ('Amerophobic') or *'Gharb-setiz'* ('Europhobic'). I am going to cite from a recent source at the Smithsonian Institution, with no claims or connections to any anticolonial criticism or postcolonial scholarship. In this source we read:

> In 1952, a group representing the most important trade, university and educational publishers in the United States met in New York City to incorporate Franklin Publications. Some of the men (and they were all men) had been active in the Council of Books in Wartime during World War II. Then, they had helped to produce the Armed Service Editions that took popular books to the fighting troops, and the Overseas Editions that had taken American books in translation into liberated Europe.[30]

So that is the origin of Franklin Publications. But what exactly were they up to? 'Funded by the US government, Franklin Publications was viewed as pushing imperialist propaganda.' But then we read something more specific about things Franklin Publications were doing in places like Iran:

> When Franklin decided to produce Arabic and Persian editions of Edward R. Murrow's popular anthology *This I Believe* . . . some chapters were replaced with those that highlighted the views of prominent Islamic and Middle Eastern figures. The text also helped to assist the United States'

broader vision of promoting Islam and religious faith as a counter to Communist irreligiosity.[31]

Al-e Ahmad had no precise knowledge of these facts and was drawn to his misgiving of what this American project was by his precise theoretical suspicion of US imperialism. And he was not the only one. From the same source we read:

> But as much as Datus Smith [the head of the Franklin Publications] declared that he was in no way an American imperialist or an Ugly American, the realities of operating abroad made such assertions questionable. For example, Franklin's work came under fire in Egypt from nationalists who saw American culture as a fundamental threat to Arabic culture and the sale of imported books as crippling to an Egyptian cultural industry. As one Egyptian journalist wrote: 'National thought must be allowed to live and flourish'. In Indonesia, initial public support for a program to help the country reach its educational and literacy goals changed as Indonesian nationalism increased: under the Sukarno regime, educational and cultural development was to be state-directed and not imposed or aided from without. Like the USIA's libraries, which were sometimes the target of protests, Franklin books, even if in translation, were regarded as potent symbols of American power.[32]

The second piece of the confession and the first *Chaleh* (Pit) is a critique of Ibrahim Golestan, his close friend and comrade ever since his Tudeh Party years and a Shirazi family friend of his wife Simin Daneshvar. Much of this account is comprised of personal grievances with occasionally brilliant critique of Golestan's prose and his cinema.[33] But the key issue here too was the fact that when Al-e Ahmad was writing his monograph on Kharg Island, Ebrahim Golestan had asked him to work with the Iranian Oil Consortium, from which transaction Al-e Ahmad had received almost three thousand tumans (almost 400 dollars at today's rate) with which he had painted his house, and he had bought a heater for his house with the one thousand tumans (almost 140 dollars at the same rate) that San'ati-zadeh had previously given to him. So, he felt guilty and thus compelled to confess through the publicity of this autobiographical account of the mistake of having accepted that money from Golestan. One might think Al-e Ahmad utterly insane for such thoughts. But we need to know what this 'Consortium' was, and why Al-e Ahmad would be concerned to be affiliated with it through Golestan. Soon after the coup of 1953, the US moved to secure its strategic and oil interest in Iran, and thus the infamous Anglo-Iranian Oil Company yielded to the formation of a multinational oil consortium to take advantage of the post-coup bonanza. As early as August 1953, days after the coup, the US Secretary of State John Foster Dulles was moving to secure US oil interest in post-coup Iran. Comprador intellectuals like Golestan had no qualms working with and for this consortium, making propaganda films for them and, to protect themselves, implicating others like Al-e Ahmad too. At issue, again, is the sanctity of his pen, the fact that his pen is not supposed to be for sale, that he is an honest public intellectual. Golestan had voluntarily sold his soul to the colonialists on his homeland, making a bundle of money, and so had Al-e Ahmad been implicated for a few hundred dollars to paint his house! This is the issue that bothered Al-e Ahmad, and which he felt compromised his integrity.

The third piece and second *Chaleh* is about a friend, Nasser Vosoughi (1922–2010), a lawyer and a judge with an enduring interest in literature and culture who had established a leading journal called *Andisheh va Honar* (*Thought and Art*). Al-e Ahmad had known Vosoughi since his Tudeh Party years and then as part of the party they had formed with Khalil Maleki, the so-called Zahmatkeshan Party. They had a friendship until Vosoughi had suggested they devote an issue of the journal he was editing to Al-e Ahmad, which had turned out to be a nasty trap to discredit and dismantle his monumental popularity. This had deeply hurt Al-e Ahmad and here he blames himself for having given way to his own vanity and fallen into this trap. At issue here is the vainglory and narcissism of an intellectual that can fool and derail him. He should have known better, he thinks.

What we notice here is how Al-e Ahmad's evident obsession with the sanctity of the pen is a substitutionary sacred object projected from his lapsed Shi'ism onto his prophetic zeal as a public intellectual – the passion with which he wrote, and the writing that dwarfs almost the entirety of the mediocrity attacking him, was no ordinary passion. He spoke from the certainty of a conviction that emerged not from the divine certitude of his parental pieties but from the earthly struggles of a people he called his own and saw as the manifestation of an earthly truth. He was and remained a Muslim intellectual warrior – and those who attacked or hurt him were no match for him. Crucial here is to see Al-e Ahmad's notion of *the sacred* transferred and projected from his ancestral faith onto his public political and moral commitments. This sense of sanctity was lost on those with whom he did not share his deep-rooted Islamic convictions. Convoluted and self-referential as this was, even he could not see why he was so particular about the 'sanctity' of his pen. He may have thought he had abandoned his father's faith. He had not. The world had taken him out of his father's house, but not his father's house out of him.

In 'Philosophy as Autobiography: The Confessions of Jacques Derrida' (2000), Joseph G. Kronick writes of the speculative place of what he calls 'spectral logic' as the philosophical predicate of autobiography:

> There are many texts by Derrida, besides *Specters of Marx*, that analyze this spectral logic wherein truth, testimony, self-representation, history, and so on, are attached to the simulacrum that haunts the original. Without this possibility of doubling or perversion, there can be no truth, history, testimony, or self-representation . . . History and, with it, freedom and action depend upon that which resists totalization, ontology, and phenomenology. Faced with the absolutism of principles and identity, we must bow down in worship as do the people, in Dostoevsky's 'Legend of the Grand Inquisitor,' before miracle, mystery, and authority . . . In short, without the threat and chance of the lie, secrecy, the simulacrum, history and politics would be 'the irresponsible action of a programmatic machine.'[34]

This *simulacrum* is not scripted and perforce oscillates from culture to culture, politics to politics, and circumstance to circumstance. The key question is what that simulacrum is that enables the mind to think, provides the morality to be ethical and politics to resist rather than to will power. The central metaphor of Al-e Ahmad's autobiographical prose is the sanctity of his pen, both in the physical and allegorical sense of the object. He had transferred the sanctity of his father's word of God to his own word of and for the people. That sanctity had remained constant, varied the place and purpose of the prose, with which Al-e Ahmad breathed and prayed in his own specifically

Muslim way. He was making being a Muslim worldly – though he would not recognise this until he made his Hajj pilgrimage.

The Amen-saying Bird

Al-e Ahmad was to be found at the confluence of multiple historical forces: the height of European colonialism in Iran of the 1910s resulted in the lyrical poetry of Aref Qazvin, whose beautiful inspired response in turn yielded into the Allied militarism of the 1920s to which the poetry of Nima Yushij was a soaring reaction, then came the Reza Shah proto-fascism of the 1930s to which Sadegh Hedayat's ingenious fiction was an enduring literary response, which was in time wedded to the Tudeh Party socialism of the 1940s, in which the combined forces of Nima's poetry and Hedayat's fiction came together, and then came the anticolonial nationalism of the 1950s whose failure resulted in the Islamism of the 1960s to which Khomeini was a consequence. Al-e Ahmad was emotively born and raised in the thicket of this universe. Those who call him 'nativist' are blind to this world, deeply colonised in their Eurocentric imagination, and a totally lost cause, and in fact the symptom of what Al-e Ahmad prophetically called *Gharbzadeh*, paralysed by 'the West', who could not think on their own feet unless they participated in the Euro-universalism they had inherited colonially and that diminished the rest of the world to 'nativism'.

Al-e Ahmad was at the epicentre of it all – this universe of a post/colonial pandemonium. He knew Sadegh Hedayat well, was a close friend and neighbour of Nima Yushij and a solid fellow-traveller and comrade of the towering dramatist of his time, Gholamhossein Saedi (Gohar Morad). He was married to Simin Daneshvar, the single most prominent woman novelist of her generation, was the writer of his own works of fiction and did more than his share of significant translations of important literary works. He travelled extensively inside and outside Iran, which resulted in his 'ethnographies' and 'travelogues', and then he wrote masterful essays about a range of timely issues. He was a close friend of revolutionary figures like Mostafa Sho'aiyan (1936–76), a leading Marxist intellectual and leader of his time. His presence in Iranian politics, arts and culture was omnipresent, omniscient, normatively ambidextrous.

If retrieving Al-e Ahmad's memory is not for either antiquarian or panegyric purposes, either to condemn for something he did not do or celebrate him for something he may have done, then it is rather to rediscover a world which, in the aftermath of the consolidation of the Islamic Republic, and then the cataclysmic events of 9/11 and all the hell that it broke loose, we have now lost. It is for that reason that the life and legacy of Al-e Ahmad offers a sense of historical urgency, for he is both far away from us today and yet very close. Al-e Ahmad loomed larger than life on the intellectual horizons of mid-twentieth-century Iran for over two decades from the 1940s to the 1960s. He lived a very short life and yet he had a lasting and deeply influential impact on the history of his homeland. His contemporaries, like Ebrahim Golestan and Dariush Ashuri, have happily lived long and fulfilling lives. There are, however, very few similar intellectuals one can cite to compare with him in Iran or elsewhere. A combination of Jean-Paul Sartre and Michel Foucault in France, or of Edward Said and Noam Chomsky in the US, perhaps might be helpful in coming to terms with who and what Al-e Ahmad was in Iran. Such revolutionary figures as Frantz Fanon and Malcolm X, C. L. R. James, James Baldwin, Aimé Césaire or José Martí must also come together to help us understand the place of Al-e Ahmad in Iranian intellectual history.[35]

Because he wrote in his native Persian and the English translations of his work were limited to the obtuse field of 'Iranian Studies', scarcely anyone outside his homeland knew Al-e Ahmad or the significance of his work. When the scattered, random, entirely inadequate translations of his work eventually appeared in English he did receive some elementary attention, and even made it to Edward Said's *Culture and Imperialism* (1993). When I wrote one of the earliest accounts of his life and legacy in my *Theology of Discontent*, my chapter was almost entirely based on Al-e Ahmadi's own original sources. Soon after, other scholars also wrote on his work from various perspectives. Most of these writings however, remain limited to the presence of Al-e Ahmad in the Iranian scene – lacking in how to read him in connection to the larger world.

The origin of this limitation of vision has to do with Al-e Ahmad having made it into the global scene mostly through the lens of the Iranian revolution of 1977–9. As a result, most of the attention to Al-e Ahmad has been domestic or at best regional for the obvious reasons. The traumatic impact of the 1979 revolution and the Iran–Iraq war (1980–8) associated with the name of Ayatollah Khomeini brought the name and reputation of Al-e Ahmad to wider attention. Most of the world's attention was focused on that traumatic event and we were almost myopically fixated on the immediate contexts and the close environment of Al-e Ahmad's lifework. Some of our observations were accurate, some of it coloured by our particular prejudices and predilections. Forty years after those historic revolutionary years, and half a century after the sudden passing of Al-e Ahmad, we are in a far better position to look back at Al-e Ahmad's life and legacy. After the militant Islamisation of the Iranian revolution of 1977–9 and the bloody consolidation of the Islamic Republic in Iran, the world that had given birth to those momentous events is consistently and systematically lost. That world is no longer visible, evident, or even traceable. Very few of us students and scholars of modern Iran are still left active and perhaps capable of retrieving that world. If we are to think of a post-Islamist theology of liberation we must begin with a pre-Islamist Islamic liberation theology: one I have spent a good portion of my academic career mapping out. The significance of Al-e Ahmad was not, could have never been, in the totality or the total veracity of everything he thought and said. It was in the healthy dialogical environment where he uttered his thoughts and to which he had to respond. This responsiveness gave his prose a hidden or manifest dialogical poise. Immediately related to this environment was the global context of similar thinkers like Aimé Césaire, Frantz Fanon and Jose Martí, to whom we must now think how Al-e Ahmad is related.

The task at hand is therefore neither to eulogise nor to malign, neither to accuse nor to excuse, a man long since rushed to meet his creator. What would be the point? The task we face is the legacy of that man, and what that legacy means for the posterity of a nation, a region and by extension a world in the grips of a malignant monarchy when he died, and then in the tight grips of theocratical sectarianism he was no longer around to either endorse or denounce. One need not either believe my word that he would have opposed the formation of an Islamic Republic from day one, nor the word of the ruling Islamists in Iran who propose he would have been in their camp. The task facing us is to take his legacy and see in what particular ways it dovetails with the making of a future he would have recognised as the sustained extension of his restless, impatient and relentless mind, and even more importantly the world in which that mind dwelled.

In that mind and in his abiding prose and politics Al-e Ahmad became the omniscient narrator of his time – good and bad, the all-knowing character of an unfolding drama – the tragic hero that was out and about to learn of a traumatised world and write it up speedily for his people to read and learn. He was narrating the world and integrating his home and his world – and that is precisely why his travelogues in and out of Iran ought to be read together either as travelogues or, if ethnographies, then also as ethnographies of the world. In his sojourn through this life, Al-e Ahmad became the narrating voice of both faith and unbelief, of this world and the next, of the literary and the literal. He was mapping a cosmopolis. He had become the *Morgh-e Amin* of which Nima wrote:

Morgh-e Amin dard-aludi ast keh . . .

The Amen-saying Bird
Afflicted with pain
Homeless and forlorn –
Has flown to the thither end
Of this world of injustice
And returned –

Paining for his people
He has lost all his appetite
For water or feed
Awaiting the day of delivery
Thinking of salvation –

The Bird knows – omniscient as it is –
The hidden ear of our world –
The wretched of the earth –
With his refrain of 'Amen! Amen!'
The familiar bird
Brings them together
Reducing their afflictions and pains
Gathering their hidden hopes closer together.

In its throat the Bird has kept

The story of its people –

Linking them all together

Dismissive of all the faults they found with him –

Carrying in its beak

The tip of their unwounded skein.[36]

Notes

1. Jalal Al-e Ahmad, *Masalan Sharh-e Ahval* (*Something of an Autobiography*), in Jalal Al-e Ahmad, *Yek Chah-o-Do-Chaleh* (*One Dug Well and Two Pits* and *Masalan Sharh-e Ahval/Something of an Autobiography*) (Tehran: Ravaq Publications, no date): 46–54.

2. The full names of Jalal Al-e Ahmad and his father and grandfather are best recorded in the documents published by the secret archive of the Shah's intelligence ministry. See Anonymous (ed.), *Jalal Al-e Ahmad beh Ravayat Asnad SAVAK* (*Jalal Al-e Ahmad Based on the SAVAK Archive*) (Tehran: Markaz Barresi Asnad Tarikhi-e Vezarat-e Ettela'at, 1379/2000): 9.

3. For a brief and reliable account of Al-e Ahmad's life and career see the entry 'Al-e Aḥmad, Jalāl', in *Encyclopedia Iranica*. Available online here: http://www.iranicaonline.org/articles/al-e-ahmad-jalal-1302-48-s.

4. A solid source of information on Al-e Ahmad's biography based on extensive research in Persian is Hossein Mirza'i, *Jalal-e Ahl-e Qalam: Zendegi, Asar, va Andisheh Jalal Al-e Ahmad* (*The Glory of Writers: The Life, Work, and Thoughts of Jalal Al-e Ahmad*) (Tehran: Soroush, 1380/2001).

5. Al-e Ahmad gives a brief account of his stint with the Tudeh Party in his *Masalan Sharh-e Ahval* (*Something of an Autobiography*).

6. The most recent and reliable account of the CIA–MI6 coup against Iranian democracy is Ervand Abrahamian's *The Coup: 1953, The CIA, and The Roots of Modern U.S.–Iranian Relations* (New York: The New Press, 2013).

7. For a detailed study of these 'ethnographies' see Franz Lenze, *Der Nativist Galal-e Al-e Ahmad und die Verwestlichung Irans im 20. Jahrhundert* (Berlin: Klaus Schwarz Verlag, Islamkundliche Untersuchungen Band 284, 2008). The assumption that Jalal Al-e Ahmad was a 'nativist' is now a common cliché, and categorically flawed. Before Lenze, Mehrzad Boroujerdi had articulated this ill-conceived idea in his *Iranian Intellectuals and the West: The Tormented*

Triumph of Nativism (Syracuse, NY: Syracuse University Press, 1996). For these scholars anything other than the colonially conditioned European universalism is 'nativist'. For my critique of Euro-universalism see, among other places, *Can Non-Europeans Think?* (London: Zed Books, 2015).

8. For an excellent essay about the proclivities of Iranian to conspiracy theories see the entry under 'Conspiracy Theories' in *Encyclopedia Iranica*. Available online here: http://www.iranicaonline.org/articles/conspiracy-theories. Iranians of course are not the only people prone to such theories. Conspiracy theories regarding the assassination of John F. Kennedy or the events of the 9/11 are vast industries in the US. For my take on conspiracy theories in the US see my essay, 'The Garden of Americanly Delights' in *Al Jazeera* (20 September 2016). Available online here: https://www.aljazeera.com/indepth/opinion/2016/09/hamid-dabashi-election-2016-garden-americanly-delights-160919121423765.html.

9. See Anonymous (ed.), *Jalal Ale Ahmad: Mardi dar Keshakesh Tarikh-e Moaser (Jalal Al-e Ahmad: A Man in the Vicissitude of Cotemporary History)* (Tabriz: Kaveh Publications, 1357/1978).

10. Ibid: 3.

11. Ibid. 10.

12. Ibid: 16.

13. Ibid: 22.

14. Ibid: 24.

15. Ibid. 27.

16. Ibid: 33.

17. Ibid: 35.

18. Ibid: 40.

19. Ibid: 45.

20. Ibid: 49.

21. Ibid: 54.

22. Ibid: 124–5.

23. See *Jalal Al-e Ahmad based on SAVAK Archive*: 4.

24. The marginal note at *Jalal Al-e Ahmad based on SAVAK Archive*: 10.

25. Al-e Ahmad, *Masalan Sharh-e Ahval* (*Something of an Autobiography*) (Op. Cit.): 52.

26. Paul de Man, 'Autobiography as De-facement' (*MLN*, vol. 94, no. 5, December 1979): 919–30.

27. Ibid: 920.

28. Al-e Ahmad, *Yek Chah-o-Do-Chaleh* (*One Dug Well and Two Pits*) and *Masalan Sharh-e Ahval* (*Something of an Autobiography*): 9.

29. Ibid: 16–17.

30. See Amanda Laugesen, 'This Cold War-Era Publishing House Wanted to Share American Values with the World'. (Smithsonian.Com, 13 July 2018): Available online here: https://www.smithsonianmag.com/history/cold-war-government-funded-publishing-house-took-american-literature-world-180969624/.

31. Ibid.

32. Ibid.

33. Yek Chah-o-Do-Chaleh: 25.

34. Joseph G. Kronick, 'Philosophy as Autobiography: The Confessions of Jacques Derrida' (*MLN*, vol. 115, no. 5, December 2000): 1002.

35. In her excellent book, *The Intellectuals and the State in Iran: Politics, Discourse, and the Dilemma of Authenticity* (Gainesville: University Press of Florida, 2003: 84) Negin Nabavi rightly sees the connection between Al-e Ahmad and Césaire and Fanon, and also includes Jean-Paul Sartre. But she suggests a causal relation between them and Al-e Ahmad and places him at the receiving end of these figures in the category of 'Third-Worldist intellectual'. She also believes the idea of a 'committed intellectual' came to Iran from France and specifically from Sartre. All of this is of course the result of too-Eurocentric an imagination and categorically flawed. The relation of Al-e Ahmad to Césaire or Fanon was coterminous rather than causal, and Sartre had a very minimal presence here. But far more crucially the history and significance of Russian intelligentsia and the revolutionary mobilisation of intellectuals in the Central Asian regions in the nineteenth century that includes Iranian intellectuals like Fath Ali Akhondzadeh, Mirza Habib Isfahani and Mirza Agha Khan Kermani is much older and far more influential than Sartre and his nevertheless minor significance in the time of Al-e Ahmad. St Petersburg, Istanbul, Cairo and Delhi are far more crucial places of origin for this intellectual history than Paris and London, put together. For a sustained critique of this enduring Eurocentrism in Iranian historiography see my *Reversing the Colonial Gaze: Persian Travelers Abroad* (Cambridge: Cambridge University Press, 2020).

36. From Nima Yushij, 'Morgh-e Amin', My translation.

3

Her Husband Jalal

It was at this time that I married. When you give up hope in society at large, you build a smaller one at home – running away from my parental home to political life, and then from there to private home. My wife is Simin Daneshvar whom you all know well – a learned woman and a professional writer, an assistant professor of aesthetics, the author of countless books of her own and translations. In truth she is a friend and a comrade to the writer of these lines. Were it not for her, how much gibberish I would have published (have I not already?) From 1950 onward I have not published a word without Simin having first read and evaluated it.[1]

Jalal Al-e Ahmad, *Something of an Autobiography* (1967)

He died beautifully, just as he had lived beautifully, and he died hurriedly, just like the dying of a lantern, and right in the midst of ordinary people whom he loved and fought for . . . and now I understand why during all those years I had known him he was always in a rush – he knew the time was short, so he was always in a hurry to read, and learn, and touch, and experience, and build, and make a record, and drink the cup of every instance fully, and welcome the minutes with open mind and open arms . . .[2]

Simin Daneshvar, *Ghorub-e Jalal* ('Jalal's Sunset') (1969)

Before I go any further and in this chapter explore the relationship of Jalal Al-Ahmad and his wife Simin Daneshvar, a seminal aspect of both their lives and characters, let me briefly recap the major points I have been driving home so far as I write this book on the person I have suggested we consider 'the last Muslim intellectual'. You recall I have shared with you my primary concern in this book is to think through the prospects for a *post-Islamist liberation theology* by going back to a pre-Islamist period before the rise of the Islamic Republic in Iran, retrieving the pre-revolutionary world where Al-e Ahmad lived and wrote. By *Islamism* I mean the aggressive and violent transmutation of Islam as a multifaceted worldly religion into a singular sight of ideological resistance to 'the West'. And by *post-Islamism* I mean a period when Islamism has performed all its ideological functions and politically exhausted itself. This task I perform via actively de-nativising Al-e Ahmad against the grain of a sustained history of reading him as a nativist, which is exactly the opposite of who and what he was. There is a prevalent misreading of postcolonialism (as a mode of critical thinking), mostly by those alien to it, as a celebration of nativism, whereas at least in my own work I have sought to de-universalise Euro-universalism via a theoretical documentation, archiving and theorising of alternative universes rather than a celebration of nativism grounded in *ressentiment*. In identifying Al-e Ahmad as a Muslim intellectual I have therefore suggested the history of African slavery, the predicament of global coloniality and the victims of the Nazi Germany as the only types of seriously radical intellectuals that would call for a comparative understanding. This places Al-e Ahmad as much next to Theodor Adorno and Hannah Arendt as it does next to Aimé Césaire and C. L. R. James, or W. E. B. Du Bois and James Baldwin, Ngũgĩ wa Thiong'o and José Martí for a far better comparative and global understanding of who he was and what he meant. Once we do so, again against the grain of much scholarly writing on Al-e Ahmad by the professional enemies of the Islamic Republic, we see the rise of a far more global and worldlier universalism hitherto hidden under Eurocentric provincialism.

Instrumental to this violent nativisation of Al-e Ahmad is of course the Islamic Republic itself. Over the last four decades the ruling echelons of the Islamic Republic have claimed and thus distorted the legacy of Al-e Ahmad for their own benefits, as have the enemies of the Islamic Republic who have picked on Al-e Ahmad as their *bête noire*, holding him responsible, entirely illogically, for its atrocities. These two opposite sides cancel each other out and leave us plenty of room to think Al-e Ahmad anew. Against these misguided but prevalent tendencies, I have sought to retrieve *the spirit* of the age Al-e

Ahmad lived in, in the vicinity of the two towering figures of Nima Yushij and Sadegh Hedayat. In this context I have also proposed Jalal Al-Ahmad's prose, formed in their neighbourhood, works through a systematic act of 'defamiliarisation' or *ostranenie* as the Russian formalist Victor Shklovsky would term and theorise it. I will have more occasions in the next few chapters to return to this issue and develop it further, for I believe in his prose the form of the familiar narrative, *the prose of our historicality* as Ranajit Guha would call it,[3] becomes unfamiliar, the ordinary strange and the common twisted to yield the alterity of identity politics. In this context I have also suggested that Al-e Ahmad's turn to autobiographical accounts are acts of public performances, whereby he stages himself, and this staging is integral to

Figure 3.1 Jalal Al-e Ahmad and Simin Daneshvar's wedding, 1950. (Photo courtesy of Ali Dehbashi, from the *Bokhara Magazine* archive) The newlyweds typify the young couples of their time and class. Daneshvar hailed from the provincial capital of Shiraz from a learned bourgeois family, Al-e Ahmad from a clerical coterie of Shi'i mullahs residing in the capital of Tehran. Neither of them had married up or down, but sideways, having come from learned families of differing sentiments and proclivities. The expansion of urbanisation and social mobility from the early twentieth century onwards had occasioned organic expansion of nuclear families.

his public persona, to his ability to speak in the voice of a public intellectual. He in fact constitutes that public space by crafting and performing (in) it. Such literary moves are integral to my attempt to pay as much attention to the *forms* of his work as to their *substance*. Without such detailed attentions to forms we might not be able to see how his substitutional transference of the sacred takes place from the *Theos* to the *Demos*, from *God* to *the People*. All his protestations notwithstanding, he did follow his father's profession after all!

Leili and Majnun, etc.

How would an Iranian couple form an ideal prototype for their society at large? I was born to a working-class family a year after Jalal Al-e Ahmad and Simin Daneshvar were married in 1950. We grew up without it even occurring to us that a married couple had to have an ideal-type to which they might approximate their lives together – with respect, love, mutual admiration, friendship and even comradery. Our parents were our most normative ideal types. Boys grew up to be like their fathers and girls like their mothers. But the world at large was changing around us and Iran with it. Consistent patterns of urbanisation and labour migrations from villages and small towns to cities like Ahvaz where I was born, or Shiraz where Simin Daneshvar was born, or Tehran where Jalal Al-e Ahmad was born, meant that these and other major cities were undergoing sizeable demographic changes. My mother was the first child of a migrant labour couple from Dezful to Ahvaz. Her parents, my maternal grandparents, were so concerned about their move to a major city they did not send their elder daughter, my mother, to any formal state-run schooling. Her younger sisters, my maternal aunts Gohar and Qadam, however, were born at a time when the migrant couple were more confident about their new urban environment and, therefore, they received formal schooling. My aunts received a proper high school education and married middle-class bourgeois professionals, while my mother was married off to the first simple labourer at the railway crossing my grandparents could get hold of and entrust their elder daughter to his care. It did not occur to them, given their class origins, or to us their children that a couple might have an 'ideal-type'.

These were the circumstances of marital lives and parental care in the Iran of the 1950s when Jalal Al-e Ahmad and Simin Daneshvar met and soon married. But what about love, you may wonder. Well, there was love, to be sure, but all in a very abstract and remote and unearthly kind of a way. We were born to and grew up with the phantasmagorical love stories of Leili and Majnun, Khosrow and Shirin, Vamegh and Azra, Vis and Ramin, Bizhan and Manizheh – all on the prototype of Adam and Eve, or their Zoroastrian counterparts, perhaps to be more precise, Mashya and Mashyana. They were not real. These were all magnificent love stories, and still remain beautiful love stories preserved for us by master Persian poets like Nezami, Ferdowsi, Gorgani and others. We read these love stories when we grew up in our high school textbooks. They were passionate, moving, performed in sublime Persian poetry and made us wonder – but they were just stories, and we could never imagine Leili and Majnun as a married couple or Khosrow and Shirin as a pair of parents. They were unreal and, in their unreality, they formed the poetic subterfuge of our normative sense and sensibilities, as our heroes and heroines, in the deep background of our budding sense of Eros and eroticism.

Things were changing, however. The lyrical poetry of the Constitutional period (1906–11) had now entered the public domain. With the emergence of the first generation of female vocalists like Qamar al-Moluk Vaziri (1905–59) and Moluk Zarrabi (1910–99) and the establishment of Tehran Radio in 1930, people could actually hear a woman sing of love and passion and desire openly for the whole world to hear. The eventual introduction of Indian, Egyptian and Hollywood musicals in the 1930s through to the 1960s widened the horizons of exposure of female singers, dancers and visual topographies of heterosexual couples. With the emergence of Parvin E'tesami (1907–41) as a prominent poet, people could now read that a woman could also be socially engaged, politically conscious, morally imaginative, poetically gifted. But without a doubt something far more serious happened with the emergence of Forough Farrokhzad (1934–67) as a celebrated and scandalised poet. Her poetry was real, her passions palpable, her eroticism bewildering. People could now hear and read a woman write poetry of the most sensual power and poignancy. My elder cousins Sharifeh and Fattaneh were devotees of Forough Farrokhzad and would recite her poetry for the rest of us, little rascals in the neighbourhood of their puberties and disquieting desires.

By the time of Jalal Al-e Ahmad and Simin Daneshvar's marriage, Iran at large had also become aware of more famous couples whose married life had stimulated something of a global awareness. Diego Rivera and Frida Kahlo, Rosa Luxemburg and Konstantin Zetkin, Franz Kafka and Milena Jesenská, Jean-Paul Sartre and Simone de Beauvoir, and later Martin Heidegger and Hannah Arendt – the figures of Simin Daneshvar and Jalal Al-e Ahmad began to resonate with other famous couples around the world – whether married or just romantically involved. The issue in Iran however at the time of this marriage was how to be a married couple and to see how their love was made public. Limited as it was mostly to literary and intellectual circles in Tehran, the couple soon assumed an iconic significance beyond their own immediate reaches. For that kind of marriage, we did not have a history, a model, or a predecessor. We had the case of Ebrahim Golestan and Forough Farrokhzad as two renowned lovers, but that was an illicit love affair between a married man and a famous poet, and not the public life of a married couple. Golestan was a prominent filmmaker and novelist. Farrokhzad was a divorced and single woman emerging as the most gifted poet of her time. Their liaison was scandalous for any couple, rather than normative. The issue with Al-e Ahmad and Daneshvar was how, in the absence of any drama or scandal, their marriage was emerging as the prototype of an ordinary heterosexual marriage – very normative, heteronormative in fact. That kind of marriage was supposed to be boring and banal and yet Al-e Ahmad and Daneshvar's marriage was nothing of the sort. This is how it was that their increasingly public marital status became normative for an entire generation of aspiring middle-class couples in whom love, affection, friendship and comradery were made possible, visible, palpable. In them Mashya and Mashyana had come back to earth to converse with the earthlings. In them we were witness to a modern mythology.

At issue was also the prospect of modern marriage in general with the couple constantly negotiating love and affection and even eroticism while addressing issues of parity between two intellectual equals and political comrades. That kind of role model did not exist. That was not part of any public conception of marriage.[4] We had marriage of the designated couples, mostly members of the same family, or in the neighbourhood, or even professional acquaintances in a hospital or high school, etc. In this case, Al-e Ahmad and Daneshvar had met during a bus ride between Shiraz and Tehran and fallen in love, and this was rare – but possible – for the emerging bourgeois public sphere had made it possible for young girls to go to pursue their education from their hometown to the capital.

Simin Daneshvar Enters Jalal Al-e Ahmad's Life

Let us now pay a closer attention to the relationship between Jalal Al-e Ahmad and his wife Simin Daneshvar. The couple were central figures in much of the social and intellectual life of their time. A few seminal texts are crucial here, firstly an extraordinary autobiographical book Al-e Ahmad wrote, *Sangi bar Guri* (*A Tombstone*) (written in 1963, published in 1981), in which he offers a rare glimpse at deeply personal aspects of their married life together. This text is to be read in conjunction with two other biographical sketches that Simin Daneshvar wrote, *Shohar-e Man Jalal* (*My Husband Jalal*) (1961) and *Ghorub-e Jalal* (*Jalal's Sunset*) (1982). The letters of the couple to each other have also been edited and published, and these are equally important. A spectacularly successful novel that Simin Daneshvar wrote, *Savushun* (*Requiem*) (1969) is also important in this regard for the central two characters of the novel, Zari and Yusef, are also a fictive rendition of Simin Daneshvar and Jalal Al-e Ahmad. These sources put together offer a unique and deeply moving account of the life of the couple and what they meant to each other and to posterity. Prompted by a blasé liberal feminism combined with the post-mortem hostility towards Al-e Ahmad by his liberal detractors, these sources by the husband and wife have always been read against each other. I intend to read them in tandem.

There is no exaggerating the significance of Simin Daneshvar in her own right as a towering literary figure, but also for our purposes in this book her seminal significance in Al-e Ahmad's life and legacy. When read together Al-e Ahmad and Daneshvar configure a far different portrait from when they are pitted against each other, as their liberal readers have habitually done. Simin Daneshvar was born on 28 April 1921 to a deeply learned, cultivated and prominent family in the southern city of Shiraz.[5] By the time of her death on 8 March 2012 at the age of ninety-one, she had established herself as a towering literary figure in her homeland – a novelist, short story writer, essayist and academic. Iranian literary critics have noted how, when the entirety of a nation was deeply influenced by Jalal Al-e Ahmad's prose and politics, she sustained her own signature prose, uncompromising attention to literary details and an admirable independence in her own erudition and diction. This is only partially true and made paramount if we insist on reading the couple against each other. There is an alternative way of reading them in tandem that I believe is more insightful for understanding the literary career of both writers. Simin Daneshvar's confidence was rooted in her exquisite upbringing long before she met Al-e Ahmad. Daneshvar's father, Mohammad Ali Daneshvar, was a prominent physician; her mother, Qamar al-Saltaneh Hekmat, was an accomplished painter. From her mother's side she was connected to a prominent clerical family in Shiraz. Her father had studied traditional medicine in Iran and modern medicine in Germany and France. As a major cosmopolitan city in southern Iran, Shiraz was no ordinary city. The birthplace of two towering Persian poets, Sa'di and Hafez, the city was renowned for its long and illustrious history of learned literati. The Daneshvar family, the father's library and the mother's atelier, were the location where Daneshvar and her siblings built their childhood and youthful confidence and moral rectitude.[6]

Daneshvar's love for learning and the arts was cultivated right there in her home, in their family's library and atelier. She soon commanded a solid knowledge of English through which she read masterpieces of European literature, from Mark Twain to Johann Wolfgang von Goethe to Charlotte Brontë. Upon graduation from high school she accompanied two of her older siblings to Tehran where she first studied English in an American boarding school, and then entered Tehran University to work on her bachelor's in Persian literature. She was blessed with progressive parents who were even thinking of sending her abroad for her higher education. She soon became a known figure to her literary contemporaries. 'Tell you the truth, I was quite cheeky and talkative in those days. Now I am learning silence.'[7] While still in Shiraz she had met with Sadegh Hedayat, in Tehran she met Parvin E'tesami. The leading novelists and poets of her time were now on her radar. Her first collection of stories appeared in 1948, called *Atash-e Khamush* (*Burned Fire*). In the same year of 1948, she met Jalal Al-e Ahmad on a bus journey to Tehran. They were immediately drawn to each other. By then Daneshvar knew Al-e Ahmad because by then he had already been established as a writer. Two years later they were married.

Simin Daneshvar wrote her doctoral thesis on aesthetics in Persian literature with professor Fatemeh Sayyah (1902–48), the first professor of comparative literature at Tehran University.[8] When Fatemeh Sayyah passed away at a very young age, Daneshvar continued her work with the eminent doyen of Persian literature Badi' al-Zaman Foruzanfar (1904–70). This means her command of Persian and comparative literature was the result of close work with the most eminent master of the field at her time. She defended her dissertation in 1949, just a year before her marriage to Al-e Ahmad in April 1950, who was two years younger than her. Both professionally and in formal and disciplined education and scholarship she was more accomplished than her husband. Al-e Ahmad's family initially did not approve of this marriage for she was not from their clerical class or from the merchant's class in the bazaar (which they would have equally approved), but most particularly because she had already dispensed with the customary hijab still much favoured by those two classes. She was deeply learned, widely cultivated, intellectually on par if not entirely superior and professionally more accomplished than their son – and they had no idea how to handle those facts. The fact that she was *bi-hijab* ('hijab-less') was just the iconic register of those other issues. Al-e Ahmad's family, however, eventually learned deeply to love and admire their daughter-in-law.

Taking advantage of a Fulbright Fellowship in 1952, Simin Daneshvar travelled to the US and studied fiction at Stanford University. She worked closely with Wallace Stegner (1909–93), the Pulitzer Prize-winning American novelist who had initially taught at the University of Wisconsin and Harvard University and eventually settled at Stanford University, where he founded the creative writing programme. Among his many prominent students were the future Supreme Court Justice Sandra Day O'Connor. This experience had an enduring effect on Daneshvar's creative writing and professional career. It also meant she had more than a passing command over English as a literary language. Translating literary works from English to Persian, sometimes in collaboration with Al-e Ahmad, became a steady source of income for the couple. The couple were by now comfortably multilingual, with fluent command over Persian, Arabic, English and French. While Daneshvar was in the US, her husband was busy building her their dream house, a legendary home that became the iconic destination of the leading literati and poets of the time. The deeply passionate and beautiful love letters Al-e Ahmad and

Daneshvar wrote to each other in this period have survived as a masterpiece of epistolary literature in Persian.

In 1957, Daneshvar and Al-e Ahmad travelled abroad, and she delivered a speech at the American University in Beirut (AUB), from where they travelled to Italy and France for a few months sightseeing and visiting museums. All such experiences were crucial for her when, in 1958, she started teaching aesthetics at Tehran University. It is crucial here to recall Daneshvar began writing her doctoral dissertation with Fatemeh Sayyah, the first woman professor at Tehran University. Sayyah was a product of Russian higher education, with a native command over Persian language and literature. Daneshvar at this point is almost entirely a product of Iranian higher education, with short but important visits to the Arab world, Europe and the US. These are inaugural instances in the momentous history of women's achievements in higher education, and Simin Daneshvar has an iconic place in this history.

In 1961 Daneshvar published a collection of ten short stories called *Shahri Chon Behesht* (*A City Like Paradise*). This collection staged Daneshvar's gift of quick and effective plotting of a short story and her exceptional command over character building. Slave girls in southern Iran, American families visiting the country, poor women at the mercy of their careerist husbands, manifestations of urban pieties, lives of midwives, budding loves among teenagers, marital infidelity, class differences and racialised tensions are among the issues she explores in this collection of short stories. The collection consolidates Daneshvar's place as a seminal literary figure. By this time Al-e Ahmad had already established a solid name for himself in emerging contemporary fiction, with *Modir-e Madreseh* (*School Principal*) (1958) as his seminal achievement. Daneshvar meanwhile had her own distinct creative character, by having effectively cultivated a direct link to Sadegh Hedayat in her own distinctive prose.[9]

Daneshvar spent the summer of 1963 at Harvard University in Boston, Massachusetts as the guest of a summer programme organised by the future US Secretary of State, Henry Kissinger. While in the US, she also met with the eminent American novelist Ralph Ellison (1914–94) and others. Two years later, in the summer of 1965, Al-e Ahmad would also come to join the same summer programme at Harvard. In a short piece written for Harvard Crimson in August 1969, just a few short years after Daneshvar and Al-e

Ahmad had visited Harvard, Robin B. Wright, who later became a prominent journalist, wrote about the rise and demise of this Harvard seminar.[10] Wright writes:

> The idea of the International Seminar was conceived by Professor William Elliott in 1951. But for all practical purpose the program's success is accredited to Professor Henry A. Kissinger who has served as director and chief fund-raiser during the seminar's 18-year history.

From the same report we learn:

> A serious drawback to the seminar this year is Kissinger's absence. Because the program is sponsored by a single professor, not directly by Harvard, the funds come from outside sources. Without what has been described as 'the magic of Kissinger's name', it is difficult to raise the $80,000 necessary to fund the participant's transportation, room and board and $15 a week spending money.

At the height of anti-war protests and the Civil Rights Movement in the US and around the globe, the function of these summer programmes was now threefold: Kissinger wanted to know the state of mind of critical thinkers from around the world, he wanted to implicate and ingratiate his guests in 'American generosity' and he hoped to plant pro-American intellectuals in 'the Third World'. His success on these three fronts is quite dubious.

Early in the summer of 1969 Daneshvar's masterpiece novel *Savushun* was published; later that summer her husband Jalal Al-e Ahmad died of a sudden stroke. *Savushun* rightly established the name and reputation of Daneshvar as the preeminent novelist of her generation, in the same ranking as Sadegh Hedayat, Ebrahim Golestan and later Houshang Golshiri and Mahmoud Dolatabadi, perhaps even more prominent than that of Al-e Ahmad. Set in Daneshvar's hometown of Shiraz while under British occupation during World War II, *Savushun* is the story of Zari, the young wife of a member of the landed gentry Yusuf, herself from a leading local family. Fully aware of the political forces at work beyond her control, Zari seeks to safeguard her own home from the horrors of the outside world. She raises her children lovingly, attends to the political whims of her husband and does social work for the needy in the city. One disruption after another leads to a final tragedy that tests Zari's threshold of sanity and grace. The novel is so exquisitely poised, so quietly elegant, so politically perfectly pitched that it pushed the boundaries established by Hedayat into decidedly female spaces and voices.[11]

Daneshvar survived Al-e Ahmad by decades and lived a long and rich and fulfilling life to the mature age of ninety-one, loved and admired by generations of her readers, widely translated and having found readers around the globe.[12] Towards the end of her life her final book *Jazireh Sargardani* (*Wandering Island*) (1993) was published. In this novel, presumed to be the first in a trilogy, Daneshvar experiments with multiple perspectives, flash-back, fusion of varied times and narratives, which all come together to project

Figure 3.2 Jalal Al-e Ahmad and Simin Daneshvar's wedding, 1950, with Simin Daneshvar's sister Victoria Daneshvar. (Photo courtesy of Ali Dehbashi, from the *Bokhara Magazine* archive) The festive painting on the wall, the bottles of wine on the table, the tie and pocket square of Al-e Ahmad, Daneshvar's necklace and dress and her sister's gold bracelets all come together to mark the changing accoutrement of class distinction. Daneshvar and her sister's body language exudes women's confidence only a few years after Reza Shah had banned the chador. Al-e Ahmad sparkles in his brand-new wedding suit despite the fact that in his writing he was fully self-conscious of having very recently abandoned the clerical robe for European chic.

a politics of contemporary Iranian life and memory where the personal and the political, the past and the future, fuse together. The second instalment of this trilogy, *Sareban-e Sargardan* (*Wandering Cameleer*) (2001), was reported to be followed by *Kuh-e Sargardan* (*Wandering Mountain*), but for unknown reasons this never materialised. With her passing an entire era came to a desolate ending.

My Husband Jalal

This brief introduction to the life and significance of Simin Daneshvar is only in the context of this book on Jalal Al-e Ahmad. She richly deserves, and has in fact received in Persian among Iranians, much more detailed attention to her work with perhaps a minor chapter to her marriage to Jalal Al-e Ahmad. I very much hope the extensive material available in Persian will be carefully read and expanded to unpublished and archival material so a richly deserved biography in Persian and other languages will be prepared on Simin Daneshvar to salvage her literary significance from the jaundiced liberal feminism sporadically thrown at her. For my purposes I must rather draw attention to those priceless moments when she wrote specifically about her husband, the subject of my investigation in this book. Beyond that I am also eager to explore the dialogical disposition of their respective prose framing each other. The couple were like two mirrors constantly placed in front of the other. That reflective dialectic remains an entirely unexplored dimension of their literary characters. The question is not a cliché characterisation of who 'influenced' whom, but rather how their binary disposition embedded their creative proses. In other words, I propose to read the two not *in opposition to* each other as they have often been, but *in apposition with* each other as they should be.

Simin Daneshvar's *Shohar-e Man Jalal* (*My Husband Jalal*) (1961) was written and published when Jalal Al-e Ahmad was still alive.[13] This fact in and of itself is crucial, for writing about one's husband is not something an Iranian wife does, the genre does not exist, the format is not mapped out, and prior to this extraordinary text the very language of a woman writing publicly about her husband was unavailable. Immediately related to this rarity is the way Daneshvar refers to her husband, as 'My Husband Jalal', when just about a generation earlier, or even simultaneous with her, husbands and wives did not refer to each other publicly by their first names. Such references as *Aqa* ('sir'), *Madar-e Bachcheh-ha* ('the mother of the children') or else the husband's last name, 'Al-e Ahmad', or his professional title, 'the doctor', 'the engineer', and so forth, were the common ways for a wife publicly to referring to her husband. Just a generation after Daneshvar, however, even the term *Shohar* ('husband') would become a derogatory term for a certain brand of bourgeois feminism that took hold of a class of Iranian feminists. They consider it demeaning and beneath them to call someone their '*Shohar*' or even '*Hamsar*', which had become a more common and palatable term among the educated middle class. In these circumstances, Daneshvar opted for the classical and solid term '*Shohar*'. By and large in public documents, Al-e Ahmad referred to his wife as 'my wife Simin', and Daneshvar to her husband, as in this case, 'my husband Jalal'.[14] The reference in both cases is endearing, disarming, real, evident, something that only a creative writer would dare to declare so publicly. From Daneshvar's pen, in other words, Al-e Ahmad emerges as a character in a work of fiction, *her* work of fiction, except real.

In *Shohar-e Man Jalal*, Daneshvar tells us how usually wives do not have much interest in their husband's artwork, but she does so because she does not distinguish between her husband and his work, except she knows him as the first draft of her work and others know him as the final clean version.[15] In making this distinction between the first and the final draft of Al-e Ahmad she in effect demarcates the private and public personae of the writer – both herself and her husband – one rehearsed, the other performed. Opting to describe the public, she describes Al-e Ahmad's writing as 'telegraphic, sensitive, precise, insightful, angry, absolutist, violent, blunt, sincere, puritanical and incident-prone'. She compares him to the hero of a story, but a contemporary story, a character in search of dramas. She speaks with humility and love of her first meeting with Jalal Al-e Ahmad in the spring of 1948, and how they fell in love, and the fact that they have shared their lives together now for fourteen years at the writing of this essay in 1961, and tells us how Al-e Ahmad built the house in which they live almost all by his own hand. What we are reading here is really a short love story, with Simin Daneshvar as both the omniscient narrator and protagonist. This little piece is in fact the reversal of thousands of years of women being the objects of desire not the subjects of loving, caring, of admiring the man they love, of desiring him body and soul. The Al-e Ahmad that emerges in this piece is an object of affection, not an *Asheq* (lover) but a *Ma'shuq* (beloved). This is putting Persian lyrical poetry on its head.

Daneshvar speaks regretfully of her and Al-e Ahmad not having had a child together, which would have made her husband more tolerant of adversities.[16] She tells us that Al-e Ahmad was a thoroughly religious believer in his youth, that he then joined the Tudeh Party and that he had just left the party when they met and soon married. She writes lovingly of his travels, of his compassion for ordinary people, of his total devotion to his research, when getting ready to write, all at the cost of attending to his own health, to the point that in his forties all his hair has turned white and he is exceedingly thin and weak. She shares with us how Al-e Ahmad totally gets himself lost and immersed in his work, for example when he was writing on beehives and was stung by bees many times, and he even wanted to have a beehive at home (with which his wife disagreed 'for I was afraid he may soon want to write about bigger animals and before we knew it our home would turn into a zoo').[17] The master storyteller, the quick wit of her proverbial Shirazi humour, is here fully at work endearing her husband, portraying him as an ascetic revolutionary, a gift to the world, all seen from her own loving eyes. It no longer matters if Al-e Ahmad himself measures up to what Simin Daneshvar tells us he is. Al-e Ahmad himself, the real person, disappears into the persona the most gifted woman novelist of our age made him out to be.

Daneshvar shares with us how Al-e Ahmad is prone to prolonged periods of depression, followed by fits of anger, followed by a heightened desire to travel. She compares him to a caged bird.[18] Occasionally he has tried to work with institutions but has failed, but they keep trying various avenues because their combined salaries are not sufficient for them to self-publish. Like a bipolar person Al-e Ahmad then comes out of these periods of seclusion and becomes excessively social. Daneshvar speaks of the astonishing range of their friends who come together to be with them. Here is where we see how Al-e Ahmad's charismatic presence as a public intellectual attracts a whole range of learned and common characters to him. His stubbornness, she says, is like his father who had not come to visit them for ten years after their marriage until the elder Al-e Ahmad became ill. But Al-e Ahmad had a very close and loving relationship with his mother. Line after line, Daneshvar reveals the key character of her own life story, the protagonist of her sojourn through life, Jalal Al-e Ahmad, who becomes a full, complete, vulnerable, real, phantasmagorical, flawed, and yet only too human figure, sketched from her caring, loving, forgiving pen. At this point we realise Al-e Ahmad and Daneshvar are two public personae entirely contingent on each other, living and pairing and performing each other in public.

When Daneshvar's sister Homa Riyahi commits suicide, Al-e Ahmad drives them both furiously from Tehran to Kermanshah to get to her where she lived but she dies before they get there, and Al-e Ahmad sobs like Daneshvar had never seen him cry. Writing about his fast driving on this occasion, Daneshvar tells us how Al-e Ahmad never waits for the events to happen but always rushes to embrace them. From the dignified quietude of her writing pad, Daneshvar sketches out the central protagonist of a novella she was living and no one else could see or read or write as she did. Every incident, every characteristic, she shares with us is at once true and yet indicative of something unusual, strange and yet strangely common. Al-e Ahmad, or more precisely 'Jalal', the way she saw and described him, was perhaps her greatest work of art.

Daneshvar's portrayal of Al-e Ahmad as an ascetic revolutionary is consistent. He dressed, she tells us, frugally and only upon his wife's insistence would he go to get himself a new suit. He has a saintly patience when gardening and loves to stare at their little pond and count their goldfish, who all die during the winter but he replenishes them by the spring so their little pond is always full of goldfish. She writes warmly and lovingly of their reading the masterpieces of Persian literature together during the long winter nights, or else they would listen to classical Persian music. Al-e Ahmad loved to work around the house, attending to electrical chores or other little machines around the house that needed repairing, mending, fixing. He was evidently quite a handyman. Daneshvar is particular in giving her readers a domestic view of the public intellectual, making him look ordinary in his extraordinariness. As we read Daneshvar we realise we knew only half of the man, half a truth, half a phenomenon – but now she completes him, writes the other half, completes the visible with the invisible. Now we suddenly realise no human being is complete without the interiority of his exteriority discovered and told by a caring loving chronicler. Now Daneshvar can let us go and read the loud and defiant man. She has completed the picture. Without this loving narrative, and there is the rub, we could never, we have never, read the man. Al-e Ahmad as a phenomenon, as a public figure, would have been impossible to imagine without this imagining of his hidden half, written by his better half.

Al-e Ahmad went mountain climbing, she tells us, and on his return he would bring his wife wild flowers he had picked on the mountaintops, or even on an occasion a branch of olive tree.[19] The prose thus folds and unfolds and then she concludes:

> ... and let me say this and end, despite his apparent harshness, at the bottom of his heart he is a poet and even a bit romantic, and perhaps that is the only difference between him and his writing. Although I have seen many traces of poetry in his work, never have I seen any hallucinations or running away from bitter reality.[20]

Did she see that, or did she just invent it? After this 'My Husband Jalal', it is impossible to read Jalal Al-e Ahmad except as Simin Daneshvar's husband, the object of her enduring love and ennobling affection.

A Childless Pair

'*Hamid-e Azizam* (My Dear Hamid), this book is a truly stupid book.' The handwritten note written by pencil in Persian on the first blank page of my copy of Al-e Ahmad's *Sangi bar Guri* (*A Tombstone*) (1963/1981) brought an avalanche of memories back to me. I had just opened to reread it while working on this chapter when I remembered this note and continued to read:

> But for two reasons I am sending it to you. First of all, as soon as I saw it, I bought two copies one for you and the other for me. Second, because it is very important you read this book and be aware of the backwardness and corruption of the mind of this gentleman who never thought much of anyone else, and considered himself made of a superior fabric. It'll make you wonder, and you'd no longer be surprised by what calamity has befallen us [the Islamic Republic], for when the so-called responsible and committed intellectuals of a nation is someone like this person then that nation deserves whatever calamity happens to it, (everything except salvation). At

any rate, read and learn, and if you were about to throw up or something similar, just endure it for (as the poet says): It would be good if we were to have the measure of experience/So the impure are scandalised.

At the bottom of her note in Persian I had added, after having read the book, also in Persian, 'Alas, . . . as usual I disagree with you!'

The writer of that hand-note is a dear friend, with a PhD in Persian literature from Tehran University and an exceptionally well-read and erudite member of my extended family. This exchange some forty years ago on the front pages of a copy of Al-e Ahmad's controversial book is very much typical of the debates among the rest of Iranian educated class soon after the publication of *Sangi bar Guri* in 1981, roughly two years after the Islamic Republic took over the Iranian revolution of 1977–9. Ever since, this book has remained a deeply divisive text, with some raising serious questions about its language and tone, others about its substance, and yet most concur this is a seminal book, central to some serious issues in Iranian social and political culture.

From the last dated page of *Sangi bar Guri* we learn that Al-e Ahmad had finished the first draft of the book on 1 Mordad 1342, which corresponds to Tuesday, 23 July 1963, and the second and final draft he finished on 20 Dey 1342, which corresponds to Friday, 10 January 1964. The book had remained unpublished until 1981, about twelve years after Al-e Ahmad's passing. So obviously Al-e Ahmad himself did not publish the book, and it is not clear whether if he were to have lived a year or two after the revolution, or even later, he would have ever published the book himself. Al-e Ahmad was an obsessive writer, but not everything he wrote was for public consumption. Much of his writing was private correspondence, others his ruminations. He may or may not have published this book were he to be alive. The book was published posthumously by his brother Shams Al-e Ahmad, fanatically pro-Islamic Republic, against the wish and will of Al-e Ahmad's wife. Shams Al-e Ahmad had decided to publish this book for reasons only known to him, probably to humiliate his sister-in-law, perhaps out of a sense of duty to his brother's legacy. It is hard to tell. But once it was published it had entered the public domain and there was nothing that could or should have been done to unwrite the text. Simin Daneshvar has later written that Al-e Ahmad had given the text to her to read, and reading it had deeply disturbed her. After all is said and done, *Sangi bar Guri* is a remarkable text, a unique, daring and troubling testament, whether you like or dislike it, and the contemporary history of Iran is richer for having it in public domain than not.

I still have my own copy of the very first edition of the book that my family friend had sent to Philadelphia from Tehran upon its publication. I first finished reading it on 6 Dey 1360, which corresponds to Sunday, 27 December 1981, which is exactly the year it was published, some eighteen years after Al-e Ahmad wrote it, and thirty-eight years before I read it again and finished it on 7 November 2019, as I was preparing to write this chapter.[21] The fact that I signed my first reading of the book in the Persian calendar very much describes my state of mind as a graduate student and a recent immigrant still living according to the calendar of my homeland while living in the US. More than forty years into my life in the US, I have now completely lost contact with both the Islamic and the Persian calendars, except for academic writings and scholarly purposes. The colonial conquest of the times of our lives has by now in fact reversed itself. The postcolonial world has confiscated the commonality of that European/Christian calendar to strike a chord of solidarity among all of us in Asia, Africa and Latin America. That fact and the full recognition of its veracity is one fundamental difference between me and Al-e Ahmad. He was too close to the particularity of his nation's encounter with the tragedy to realise we have triumphed over it.

Before the text of *Sangi bar Guri* starts, there is a quote attributed to someone Al-e Ahmad calls 'Faqfiqa' Bani' and the phrase is: 'Every man is a tombstone to his father.' The more I tried to figure out who this 'Faqfiqa' Bani' was, the quicker I realised Al-e Ahmad had just made him up.[22] I have concluded this is a fictitious quote from a non-existent character. This is a faux quote. There is no such Hebrew Prophet, though Al-e Ahmad fakes that impression. The giveaway is the verse number that is supposed to be 'The first and final verse from Section 31' of a Biblical book, again an entirely made-up citation. 'The first and final verse' means this is a chapter of a Holy Book, the Qur'an or the Bible, which has only one verse, and Section 31 might allude to the 30 Sections of the Qur'an. So, this is a chapter that has only one verse and comes at the end of the Qur'an, to follow the fictitious apocryphal character of Al-e Ahmad's false flag. The presumed person or the prophet is therefore

Al-e Ahmad himself, who repeats this phrase a few times towards the end of the book. This whole allusion is altogether a playful citation of a source that does not exist, and Al-e Ahmad is just making it up to feign the thunder of a Biblical moment. The false citation and its implicit blasphemous imprint, however, match well with the angry overtone of the text itself.

The short text of *Sangi bar Guri* is divided into six chapters. Each chapter addresses one particularly thorny aspect of the central issue of the book which is the fact of Al-e Ahmad's infertility, which in certain quarters of Iranian society was falsely but strongly identified with sexual impotence. The first chapter is an emotional rollercoaster in which Al-e Ahmad unleashes his violent thoughts about not having a child, his tensions with his wife, his having soon discovered the medical explanation that this was his fault for his sperm count was too low to result in any pregnancy. His low sperm count is the cause of this trauma. This fact deeply troubles, angers and frustrates him. Al-e Ahmad tells us about his frequent visits to labs where he is asked by physicians to masturbate to ejaculate for his semen to be analysed, under a microscope, after which his legs get weak and he cannot walk properly. He gives details of how he has watched his own sperm through the microscope and realised how weak and fragile and hurried they are, just like he himself, he interjects, always in a rush.[23] He tells us he once even visited an Austrian expert when he and his wife were in Europe, who told them the same thing. At this point he goes through his entire parentage and how they have all been lucky with many children except for him. His tone is angry, frustrated, sarcastic, occasionally even vulgar and feisty. There are moments when he yearns for children, and then there are moments when he denounces the entire human race. He is an angry creature facing his creator with unrelating fury against his fate.

The second chapter is equally, if not even more, furious, this time on the subject of trying to adopt a child, when the couple finally conclude they cannot conceive their own. Al-e Ahmad and Daneshvar were inclined to consider this possibility until they discover the child they had in mind was the bastard son born from a rich member of an elite family with a vulnerable woman who was putting her son up for adoption. This unleashes Al-e Ahmad's invective against the rich and the powerful. He denounces the whole business of orphanage as a sham to make the elite feel even more powerful and privileged. Towards the end of the chapter, Al-e Ahmad has a nasty revelation about how he told his wife she can go have sex with anyone she wants and get pregnant, at which point she bursts into tears. Before this chapter comes to an end we read Al-e Ahmad reflecting on the very meaning of a couple of having a child.

> When I think of it, I believe there must be a thing, nay a person, for whom we two [he and his wife] can sacrifice our lives. We have tried everything, all the abstract ideals, but which ideal would be worth the life of one human being so you can sacrifice yourself to and grow old with him/ her? Now that you and your wife will have to grow old anyway what reasons do you have to grow old, and even more fundamentally what reason even to exist, to preserve yourself? . . . From morning to evening, the two of us, husband and wife, sit in front of each other just like two mirrors witnessing a space full of nothing, or else full of failures, but something must run along in between these two mirrors so we can have a vision of the infinity, but right now the fact is that we just look like two walls with no street between us for there is no one to cross that street.[24]

In chapter three, Al-e Ahmad tells us about the occasion when he took his wife to see a gynaecologist, a male gynaecologist, and the very idea drove him mad and made him feel like a pimp as he had to sit by his wife's head while the gynaecologist examined her. Throughout the short book this scene returns and troubles him deeply. They then turn to folk medicine and remedies all to no avail, including a visit to the site of the Tomb of Daniel in Susa where Al-e Ahmad forgets all about his issue and starts reflecting on the history of Esther and Mordecai.[25] He always return to the serenity of the home he has built for himself and his wife. Here he corroborates Daneshvar's report elsewhere that he loves looking at the goldfish in their pond.[26] As in a violent opera, such moments of calm make the weight of his rage even more pronounced. Eventually he turns back to modern medicine and now he unleashes his anger against the European-educated physicians and the pharmaceutical companies they serve, whom he believes to be as charlatan as the magicians and medicine-men of other cultures. He is finally fed up with abusing his body so much with needles and subjecting himself to physicians' whims that in a moment of uncontrollable rage he has a fist fight with two people, a student and a metalworker. He tells us how he savagely beat them both.[27]

The fourth chapter deals with the social and familial consequences of not having children and the dilemma of how to deal with the children of the family members. If you play with them at family gatherings they say because you don't have the children of your own and pity you, if you don't play with them, they say because you're bitter and childless. Then comes perhaps the most powerful moment of the text, when Al-e Ahmad describes their receiving the news of his sister-in-law's suicide by self-immolation. This is Al-e Ahmad's fast-paced prose at it best. He forgets about his own pain and anger and shifts gears into how to deal with this tragedy. His pen is furious, fast, powerful, soaked in tears of the calamity that has befallen them. On their way to Kermanshah where the suicide had occurred, and towards which he drives like a maniac, they pass by the earthquake-ravaged areas where he sees countless homeless orphans and bursts into a tirade against himself that he could be the father of all these children. He even suggests to his wife to adopt two of these children. She is too grief-stricken to agree. With a reference to *Les Nourritures terrestres* (1897), a prose-poem by André Gide he had helped translated into Persian, he writes: 'at this moment it occurred to me. Why should I not be a father to all these children? Do you see these children, these inheritors of earthly delights bereft of their shares?'[28] He writes as fast as he drives, and he drives as madly as he writes – all through the misery of people stricken by earthquakes rushing for aid that is coming their way. By the end of this trip they briefly consider the prospect of adopting the children of his deceased sister-in-law but ultimately opt against it. They drive back to Tehran – resigned to their fate.

In chapter five, Al-e Ahmad confesses to his marital infidelities in Europe, particularly with a woman in Amsterdam with whom things get serious and he is even hoping to have a child from that encounter, but nothing happens. Upon his return to Iran, he confesses to his wife who had suspected as much. The expression he uses for his affair in Europe is *Lor-e dough nadideh* ('a lout in a fancy restaurant'). Here he confesses: 'I was picking up hookers right in the middle of the streets.'[29] Here again he splits his character into two, a traditional man versus his own person, one insisting he takes advantage of his Muslim heritage and the other putting up resistance.

Whenever he succumbs to temptations and has sex with someone, he says 'the second person (*shakhs-e dovvum*)' takes over.[30] His interior dialogue eventually becomes entirely existential, almost nihilistic. 'You live to write', he tells himself, 'while others just live . . . You have confined the power of action to the space of the writing paper.'[31] The compulsive writer, the temptation to indulge in illicit sex, the urge to sit down and write a confessional and have his wife read it through, all of these come together to electrify and bewilder the prose.

In the sixth and final chapter, Al-e Ahmad goes to the cemetery where his parents, sisters, nieces and other family members are buried. He sits by his parents' and sister's grave and he ruminates in magic-realist terms:

> My mother is sitting by the central grave and her shoulders are shivering under her chador. My sister sitting next to her reciting the Qur'an, quietly, gently, for the father is asleep, and our other sister does not like commotions either, just like me, she too had no children, and my nieces are there too . . .[32]

Here he deeply identifies with his sister who had died of breast cancer but had refused to allow a male gynaecologist to touch her body. She too had no children. Here his voice becomes a ventriloquist and speaks for his sisters. Through her he starts talking for childless women, both his sister and an old auntie, Ammeh Qezi, a family friend who also had no children. He walks among the dead speaking with his mother, his sister and his father. He comes to the grave and rests his case with Ammeh Qezi, an old maiden storyteller who had taught him storytelling and who was also childless. Again: Al-e Ahmad was a more complicated thinker and writer than his belated liberal readers have had reasons to muster the necessary patience to read him carefully. This entire surreal ending of *Sangi bar Guri* does not quite jell with the way this book has been presented to a public too busy actually to read the text.

Once we finish reading the text of *Sangi bar Guri* carefully a crucial feature of the book reveals itself. Five women emerge at the centre of the narrative of this short and powerful book – his wife, his mother, his sister, her sister-in-law who had committed suicide, and finally and perhaps most poignantly his childhood storyteller aunt. Towards his wife he has a daunting and paralysing sense of guilt and shame for not having been able to bear her a child. The entire text is a public act of self-humiliation and self-flagellation out of guilt and shame for having failed to answer the motherly desires of one woman he deeply loved and admired. He loves his wife with every fibre of his guilt-ridden prose and he is paralysed by fear and anger that he has failed to help her fulfil her one true desire not as a wife but as a mother. That paralysing guilt draws him back to the grave of his mother by projection for his having been the fulfilment of his mother's wish for a son – and that draws him to his sister for having yielded to cancer rather than subjecting herself to the humiliations he went through, which brings him to his storyteller aunt figure who also died childless. But the most traumatic moment of the entire book is the death by suicide of his sister-in-law, in the face of whose tragic death he feels particularly impotent to do anything. His mad driving towards the final encounter with that death is the inferno where he and these five women come to a tragic encounter – his life among the dead and dying souls, all of them women, all of them definitive to his authorial voice.

The text itself is purgatorial – both publicly and privately. When Al-e Ahmad was writing it, he was actively imagining himself performing it in public – and that is the reason it has his signature speed – but by not publishing it he was hoping to avoid his own and his wife's humiliation. By having appointed both his wife and his brother Shams as his executors he had projected that ambivalence to a posterity when the two of them would decide the fate of the book after his death. By publishing the book against Simin Daneshvar's wish, Shams Al-e Ahmad put his own personal will over his brother's ambivalence. Having been published, the text remains the historic testimony of a restless and defiant man deeply guilt-ridden and ashamed at having failed one woman he truly loved and yet was unable to make happy. Read closely, the book is not about the wounded pride of a patriarchal man. It is about the tortured soul of a man-in-love having failed in the most physical testament of his desires for the woman he loved. Yes, there are moments of revolting vulgarity in the text, but precisely in those moments Al-e Ahmad allows the world a glimpse of his tormented soul. Not a single leading intellectual of his generation or after would dare, could dare, go anywhere near exploring in in public such darkest corners of their own mediocre souls.

Trouble in Paradise

The publication of the collected volumes of Simin Daneshvar and Jalal Al-e Ahmad's letters in 2004–6 is a historic event that will take generations of scholarship to decipher and read for their consequences on how we understand this iconic couple.[33] This exquisite scholarly service is the work of Mas'ud Ja'fari Jazi whose collected volumes *Nameh-ha-ye Simin Daneshvar va Jalal Al-e Ahmad* (*The Letters of Simin Daneshvar and Jalal Al-e Ahmad*) have gifted the world an extraordinary collection of primary material to read and assess. It is however an unfortunate fact that very rarely do works of scholarship undertaken in Persian (or Arabic or Turkish) appear in the professional output of North American and western European professoriate, who either disregard or else abuse these sources without citing them.

This collection of letters that we now have thanks to the hard work of Mas'ud Ja'fari Jazi consists of three massive volumes, and volume II consists of two bulky tomes – altogether four heavy volumes that require a small handbag to carry them around. The content of these volumes are as follows: Volume I: Daneshvar's letter to Al-e Ahmad during her visit to the US 1952–3; volume II: (1) Al-e Ahmad's letters to Daneshvar during her visit in the US 1952–3; volume II: (2) Al-e Ahmad's letters to Daneshvar during her visit in the US 1952–3; volume III: Daneshvar and Al-e Ahmad's letters to each other during their respective short trips 1962–5. I am looking at these four volumes sitting imposingly on my writing desk and just laugh at the enormity of what was there, and we did not know.

It is beyond the scope and purpose of this chapter and this book to read this massive body of exchanges between Daneshvar and Al-e Ahmad in two crucial periods of their lives together. They need a whole different set of circumstances to be read patiently and purposefully. These precious volumes will engage generations of scholars to come. But what becomes evident from a first glance at these private letters now made public is the deeply passionate love affair at the heart of Al-e Ahmad and Daneshvar's marriage. The depth and intensity of their love for one another completely changes the character of much we have known or perceived about their marriage. There is an expression of love and affection, desire and longing, rarely seen in public between a young couple, now made palpably evident. They were both passionately in love and these letters reveal their deeply physical, emotional, at once erotic and intellectual attraction to each other. Though much to my regret I soon discovered in the editor's introduction that the calamity of censorship is still evident even in this historic document. Here the editor informs us that he has censored passages in the letters that have to do with 'marital' (*zanashu'i*) issues, which means when the letters become explicitly sexual, or passages in which they use curse words![34] The editor tells us on such occasions he has placed ellipsis marks between brackets [. . .], which is a very kind help as we can surmise from each such occasion the sexual nature of those deleted passages. In the first part of the second volume in one of Al-e Ahmad's letters to Simin Daneshvar, dated 1 January 1954 we read, 'My sweetheart Simin my Beloved, I just came out of the bath [. . .] and put on my underwear that I had not been using for a while . . .'[35] It is obvious the deleted and censored part of this sentence is not about the brand of the underwear. Such omissions alas are most unfortunate, irresponsible and damaging to an otherwise excellent editorial work. We don't know if this act of irresponsible censorship was the editor's decision, Simin Daneshvar's demands, or the grand wisdom of the official censorship of the Islamic Republic. Either way this is a serious flaw in the otherwise excellent service these volumes have made to Simin Daneshvar and Jalal Al-e Ahmad scholarship.[36]

These letters cast a whole different light on these two seminal characters in contemporary Iranian history. But before reading them closely, as generations of scholars will do in future, the tonality of their language must first be understood. These letters first begin as innocent private correspondence between two young people deeply in love with each other, but eventually both authors become aware of their historical significance and thus their prose becomes self-conscious of these letters' future readers, if not immediately then in the posterity. Therefore, there is a private publicity, an initially hesitant but increasingly evident performativity in these letters, that makes them doubly precious. The authors soon begin to compile, file and chronologically order their exchanges, and they say so, as the editor informs us, on multiple occasions.[37] As the editor also notes, these letters combine multiple prose style, such as personal love letters, travelogues, literary criticism, ethnographic reportage and more. But far more important, and a gift for those who have the patience to read these letters cover to cover, is the domesticity of the prose that emerges. Far more important than when the authors start performing for a future public readership of their private letters is when they engage in entirely domestic chitchat, making tea, taking a shower, buying gifts for family members, or gossiping about the illicit love affair of Ebrahim Golestan and Forough Farrokhzad.

Let us take a look at the complete structure of these immense volumes, for although we will not have reasons or space to discuss them all we must know their context. The first volume contains two utterly precious letters from Daneshvar to Al-e Ahmad before their marriage, where she addresses him 'Dear Mr Al-e Ahmad', and signs 'Simin Daneshvar'. In the second letter she addresses him as 'My dear friend' and still signs Simin Daneshvar.[38] The next letter in this first volume jumps by three years to 2 September 1952 when they are now married and Daneshvar is on her way to the US and is sending a letter to 'My Dear Jalal' and signs it as 'Your Simin'.[39] But again she becomes bashful almost on the same day and signs the next letter 'Simin Daneshvar', until she reaches New York when she is still Simin Daneshvar, but just about a day later on 9 September she becomes Simin again, and continues as Simin and then occasionally as 'Your Simin'.[40] By the time she is in Palo Alto, California, she is thoroughly *Simin-e To* ('Your Simin'). Later she signs *Simin Zan-e Tanha-ye to* ('Simin Your Lonely Wife').[41] Depending on her mood, we may even come across *Zanat Simin* ('Your Wife Simin').[42] This entire collection can be canvassed just on the manner in which the two lovers address each other and sign their names.

A good example of her letters from the US, where Daneshvar was at this time on a Fulbright Fellowship to study creative writing at Stanford University, is the one she sends on 30 November 1952, in which she first writes she is not going to send it to him because it is bitter. The letter consists of three reasons why she left Al-e Ahmad to come to the US on this scholarship. First she says she was fed up with his family's disrespectful treatment of her, second his devotion to Tudeh Party was becoming detrimental to their marriage and third she felt she was underappreciated by him.[43] Here we read a young woman, thirty-one years old at the writing of this letter, having already received her doctorate degree in Persian literature, been married to Al-e Ahmad for about two years, deeply in love with her husband, terribly missing him, being lonely and forlorn in a faraway country. She is pleasantly talkative, normal, verbose, occasionally coquettish and as she is writing this letter she is on what she calls 'telephone duty' in her dorm, which means she must answer the phone where other girls in her dorm receive gentlemen callers to go on dates. After each phone call she comes back and resumes writing the letter. He is vicariously with her, like a 'date', her gentleman caller, as it were.

In a previous letter she has already sent him a diagram of her room, where we see on a shelf immediately after she enters the room there is a picture of Al-e Ahmad in a bookcase, next to it her writing desk, then the window, then her bed and then her closet.[44] Next to her bed, she writes, there is a small nightstand on which she keeps a brown box in which she keeps his letters, right next to a Divan Hafez from which she does bibliomancy. She also has a small mirror in one of her bookshelves in which she keeps a second, smaller, picture of her husband. There is no exaggerating the precious power of these passages. This is the beautiful mind of a novelist at work, detailing the paraphernalia and physiognomy of her love nest away from the man she loves, on a mission away from her homeland to make her literary gift worldlier than it already was. Without coming to terms with the intensity, sincerity and omnipresence of this love between the couple, much about their public relationship will be subject to abusive misreading.

Another good sample of her letters from this period is dated 20 February 1953 in which she expresses happiness to have just received two letters from Al-e Ahmad, then expresses concern for political turmoil in southern Iran, then apologises for having bothered him with complaints about his mother and sister and such.[45] She complains of what she sees as loose girls around her on campus who openly flirt and kiss and maybe even have sex with multiple boyfriends. Then she shares with him how an Iraqi young man was making a pass at her, and then she writes of an old Norwegian professor who too was making passes at her. This is how she puts it:

> My dearest, for the thousandth time, if you ever lacked confidence in me have confidence in me. I swear by our love that no one has cast an inappropriate look at your wife. I am not writing these to boast or tell you how many people are in love with me. A rat-eating Arab or a Norwegian senile dog[46] are not much to boast about – this is just since you asked for details

I wanted to assure you I know how to protect myself and you don't know how much pleasure this gives me, how it soothes my conscience and calms my mind when I stand up to them like this! How much I am pleased with myself! This is enough for me. Just sending you love letters is not sufficient, I must prove my love to you by remaining loyal to you in this loose environment of American society. You must know that if one day as much as I kissed someone, I will never write you any more![47]

Al-e Ahmad's letters are far blunter, more verbose and quite expressive of his frank and forward prose unsheathed here privately for his wife. He also wrote twice as much as she did, as the sheer two volumes of his letters show in comparison to her one volume from this period. 'Simin my sweetheart, the Little Pitch-Black Shirazi Girl, what can I call you, my life, I was breathless until your letter arrived.'[48] On another occasion: 'My sweetheart what have I not done to have you all to myself!'[49] On another occasion: 'Well my sweetheart, one more day passed, today is exactly fifty-three days since you have left.'[50] Then again: 'My Sweetheart Simin, My life, my true soul, how your precious eyes kill me!'[51] Here we read how Al-e Ahmad obsesses over Daneshvar's letters, as in the case of a letter he receives while he is away from Tehran, travelling in the south, staying with a friend, and after waking up and starting to write a letter to her he begins pacing at the door waiting for the postman, and when he does not come he goes walking with another friend, but keeps calling the servant of that friend to see if the postman has come. When the servant does not answer he borrows a bicycle and bikes back to his residence, where he finds the door locked and the servant gone. He climbs the wall, and finds the windows sealed, and ends up tearing the window screens to get to the room and pick up her letter and start reading it.[52] For the duration of Daneshvar's sojourn in Stanford, the couple lived vicariously through their letters. They were narratively cohabiting with each other.

Here is another letter dated 10 May 1953 to give a taste of how he wrote back to Daneshvar:

My sweetheart, I am waiting for the tea to brew and meanwhile writing to you. I am staying up at home hoping your letter will arrive, until 7 or 7:30 p.m. Just came back from our home we are building, may it be blessed for you! I took the doors upstairs (this afternoon), and while I was there, they installed three of them. Altogether I took upstairs fifteen frames for doors and windows. This morning too I was there – from morning till sunset. For lunch I came back to Tehran. I went to your family house. But why am I writing in such a rush? Let me write in details. But first let me see how my tea is doing, and have a bit of bread, butter and honey with it and then I shall come back. Perhaps your letter may arrive meanwhile. For now, Bye! Bye![53]

He comes back and continues writing, having had his afternoon tea. He reports that his Pangaduin syrup has been finished – this was a famous syrup at the time supposed to increase appetite. He reports that his appetite is good, and he is full of energy, and that he has spent the whole day working like a mason's apprentice. Then he interrupts and says her letter has not yet arrived, and proceeds to give her a full itinerary of his day. He then concludes by saying the next day he plans to kill a sacrificial lamb to sanctify their new home. Then that, he does not know why, he remembers a poem of Nima's – which he writes for Daneshvar:

Nazok Ara ye . . .

The thin body of the stem of the flower
I planted with my soul
And with my soul watered it . . . [54]

He continues to write, drinks tea, waits for her letter – which doesn't arrive. Then he writes to her that, alas, he has to go to a Tudeh Party meeting, 'the hell with them', he interjects, he wants to abandon all his party responsibilities, then he gets up and reports he is standing up naked in his underwear and a pair of pants and off he goes.[55] This letter was done by 6:30 p.m. By 7:30 p.m. he writes again that he has dressed and waited for her letter, which still did not arrive. He says he has to go out, 'Bye! Bye!' By 10:30 p.m. he writes again, reporting that her letter finally arrived, and continues to write, obsessively, almost minute by minute of his daily activities. This is a typical letter-writing habit for Al-e Ahmad, less so for Daneshvar, but still both of them were compulsive in their habit of writing the details of their daily activities for one another, vicariously in effect living together through these pages.

It is in the third and final volume, which contains their correspondence during the years 1962–5, that we learn more details of Al-e Ahmad's extra-marital affair – to which he had referred in his *Sangi bar Guri*. The first time we hear about 'Hilda', the woman with whom Al-e Ahmad had an affair, is in a letter from Daneshvar to Al-e Ahmad dated 26 January 1962 in which we learn someone had been writing to her from Amsterdam in Persian telling her about Al-e Ahmad's intimate relationship with a woman named 'Hilda'. He is in Europe and this 'Hilda' has been his host, a task to which she was appointed by those who had invited him.[56] Al-e Ahmad and Daneshvar are both on their way to Israel, he from Europe and she from Iran, and she is not sure if she will go to Israel after the revelation of these letters. In her moment of anger and despair she goes to Al-e Ahmad's mentor Khalil Maleki and his wife and tells them the story. Malaki's wife is furious, Maleki himself sarcastically declares that Al-e Ahmad wrote a book about *Gharbzadegi* (Westoxication) and now he falls for a *Gharbi* (Western) woman! But Maleki convinces her not to rush to judgement or file for divorce and insists she should go to Israel and show him the letters she has received anonymously, though confirmed by the letter Al-e Ahmad's host had also written to her informing her of this incident.

The rest of Daneshvar's letter is a powerful indictment of Al-e Ahmad, asking him in a deeply moving prose why he did this, turning to a beautiful Arabic phrase 'Why did you abandon me?' She says perhaps he turned to 'Hilda' to have a child? And then bitterly adds: 'Jalal, you will not have a child, especially with a woman in her forties.'[57] She tells him the reason he keeps seeing Golestan in his dreams, as he had told her in a letter, is that he too has done to her what Golestan did to his wife Fakhri, betraying her with Forough Farrokhzad. But she assures him she is not like Golestan's wife and will file for divorce.[58] She assures him she plans to be a role model for Iranian woman, not accepting such humiliation. The letter is painful, hurtful, deeply moving:

> I am grateful for the beautiful times we have had together. I am grateful
> for the few times you told me I am your compass . . . I am grateful for the
> time we saw two cuckoo birds making love and you said the fat one looks
> like me and the thin one like you. I am grateful to you for ridding me of
> my laziness, and make my life exciting. This was my share of love, my share
> of eternity.[59]

The following day at 6 a.m. she writes she may not come to Israel and that she will file for divorce and he should marry 'Hilda' and stay in Europe, but she still concludes by saying if this has just been a fling she is willing to forgive him.[60] She tells him to tell 'Hilda' she won – and she signs the letter 'Simin Daneshvar'.

She goes to Israel anyway and something happens in Israel that makes her forgive Al-e Ahmad. The next time we hear the name of 'Hilda' is in a letter dated 26 June 1963 from London on her way to the US, and now she is back to 'Jalal Janam/Jalal My Sweetheart'.[61] By 27 June 1963, on board the ship on her way to the US, she terribly misses her husband and bemoans 'what stupidity I committed once again getting myself separated from you'.[62] By 3 July we learn how Al-e Ahmad had welcomed her in Tel Aviv airport so warmly and enthusiastically that it made her forgive him.[63] In the same letter, dated 3 July, she tells him how offended she was when she read the yet unpublished text of *Sangi bar Guri*,[64] and accuses him of still being in love with 'Hilda'. But still she proceeds to tell him about his visit to Harvard and signs: *Simin-e to beh qorbanat* ('Your Simin dies for you!')[65] By 6 July from Boston she tells him 'Jalal my sweetheart I miss you dearly' and later,

> how are you my sweetheart, my little mouse, my little sparrow, now you say I am possessive. Say it! You are mine, as I am yours, am completely yours. Look right now I am the only woman among about forty men, all of them *creme de la creme*, and they are all very kind to me, but none of them is my own cantankerous Jalal.[66]

Al-e Ahmad repeatedly and profusely apologises to Daneshvar for his affair and begs for her forgiveness. In a letter dated 7 July 1963 sent to her while she is at Harvard, he pleads with her to forgive him. He writes that her letter smells of 'disgust' (*bizari*), and that he prefers 'hatred' (*nefrat*) to disgust. He confesses he made a blunder and refers to his affair as *qaziyeh an zanak* ('the story of that little woman thingy').[67] Then he pleads with her:

> I am a man like all other men. I am not an angel. I made a mistake and you made it worse by your letters. I have told you before, this is finished . . . I have made one mistake and even that out of desperation. Even prophets have made mistakes, even Jesus Christ. What else can I do for you to forget that story?[68]

Figure 3.3 Jalal Al-e Ahmad and Simin Daneshvar's Wedding, 1950, with a few close
friends including Al-e Ahmad's younger brother Shams Al-e Ahmad to the far left. (Photo
courtesy of Ali Dehbashi, from the *Bokhara Magazine* archive) All the men are clean-shaven
except the man to Al-e Ahmad's right, Parviz Daryoush, who was a prominent translator and
a close friend of Al-e Ahmad's. The moustache he is sporting was known at the time as '*Sibil
Stalini*' ('Stalin-style Moustache').

He then proceeds to correct her English and tells her 'Trade Union' is not
'Common Market', but a kind of 'Labour Union'.[69] And he signs the letter,
'Your Jalal'.

'Jalal's Sunset'

There were feeble minds around Simin Daneshvar expecting and in fact
encouraging her to write angrily 'in response to' the publication of *Sangi bar
Guri* years after her beloved husband's passing. Those feeble minds, never the
author of anything memorable, had no clue who Daneshvar was, what Al-e
Ahmad meant to her and how she would choose to honour his memory. They
scarcely read what she actually wrote. They just wished they could use her
iconic voice to denounce Al-e Ahmad. It never happened.

In one of the most iconic texts of Persian literary history, '*Ghorub-e Jalal*' ('Jalal's Sunset'), Simin Daneshvar left behind a document of unsurpassed power and grace. 'Jalal's Sunset' begins with a disclaimer, with a refusal to turn Al-e Ahmad into a saint, as she immortalises her husband as a mortal demigod full of fleeting virtues punctuated with forgiven vices. Here she praises him as a principled intellectual, who had been disappointed with Marxism and existentialism and turned to religion as a mode of resistance to cultural imperialism.[70] It is crucial to keep in mind the date of this magnificent essay, 1361 according to the Iranian calendar, 1982 on the Gregorian calendar, meaning about four years after the Iranian revolution of 1977–9, when Daneshvar knew full well the ruling regime in Iran was unjustifiably turning Al-e Ahmad into an icon of their legitimacy:

> I have never sought to turn him into an idol. Idolatry is a characteristic of our people, but it is not, nor can it ever be to the benefit of the person that has been idolised, and it is at the end of the day against the interest of people too. I have never turned Jalal into a saint. Jalal was a responsible writer, a disciplined man, to the point of sacrificing himself.[71]

She then goes on to write a moving account of the day Al-e Ahad died, Wednesday, 18 Shahrivar 1348/9 September 1969. He was busy those days repairing a handmade heater he had designed and built himself in the little cottage home they had in Asalem in the Gilan Province in northern Iran. He was also attending to his little patch of garden where he had planted some vegetables.

> Jalal was always a gardener. A gardener for his readers, a gardener to his students whom he always considered like a tree needing attention. A gardener to anyone he would encounter and see something promising in him . . . he did not know the flower was himself, his whole life was like a flower. At least for me he was like that. On the day of his burial his mother told me, 'Don't cry my sweetheart, God is a florist.'[72]

She lovingly recalls a day they were travelling in the north together and they came across a rice paddy, when he started taking notes. She asked him what he wrote, to which he replied: 'the main staple of people in the Far East is rice, and rice paddies are the source of the gentility of their artists' inspiration.

Most other people eat wheat which is much rougher than rice.' She asked him why she didn't think of that. He said, 'look how graciously the rice paddies dance with the breeze!'[73]

She writes lovingly of how life with Al-e Ahmad was so fulfilling and so full of joy for her, that she laughed when people thought she could not have children – and even here she uses the turn of phrase (*ojaqam kur bud* ['my oven was cold']) that blames her for their not having children – whereas the issue was Al-e Ahmad's infertility. She remembers how once he had asked her and a friend where they would like to live. 'Wherever you are,' she told him, at which she recited a poem for him to that effect. And then the sheer power of grief gets hold of her, she exits the narrative of telling us how her beloved husband died and tells us how she wished to die. 'I still think the same way, and the fulfilment of this wish is not too far away. Every day I feel I am melting. Bury me in Jalal's grave. I have arranged the official documentation.'[74]

The structure of this extraordinary act of mourning is somewhere between Antigone burying her brother Polynices, and Zainab lamenting the death of her brother Imam Hossein, though with both those cases we read about sisters mourning their respective brothers, while in this case we are reading a bereaved wife remembering her husband – something quite rare and precious in Persian literature. From her pen the unfolding drama of Al-e Ahmad's dying has the character of a tragedy unfolding. Her act of public mourning is a lyrical lamentation, a *marthieh* in poetic prose – both at the time when it was happening in 1969 and then in 1982 when she is remembering and writing it.

> I looked at Jalal. He was staring at the window, gazing through the windowpanes, cutting through the darkness covering the alder trees, trying to reach the seashores. He was smiling – peaceful and calm. As if he had discovered all the mysteries, as if the two curtains had been lifted and let him see the secrets, and now he was smiling, smiling and telling us 'Oh how I fooled you all and left.' This is the worst thing he ever did to me.[75]

At the height of her mourning she recalls the day Jalal drove them to Kermanshah for the funeral of her sister Homa Daneshvar – 'no one could love with the very breath of truth like he did, and no one could roar like thunder as he did'.[76]

She tells us in a very simple, compelling and straightforward way, cutting through all nonsensical conspiracy theories, that Al-e Ahmad had died of either pulmonary embolism or brain aneurysm.[77] Then comes the moment for saying goodbye:

> I neither wailed nor did I cry, I had promised, I kissed him and I kissed him, in this world very few people have been as lucky as I am to have found their soulmates, just like two migrant birds who had found each other, keeping each other company in a cage, making the cage tolerable for each other.[78]

The ending of 'Jalal's Sunset' is like the finale of Daneshvar's masterpiece *Savushun* (1969). The two texts – one factual the other fictional – approximate to each other. We see the same structure at work at the end of *Savushun*, an allusion to the death of Imam Hossain in Shi'a martyrology, or in Seyavash in the *Shahnameh*, or John the Baptist in the Bible (Daneshvar was deeply familiar with the Bible and had studied it closely). Daneshvar did not turn Al-e Ahmad into the *tabula rasa* of any saint by disregarding or covering up his faults. She did something far more serious. She immortalised him by writing a memorial prose that is replete with the most sacred prose narratives of multiple cultures – Iranian, Greek, Islamic and Christian. Her pen was writing history as she mourned her lover, her friend, her comrade, the joy and sorrow of her soul. Tapping into the memories of Zainab and Antigone in particular, she wrote in a poetic prose that immortalised her husband for a posterity that will have a very difficult time disregarding her monumental memorial when alternatively valorising or vilify him. In the edifice she erected with her prose for her husband, Al-e Ahmad became a tragic hero beyond the reach of all earthly measures of good and evil. Above all, Al-e Ahmad was Simin Daneshvar's *Shohar-e man Jalal* ('My husband Jalal').

'In Memory of the Friend'

The publication of Simin Daneshvar's undisputed masterpiece *Savushun* coincided with the death of Jalal Al-e Ahmad – who died in northern Iran just a few months after the book was published in Tehran. Two preliminary passages, and one final phrasing of this seminal event in the history of modern Persian fiction, embrace the substance of a book that is both an allusion and a testimony to the ability of Simin Daneshvar to sublimate the story of her love affair with her husband into an allegory of modern Iranian history. *Savushun* is both a narrative realism of unsurpassed power and precision and yet so symbolic of an entire nation that in one creative act she wed her beloved husband and the fate of her beloved homeland to eternity. If Al-e Ahmad had done nothing else in his life than just being in the vicinity of Simin Daneshvar when she crafted this jewel of a novel, and having a smidgeon of his character projected into its male protagonist, he would have done enough.

The publication of *Savushun* in 1969 was a major literary event in the history of Persian fiction, the first novel written by a woman, and a novel that was printed and reprinted countless times as one of the most widely read and acclaimed at a level unmatched by any other similar work of fiction.[79] The origin of the Persian novel goes back to the late nineteenth and early twentieth century, though it is not until the appearance of Mohammad Ali Jamalzadeh (1892–1997) and Sadegh Hedayat (1903–51) that the genre finds its bearings in Persian. Daneshvar knew Jamalzadeh and Hedayat in person. The success of her novel had to do with two complementary facts: (1) her ingenious literary craftmanship and (2) the sizeable women's readership that welcomed, loved and celebrated the novel. The active presence of high school- and university-educated women in the public sphere at this point in the 1960s was ready and eager to welcome and celebrate women poets, novelists, dramatists and filmmakers. While poets like Parvin E'tesami, Forough Farrokhzad and Simin Behbahani emerged as the gifted social consciousness and the provocative lyricist of their generations, Simin Daneshvar delivered a similar expectation in fiction. After her a whole range of women novelists emerged, Mahshid Amirshahi and Shahrnoush Parsipour chief among them. But none of them achieved the height of Daneshvar's popularity.

When we open the book to read *Savushun* we see it cast under the shadow of two framing citations. First the dedication page of the book that reads: *Beh Yad-e Dust keh Jalal-e Zendegi-am bud va dar Sugash beh Savushun Neshasteh-am* ('In Memory of the Friend who was the Glory of my life and in whose mourning, I have sat in *Savushun*.') This dedication is followed by an utterly shattering line from a famous *ghazal* of Hafez: *Shah-e Turkan Sokhan-e Modda'ian mishenavad/Sharmi az mazlameh-ye khun-e Seyavushash bad!* ('The King of the Turks hears the grievance of the accusers/Shame of the blood of Siavash be on him!')[80] On the dedication page the name of Jalal Al-e Ahmad is worked into the etymological meaning of the name Jalal ('glory'); and in the citation from Hafez the title of the book, *Savushun*, finds its poetic allusion. Now that her letters from Stanford in the 1950s are published we remember that small nightstand by her bed in her dormitory room, where she kept Jalal Al-e Ahmad's letters and her copy of Hafez's *Divan* next to each other right where she slept. On the dedication page, Jalal Al-e Ahmad is pointedly identified with Seyavash, for whose loss Daneshvar is now in mourning. In the line from Hafez the political point of the novel places the ruling Pahlavi monarchy on the defensive.

In *Savushun*, Simin Daneshvar has written perhaps the single most powerful work of fiction chronicling in exquisite detail the city of Shiraz towards the end of World War II under British occupation. While aware and attentive to the politics of occupation and resistance outside her home, Zari, the central protagonist of the novel, attends to her own home and household – trying to shield it from the outside chaos. In the company of her son Khosrow, her twin daughters and her sister-in-law, Zari sustains an oasis of love and confidence in the midst of a desolate politics of despair. Zari's husband, Yusef, is a central figure in the local resistance against the British occupying forces and their domestic collaborators among the Qashqai tribal leaders. Yusef's heroic resistance, to which Zari is beholden, results in his assassination, and crescendos towards the tragic end of the novel, where Zari's grief for the loss of her husband results in the transformation of her private mourning into political rebellion against the ruling regime. The revolt is aborted, and Zari's grief transforms into a hallucinatory poetic end to the novel. The novel thus uses the factual evidence of colonial occupation and abuse of local crops for the occupying forces to recast ancient Persian and Islamic fusion of Seyavash and Hussein into a martyrology of revolt.

Daneshvar places the finale of the novel in the words of McMahon, an Irish poet friend of the family, a character with similar colonial background who understands the trauma of colonisation:

> *Geryeh nakon khaharam* . . . don't cry sister, in your home a tree will grow,
> and even more trees in your city, and millions more trees in your homeland,

and the wind will carry the message of every tree to the next and the trees shall ask the wind: on your way here did you see the dawn rising?

It is crucial to see here how Daneshvar gives her last words to an Irish poet to speak the pain of colonisation, as well as the hope of triumph. Among other critics, Houshang Golshiri has drawn comparisons between Al-e Ahmad's *Gharbzadegi* (*Westoxication*) and Daneshvar's novel.[81] The comparison is actually quite crude, for the two texts speak very differently. Al-e Ahmad's text is definitive, conclusive and combatant. Daneshvar's novel is expansive, liberating and open-ended. But it is true they both speak from the depth of the colonial conditions against which they revolt, one in a decidedly critical, the other in a pointedly creative mood.

Central to Daneshvar's novel is the enclosed garden that is Zari and her family's home, and that house has a real-life doppelgänger in the home Al-e Ahmad built for his wife Simin Daneshvar while she was away studying in Stanford. Al-e Ahmad built that house literally with his own hands, with thousands of red bricks, as he once put it in a letter, and wrote a daily account of his labour of love to Daneshvar in thousands upon thousands of words – in bricks, words, prose, poetry, hopes, passions and impatience. The house in *Savushun* is the fictionalised version of the house Al-e Ahmad made for the woman he loved. Soon after Daneshvar and Al-e Ahmad moved into that house it became the epicentre of national and regional politics and culture. It is crucial to remember that while the CIA–MI6 coup of 1953 was taking place Al-e Ahmad and Daneshvar were preoccupied building this house and making a home for themselves. In this house the first meetings of the Association of Iranian Writers took place. To this house frequently came the founding father of modernist poetry, Nima Yushij, who lived just a few houses down the street, to read his newest poems – as did Sadegh Hedayat. To this house came Seyyed Mahmoud Taleqani (1911–79) a leading revolutionary cleric who would later become instrumental in toppling the Pahlavi monarchy. The ground-breaking children's stories icon Samad Behrangi (1939–67) came to this house, as did Imam Musa al-Sadr (1928– disappeared in 1978), and the legendary Lebanese-Iranian Shi'a cleric, as did the leading revolutionary ideologue of the time Ali Shariati, as did the most distinguished dramatist of Iran in this time, Gholamhossein Sa'edi

(1936–85).[82] This house, where Simin Daneshvar and Jalal Al-e Ahmad lived, was the iconic home of the brightest stars in a constellation of thoughts and sentiments to which the Islamist fanatics that took over the Iranian revolution of 1977–9 put a decisive end.

The Anima and the Animus

Any assessment of Al-e Ahmad and Daneshvar together, as an iconic couple who lived their lives in public, brings us face to face with the dominant politics of 'intellectuals' inside and outside Iran – the fact that the very idea of 'the intellectual' is irretrievably masculinist. The question we face in general is quite daunting: why is it that we categorically consider Jalal Al-e Ahmad 'an intellectual', Muslim or otherwise, but his eminently learned and accomplished wife Simin Daneshvar we consider a novelist, a translator, a professor of aesthetics but not 'an intellectual?' Whence and wherefore this masculinist prejudice embedded in the very term 'intellectual?' The question turns around the fact that by every measure of their achievements Simin Daneshvar was an intellectual but the phenomenon of the overriding masculinity of the very term continues to trouble the term 'intellectual'. But at issue is not why a towering character like Simin Daneshvar is not considered an intellectual. The question is the failure and shortcoming of a critical consciousness that, upstream from the term 'intellectual', does not have a conceptual category for a woman of her literary and moral stature.

The immediate answer to this question resides in the fact that the *public sphere* upon which the very idea of an intellectual has been formed is masculinist, and this is not limited to Iran or Islam or any other particular religion. Consider the question once put to the French philosopher Jacques Derrida: 'If you had a choice, what philosopher would you like to have been your mother?' Derrida pauses a moment and thinks for a while.

> I don't know how to answer this question. Give me some time. My mother? [laughs] It is a good question. It is a good question, in fact. [Thinks]. It is interesting for I try to tell you why it's impossible for me to . . . to have any philosopher as a mother . . . my mother . . . my mother couldn't be a philosopher [switches to French] . . . 'A philosopher couldn't be my mother. That is a very important point. Because the figure of the philosopher, for

me, is always a masculine figure. This is one of the reasons I undertook the deconstruction of philosophy. All the deconstruction of phallogocentrism is the deconstruction of what one calls philosophy, which since its inception, has always been linked to a masculine and paternal figure . . . So, a philosopher is a father, not a mother. So, the philosopher that would be my mother would be a post-deconstructive philosopher, that is myself or my son. My mother as a philosopher would be my granddaughter, for example. An inheritor. A woman philosopher who would reaffirm the deconstruction. And consequently, would be a woman who thinks. Not a philosopher. I always distinguish thinking from philosophy. A thinking mother it's both what I love and try to give birth to.'[83]

There are a number of obvious issues with this response – first and foremost the fact that Derrida must borrow the metaphor of giving birth to a woman philosopher – and he does not even see the irony of him as a man giving birth to a woman who thinks. The second issue is the fact that even a post-structuralist woman can only think, not do philosophy, a task that therefore remains exclusively male. The admission that the figure of European philosopher is quintessentially masculine overrides even the Derridean deconstruction after which a woman can think but not become a philosopher, because the masculinity of the figure of philosopher remains intact even after the deconstruction of its phallogocentrism. The other issue, that concerns me more here, is the fact that even the master of European deconstruction can only think in monological terms, either masculine or feminine, and not dialogically, so that a philosopher's voice, or more accurately the voice of a thinking person, must be either this or that and therefore could not be dialogically transcended.

Once we thus de-Orientalise the issue of gender as the thinking voice of the author, the dialectic between Jalal Al-e Ahmad and Simin Daneshvar as a couple who performed themselves publicly assumes a far more serious character. In this mirroring image, Al-e Ahmad emerges as a character type, a persona rather than a person, thus marking the difference between the two authors: while she wrote fictively even when she was writing for real, he wrote for real even when he was writing fiction. The dialectic of the two puts a twist to Shklovsky's idea of *ostranenie*; in other words we have always (though unbeknownst ourselves) read them together rather than against each other.[84] He begins with fact and moves to fiction, while she begins with fiction and moves to approximate truth. They were the narrative Yin and Yang to one another, coterminous to making the other at once incomplete and yet completed in the presence of the other. Together they did not just become complete but transcended the fictive binaries of gender.

What I propose here happening between Al-e Ahmad and Daneshvar dialogically is akin to what Gayatri Chakravorty Spivak performs in one of her signature essays. In 'Moving Devi' (2001), Spivak writes:

> Every critical conviction persuades me that if I were representative of anything, I would not know that I was. Yet, surely, I must at least represent the passage, in migration, from *ethnos* to *ethnikos* – from being home to being a resident alien – as I write on the great goddess as she steps into a great U.S. museum I will allow 'myself' to occupy this stereotype as I think about her. Surely, it is because of this stereotype that I was asked to be part of the catalog. I have moved from a Hindu majority in the center of Hinduism to a Hindu minority in a new imperialist metropolis where Hinduism was, until the day before yesterday, in the museum. Yesterday, when the active polytheist imagination accessed the mind-set of the visitor in the museum, a colloidal solution, shaken up between here and there, was surely the result. I want to ruminate upon this transference from careless participant to uneasy observer. I speak of Devi, from somewhere upon this transference circuit, although not as an expert among experts. I have no disciplinary access to knowledge upon this topic.[85]

This passage Spivak calls from '*ethnos* to *ethnikos* – from being home to being a resident alien' is the dialogical impersonation of a dual voice speaking in her signature prose here and elsewhere. The dialogical voice oscillates between 'myself' and the 'stereotype', or between 'here and there', or between a 'careless participant' and an 'uneasy observer'. When she concludes, 'I speak of Devi, from somewhere upon this transference circuit', the voice that speaks is already richly inconclusive. This dialogical voice, this contrapuntal phrasing of a woman thinker, is missing in Derrida's philosophising the absence of the women philosopher. That dialogical voice speaking in the prose of Spivak becomes specular in the interface between Daneshvar and Al-e Ahmad.

A similar argument can be seen in Kimberlé Crenshaw's idea of 'intersectionality' where she in effect posits multiple and shifting sites of subjectivity. As she formulates it:

> The concept of political intersectionality highlights the fact that women of color are situated within at least two subordinated groups that frequently pursue conflicting political agendas. The need to split one's political energies between two sometimes opposing political agendas is a dimension of intersectional disempowerment that men of color and white women seldom confront. Indeed, their specific raced and gendered experiences, although intersectional, often define as well as confine the interests of the entire group.[86]

She therefore uses 'intersectionality as a way of framing the various interactions of race and gender in the context of violence against women of color', or 'intersectionality as a way to articulate the interaction of racism and patriarchy generally . . . to describe the location of women of color both within overlapping systems of subordination and at the margins of feminism and anti-racism'.[87] This transcendental voice of the critical thinker has now become positively ventriloquist. It speaks, thinks, reads, writes, advocates and theorises in an orchestral mobilisation of voices that brings race, gender, critique of patriarchy and class struggle to speak to each other. In both Spivak and Crenshaw's case the singular voice of the critical thinker has become plural, orchestral, polyvocal, consistently dialogical. In the case of Daneshvar/Al-e Ahmad the two personae perform this dialogical speech act simultaneously.

Let us put the case of Al-e Ahmad and Daneshvar in a larger comparative context where we can see how it resonates with a whole host of other couples around the globe having had simultaneously amorous and intellectual relationships with each other: John Adams and Abigail Adams had a deeply loving and political relationship, Voltaire and Émilie du Châtelet had both a romantic and an intellectual relationship, as did Harold Pinter and Lady Antonia Fraser, Sylvia Plath and Ted Hughes, Georgia O'Keeffe and Alfred Stieglitz, Martin Heidegger and Hannah Arendt, Peter Abelard and Héloïse d'Argenteuil, Beatrice Webb and Sidney Webb, Mary Wollstonecraft and William Godwin, Jean-Paul Sartre and Simone de Beauvoir, Diego Rivera and Frida Kahlo. But what I propose here in the case of Al-e Ahmad and Daneshvar is not just their amorous presence in their literary and intellectual and above all public life together. It is the appositional cross-creativity of their respective voices that matters most here – and perforce it genders the figure of the 'public intellectual'. For something of her voice was in his and something of his in hers.

In the case of Al-e Ahmad and Daneshvar, therefore, I would suggest a much more dialogical and contrapuntal reading of their relationship, something of an 'anima and animus' in their creative psyche, the way Carl Gustav Jung theorises it in his analytical psychology as part of his theory of collective unconscious. As a couple, Al-e Ahmad and Daneshvar become each other's anima and animus. Jung considered the animus as the unconscious masculine side of a woman, and the anima as the unconscious feminine side of a man, each transcending their respective personal psyche and gender identity. The phony liberal feminism thrown at the couple has systematically concealed and distorted the dialectic of their creative egos. As two anthropomorphic archetypes of the unconscious mind, Jung saw anima and animus as the interactive components of the Self. That Self always contains an Other – the masculine a feminine, the feminine a masculine, the sedentary a mobile, the mobile a sedentary and so forth. Another way of looking at their relationship is to think of the mystical idea of '*al-Insan al-Kamil*', or 'the Perfect Person' as theorised by mystics like Ibn 'Arabi, Aziz Nasafi and others. In this sense, the Perfect Person is not an entity but a goal, an archetype and not a persona – the gathering of divergences. Though mystics like Ibn 'Arabi meant the concept in the context of their notion of *Wahadat al-Wujud* ('Unity of Being'), here I see the idea as two mirrors that, facing each other, contain each other, as Al-e Ahmad himself uses the metaphor for his relationship with Daneshvar when lamenting their not having a child. Their respective voices and proses, as it were, became their 'twin' offspring.[88]

Notes

1. Jalal Al-e Ahmad, *Masalan Sharh-e Ahval* (*Something of an Autobiography*), in Jalal Al-e Ahmad, *Yek Chah-o-Do-Chaleh* (*One Well and Two Pits*) and *Masalan Sharh-e Ahval* (*Something of an Autobiography*) (Tehran: Ravaq Publications, no date): 50–1.

2. Simin Daneshvar, '*Ghorub-e Jalal*' ('Jalal's Sunset') (1969) in Simin Daneshvar, '*Ghorub-e Jalal*' ('Jalal's Sunset') (Tehran: No publisher, No Date): 21.

3. See Ranajit Guha, *History at the Limit of World-History*, Italian Academy Lectures (New York: Columbia University Press, 2002): 7–23.

4. There is a growing body of excellent literature on modern marriage in Iran. There is a brilliant MA thesis on marriage by Maral Sahebjame, 'Marriage: An Authentic Iranian Experience with the Modern' (California State University, Long Beach, December 2012). It contains important insights and a thorough review of the literature. Equally insightful is Soraya Tremayne's 'Modernity and Early Marriage in Iran: A View from Within' (*Journal of Middle East Women's Studies*, vol. 2, no. 1, Winter, 2006): 65–94.

5. There is unfortunately no solid study of Simin Daneshvar's life and literary significance available in English. For a preliminary sketch from a liberal feminist perspective see Farzaneh Milani, *Veils and Words: The Emerging Voices of Iranian Women Writers* (Syracuse, NY: Syracuse University Press, 1992). This study is seriously outdated and far more important works have now appeared in Persian and are in need of a thorough examination of the figures Milani covers in this book. For a collection of personal reflections, memoirs and insightful literary comments on Simin Daneshvar and her work see the special issue of the journal *Bokhara* (12: 75, Farvardin–Tir 1389/March–July 2010).

6. There is an excellent autobiographical account Simin Daneshvar has shared with Naser Hariri in *Honar va Adabiyat-e Emruz: Goft-o-Shonudi ba Simin Daneshvar* (*The Art and Literature of Today: A Conversation with Simin Daneshvar*) (Babol: Ketabsara-ye Babol, 1987). This magnificent autobiographical account is marred by a false humility at the very beginning of it in which she says she does not like to indulge in '*man-nameh*', literally 'I-writing'. Later this phrase was chiefly applied to Al-e Ahmad and he was 'accused' of '*man-nameh-nevisi*' ('writing the I'). Today we think of such deliberate and purposeful self-consciousness of the knowing subject in its colonial and postcolonial contexts as a profoundly liberating prose. But in Iran and under the multiple frames of self-denial and self-deprecation it has been criticised and shunned. There is absolutely nothing wrong with '*man-nameh-nevisi*'. It is a beautifully liberating voice. We should have more of it.

7. Hariri, *Honar va Adabiyat-e Emruz: Goft-o-Shonudi ba Simin Daneshvar/ The Art and Literature of Today: A Conversation with Simin Daneshvar* (Op. Cit.): 17.

8. The life and achievements of Fatemeh Sayyah are the subject of a full chapter in

my *Reversing the Colonial Gaze: Persian Travelers Abroad* (Cambridge: Cambridge University Press, 2019).

9. By far the best critical reading of Simin Daneshvar's work is Houshang Golshiri's *Jedal Naqsh ba Naqqash dar Asar-e Simin-e Daneshvar* (*The Battle of the Form and the Former in the Works of Simin Daneshvar*) (Tehran: Agah Publications, 1997). In the title and content of the book, Golshiri employs the word '*Naqsh*' playfully and pointedly. He uses it as 'role' or 'share' or 'form' and thus '*Naqqash*' (usually meaning 'painter') here becomes 'role-maker', 'form-giver', etc. Altogether the state of critical reflections and archival work on Simin Daneshvar in Persian is far superior to anything sporadically done in English or any other European language, where alas still the remnants of neo-Orientalism, Area Studies, or else an outdated liberal feminism are dominant. An excellent exception is Razi Ahmad, 'A Postcolonial Reading of Simin Daneshvar's Novels: The Spiritual and the Material Domains in Savushun, Jazira-ye Sargardani, and Sarban-e Sargardan', in Kamran Talattof (ed.), *Persian Language, Literature and Culture New Leaves, Fresh Looks* (London: Routledge, 2015): chapter six.

10. See Robin B. Wright, 'International Seminar Introduces Foreign Dignitaries to United States' (Harvard Crimson, 12 August, 1969). Available online here: https://www.thecrimson.com/article/1969/8/12/international-seminar-introduces-foreign-dignitaries-to/.

11. I have a long essay in Persian on *Savushun*, see Hamid Dabashi, '*Hejab-e Chehreh Jan: Beh Jostojui-ye Zari dar Savushun-e Simin Daneshvar*' ('The Veil upon the Face of Soul: In Search of Zari in Simin Daneshvar's *Savushun*') (*Nimeh-ye Digar*, no. 8, Autumn 1366/1987): 65–118.

12. Read my obituary on Simin Daneshvar when she passed away on 8 March 2012: 'Simin Daneshvar: Death of the Storyteller' (*Al Jazeera*, 13 March 2012). Available online here: https://www.aljazeera.com/indepth/opinion/2012/03/20123126453243315.html. Soon after her passing another useful memorial volume was published in her honour. See Mohammad Reza Zadhoush (ed.), *Yadnameh Dr. Simin Daneshvar* (*A Memorial Volume for Dr. Simin Daneshvar*) (Isfahan: No Publisher, 2012).

13. For the original text of the essay see Simin Daneshvar, '*Shohar-e Man Jalal*' ('My Husband Jalal') (1961) in Simin Daneshvar, *Ghorub-e Jalal* (*Jalal's Sunset*) (Tehran: No publisher, No Date): 1–19. I see the younger generation of scholars usually conflate these two essays: *Shohar-e Man Jalal* with *Ghorub-e Jalal*. These are two very different texts from two different times, one written before and the other after Al-e Ahmadi's death. But they are usually published together.

14. Al-e Ahmad on occasions refers to Daneshvar as 'Ayal' – which is an old-fashioned and outdated mannerism that his detractors enamoured by liberal feminism now hold against him. The rhetorical cast of al-e Ahmad's prose is entirely lost to such an abusive reading of his prose. Al-e Ahmad deeply loved and admired his wife and was very proud to have been married to her. His affectionate mannerism assumes many verbal twists as we can see in their published private letters. But more of that later.

15. Ibid: 5.

16. Ibid: 9.

17. Ibid: 10.

18. Ibid: 12.

19. Ibid: 18.

20. Ibid: 18–19.

21. Almost a decade after I finished my book on the Iranian revolution, *Theology of Discontent* (1993), I donated all the original copies of my collection of primary sources I had used for that book to Columbia University library for safekeeping, for I knew for a fact the ruling Islamic Republic would soon ban, censor and/or doctor these sources. But intuitively I kept all my original Al-e Ahmad books in my own library, for I also knew I was not completely done with him and would sometime return to the first edition of his books.

22. I have consulted with a few learned friends to check this citation. Mahmoud Omidsalar in particular has always thought this is a faux quote and there is no such character as 'Faqfiqa' Bani'. I even tried to go through the route of Abjad and the numerical power of Arabic letters but did not get anywhere meaningful. The additional evidence that this is a fake citation is the fact that Al-e Ahmad on another occasion patently faked the biblical prose. In the second edition of his collection of short stories, *Zan-e Ziadi* (*Redundant Woman*) (1952), he has an introduction he calls 'Risalah-ye Polus-e Rasul beh Kateban' ('The Letter of Paul the Prophet to Writers') which is a kind of manifesto on the sanctity of the pen and the duties of a writer, which is an entirely fake impression of the New Testament, on the model of Paul's letters. See Jalal Al-e Ahmad, '*Risalah-ye Polus-e Rasul beh Kateban*' ('The Letter of Paul the Prophet to Writers') in *Zan-e Ziadi* (*Redundant Woman*) (Tehran: Amir Kabir, 1371/1992): 11–21.

23. Jalal Al-e Ahmad, *Sangi bar Guri* (*A Tombstone*) (Tehran: Ravagh Publications, written in 1963, published in 1981): 14. There is an English translation of this text. See Jalal Al-e Ahmad, *A Stone on a Grave*. Translated from the Persian by Azhar Moin (Costa Mesa, CA: Mazda Publications for Bibliotheca Iranica:

Literature Series, 2008). All my citations are from the original Persian of the first, now rare, edition and with my own translations.

24. Jalal Al-e Ahmad, *Sangi bar Guri* (*A Tombstone*) (Op. Cit.): 23.

25. Ibid: 42.

26. Ibid: 44.

27. Ibid: 48–50.

28. Ibid: 60.

29. Ibid: 76.

30. Ibid: 76.

31. Ibid: 73.

32. Ibid: 85.

33. See Mas'ud Ja'fari Jazi (ed.), *Nameh-ya ye Simin Daneshvar va Jalal Al-e Ahmad* (*The Letters of Simin Daneshvar and Jalal Al-e Ahmad*) (Tehran: Golshan Publications, 1383–85/2004–6). I am grateful to my research assistant Laila Hisham Fouad and to my colleague Peter Magierski, the Middle East and Islamic Studies Librarian at Columbia University Libraries for their tireless diligence in procuring for me these volumes here in New York.

34. Ja'fari Jazi (ed.), *Nameh-ya ye Simin Daneshvar va Jalal Al-e Ahmad* (Op. Cit.): volume I: 11.

35. Ibid: II: 1: 399.

36. Another structural problem with these volumes is their arrangement. All Daneshvar's letters come together and then all Al-e Ahmad's letters together. A far better arrangement would have been if the distinguished editor had gone through the trouble of collating them so the letters and their responses would come together, one after the other. It is true that sometimes more letters are sent than received by either party. But nevertheless, in their letters Daneshvar and Al-e Ahmad often refer to the letter to which they are responding.

37. Ibid: I: 10.

38. Ibid: I: 31.

39. Ibid: I: 31.

40. Ibid: I: 46.

41. Ibid: I: 174.

42. Ibid: I: 203.

43. Ibid: I: 176–80.

44. Ibid: I: 63.

45. Ibid: I: 279–85.

46. The Daneshvar–Al-e Ahmad correspondence is full of ghastly racist, anti-Arab

and anti-Semitic phrases common among their generation. They even refer to Daneshvar herself, both Al-e Ahmad and Daneshvar herself as '*Dokhtar Shirazi-ye Siah Sukhteh*' ('The Little Pitch-Black Shirazi Girl'). Fortunately, the editor has not taken these out, as he has taken the sexual references, and they remain as they are for critical reflections of subsequent generations.

47. Ibid.
48. Ibid: II: 1: 24. This is an instance when he refers to her as his 'Little Pitch-Black Shirazi Girl', and she too occasionally refers to herself as such. Obviously for them this is a term of endearment, oblivious to or negligent of its racist implications.
49. Ibid: II: 1: 61.
50. Ibid: II: 1: 165.
51. Ibid: II: 1: 209.
52. Ibid: II: 1: 438–9.
53. Ibid: II: 2: 747. Bye! Bye! Written in Persian letters.
54. This is part of a famous poem from Nima Yushij, which Al-e Ahmad remembers here for obviously it refers to the house he is building for his sweetheart.
55. Ibid: II: 2: 749.
56. Ibid: III: 345 ff.
57. Ibid: III: 349.
58. Ibid: III: 350.
59. Ibid: III: 351.
60. Ibid: III: 352.
61. Ibid: III: 354.
62. Ibid: III: 355.
63. Ibid: III: 362.
64. Ibid: III: 362.
65. Ibid: III: 363.
66. Ibid: III: 364.
67. Ibid: III: 441.
68. Ibid: III: 441.
69. Ibid: III: 442.
70. Simin Daneshvar, '*Ghorub-e Jalal*' ('Jalal's Sunset') (1981), in Simin Daneshvar, *Ghorub-e Jalal* (*Jalal's Sunset*) (Op. Cit.): 22. There is a flawed English translation of this exquisitely beautiful essay. See Simin Daneshvar, 'Jalal's Sunset', translated by Farzaneh Milani and Jo-Anne Hart (*Iranian Studies*, vol. 19, no. 1, Winter, 1986): 47–63. I read from and make my own translations based on the original Persian.

71. Ibid: 22–3.
72. Ibid: 25–6.
73. Ibid: 27.
74. Ibid: 28.
75. Ibid: 32–3.
76. Ibid: 35.
77. Ibid: 39.
78. Ibid: 40.
79. There are two excellent translations of this novel into English. One by M. R. Ghanoonparvar, *Savushun, A Novel About Modern Iran* (1990) and the other by Roxane Zand, *A Persian Requiem* (1991). As usual all my references are to the original Persian.
80. I still have my own copy of the original first edition of Simin Daneshvar's *Savushun* (Tehran: Khwarizmi Publications, 1969).
81. Houshang Golshiri, *Jedal-e Naqsh ba Naqqash dar Asar-e Simin Daneshvar* (*The Battle of the Form and the Former in the Works of Simin Daneshvar*) (Op. Cit.): 80 ff. For an excellent overview of the critical reception of *Savushun* see the entry under 'Suvashun' in *Encyclopedia Iranica*, available online here: http://www.iranicaonline.org/articles/suvashun.
82. There is a beautiful documentary on this house by Parisa Eshqi, *Khaneh Simin and Jalal/The House of Simin and Jalal* (2012–13). It is available online here: https://www.youtube.com/watch?v=Ro9gibVX4KM. Towards the end of this documentary we learn the ruling institutions of the Islamic Republic are actually quite selective in what aspects of Al-e Ahmad's legacy they choose to underline and celebrate. For example, we learn that three copies of Al-e Ahmad's personal memoires have been 'disappeared'. We also learn that Sazeman Miras-e Farhangi/The Organisation of Cultural Heritage, an official organ of the Islamic Republic, has no interest in safeguarding the house of Daneshvar and Al-e Ahmad or even the house of Nima Yushij nearby for that matter. The actual memories and legacies of these iconic figures are far more troubling for the Islamic Republic than helpful.
83. Watch the interview with Derrida here: https://www.youtube.com/watch?v=-TKRimlH5ZU.
84. As a typical example of such oppositional readings, pitting the couple against each other, the late Houshang Golshiri begins his otherwise insightful reading of Daneshvar's work first by a typical liberal feminist denunciation of Al-e Ahmad and thus pre-empting the theoretical vision of reading them dialogically. See

Houshang Golshiri's *Jedal Naqsh ba Naqqash dar Asar-e Simin-e Daneshvar* (*The Battle of the Form and the Former in the Works of Simin Daneshvar*) (Op. Cit.): 7–11.

85. See Gayatri Chakravorty Spivak, 'Moving Devi' (*Cultural Critique*, vol. 47, Winter, 2001): 121.

86. See Kimberlé Williams Crenshaw, 'Mapping the Margins: Intersectionality, Identity Politics, and Violence Against Women of Color', in Martha Albertson Fineman and Rixanne Mykitiuk (eds), *The Public Nature of Private Violence* (New York: Routledge, 1994): 93–118.

87. Ibid.

88. My task in this book is limited to an examination of Al-e Ahmad as the last Muslim intellectual by way of thinking through a post-Islamist liberation theology. The other, equally important, task of reconfiguring the character and creative ego of Simin Daneshvar will remain for the next generation of thinkers and scholars who will leave behind the outdated bourgeois feminism that has been crudely thrown at her. Fortunately, there is a new generation of scholars who have already picked up this task. Steps towards a far richer reading of Simin Daneshvar are already evident in the excellent doctoral dissertation of Atefeh Akbari Shahmirzadi, 'Disorderly Political Imaginations: Comparative Readings of Iranian and Caribbean Fiction and Poetry, 1960s–1980s' (Columbia University, 2019). I had the privilege of serving on her dissertation committee.

4

The Master Essayist

And here you are – you and these 'Hurried Evaluations'. And indeed, what else can I call this collection of essays? For I am not sure of anything else except the fact that they are essays. I call them 'evaluations' for most of them are certain impressions moving towards criticism in various fields, as you notice in their titles, and I call them 'hurried' for most of them I have written on the spur of the moment, far from any far-sightedness or caution or any other such nonsense. When I think of it, I say to myself why not, let them be! Do we breathe cautiously? Are you cautious when you are on your daily commute between home and work? These essays are the same. They are something of a daily chore. Almost instinctive – and why not?[1]

Jalal Al-e Ahmad, *Arzyabi-ye Shetabzadeh*
(*Hurried Evaluations*) (1964)

Our conclusions towards the end of the last chapter open up new ways of thinking about Al-e Ahmad's prose and politics as we move steadily towards considering his legacy for the posterity of a post-Islamist liberation theology. The question of gender remains central and even definitive to the moral imperative of that liberation theology. If that liberation theology will remain pathologically masculinist and its politics ignorant of the gendered disposition of being a Muslim, let alone an intellectual, then that liberation could never shed its reactionary disposition. It is of course absolutely necessary and indispensable for women of different classes and races to be integral to the social and political disposition of that liberation – in the formation of the very *public sphere* upon which that theology is to be articulated. But by the same token that the politics of race and class must be integral to the reading of the gender central to that politics, lest a habitual bourgeois feminism takes hold of it and speaks for 'Women', then the perceived masculinity of the male voice will also have to be critically reassessed. The result will be a trans- and cross-gendered reading and articulation of the prose and politics of that liberation theology – as we are working towards here in this rethinking of Al-e Ahmad's legacy. The whole binary of male–female will then resolve into a much richer and more diversified tapestry of gendered pluralism. If gender is socially constructed, as it is, as we know from the works of leading critical thinkers from Simone de Beauvoir to Judith Butler, then it is the reconstitution of the *public sphere* upon which such social constructs are projected that can alter the terms of the gendered prose and politics of our present historicity.

I have already suggested that the few autobiographical texts that we have from Al-e Ahmad are the signs of his *performing* himself (as all public intellectuals do) publicly, staging himself, and how that performativity and staging are integral to his persona as a widely read and discussed (liked or disliked) intellectual. From the previous chapter detailing the relationship between Al-e Ahmad and his prominent wife Simin Daneshvar I have then suggested that their voices are in fact formed and ought to be read dialogically, for in effect they think, read, write and speak contrapuntally – for, from and towards each other. We have indeed been reading them cross-referentially all these years and yet we did not know. There is a reason why the main two protagonists of Simin Daneshvar's *Savushun*, Zari and Yusef, are consistently interpreted as the fictional versions of Daneshvar herself and her beloved husband Jalal. Al-e Ahmad was so revered in a cultic way from one end or despised and reviled from another, and she had been so widely abused by a tired and cliché-ridden liberal feminism that was hurtled her way, that we were denied the mere prospect of reading them together, not against each other. But the simple fact is that it is impossible to imagine one of them without the other, or therefore to read one without the other. Al-e Ahmad had not published much before he and Simin Daneshvar met and married and after their marriage she was his first reader, but far more importantly in fact she was his hidden and evident interlocutor – as in fact he was hers. He was writing for her to read and approve. She was his significant other, her presence and interlocution integral to his dialogical self. They were, I have suggested, like the Jungian anima and animus, the male and female sides of each other, collapsing and qualifying the gendered voice of each into the other. They went through his brief marital infidelity and emerged triumphantly, more loving and embracing of each other, thus, to leave for the posterity the fusion of their cross-gendered voices. This is not to suggest their dialectic was peaceful, but that it was productive and purposeful.

The Dialogical Self

The contrapuntal reading of Al-e Ahmad and Daneshvar's respective voices I propose here is predicated on the idea of a *dialogical self*, as has been theorised in the work of George Herbert Mead, Mikhail Bakhtin and others, making the prospect of an intersubjectivity in Persian prose and Iranian politics evident. This is not to say that Al-e Ahmad did not have some, for his time, 'progressive ideas' on women because of his proximity to Daneshvar – as perhaps most evident both in his works of fiction and critical essays. What I suggest is something entirely different. I propose that he had a dialogically gendered voice, that he wrote for Simin Daneshvar to read, as he said so clearly, that Simin Daneshvar was looking over his shoulder whatever he wrote, that their voluminous and almost obsessive correspondence clearly show they had a dialogical disposition to their creative and critical egos, but even more importantly that we have always read them that way together and co-creatively. They could not have so obsessively written for each other and then the alterity of their creative ego just disappears into the thin air once they turned to write their respective works of fact or fiction. They were integral to each other's creative egos. Like a palimpsest or pentimento, to use two complementary metaphors, the couple ought to be both read and seen together, not in opposition but in apposition, with the hidden traces and echoes of one present and evident in the other, not one against the other, or one overwriting or overdrawing over each other, but both together, so through both their writing we can see the dialogical formation of a third space, a third prose, one intersubjectively always present in the other, evident from where we read them together, like the two lenses of a binocular.

In an interview Daneshvar recalls how she and Al-e Ahmad used to play a game when walking together. A passer-by would approach, and they would say to each other let us tell his or her story. They would then exchange their stories and be amazed by their differences.[2] The point here is however different their accounts may have been they were in effect performing these sketches for and in the presence of each other. Their dialogically embedded voices had become in effect second nature to them – even when they were not in each other's physical presence. What pre-empts and dismantles the aggressive nativisation of Al-e Ahmad by his friends and foes alike is precisely this dialogical voice embedded in his prose and perforce politics. It is crucial to keep in mind that both Al-e Ahmad and Daneshvar were primarily literary figures, however different their predilections – and as literary figures they wrote with an open-ended signification to their respective voices. The result in both their cases was a mode of *dialogical defamiliarisation*, if we were to put Bakhtin and Shklovsky together – as here I propose we do.

In this chapter therefore, I wish to carry that contrapuntal and cross-gendered voice of Al-e Ahmad's writing forward and concentrate on the defining character of his prose, namely his widely read and admired essays. He was a master essayist with a powerful and poignant pen the likes of which Iranian literary culture had not seen before or since. Al-e Ahmad effectively invented a unique prose signature that many tried to mimic but no one could ever match. His earliest essays date back to the mid-1940s, followed by a succession of essays that were definitive to the political culture of the post-1953 CIA-sponsored coup against Iranian national self-determination: *Haft Maqaleh* (*Seven Essays*) (1954) and *Seh Maqaleh-ye Digar* (*Three More Essays* (1962), which was then topped by his most famous essay, *Gharbzadegi* (*Westoxication*) (1962), which has to be read in the context of this constellation of essays and in their genre. After *Gharbzadegi* came another collection of essays, *Karnameh Se Saleh* (*The Three Year Balance Sheet*) (1962), and then *Arzyabi-ye Shetabzadeh* (*Hurried Evaluations*) (1963) and the autobiographical pieces in *Yek Chah-o Do Chaleh* (*One Dug Well and Two Pits*) (1964), all of which culminated in his last major essay, *Dar Khedmat va Khiyanat-e Roshanfekran* (*On the Services and Treasons of Intellectuals*) (1964–8), which was published posthumously. These essays are definitive to his political legacy and integral to the active articulation of a Persian prose that his friends and foes alike to this day debate, dismiss, or celebrate. It is a mistake to read these essays as works of scholarship, or the results of a disciplined mind. They must be read instead, as he insisted, as the highly accurate impressions of a critical mind – like when a horse senses the coming of an earthquake, he once quipped, long before a seismograph registers its precise magnitude.

I will leave the two seminal and lengthy essays of *Gharbzadegi* (*Westoxication*) and *Dar Khedmat va Khiyanat-e Roshanfekran* (*On the Services and Treasons of Intellectuals*) for the next chapter for they require a more concentrated attention. Here in this chapter I want to dwell on the very genre of *Maqaleh* (essay), which he brought to perfection.

The Essayist as a 'Self-liberated Man'

The history of roughly the last thousand years of Persian prose encompasses a wide range of literary and scientific traditions that remain to this day the pride and joy of the language. From the earliest records of Persian prose after the Muslim conquest of Iran in the seventh century, through its long and illustrious history, and down to its resurgence as a language of effective and potent communication in the public sphere, Persian has witnessed master prose stylists of different genres. In such genres as the *maqamah*, *risalah* or *majales*, Persian prose has shown its hidden and manifest capacities for precise and probing purposes. *Golestan* Sa'di, *Safarnameh* Naser Khosrow, the *Letters* of Ayn al-Qudat al Hamadani, and the philosophical allegories of Shahab al-Din Yahya Suhrawardi are prime examples of such a precise and powerful prose. In more recent times, Mirza Abolghasem Ghaem-Magham Farahani (1779–1835) is one of the earliest prose stylists who deliberately simplified Persian prose and placed it squarely in the service of a more public communication in the course of the Iranian encounter with colonial modernity. Mirza Aqa Khan Kermani (1854–97), chief among a whole host of other evolutionary thinkers of the nineteenth century, brought that simplified Persian prose to full political practice. Predicated on a long and illustrious period of pioneering journalism throughout the nineteenth century, Ali-Akbar Dehkhoda (1879–1956) perfected that prose in a delightful satirical register. Major literary figures like Mohammad-Ali Jamalzadeh and Sadegh Hedayat had discovered and staged the capacity of Persian prose for discovering the hidden corners of Iranian life and social presence. Al-e Ahmad was the inheritor of all these and more master practitioners of the Persian prose. To all of that, however, Al-e Ahmad put a unique and precise signature, pushed it forward to meet the moral and political demands of his time. He wrote as he spoke, with an 'I' that was the personification of an entire age of revolt.

Let us now exit the Iranian context briefly and ask in a larger context what an 'essay' is, and who, indeed, an essayist is? In an introduction to a collection of his essays, the legendary essayist E. B. White writes:

> The essayist is a self-liberated man, sustained by the childish belief that everything he thinks about, everything that happens to him, is of general interest. He is a fellow who thoroughly enjoys his work, just as people who take bird walks enjoy theirs. Each new excursion of the essayist, each new 'attempt,' differs from the last and takes him into new country. This delights him. Only a person who is congenitally self-centered has the effrontery and the stamina to write essays.[3]

This is correct as far as it goes. But there is something more than just a 'childish belief that everything' the essayist thinks 'is of general interest'. The essayist, such as in the case of Al-e Ahmad, comes to personify and his or her pen to represent, or more accurately constitute, the simulacrum of a representation of the public weal. There is a dialectic at work here: the essayist represents the society and the society eventually begins to look as the essayist says it is. There was *Gharbzadegi* in Iran and the rest of the colonised world before Al-e Ahmad theorised it in a major essay, but once he had thus theorised it, his diagnosis became definitive of an entire age. Off the top of my head I tried to put together a quick list of essayists I have always enjoyed reading: Ralph Waldo Emerson, Samuel Johnson, Marcel Proust, Leo Tolstoy, Fyodor Dostoyevsky, George Orwell, Flannery O'Connor, James Baldwin, Langston Hughes, Gore Vidal, Susan Sontag, Amrita Pritam, Adrienne Rich, Zadie Smith, Jamaica Kincaid, Joan Didion, Angela Davis, Asia Djebar, Cherríe Moraga . . . There is something about the genre that is indeed best captured by what E. B. White calls: 'the childish belief that everything [the essayist] thinks about, everything that happens to him, is of general interest'. But that belief, that 'childish' conviction, constitutes a *tabula rasa* of reading the world anew. All of these essayists, whatever else they did, were definitive to their age and its central traumas.

I cannot think of a single contemporary member of the literati at the time of Al-e Ahmad who was so liberated as he was – so in tune with the central political traumas of his time, so free, flamboyant, self-confident to articulate and speak his or her mind. There were others more erudite than him, some like Khalil Maleki he admired and others like Ehsan Yarshater he loathed, some like Ahmad Fardid and Mahmoud Houman he befriended and ingratiated. But no one wrote as he did. His prose and politics were identical and in his confident voice he was the liberated postcolonial subject who could think and speak that voice in precise staccatos of truth and dare, nerve and narrative. He could say 'I' in a way that no single one of his contemporaries could say 'I'. His 'I' had become collective, communal, national, global, worldly. His 'I' was in the present perfect tense of defiance and agency. He roamed through subjects and he wrote with precision and poise. He knew enough to write – not too much to paralyse him, not too little to make a fool out of himself. His army of jealous critics could pick many holes in his arguments. But none of them could even repeat that 'I' that spoke in him let alone command it. That confidence was precisely because he was not intimidated by too much learning. He knew just enough to enable him to breathe and write – not too little to make him conscious, not too much to silence and give him a pause of humility. His character and erudition were pitch-perfect for a bold essayist.

To be sure, we had a number of masterful practitioners of Persian prose at the time of Al-e Ahmad. Ebrahim Golestan commanded a magnificent poetic prose, Mostafa Rahimi a solid probing diction, Ahmad Shamlou a playful prose of uncommon power and poignancy. Shahrokh Meskoub wrote a magnificent literary prose. There were master scholars like Abdolhossein Zarrinkub who could bring a monumental literary learning to their fluent and readable prose. The list can go on and on. But none of them came anywhere near Al-e Ahmad with the flawless spontaneity of his prose, the fluency with which he flew from one urgent subject to another. Everyone speaks of the power of his prose, without knowing precisely what this power was. His prose was powerful because in his written textuality he mimicked orality, intimacy, conversational proximity, the presumption that he was talking to you, that you were having a cup of tea with him. He wrote as if he was speaking. This mimicry of orality is where the power of his power presides.

In his classic essay 'Plato's Pharmacy' (1968), as indeed in much of his other work, Jacques Derrida goes after Plato and with him the entire course of

European philosophical mistrust of writing.[4] 'A text is not a text', he stipulates at the very beginning of the essay, 'unless it hides from the first comer, from the first glance, the law of its composition and the rules of its game.'[5] From here he proceeds to dismantle the presumed primacy of orality over textuality. The origin of Plato's denunciation of texts versus orality in the *Phaedrus* was of course his teacher Socrates, who never wrote anything and believed truth was accessible only through oral communication and dialogical conversation. Derrida's central polemic narrows in on the opposition between speech and writing, or ultimately between presence and absence. He thus accuses the entire range of fields from philosophy to literature of being fraught with phonocentricism and logocentricism, which for him involved a desire for transcendental authenticity. Students and followers of Derrida have also seen this proclivity for logocentricism as the manifestation of egocentrism.

What is crucial to Al-e Ahmad's essays (all in written forms) is their successful mimicry of orality, feigning conversational intimacy, of approximating transcendental authenticity. For Al-e Ahmad this was getting closer to the Qur'anic speech as truth. Is the Qur'an oral or textual? The Qur'an both refers to itself as '*Hadha' al-Kitab*' ('This Book'), and the first revelation of the Qur'an command the Prophet to '*Iqra*', to recite, to say, rather than to read or write. Somewhere between textuality and orality, therefore, the primal text of Islam both authenticates and lets loose the theo-textuality of the transcended signifier. Al-e Ahmad stands there, somewhere in the proximity of the transcendental authentic of the spoken word, hidden in the Qur'anic authority of the 'Word of God'.

The Essayist at Work

Let us now look at one of Al-e Ahmad's most famous collections of essays, *Haft Maqaleh* (*Seven Essays*) and its composition.

The collection begins with Al-e Ahmad's famous essay, '*Hedayat-e Buf-e Kur*' ('The Hedayat of the *Blind Owl*) (November 1951), which he wrote just a few months after Hedayat's suicide in Paris in April 1951. The essay starts by making a distinction between the 'I' of Hedayat as a person, that could be degenerate and clownish, and his literary 'I' – the author who wrote his literary masterpieces, and Al-e Ahmad identifies his *Blind Owl* (1937) as an entirely unique prose.[6] The literary world in Iran had just been shocked by

Figure 4.1 Jalal Al-e Ahmad and Nima Yushij and other friends, 1951. (Photo courtesy of Ali Dehbashi, from the *Bokhara Magazine* archive) Al-e Ahmad is at the centre of the photo. Nima is sitting to his left, to his right is his other close friend, the prominent translator Parviz Daryoush. The child standing in the left corner of the picture is Nima Yushij's son Sheragim Yushij. Years later, when he was a grown-up man, I met Sheragim Yushij in Austin Texas where I was a visiting professor at the University of Texas in Austin. He was a cameraman working at a local television station.

the news of Hedayat's suicide, and the air was full of anticipation regarding how best to measure and register his literary significance. Two monumental figures were definitive to the late Reza Shah, early Mohammad Reza Shah periods: one was Hedayat and the other Nima. This is the gist of what Al-e Ahmad thinks of Hedayat's major novella:

> What is it we are reading in *The Blind Owl*? What does it mean? *The Blind Owl* is a compendium, a mixture of the ancient Aryan doubts, of Buddha's Nirvana, of Iranian mysticism, of the ascetic isolationism of the oriental person, of a scape that an Iranian person, an oriental person, makes towards his inner self. *The Blind Owl* is an escape route for the pains, shortcomings,

woes and sorrows of the author. It is an attempt to grasp the eternity of beauty. It is the revenge of the mortal temporal person, against this life, this world. It is the revenge of the mortal person against mortality and decay. *The Blind Owl* is the cry of revenge – a cry of revenge that rises only internally and makes a commotion. It is a cry that echoes only under the roof of the mind, and like a whip comes down on the back of memories. *The Blind Owl* is the crystallisation of all the hatred that an impotent person has towards those who have power, a hatred that rises from depravation.[7]

Al-e Ahmad loves and admires the simplicity of Hedayat's Persian prose in which the surreal ambience of the novella becomes most compelling. He compares Hedayat to the German poet and novelist Rainer Maria Rilke (1875–1926), praises Hedayat's fusion of realism and surrealism, and detects traces of ancient 'Aryan cynicism', as he calls it, and Khayyam in them. 'Hedayat is the child of the constitutional period and the writer of the era of dictatorship,' he famously proposes.[8] Al-e Ahmad recalls how Hedayat published his *Blind Owl* in only a few copies in India in 1937, reminding his readers of what he believes to have been the aborted constitutionalism of the early twentieth century in Iran, and the rise of the dictatorship of Reza Shah. He navigates through all Hedayat's stories and proposes to read them as the mirror image of his time. He traces Hedayat's thinking to India, to Buddha and to his vegetarianism. Khayyam and Buddha are the main sources of Hedayat's thoughts, he proposes. He then tells us he believes Anton Chekhov, Edgar Allan Poe and Rainer Maria Rilke are all present in Hedayat's work.[9] Al-e Ahmad's essay navigates a literary and cultural archive that was vibrant and effervescent both at the time of Hedayat's passing and his own essay.

The next important essay in this collection is his famous piece on the legendary poet of his time with whom he was very close and in fact a neighbour – and among his earliest supporters. Al-e Ahmad's '*Moshkel-e Nima Yushij*' ('The Problem of Nima Yushij') (Ordibehesht 1331/April1952) remains to this day not only a pioneering essay on the poet but still valid in its pioneering insights. The 'problem' with Nima, Al-e Ahmad tells us, is his new poetic language, his unpresented poetic voice and the themes of his poetry – either one of which issues would have deeply disturbed the reactionaries especially among Iranians who each think themselves experts on poetry.[10] Al-e Ahmad defends Nima for having overcome the classical prosody, for the world has changed, he says, people have changed, speed has changed and so must the prosody of the poetry that seeks to reflect such changes. Al-e Ahmad uses the example of poets like the French Arthur Rimbaud (1854–91) and the American T. S. Eliot (1888–1965), and suggests a young Iranian reader reads these European and American poets and becomes hateful of his own classical poetry. 'The economic hegemony of the West inevitably brings about their cultural hegemony,' he tells us, 'and that precisely is the problem of Nima. Could we address this issue by opting for cultural isolationism and be content with our past?'[11] Al-e Ahmad is aware that Nima is becoming a fad without any critical assessment of his poetry. There is no body of critical reflections on Nima's oeuvre to which Al-e Ahmad can refer. He is effectively making that critical assessment possible as he writes this pioneering essay.

He charges Nima with publishing too much whereas his real audience, Al-e Ahmad believes, is not yet ready for him. He shares a priceless memory of how Nima recites his poetry for his privileged few visitors. Nima goes to a backroom and comes back with a massive piece of paper that has been folded multiple times. He spreads it, sits on it and rolls all over it (*milulad* is the word Al-e Ahmad uses in Persian – a verb usually used for worms) until he finds a poem he wants to read to his visitor. Nima does not write poetry, Al-e Ahmad tells us. He 'spreads it' like seeds.[12] Al-e Ahmad gives a short biography of Nima, for he is not much known at this point. He speaks of his son Sheragim, and of his opium addiction. He provides something of an 'ethnography' of the poet and his habitat in Mazandaran. Then he turns to Nima's poetry and gives a genealogy of its origins, complains of the difficulty of getting hold of his early poetry, gives details of the earliest records of Nima's poems. He considers 'Afsaneh' to be the true origin of Nima's poetry, while he believes Nima's major essay on poetics, *Arzesh Ehsasat dar Zendegi Honarpishegan* ('The Significance of Emotions in the Life of Artists') (1939–40) an insufficient defence of his poetry.[13] He goes through all the various magazines and literary journals in which Nima had published his earliest poems. He believes the French poet and critic Stéphane Mallarmé (1842–98) was influential on Nima's poetry. He thinks Iranians might as well learn and adopt free verse and blank verse. He proposes a link between Hedayat's *The Blind Owl* and Nima's projection of himself as 'an old owl' and they both reflect the tyranny and pessimism of the Reza Shah period. He thus proceeds between poetry and sociology in understanding Nima's significance. He finally turns to a letter of Nima's in which aspects of his poetics are discussed. He writes with critical intimacy and close familiarity with both the revolutionary poet and his work.

These two pioneering essays on Hedayat and Nima in effect lay the foundation for modern literary criticism in Iran. Hitherto there had been no other major essays on either of these two seminal figures for the very language of literary criticism of this range and engagement did not exist in Iran. Al-e Ahmad's contemporary was Fatemeh Sayyah (1902–48) who taught comparative literature at Tehran University and with whom Simin Daneshvar wrote her doctoral dissertation, but Sayyah was entirely clueless about these seminal contemporary figures. She had a solid command over Russian and French literatures and, for her, 'literary theory' meant for the contemporary Persian literature to hurry up and catch up with civilised Europeans, which is to say the precise opposite of Al-e Ahmad's critical positions.[14] Writing on Hedayat and Nima required a critical intimacy with both that very few people other than Al-e Ahmad had or could muster.

The rest of the essays in this book are actually mostly translations. There is an essay on W. H. Auden in which Al-e Ahmad translates Auden's poem 'Refugee Blues' (1939). Another piece in this volume is a translation of a travelogue to Greece he had read in *Les Temp Modernes*, the February 1952 issue. *Les Temps Modernes* (*Modern Times*) was a leading French journal founded by Simone de Beauvoir and Jean-Paul Sartre and was deeply influential among the French and the Francophone literati around the globe. It first issue was published in October 1945. From another issue of the same French periodical Al-e Ahmad translated a chapter from the French translation of *The Autobiography of Mother Jones* (1925). What his own short notes to both Auden and Mother Jones emphasise is the fact that these two seminal figures were both against party politics but progressive in their own independent positions.[15] He also translates a short story by the Egyptian-French writer Albert Cossery (1913–2008), which he took from a French book called *Les Hommes oubliés de Dieu*. He then turns to Jean Cocteau (1889–1963) and translates his libretto to the ballet *Les mariés de la tour Eiffel* (1921). In other words, the future author of *Gharbzadegi* (*Westoxication*) is thoroughly

Francophile and Europhile in his literary and critical choices for translation and dissemination into his own mother tongue. For the rest of his short but highly influential life Al-e Ahmad was never able to resolve or even to understand this paradox.

What is evident in these essays is that Al-e Ahmad is an impatient reader. He reads and learns something and he wants instantly to share it with a critical twist. The range of translations he makes in such a volume of essays has multiple meanings. At this point the severe censorship of the Pahlavi regime would make it easier to translate than to compose original pieces. These translations therefore always carried multiple meanings and implied certain political innuendoes. Be that as it may, the preponderance of French, European and North American sources still revealed the power the 'West' exercised over the creative and critical mind of the very author of *Westoxication*! In effect Al-e Ahmad was both the product and the critical reaction to a global condition of coloniality in which the postcolonial subject is yet to reach full critical consciousness to see alternative universalities beyond 'the West and the Rest'.

He Was in a Rush

Let us now look at another signature collection of his essays, *Arzyabi-ye Shetabzadeh* (*Hurried Evaluations*) (1964), a compilation of eighteen pieces he readied for publication late in 1964 and published early in 1965. The collection begins with a short introduction he calls 'Serkeh-ye Naqd Ya Halva-ye Tarikh' ('The Vinegar of Criticism or the Sweet of History') (1964). The title comes from a common Persian idiom that means it is better to have even a bad (sour) thing like vinegar now than to wait for the promise of a very good (sweet) thing like confectionery in future. He then divides the essays into six categories: On Poetry and Poetics, On Writing, On Drama, On Painting, On Anthropology and Sundries. The most famous piece in the first section is his now legendary essay on the occasion of the passing of Nima Yushij, 'Pir-e Mard Chesham-e Ma Bud' ('The Old Man Was our Eyes'). In the second section he has a pioneering essay on Dostoyevsky and nihilism, in the third part, he writes on a few theatrical pieces he has either seen on the stage or read in print, in the section on painting he has a probing essay on the prominent Iranian artist Bahman Mohassess (1931–2010), in the section on anthropology he has a travelogue to Yazd, a report from the seventh congress of ethnography in Moscow in August 1964, and then comes a review of an essay on the function of religion in Iran, and then a report of a festival in Ardahal. At the end under the section he calls 'Sundries' he has an essay on Gandhi, a critical short piece on rapid urbanisation and finally a report of an encounter with a French Trotskyist who had visited Iran.

What strikes us most today when reading these essays is the wandering soul of their author, his impatience, his urge to attend to everything, to have a full bird's-eye view of his homeland and the world. In 'The Vinegar of Criticism or the Sweet of History', dated 1964, he argues for the urgency of writing the present as opposed to waiting for the historical comprehensiveness of the posterity. The essay is a manifesto for the urgency of recording the here and now, rather than waiting for there and then.[16] In another essay, dated 1958, he lashes out against writing endorsements for young poets or writers by giving himself as an example.[17] He then proposes this malady is due to the absence of literary criticism in Iran. But he ends up turning the piece into a letter to a young poet on the model of *Rainer Maria Rilke*'s 'Letters to A Young Poet' (1929). In a piece dated 1959, he brings Tibor Mende (1915–84), the Hungarian-French journalist and author of *Entre la peur et l'espoir, réflexions sur l'histoire d'aujourd'hui* (*Between Fear and Hope: Reflections on Today's History*), and places him next to his political guru Khalil Maleki and a leading Iranian poet Mehdi Akhavan-e Sales' poem '*Akhar Shahnameh*' ('The End of Shahnameh'). The essay shows his uncanny ability to place Iran and the world together in meaningful but still surprising frames of references.

In another piece on Nima, dated 1959, he gives a genealogy of the poet's time and those other seminal poets of the period like Ahmad Shamlou and Mehdi Akhavan-e Sales who followed him. Then comes a moving piece, 'The Old Man was our Eyes', dated 1961, on how Nima died and Al-e Ahmad prepared his body for burial. In a speech he gave at the Technical School of Abadan in the same year he gives his panoramic view of his contemporary Persian literature with detailed and intimate knowledge of the field. Then follows a long interview with Al-e Ahmad dated back to early 1964. This interview is mostly a reflection on his own work. Periodically he has such overviews of his work that give him an occasion to reformulate and sum up what he has been up to over the course of his literary and critical career. 'I am scared of Dostoyevsky. He petrified me, I might even say.' This is how he starts an article on Dostoyevsky and nihilism, dated 1964.[18] The essay is a clear indication of his deep-rooted attraction to existentialism, which we also see in his close attention to Jean-Paul Sartre and Albert Camus.

Read back to back, these essays in fact mark the course of his regular life and what he reads or sees or observes. He goes with his wife to see a play, he comes home and writes on it in the autumn of 1961.[19] In the autumn of 1964 they saw another play and he went to sit somewhere to write on it. He writes another essay on Vincenzo Bianchini (1903–2000), a doctor, painter, sculptor, writer, poet and philosopher who used to visit Iran regularly.[20] Bahman Mohassess was a prominent painter who was also his close friend, so he writes a piece on him in autumn 1964 and uses the occasion to reflect on modern painting. He is not a contemporary or modern art historian, he is not an art critic, he is an essayist, and writes cogently and plausibly on any issue with which he chooses to engage. He travels to Yazd with his brother Shams, so he writes on that magnificent city – again not as a trained anthropologist or professional ethnographer, but as an essayist. In late summer 1964 he goes to Moscow to attend an ethnographic congress and writes a report on his experiences – not as a scholar or even a graduate student, but as an essayist. Early in the autumn of 1964, Brian Spooner, a professor of anthropology at my own alma mater the University of Pennsylvania, had published a short essay on 'the Function of Religion in Iranian Society'. Al-e Ahmad reviews it in autumn 1964. In the same year he writes on an ancient festival in Mashhad Ardahal. Next year in 1965, he writes a short biography of Gandhi. In the autumn of 1958 he had already written a scathing critique of the urban design of Tehran. In the summer of 1964 he writes of his encounter with a Trotskyist. There is no rhyme or reason to any of these choices except the logic and rhetoric of a deeply engaged public intellectual mastering the prose of an essayist to engage with his people, stir them, inform them, jump-start them into becoming aware of their surroundings.

Prose of our Historicality

Let me now write more on the particularities of his prose. Al-e Ahmad was a master of speed, precision and brevity – but above all of emotive writing, of making you breathless trying to catch up with the velocity of his runaway thoughts, but also the punctual precision of his universe. This is how he describes the moment of Nima's death in a famous essay dated 1961.

> Tell me, you mean I have lost my Nima? How could I say yes? I sent Aliyeh Khanom [Nima's wife] and Simin [Daneshvar, his wife] to our house to call the doctor. Before I had arrived, they had sent his son to 'Ezam al Saltaneh his brother-in-law. The maid of the house and I helped bring his body – that had become very light – from under the homemade heater and laid it towards the Qibla. I saw the fear of death in the maid's eyes. I said: 'go get the samovar ready. The family will be here shortly.' As the samovar was heating up I asked her to get me the Qu'ran and I sent her after [a mutual friend] Sadiqi who was not a fan of Nima until one night he heard part of '*Qal'eh Seqrim*' [a famous poem of Nima's] from the mouth of the Old Man himself. Until Sadiqi arrived I opened a page of the Qu'ran and began reciting: '*wa al safat al Safa . . .*' ['By those [angels] lined up in rows/ And those who drive [the clouds] . . . ']²¹

You just try to keep pace with the prose, piercing from the sublime to the prosaic – from the Qur'an to the samovar, interrupted by reminding us of one of the most beautiful poems of Nima. But the point is that you cannot stop and think and tally. You must just let go of control and let him take you for the ride.

Let us look at another example. This is how he writes about Bahman Mohassess, a major painter and a close friend of his:

> I have known Bahman Mohassess since early 1950s – known him consistently, traveling or at home, and this has of course occasioned an intimacy between us. But in addition to this I just like him, because he is warm, learned and more than anything else he is a phenomenon unto himself. He is a Rashti [a native of Northern Iran] who has become Italian! And I don't believe such a phenomenon has ever been seen anywhere else at any time in history – if one can generalise from the particular, the story of Bahman Mohassess is the story of contemporary art.²²

Thus he takes the personal and makes it palpably political and turns the result into an aesthetic observation on the phenomenon of (artistic) modernity. The point here is not to agree or disagree with his assessment, but to configure the speed and precision of his staccato moves to make his arguments clear. This was a unique prose. There were those who could write on friendship, on art, on literature, on poetry, but absolutely no other person than Al-e Ahmad could zip through a prose like this and sustain the course of your credulity. He was fully aware of the uniqueness of his prose and the manner he wrote his essays. This is how he defended the genre of essay writing:

> I write about anything about which I have the right to say something – such as dialect or travelogues or anything else. Let me cite for you something that Sartre said when he started *Les Temps Modernes* . . . It is about the responsibility of a writer . . . Who must write even on those issues that are beyond his expertise . . . Because in our time the machine has turned in issues for which you need no expertise, even for painting, even for film . . . music, if an instrumentalist is shitting all over the place, I have the right to tell him and I am not a musician . . . I have ears I have eyes I watch a movie just as a viewer not as an expert.[23]

The issue of the range and variety of Al-e Ahmad's essays and the speed with which he wrote and published them reaches a crescendo long after his death, when in 1994 Mostafa Zamani-Nia, a scholar of Al-e Ahmad's work, collected, edited and annotated a comprehensive collection of his essays.[24] This was a threshold in Al-e Ahmad studies that has required a much closer attention to the intensity of his preoccupation with this genre. The publication of this collection was supervised by Shams Al-e Ahad, Jalal Al-e Ahmad's brother. This was a crucial publication that introduced Al-e Ahmad to a new generation of readers. This publication was a mixed blessing – both enriching and expanding our understanding of Al-e Ahmad, and yet forcing us to confront the issue of how he wanted himself remembered by posterity. The generation of Al-e Ahmad's readers who came to critical thinking with his publications now had given way to a new generation that was reading him at a long historical distance. Many of these essays that Zamani-Ni collected here were in fact scattered in diverse places and eventually lost their bibliographical references. We now needed to rethink Al-e Ahmad's famous essays and iconic collections he had published himself as part of a much larger and more comprehensive body of work.

Zamani-Nia's voluminous collection brought all these known and unknown essays together. Many of these pieces had not appeared in the selection of the essays that Al-e Ahmad published himself during his lifetime, which means he was selecting and choosing what he wanted to leave behind and discarding the rest. Perhaps there were also censorial reasons why he was not reproducing such pieces, for the official Pahlavi censorship was much harsher with books than with sporadic essays in obscure periodicals. In these posthumous volumes, Zamani-Nia has collected and published them all – or almost all, for even he is not sure he has collected all of Al-e Ahmad's pieces. When we look at these imposing volumes, we realise Al-e Ahmad was the author of much more than 'Seven' or 'Three More' essays – that in fact he was the author of scores of such essays, at least some of which have been collected in these four volumes, digging deeply into out-of-print, obscure and rare or altogether non-existent originals that have by now disappeared.

Zamani-Nia has divided these four volumes into sections on autobiography, literature, poetry, language, myth, legends and epics, contemporary fiction, art, architecture, media, textbooks, music and drama. Important as this collection is, one should not assume its publication in 1994 is an entirely innocent deed. Supervised by Al-e Ahmad's staunchly pro-Islamic Republic younger brother Shams Al-e Ahmad these four volumes contain obscure and out-of-print articles that, gathered together, might project a far more palatable image of Al-e Ahmad to the ruling regime if we were to forget that in these essays, as indeed in all his writings, Al-e Ahmad is in fact in conversation and contestation with all the vital issues and intellectual trends of his time – issues and trends that were subsequently repressed and silenced by the Islamic Republic in the interest of their proto-fascist Islamism. Be that as it may, the self-same collection also expands the horizons of our understanding of Al-e Ahmad's work – though not in a qualitative manner, corresponding to the quantity of articles published here. In these expansive collections of essays, we remain in the presence of the self-same restless mind writing on just about any subject that tickles his critical or creative fancies. In other words, this collection of essays offers us more of the same issues Al-e Ahmad usually wrote about, and does not introduce any new subject or genre.

If we put these four volumes next to a short piece that Simin Daneshvar published soon after they appeared, it shows the depth of the ideological battle over Al-e Ahmad's legacy. The publication of one particularly poignant piece by Simin Daneshvar in 2003 could be read as a response to such attempts. In this short essay Daneshvar seeks essentially to put an end to the baseless rumours that Shams Al-e Ahmad had initiated in which he had even accused Daneshvar herself of having killed her husband, and when that idiocy did not wash then accused SAVAK of having done so. Daneshvar specifically dismisses this charge too, and reports how the Shah's secret police had assured them they would not kill Al-e Ahmad to avoid turning him into a martyr. She writes of the medical history of Al-e Ahmad, and confirms that he was a heavy smoker. She further testifies that, like his guru Khalil Maleki and his follower Gholamhossein Saedi, Al-e Ahmad was also an alcoholic, and then to top everything off she opts to change the subject completely and turn to her love for Al-e Ahmad and concludes:

> If I were to come back to life I would still marry Jalal, of course I wish I could marry Hafez, Rumi, or Shams . . . even as a co-wife . . . In the world of cowardly men, Jalal was a singularly chivalrous and kind man. How well he knew how to love, how to caress, and how to soothe.

And she then goes on to tell her readers how much she loved his gift, his attentiveness, and their mutual love for each other. How he would fix her plate for her in parties and gatherings and then come and sit by her feet, and how Maleki had said after all these years that Jalal and Simin are still in love.[25]

Jalal Al-e Ahmad was blessed with a wife like Simin Daneshvar, and we are lucky she survived him for decades after his passing and remained true and steadfast in safeguarding his legacy against a state-sponsored project to steal and appropriate his memory, with his fanatically Islamist younger brother at the full service of the project. What shines through all these disputations is Al-e Ahmad's own prose, the very prose of our historicality, and how it was that even beyond Al-e Ahmad's own imagination and capacities we inherited the seeds of his postcolonial agency. In his elegant little book, *History at the Limit of World-History* (2003), Ranajit Guha gently but firmly goes after Hegel's philosophy of history as the modus operandi of imperial historiography. Guha dismantles Hegel's notion of 'World History' cast in the domain of imperial narratives. Hidden from that history, Guha argues, is the course of the voiceless agency of the subaltern. Guha's concern was the course of British colonialism in India and the necessity of putting literary twists to the prose of our historicality. But the same argument could be extended into any other colonial context when the condition of historicality trumps the Hegelian *Aufhebung*. 'Historicality as the true historical existence of man in the world', Guha proposes, 'is converted by the act of superseding into philosophy of history and the concreteness of the human past made to yield to the concept of World-history.'[26] Al-e Ahmad's legacy, his essays perhaps in particular, are the living evidence of that concrete historicality.

The Postcolonial Knowing Subject

To think towards a post-Islamist liberation theology, we need to think back over the very recent history when Islam and Muslims were in active conversation with non-Islamic facts, phenomena and forces of their world and worldliness. As you can see from the range of his essays, Jalal Al-e Ahmed was one such potent example of when Muslims were in active conversation with the world, where their *identities* were not formed or fixed but entirely contingent on the *alterities* they encountered. This is the main reason for my current interest in reconfiguring his life and legacy so many fateful years after his passing. In my *Islamic Liberation Theology* (2008) I turned that worldly engagement of Muslims with their alterities into a moment of *theodicy*, when Muslims have had to not just account for the others they encounter but in fact to embrace them as the primary site of their own critical consciousness. The events of the Arab revolutions of 2011 and beyond, and of the Green Movement before it in Iran, were the site of that recognition of the Other as agonistic rather than antagonistic, to follow Chantal Mouffe's thinking. But the violent events of counterrevolutionary mobilisations that soon followed those momentous events showed how reactionary regimes were obviously threatened by that prospect and sought to destroy it by violently rekindling the dying flames of sectarianism and thereby re-validate their outdated Islamism.

There is also a palpable autobiographical aspect to this recollection of Al-e Ahmad's life and legacy – which points to multiple generations of critical thinkers prior to the Islamist takeover of the Iranian revolution of 1977–9. I was born and raised in Al-e Ahmed's world where his (or my) Marxism and his (or my) being a Muslim were not in contradiction, but in fact complemented and corroborated and corresponded to each other. But in the aftermath of the Islamist takeover of the Iranian revolution of 1977–9 that cosmopolitan worldliness was systematically destroyed, and Iranian Islam degenerated into a pathologically paranoid clerical sectarianism. By actively remembering that cosmopolitan worthiness as I write this book on the life and legacy of Jalal Al-e Ahmad, I wish to retrieve the moral, intellectual and imaginative condition in which such a towering public intellectual was made possible. The life and legacy of Al-e Ahmad between the 1920s and 1960s gives us a prototype of a cosmopolitan culture when Islam was neither at war nor at peace with the world but instead in active and robust conversation with it. It is the spirit of that conversation that remains exemplary. Exemplifying the moral agency that occasions that conversation is the knowing-I of the public intellectual, here personified in Jalal Al-e Ahmad.

At the epicentre of Al-e Ahmad's essays is his knowing-I; his probing, searching, learning, inquisitive, teaching, wondering-I. Who and what could that I be, that postcolonial knowing subject, when questioning the very assumption of a unitary and autonomous subject was at the heart of the philosophical project concomitant with that capitalist modernity? Doesn't the deconstruction of the knowing subject extend to the colonial consequences of that capitalist modernity? The poststructuralist collapse of the world and the subject onto each other, in the signature 'Dasein' move of Heidegger, embraces both the colonised and the colonising worlds – though not in identical ways. If the subject is a *transitory* and *contingent* social construct, then the postcolonial uncertainty of the ideological apparatus that governs it is a gateway for an open-ended if not autonomous subject. The open-endedness of that knowing subject makes all its agential moves at once valid and contingent.

In 'The Subversion of the Subject and the Dialectic of Desire in the Freudian Unconscious', Jacques Lacan (1901–81) sustains his cogent critique of the assumption of a 'unified, Cartesian subject'.[27] It is crucial to keep in mind that this 'Cartesian subject' never included the colonial person, and thus they had no control over the postcolonial persona whose literary, poetic and other subversive moves were entirely outside the purview of the Cartesian cogito. As Jonathan Scott Lee succinctly summarises Lacan's position in this seminal essay,

> in many respects the lecture simply repeats . . . leading themes of his work
> of the 1950s, emphasising in particular the way in which Freud's concept

of unconscious desire radically undermines the philosophical tradition's largely unquestioned reliance on a theory of consciousness as the centre of the human subject.[28]

Again, in that European philosophical project the colonial person, and perforce postcolonial persona, has had nor indeed could have had any possible place. We postcolonial persons were persona non grata in the domain of that Cartesian cogito. We were and remain its wild card. Unscripted in the Cartesian wholesome cogito we remain outside the postmodern 'crisis of the subject', and thus free, or more precisely open-ended, in our postcolonial shanty towns.

After Marx and Freud, it is almost impossible to assume the autonomy of any knowing subject if we are confined within the self-centring domains of a Eurocentric philosophical imagination. 'The structure of the subject', as Lacan puts it, is evident in the 'discontinuity of the real'. From this it then follows that 'the human being [is envisioned] as a *coupure* (cut), *faille* (fault), a *fente* or *refente* (slit), or a *béance* (gap)'. Therefore: 'It is precisely the concept of the subject as a sort of Aristotelian "substance" that is ultimately subverted in "The Subversion of the Subject".'[29] The postcolonial knowing subject is outside the purview of that dismantled autonomy of the European subject. In every European philosophical movement, structuralist or poststructuralist, modernist or postmodernist, the knowing subject is a decidedly European subject. The world outside Europe is a knowable world for that European knowing subject – a world thus rendered decidedly incapable of any agency of its own. By definition we in that world cannot be a knowing subject without dismantling the entirety of their system. From outside the purview of those Cartesian, Hegelian and Kantian systems, and their collective knowing subjects and crises, the colonial person and the postcolonial persona know the world not within but against the Eurocentric world we have known, infiltrated, dismantled and overcome.

Notes

1. Jalal Al-e Ahmad, *Arzyabi-ye Shetabzadeh (Hurried Evaluations)* (Tabriz: Ibn Sina Publishers, 1964): 5.
2. See Naser Hariri, *Honar va Adabiyat-e Emruz: Goft-o-Shonudi ba Simin Daneshvar*

(*The Art and Literature of Today: A Conversation with Simin Daneshvar*) (Op. Cit.): 28.

3. E. B. White, *Essays of E. B. White* (New York: Harper & Row Publishers, 1977): VII.

4. See Jacques Derrida, 'Plato's Pharmacy', in *Dissemination*, translated, with an introduction and additional notes by Barbara Johnson (London: Athlone Press, 1981): 63–84.

5. Ibid: 63.

6. See Jalal Al-e Ahmad, '*Hedayat-e Buf-e Kur*' ('Hedayat of *The Blind Owl*') (1951), in Jalal Al-e Ahmad, *Haft Maqaleh* (*Seven Essays*) (Tehran: Amir Kabir, 1978, originally published in 1954). All translations from the original Persian are mine.

7. Ibid: 7.

8. Ibid: 15.

9. Ibid: 25.

10. Ibid: 27–8.

11. Ibid: 31.

12. Ibid: 33.

13. Ibid: 41.

14. For more on Fatemeh Sayyah and her importance in the nascent period of literary criticism in Iran see my chapter on her in my *Reversing the Colonial Gaze: Persian Travelers Abroad* (Cambridge: Cambridge University Press, 2020).

15. See Jalal Al-e Ahmad, *Haft Maqaleh* (*Seven Essays*) (Op. Cit.): 87.

16. Jalal Al-e Ahmad, *Arzyabi-ye Shetabzadeh* (*Hurried Evaluations*) (Op. Cit.): 6.

17. Ibid: 10.

18. Ibid: 109.

19. Ibid: 116.

20. Ibid: 136.

21. Ibid: 53. The Quranic passage is from 37:1–2 forward. '*Qal'eh Seqrim*' (Azar 1313/Winter, 1934) is a long poem of Nima Yushij. See Nima Yushij, *Majmu'eh-ye Kamel Ash'ar* (*Complete Poems*), edited by Sirus Tahbaz (Tehran: Negah Publications, 1991): 168–221.

22. Ibid: 145.

23. Ibid: 82–3.

24. See Jalal Al-e Ahmad, *Adab va Honar-e Emruz-e Iran: Majmu'eh Maqalat, 1324–1348* (*Literature and Art in Contemporary Iran: Collected Essays, 1945–1969* (Tehran: Nashr Mitra, Nashr Hamkelasi, 1373/1994). Four Volumes. I am

grateful to my friend Mahmoud Omidsalar for his uncanny ability to procure me the .pdf copies of these precious volumes.

25. See Simin Daneshvar, '*Az Ancheh Rafteh Hekayat: Nagofteh-ha-ye Simin Daneshvar az Jalal Al-e Ahmad*' ('The Way We Were: What Simin Daneshvar had not yet said about Al-e Ahmad') in Mohammad Alizadeh (ed.), *Ghorub-e Jalal: Three Essays* (Tehran: A'ineh Jonub Publishers, 1384/2005): 44–5.

26. Ranajit Guha, *History at the Limit of World-History* (New York: Columbia University Press, 2003): 3.

27. See Jonathan Scott Lee, *Jacques Lacan* (Amherst, MA: The University of Massachusetts Press, 1990): 138.

28. Ibid.

29. Ibid.

5

Gharbzadegi: The Condition of Coloniality

Thus our age is no longer the age of class conflicts within particular
borders, or of national revolutions, nor indeed is it the age of clashing
'isms' and ideologies. Under the cover of every commotion, or uprising,
or coup d'état in Zanzibar, Syria, or Uruguay we must look and see what
corporate colonial interests and their supporting states are hiding. We can
no longer even consider our regional warfare as ideological battles, even on
the surface. Today every school child sees how under the cover of World
War II were lurking the expansionism of the mechanised industries of
both parties. Even in the crisis of Cuba, Congo, the Suez Canal, or Algeria
the issues were sugar, diamonds and oil, respectively. In the bloodshed
in Cypress, Zanzibar, Vietnam also at issue was to secure a bridgehead to
protect the trade routes, for these are the first dominant issues determining
state policies.[1]

Jalal Al-e Ahmad, *Gharbzadegi* (*Westoxication*), (1962)

The study of Jalal Al-e Ahmad's arguably most seminal text *Gharbzadegi*
(*Westoxication*) has historically suffered from a mode of bizarre nativism
that has in turn projected the nativism of the Iranian or Iranist scholar onto
the presumed nativism of the subject of their studies, Al-e Ahmad himself.
Al-e Ahmad, contrary to their common assumption, was not a nativist.
Quite to the contrary: he had a wide global perspective in his prose and politics. They are nativist – these scholars who have historically, systematically
and consistently abused, misread and sought to discredit him as 'a nativist'.[2]
Despite all its flaws and limitations, the text of his *Westoxication* is still the
most compelling example of his anticolonial worldliness. A generation of
Iranist scholars that came to US and Europe in the aftermath of the US/UK

coup of 1953 were at best anticolonialist and at worst fanatical modernists, in both cases in effect consolidating the centralising trope and discourse of Eurocentric modernity, which they either loathed or loved, turning them into either fanatical Europhobes or equally zealous Europhiles, discrediting them both from any meaningful encounter with the phenomenon of 'Europe' as a self-universalising ideological project. The study of Al-e Ahmad we have received so far is the ailing by-product of this predicament. One task of this book is to liberate Al-e Ahmad from this prison-cell of 'Iranist' provincialism.

The Nativism of the Nativists

Under the very nose of these nativist Iranists writing on Al-e Ahmad, whose own work oscillates between the two compromising poles of 'Iran and the West', a whole world of postcolonial criticism was emerging of which they were blissfully unaware. Massive demographic changes were happening in both North America and Western Europe, and yet these Iranists were entirely insular and aloof from such seismic changes and their theoretical consequences. Those demographic changes were producing a widely influential body of critical literature that eventually would be called 'Postcolonial Studies' and yet these Iranists were out to lunch. If we take the publication of Edward Said's *Orientalism* (1978) as a benchmark of this field, then that date marks the crescendo of postcolonial theory reaching a barometer of a generational gap in anticolonial criticism. The previous generation were blindfolded into disciplinary formations of Political Science, History, Anthropology, Psychology, Sociology or even Third World Literature, and it never even occurred to them to have a critical stance vis-a-vis these by-and-large disciplinary products of European colonial modernity.

Even those who thought of themselves as Marxists or anticolonial activists failed to consider that they were in fact the carriers of the episteme of colonial modernity into the study of their own homelands. They thus systematically nativised, Orientalised, exoticised and perforce marginalised the study of Iran, and Iranian Studies became, and to this day remains, one of the most reactionary fields in the Area Studies fields – the very essence of self-Orientalisation. Keep in mind that by this time, in the 1970s and 1980s, the group of Subaltern Studies led by Ranajit Guha had taken Edward Said and Antonio

Gramsci's work and crafted one of the most progressive schools of historical investigation. By now Edward Said, Gayatri Spivak, Ranajit Guha and
Homi Bhabha, among many others, had crafted fields of investigation with
astonishing theoretical implications for the world at large. The conference
Gayatri Spivak and I organised in November 2000, at which Edward Said
gave the keynote speech and to which scores of subalternist scholars joined,
marked a threshold of these developments.[3] Soon serious Latin Americanists
like Walter Mignolo, John Beverley, Alberto Moreiras, Ileana Rodríguez
and Norma Alarcón had extended these fields of Postcolonial and Subaltern
Studies into Latin America, while Y. V. Mudimbe, Achille Mbembe and
Mahmood Mamdani took them to Africa, as Ashis Nandy, Partha Chatterjee
and Gauri Viswanathan into India, and Kōjin Karatani into Japan, as indeed
many other critical thinkers elsewhere from Western Asia to Eastern Europe.
By this time the classics of the anticolonial generation that included Aimé
Césaire and Léopold Sédar Senghor and José Martí were being read entirely
differently. Meanwhile Al-e Ahmad's *Gharbzadegi* was collecting dust and
living an insular, isolated and entirely irrelevant and parasitical life handled
by nativists who, in a bizarre case of Freudian projection, called the books
and critical thinkers it had joined 'nativists'!

A key task of rereading Al-e Ahmad today, decades after his passing,
is precisely to retrieve the particulars of his cosmopolitan worldlines, the
way his Islam, and his being a Muslim, were placed in the world he lived.
This is necessary because any prospect of a *post-Islamist liberation theology*,
towards which I am rereading Al-e Ahmad here, must actively imagine and
retrieve the historical moment before the sudden and traumatic rise of an
Islamic Republic on the burned ashes of the Iranian revolution of 1977–9.
Al-e Ahmad lived and breathed that world in all its perils and promises.
The aggressive and violent transmutation of Islam into Islamism helped 'the
West' to be cross-essentialised into a fetishised commodity. Al-e Ahmad had
his share of that fetishisation with and through his *Gharbzadegi*. But the cure
for that condition is also imbedded in Al-e Ahmad's larger output, and must
be brought to bear on that justly or unjustly privileged text. Thus, I read Al-e
Ahmad's *Gharbzadegi* not like an orphaned text, but one with an extended
family.

'Sixteen Tons'

Let us therefore begin by first reading *Gharbzadegi* closely and see what Al-e Ahmad was up to before we go any further. The text has been fetishised and like all other classics more cited than read cover to cover. We will read it cover to cover to get to the kernel of his argument, set the superfluous aside and examine the very core of his thinking in this book.

Al-e Ahmad's *Gharbzadegi* starts with a partial and flawed Persian translation of the lyrics of 'Sixteen Tons' (1946) a famous song written by Merle Travis about a coal miner. The version Al-e Ahmad had heard came from a 1955 recording by Tennessee Ernie Ford.[4] The original lyrics in part read:

'Sixteen Tons'

Some people say a man is made outta mud
A poor man's made outta muscle and blood
Muscle and blood and skin and bones
A mind that's a-weak and a back that's strong

You load sixteen tons, what do you get?
Another day older and deeper in debt
Saint Peter don't you call me 'cause I can't go
I owe my soul to the company store

I was born one mornin' when the sun didn't shine
I picked up my shovel and I walked to the mine
I loaded sixteen tons of number nine coal
And the straw boss said 'Well, a-bless my soul' . . .

You load sixteen tons, what do you get?
Another day older and deeper in debt . . .[5]

So, in what is in effect the first short 'chapter' of the book, Al-e Ahmad cites the lyrics of a popular song about a labourer. It doesn't matter that it is a partial and flawed Persian translation – what matters is that the lyrics tell the story of the power of corporations over body and soul of labourer, and that Al-e Ahmad shares an example from the US and not from Iran or elsewhere in the colonial world, which means he sees the structural affinity between his

'East' and 'West'. How could that be read as the sign of a nativist? It is thus fair to suggest that *Gharbzadegi* begins on a good note, identifying with the sufferings of an American labourer at the mercy of the corporations. One can only wish this structural affinity detected so early in the text would have informed the rest of the book.

From there Al-e Ahmad moves to the second chapter of the book which he calls the '*Pishdaramad*' ('Prolegomenon'). Here he gives us a genealogy of the book as to how it began in the winter of 1961 as a report to a state agency of the Ministry of Culture that did not like it. Here we also learn that, before being published and while still a typescript, the book was read by some of his friends including Mahmoud Houman, a professor of philosophy, who told him his ideas were similar to Ernst Jünger (1895–1998), and the two of them got together to translate Jünger's *Über die Linie* (*Crossing the Line*) (1951). Jünger had written this text on the occasion of Heidegger's sixtieth birthday, and in it he preaches the prospects of overcoming nihilism via nihilism. Houman's misguided allusion to this text wasted Al-e Ahmad's time helping Houman to translate it and blindsided generations of those who studied him. This false and falsifying allusion was and remains an entirely flawed and abusive suggestion that has sent generations of Al-e Ahmad scholars on the goose chase of his Heideggerianism!

Early in 1962, Al-e Ahmad then tells in this chapter, a part of *Gharbzadegi* and a chapter of *Crossing the Line* appeared in the *Keyhan Monthly*, again a false association which got the journal censored. In winter 1962 he published the book himself in a print run of one thousand copies. He then tells us he borrowed the concept from Ahmad Fardid, another putative Heideggerian whose association with *Gharbzadegi* has added to the confusion that Al-e Ahmad was a Heideggerian! Fardid may have been a Heideggerian, whatever that might mean at this point in Iran, but Al-e Ahmad was not. Al-e Ahmad was thoroughly Francophone in his intellectual disposition, and except for his brief dalliance with Ernst Jünger, was mostly unaware of the German scene. Ahmad Fardid (1910–94) is an entirely mysterious character, deeply admired by some and considered a rank charlatan by others. His putative 'Heideggerianism', however, remains highly speculative for he left behind few written documents to read and to judge.[6] All we have is a contorted shadow he has cast on Al-e Ahmad, for which he of course is primarily responsible, and that he had coined the term 'Gharbzadegi'. But such rumours, for they are precisely that, help us very little in understanding what Al-e Ahmad meant and did by the term, for which we must only rely on his own written text.

Twice Al-e Ahmad tells us he revised his Gharbzadegi, once in 1963 and then in 1964. The copy from which I am reading is this original copy with Al-e Ahmad's own handwriting from the manuscript reproduced on the first page of the book. The previous editions were bootlegged and published in US. He takes all these various editions as a sign that he has chanced upon something serious.[7] All of these points mark the bizarre circumstances of the intellectual life around Tehran University at the time when Gharbzadegi was published, when the Pahlavi's nervous censorship had exacerbated the conspiratorial environments and a simple idea was totally mystified by a mystic professor of philosophy who was rumoured to know and propagate Heidegger, and a megalomaniac monarch who was scared of his own shadow. Let me therefore get back to Gharbzadegi itself where one can read and interpret hard evidence rather than speculate and hallucinate about 'oral philosophers' and 'Heideggerian' snake oil charmers.

The third and most important chapter of the book is called 'Tarh-e Yek Bimari' ('Diagnosis of a Disease'), where Al-e Ahmad outlines exactly what he means by 'Gharbzadegi'.[8] In this key chapter he tells us that by 'the West' ('Gharb') he does not explicitly mean a geographic so much as an economic pole against 'the East', which is also an economic designation. One produces and the other consumes, while providing the other with raw material; one is a productive force, the other at the receiving end of those productivities. Iran is part of Asia, Africa and Latin America, while Europe and the US, as well as South Africa, are part of this 'West'. The battle between the USSR and the USA (meaning during the Cold War, which he experienced) has disappeared and become a battle over resources. Japan, he believes, beat 'the West' at its game and that was the reason they dropped the atom bomb on it. If Japan can today sell its products around the globe, this is because 'the West' has invested in its factories and corporations. 'The West' began calling us 'the East' from the time of the Crusaders onwards, first by bringing Christianity to us and then 'Civilisation'. Africa provided 'the West' with both raw material for its industries and raw materials for its emergent discourses of anthropology, ethnography, linguistics and so forth. Thus, *Gharbzadegi* is the cultural consequence of an encounter with the globalised machinery of domination and exploitation.

With the exception of that ahistorical reference to the Crusades, this third chapter is the best, most coherent and cogent chapter of the entire book. From here forward things degenerate. The fourth chapter is the weakest and most outlandish part of the essay, where he seeks to find historical roots for attraction to 'the West' and weaves a whole constellation of nonsense about how we have always looked to 'the West'. 'Escaping from Mother India', and 'pressure from the North-eastern tribes', 'lack of urbanism in the East' are among a whole succession of senseless verbiage he weaves together to make a case for our being drawn to 'the West'. Not a single item he presents here makes any sense, and they are all signs of undiluted historical illiteracy and delusional fantasies, and conspiratorial predilections.[9] Having just told us by 'the West' he means something very specific and something very recent, he now spends a whole chapter looking ahistorically for its historical roots, via a clichéd tour of reading premodern history, when there was no 'West' or 'East' in the way he understood them at the time he was writing his *Gharbzadegi*. But scarcely anyone among his contemporaries brought that to his attention. People either wholeheartedly celebrated or else pathologically denounced it. There was no balanced perspective – no one carefully dissecting his arguments, setting aside the cream puff and examining the actual cake. Al-e Ahmad was too much of an iconic figure to solicit such a fair assessment in his own lifetime, or especially after his passing in his own homeland.

Chapter five starts slightly better, for here he says he wants to concentrate on the last three centuries, and yet here too he falls into the trap of placing 'Islam and the West' ahistorically against each other. Islam was powerful and threatening 'the West' so 'the West' rose up and reasserted itself. We were asleep and they were awake. Sources from the Mongols to Marco Polo come together in this chapter to weaken Islam and Muslims, citing from Sa'di (1210–92) to Ibn Khaldun (1332–1406) in a chapter that was supposed to be about the last three centuries. Translate that chapter into English or Arabic or Japanese and submit it as an undergraduate paper to any half decent college and you would flunk the course. Impossible to imagine any such avalanche of nonsense to have been written, published and read with such complete impunity and straight face. It is an embarrassment. So, chapters four and five are complete ahistorical drivel. Simin Daneshvar who was his first reader, as they both testify, should have cut these two embarrassing chapters out.

That brings us to chapter six, 'The First Infestation'. This chapter too is a typical self-flagellation of *our* backwardness and *their* progress. Here he ends up defending the most reactionary Shi'a cleric of the Constitutional period, Sheikh Fadlullah Nuri.[10] In this chapter he even considers the whole Constitutional Revolution of 1906–11 as a conspiracy to steal the Iranian oil. The premise of the argument is of course entirely conspiratorial gibberish but his conclusion that oil companies become interested in Iran is perfectly correct, if not by then (soon after the CIA coup of 1953) self-evident and a truism. In this chapter he ends with a legitimate critic of globalisation and Eurocentricism, though the observation is deeply buried in a fast-paced conspiratorial dismissal of the seminal event of Iran in the early twentieth century.

By the time we get to chapter seven, we finally realise what the fundamental problem with *Gharbzadeghi* is: Al-e Ahmad is so critical of 'the West', as he should be, for by that he means the colonial domination of the world, that he keeps fetishising, totalising and ahistorically essentialising it. 'The West' ceases to be a very recent colonial concoction and stands there and we here, we have lost our identity and by imposing theirs they are dictating our identity on us. The fact that this 'West' is a globalised condition of coloniality in which we are implicated has completely escaped him. His critique of 'the West' therefore becomes integral to fetishising 'the West' into an ahistorical, almost metaphysical truth. He sets out to criticise 'the West' and ends up fetishising it. This chapter again is a critique of the 'machine' and of the mechanisation of industries, but again we see how his facilities with his prose gets the better of him.

In chapter eight, 'The Way to Break the Spell', he turns to tell us what the solution is and here suggests we have to overcome our technophobia and master the machine the same way we mastered the horse. But how exactly these two objectives are to take place within the global configuration of power he does not care to share.

That brings us to chapter nine, 'An Ass in Lion's Skin'. This chapter I love, for in its original edition of which I have a copy it appeared twice and reminded me of the catastrophe of book publications in Iran when chapters and whole sections would either completely disappear or appear twice. So much for mastering the (printing) machine! Be that as it may, in this chapter he criticises a typical Westoxicated person who comes to power precisely because he is rootless.[11] He denounces Orientalists and Iranists, which is fine but inconsequential, even though he turns his sharp tongue towards the native informers.[12]

That brings us to chapter ten, except the tenth chapter is nowhere to be found in the copy I hold in my hand, it is missing in this old original copy, again the perfect proof of the calamity of printing books in the glorious land of rose and nightingale. One chapter appears twice, another chapter does not appear at all. At least the pagination stays consistent! I had to go to my pdf copy of of another edition of the book to see what that chapter was teaching us. Turning to my pdf copy, we read the missing chapter, 'A Confused Society', in which we read his critique of the schism between the cities and the migrant tribal communities and ends with a severe critique of militarism.

From there we move to chapter eleven, which begins with a categorical dismissal of the universities and ends with why Iranian young women prefer to marry European husbands.[13]

Chapter twelve, 'A Bit about Machine-toxication', is a surprisingly cogent reflection on the dominance of machine that is conducive to the rise of fascism in Europe, and yet towards the end the chapter degenerates into moments of uncritical celebration of artists like Paul Gauguin and André Gidé going to 'the East' to seek salvation. He never heard of these artists' Orientalising enterprise and was too deep into his self-Orientalising moment to read through their oriental fantasies. The chapter begins with some cogent observations and ends in utter ignorance.

The thirteenth and last chapter, which he calls '*Iqtarabat al-Sa'ah*' ('The Hour has Come Near'), in a reference to the opening verse of the chapter 'The Moon' in the Qur'an, is on Albert Camus' *The Plague* (1947) which he says is about the machine.[14] After that reading of Camus, he turns to Eugène Ionesco's *Rhinoceros* (1959), which he again reads as a metaphor of resisting being torn by the machine. The same is true of Ingmar Berman's classic film *The Seventh Seal* (1957), in which he again thinks the Swedish master is talking about the end of time. Thus, at the end of the book he becomes completely eschatological and turns to a passage from the Qur'an (54:1) declaring: 'The Hour (of Judgment) is nigh, and the moon is clefts sunder.'

In short, the best chapter of the book is its third chapter plus a few pages of chapter twelve – those and the first citation in which Al-e Ahmad has the critical intelligence to go to the heart of capitalist modernity in the US and solicit evidence for the veracity of his argument. These crucial passages have cast a hermeneutic hook on the rest of the book and made it the centrepiece of Al-e Amad's intellectual legacy. The text as a result does have a powerful central message but it is diluted by too many unnecessary asides. What exactly is the argument here? This is how he formulates it: 'Westoxication has two ends: one is the West and the other we who are Westoxicated, we meaning a part of East.'[15] He then becomes more specific as to what 'the West' is – and lets us read it from his own pen:

> This West is the entirety of Europe and Soviet Union and the entirety of North America, or let's say advanced countries, or developed countries or industrial countries, or countries that are able with the help of machineries to turn raw material into more complicated products and present them as commodities to the market. And this raw material is not just ore or oil . . . They include mythologies too, doctrines, including music, metaphysical worlds as well . . . Instead of us as part of the opposite pole let us say Asia, Africa, let us say backward countries, or advancing countries or non-industrial countries or the sum of all the countries that are the consumers of those commodities, commodities whose raw material . . . have gone there from here.[16]

This brief passage is what *Westoxication* articulates well before it goes off track into mostly superfluous details. If we put the first citation, chapter three and a few passages from the last two chapters together we get a good solid essay in which we read a critique of colonial modernity, though Al-e Ahmad was narratively too self-indulgent to have articulated it that way. As he said, he was sensing something was wrong, not like a seismographer but like a horse fearing an earthquake. He was indeed a sensible horse. In the first citation he intuitively saw the structural affinity between the centre and periphery. In the

Figure 5.1 Jalal Al-e Ahmad in the company of two close friends, Gholamhossein Saedi and Yadollah Maftun Amini, Tabriz University, 1967. (Photo courtesy of Ali Dehbashi, from the *Bokhara Magazine* archive) Gholamhossein Saedi (1936–85) was a prominent playwright and a close friend of Al-e Ahmad. Yadollah Maftun Amini (born 1926) is a poet. A poet, a playwright and Al-e Ahmad. That is the perfect picture of Al-e Ahmad's towering intellectual presence in his own lifetime.

third chapter he had a laser-beam grasp of the systematicity of the colonial circumstances of the theft of the world, and in the final couple of chapters he could see the rise of fascism the way Max Weber did decades earlier.

How a Source becomes a Citation

Stripped of all its superfluous verbiage, Al-e Ahmad's *Westoxication* is a maximum-thousand-word exquisite essay on the condition of coloniality as seen by a sharp and inquisitive critical thinker head and shoulder above his contemporaries. The problem with the essay, however, is not just its having been padded by damaging extra fat. It is also with its reception. The essay has been systematically taken out of its more global context and nativised – by Iranians and Iranists alike. Its reception was widespread but hermetically sealed, systematically Orientalised, nativised, localised, turned against modernity but not against coloniality. Chief among these critical encounters were those offered by Daryoush Ashuri and Fereydun Adamiyyat. Let us look at these critical reactions closely.

Daryoush Ashuri (born 1938) is an amateur lexicographer without any serious formal education or disciplinary training, but nevertheless a self-taught learned man and a competent translator who made a name for himself almost simultaneously with Jalal Al-e Ahmad, though, like others in his generation, he was entirely overshadowed by him. In the piece that Ashuri wrote soon after *Gharbzadegi* was published, '*Hoshyari-ye Tarikhi*' ('Historical Consciousness') (1965), he correctly saw Al-e Ahmad's work in the same vein as Frantz Fanon and Aimé Césaire but he displays very little knowledge about those works and thinks they all seek to find out a kind of 'historical pathology'.[17] Another false assumption Ashuri makes in this essay is to presume that critical thinkers such as Fanon or Césaire were among Sartre's retinue or followers! He does not see Fanon and others as forming a critical perspective about the world, but just as *reacting* to the progress of 'the West'. He is, however, appreciative of Al-e Ahmad's reflections. His problems with the concept of '*Gharbzadegi*' are that Al-e Ahmad does not give a precise definition of the term to his satisfaction. The second issue Ashuri has with Al-e Ahmad is that he only examines the exchange of commodities and is not aware of the exchange of capital. Ashuri then psychopathologises Al-e Ahmad for lacking confidence in what he says.[18] He accuses Al-e Ahmad of conflating and confusing the geographical and historical conception of 'the West'. Al-e Ahmad does no such thing, however, and Ashuri continues making straw men to knock down. In the process he shows he has no clue what 'the West' as an idea, a concept, a myth, an allegory, is. Here Al-e Ahmad's own historical confusion and theoretical limitations lead Ashuri to become doubly ahistorical and confused. Ashuri is good in catching Al-e Ahmad red-handed with historical infelicities but, in the process, he exposes his own historical confusions. The result of reading Ashuri on Al-e Ahmad? They both cross-fetishise 'the West': one by making his criticism ahistorical, the other by nit-picking on issues that expose his own limitations without offering any alternative perspective.

Ashuri returned to *Gharbzadegi* a decade later. In a speech delivered at Columbia University in 1989, and subsequently published in 1997, '*Nazariyyeh Gharbzadegi va Bohran-e Tafakkor dar Iran*' ('The Theory of

Westoxication and the Crisis of Thinking in Iran'), he considers the very idea of *Gharbzadegi* as an amalgamation of Marxist-Leninism, nativist Nationalism, and Islamist puritanism.[19] Having by now changed his mind about *Gharbzadegi*, in this essay he completely denigrates the very idea that there is something called 'capitalism' except as an ideological assault by Marxist-Leninists. Meanwhile he conflates Jalal Al-e Ahmad and Ali Shari'ati, as he accuses them both of incurable nativism. Ashuri considers the very idea of *Gharbzadegi* a symptom of the inability of the colonised world, a term he of course does not use, to address its issues. The gist of Ashuri's argument is the outlandish, ahistorical and old-fashioned Orientalist cliché that the idea of *Gharbzadegi* is similar to the crisis Greek philosophy had caused in Islam, which he thinks finally comes to a crescendo with Al-Ghazali dismissing it as foreign in favour of revelation. This widely discredited, and entirely outdated, Orientalist delusion about the course of Islamic philosophy Ashuri picks up from the Orientalist apothecary box and regurgitates on the campus of a university where a leading historian of science like George Saliba had for decades spent a lifetime dismantling such delusions. But the amateur dilettantism of characters like Ashuri means they never bother about such things as serious scholarship, and because they perform their gibberish in Persian no one among their audience cares to correct them. The idea that Greek philosophy had caused a crisis in Islam or that Islamic philosophy came to an end with al-Ghazali is undiluted nonsense – the sheer inanity that Al-Ghazali put an end to Islamic philosophy in favour of revelation! Al-Ghazali did no such thing. Today any undergraduate student of Islamic philosophy knows that within a generation of Al-Ghazali, Averroes had dismissed his entire philosophical project, which thereafter became part of a larger frame of reference that later led to other even more powerful philosophical movements initiated by Shihab al-Din Yahya Suhrawardi and Mulla Sadra. So that part of Ashuri's argument against *Gharbzadegi* was a bizarre turn to old-fashioned Orientalism, and more to the point, it had nothing to do with Al-e Ahmad's idea.[20]

Daryoush Ashuri was and remains typical of a deeply colonised mind and white-identified critique of Al-e Ahmad whose criticism of *Gharbzadegi* was celebrated by his like-minded liberals and pitted against anyone speaking of colonialism. This liberalism either ignored or denounced Al-e Ahmad as the Iranian version of the globality of a condition European colonialism had created. What becomes evident when we read the critiques of *Gharbzadegi* by people like Ashuri is in fact the astonishingly entrapped imagination and colonised mindset, exacerbated by a structurally limited knowledge of the world immediately around them. That world in Asia, Africa and Latin America or even in North America did not exist, or existed only as a shadow of the truth of 'Europe'. They were so deeply and widely white-identified that the whole anti- and postcolonial movements, evident in such revolutionary events as the Negritude Movement or the Harlem Renaissance, did not appear on their radar. They were all wrapped up in their fascination with Enlightenment modernity and fetishised what they saw as the 'backwardness' of Iran. As a result they were incensed and deeply troubled by the fact that Al-e Ahmad was not equally enamoured with European capitalist modernity. They were convinced Iran was backward, that Europe was the destiny of humanity, and there was not a critical bone in their existence regarding *how* Iran should catch up with Europe. *Gharbzadegi* had hit them from left field, as it were, and not just surprised but deeply angered them because it screwed up their system, their episteme, of *our* backwardness and *their* progress, of their white-identified, deeply colonised mind. They wanted to be (like) Europeans, damned be (not some false conception of authenticity) the fact that Europe had become Europe on the broken back of the world, or as Fanon put it, that 'Europe' was literally the invention of the Third World.

Another major critique of Al-e Ahmad's *Gharbzadegi* came from the prominent historian of the Qajar period Fereydun Adamiyyat (1920–2008) who in a major essay he called '*Ashoftegi dar Fekr-e Tarikhi*' ('Confusion in Historical Thinking') severely criticised Al-e Ahmad's denunciation of the Constitutional Revolution (1906–11), whilst himself maintaining an entirely enamoured perspective vis-à-vis the European Enlightenment.[21] Adamiyyat represented another strain of critical thinking in twentieth-century Iran, as enamoured as Ashuri by European (colonial) modernity, which they considered the epitome of civilisation, with the rest of the world considered to be civilised to the degree that it approximated to that European ideal. His legitimate criticism of reactionary and backward ideas of the Qajar aristocracy and Shi'i clericalism collapsed squarely into the bosom of a reading of the Enlightenment modernity that was blinded to its colonial roots and consequences.

Al-e Ahmad's conspiratorial references to the Constitutional Revolution and praise for reactionary clerics like Sheikh Fazlollah Nuri (1843–1903) should have been, and were correctly, criticised. But such references are not an indication of his falling into the trap of any 'return to self', or romanticising Islam. I have already argued in some detail elsewhere how revolutionary authenticity is necessarily predicated on cultural inauthenticity.[22] A rhetoric of 'the return to the self' is first and foremost delusional and even worse categorically reactionary. What *Gharbzadegi* represents is not a call for a delusional return to self. Quite on the contrary: it points to the widespread global rising of an anticolonial critic of colonial modernity, that in and of itself constituted another contrapuntal universality. As to why Al-e Ahmad was praising the clerical reactionaries of the Constitutional period, we need to move to his next seminal work, *Dar Khedmat va Khiyanat-e Roshanfekran* (*On the Services and Treasons of Intellectuals*). For there we see him yet again in a failed but principled attempt at revolutionary mobilisation.

Dar Khedmat va Khiyanat

Al-e Ahmad wrote *Dar Khedmat va Khiyanat-e Roshanfekran* (*On the Services and Treasons of Intellectuals*) in 1964, and it was first published in 1968. It is a book put together in direct response to Ayatollah Ruhollah Khomeini's June 1963 uprising. Its structure and composition tell us much about its content. The book begins with a poem of Nima:

Man delam Sakht gerefteh-ast . . .

I am deeply saddened
In this guesthouse
That kills its own guests –
Its days darkened –
Where it has cast its guests
One against the other:
A few sleepy souls
Ruffian souls
Unconscious souls.[23]

The citation announces the feeling of Al-e Ahmad when he embarks upon writing this book, the fact that he thinks of Iran as this guesthouse in which its guests are fighting against each other, and he wishes to make peace among them. As we shall see, this is the main argument of the book.

Al-e Ahmad probably came up with the title from Julien Benda's *La Trahison des Clercs* (*The Treason of the Intellectuals*) (1927) though he made the title in Persian alliterate between *Khedmat* and *Khiyanat*, between *Services* and *Treasons*.[24] Before we ask what he meant by that title, let us look at the structure of his text and the formal foregrounding of his argument.

In the first volume, after an introduction,[25] he goes directly to the first chapter: 'What is an Intellectual? Who is an Intellectual?'[26] after which in chapter two, he asks 'Is the Intellectual Foreign or Familiar?'[27] before we read two appendices to each chapter, first appendix: Gramsci on Intellectuals: 'Formation of Intellectuals'[28] and second appendix: 'Some Statistics of Professionals and Intellectuals'.[29] After this we go to chapter three: 'The Birthplace of the Intellectuals',[30] followed by the third appendix: 'The Chinese Intellectuals and the West',[31] which is a translation of a chapter from Y. C. Wang's *Chinese Intellectuals and the West, 1872–1949* (1966). The chapter was translated by his wife Simin Daneshvar. Then follows the fourth appendix, a passage by the French Orientalist Louis Massignon.[32] This volume then ends with a few additional appendices, including a translation of a few pages of Herbert Marcuse's *One-Dimensional Man*.[33] These notes also include a reference to Ali Shari'ati's *Islam-Shenasi* (*Islamology*).[34] In these notes Al-e Ahmad also writes, 'during the first ten days of Bahman of 1347/ Winter 1968 when I was in Mashhad, I met this Shari'ati Gentleman and we had long chats. I am happy in this regard for we think very much alike.'[35]

The second volume was edited and published posthumously almost a decade after Al-e Ahmad had passed way. This volume, the publisher tells us, was based on Al-e Ahmad's scattered notes, minus annotations they could not find in his papers. The structure of the second volume is very much similar to the first volume, a couple of original essays plus a few appendices. Resuming the chapter outline from the first volume, in the second volume, chapter four is on 'Traditional Intellectuals: The Military and the Clergy',[36] followed by the fifth appendix, Mirza Agha Khan Kermani's piece '*Ay Jalal al-Dowleh*' ('You Jalal al-Dowleh').[37] This is followed by a sixth appendix, which

is Ayatollah Khomeini's famous speech during his June 1963 uprising,[38] followed by a seventh appendix, 'American Policy in Iran', by Cuyler Young,[39]
after which comes chapter five: 'Where is the Iranian Intellectual?'[40] Chapter
six: 'Recent Examples of Intellectuals'[41] comes before we get to read his eighth
appendix: 'A Few Letters',[42] followed by chapter seven: 'The Intellectual and
our Conditions Today',[43] and then the ninth appendix, 'Conversation with a
Disappointed Intellectual: Ehsan Tabari',[44] and finally the book's conclusion.[45]

Reading more like a special issue of a journal than a well thought-through
book, Al-e Ahmad's *Services and Treasons* is a flawed treatise trying to understand the nature and function of the intellectual in a country like Iran. It is a
raw book, an idea he fails to articulate and deliver, oscillating between his own
prose interrupted by scattered translations and citations that in one way or
another may or may not relate to what he wishes to convey. He understands
the word '*Roshanfekr*' ('Intellectuals') etymologically rather than conceptu-
ally or theoretically and this fatal flaw sends him on a goose chase. He was
unable to muster the patience to read, digest and think through the related
material, and write his book, and thus he continues oscillating between his
own uncooked ideas and passages from other people's works. The results are
uneven, at times incoherent and amateurish, even rushed and mechanical.
The book sometime reads like a collection of notes and citations someone
amasses before writing a book. Al-e Ahmad did not have the patience, the
poise, the perseverance, or above all the presence of mind to write a sustained
and coherent long treatise – and neither did his ardent critics like Daryoush
Ashuri. They were both dilettantes. But there was something in Al-e Ahmad
that Ashuri lacked: moral authority. It is like that passage in King Lear when
Kent comes to Lear to serve him in disguise:

> KING LEAR: Dost thou know me, fellow?
> KENT: No, sir; but you have that in your countenance which I would
>   fain call master.
> KING LEAR: What's that?
> KENT: Authority.

What Al-e Ahmad did possess was brilliant flashes of insights. He lacked
the patient wherewithal, or a disciplined mind, to flesh out those insights
in coherent ways. But when put together those staccato flashes of insights

form a formidable body of critical thinking that none of his contemporaries possessed, or at least cared publicly to share with their contemporaries.

Be that as it may, these two volumes are a crucial document in telling us Al-e Ahmad's failed attempt at self-theorisation. He is not trying to understand 'the intellectual'. He is trying to understand himself, to self-theorise. Al-e Ahmad wrote this book soon after the failed attempt of Ayatollah Khomeini in June 1963 to topple the Pahlavi monarchy. His concern here was with why the Shi'a clerical authorities and the 'secular' left had failed to come together. As the son of a prominent cleric, Al-e Ahmad was painfully aware of the rift between the Shi'a clerical class and the irreligious left. He in effect had personified that rift. In his person he thought he had represented, personified and overcome the partition between the two opposing 'guests' of this guesthouse. Why was he unique and otherwise unrepresentative of the intellectual scene at large? Underlying the *Services and Treasons* is a sense of self-alienation and thus betrayal. The Tudeh Party left had failed to support and endorse Khomeini's uprising for they thought his revolt was not theirs. Al-e Ahmad thought this was a critical and strategic mistake, and his book begins with that serious question but then goes wayward into uncharted territories.

The fundamental problem with Al-e Ahmad's conception of the intellectual as evident in this book is his theoretical inability to understand that by 'intellectual' we mean a 'public intellectual' and that a public intellectual cannot come to be unless through a public sphere of which Al-e Ahmad was clueless. Thus he went on the goose chase of finding historical antecedents for the concept in pre-modern periods, as did his critics like Ashuri who was even less learned on medieval intellectual history than Al-e Ahmad was – though this did not prevent either of them going out on a limb. The result of this categorical confusion is that anyone from Prophet Muhammad to Sa'di Shirazi becomes an intellectual! The scene of the public sphere in places like Iran, as I have argued elsewhere, was interpolated between *public* and *parapublic* because of the condition of coloniality. As Jürgen Habermas showed in his seminal book, *Strukturwandel der* Öffentlichkeit (*The Structural Transformation of the Public Sphere*) (1962), the public sphere was primarily a bourgeois proposition predicated on globalised trade. In this book, Habermas investigates the manner in which a public sphere emerged during the time of the European Enlightenment and the course of the American and French revolutions, where in the newly formed public spaces and public spheres public debates about important political issues were the premise for the rise of public intellectuals. Habermas's argument from then on is twofold, considering first how this bourgeois public sphere emerged in the first place, and then how it was structurally transformed by the rise of powerful state capitalism, or more importantly the widespread culture industry, and above all the corporate takeover of public life, whereby citizens are transformed from public persona to mere consumers. There is no public intellectual without this public sphere. This simple fact had escaped Al-e Ahmad and his critics – while the Teutophile professoriate at Tehran University were too much into Ernst Jünger and Martin Heidegger to see what was actually happening in Germany with the emerging Frankfurt School and Critical Theory.

In my *Persophilia* (2015) I extended Habermas's theory to speculate on the nature of what I there called the 'parapublic sphere' in the colonial sites informing postcolonial agencies, where the weak comprador bourgeoisie did not accommodate the rise of a robust public sphere and therefore of a public intellectual the way Gramsci speculated in his *Prison Notebooks* (1925–35) regarding 'organic' and 'inorganic' intellectuals. In this book I also demonstrated how the active formation of a transnational public sphere around the colonised world extends from the European bourgeois public spheres, but is not limited or even contingent on them. The structural transformation of that European bourgeois public sphere had an entirely different texture and trajectory in the colonial sites, compared with Europe. In the postcolonial world that structural transformation entailed a parapublic sphere in the form of orality, spontaneity and underground music, poetry, drama and so forth. Al-e Ahmad himself was a product of this conflation of the public and parapublic spheres. A crucial function of censorship was precisely this dynamic between the public and the parapublic spheres. Chantal Mouffe's critique of Habermas is quite crucial here, for she dispenses with ideas of communicative rationality and deliberative democracy and rightly introduces the crucial distinction between antagonistic and agonistic politics.[46] On the colonial site that antagonistic/agonistic dialectic is twofold, both domestically and externally from the domestic polity. That binary further complicates the organicity of figure of public intellectual on the public and parapublic spheres.

Al-e Ahmad was the last public intellectual to have lived, thought and written on the premise of this conflation of the pubic and parapublic spheres before the Islamic Republic took it over and radically appropriated and transformed it. When Russell Jacoby wrote his book *The Last Intellectuals* (1987) his basic concern was with the gradual disappearance of public intellectuals in the US. He concentrated on the post-war generation of Irving Howe, Daniel Bell and others, and tried to address why another generation of public intellectuals had not ensued. He held the universities chiefly responsible for the compromised generation of thinkers, when their concerns with the politics of their tenure had made moral cowards out of them. Consumerism and suburbanisation, he thought, were the chief reasons for this systemic degeneration of public intellectuals. But, as I have argued before, the structural transformation of public sphere in the US, as Habermas would argue, had always already pre-empted the possibility of the rise of any serious public intellectuals on the US soil, except for the immigrant critical thinkers like Irving Howe or Edward Said, or in the brutalised communities like African Americans such as W. E. B. Du Bois.

In that transnational public sphere, public intellectuals, from Edward Said to Jalal Al-e Ahmad, are syncretic propositions. Long before Russell Jacoby, and in fact Habermas, Alexis de Tocqueville in *Democracy in America* (1835–40, volume II, section II, chapter 1) wrote:

> I think that in no country in the civilised world is less attention paid to philosophy than in the United States. The Americans have no philosophical school of their own; and they care but little for all the schools into which Europe is divided, the very names of which are scarcely known to them.

Elsewhere in the same text he argues that there are certain truths about America that only foreigners can publicly dare to tell. It is for this reason that in Edward Said's *Representations of Intellectuals*, delivered in 1993 and published it in 1994, we see him, a Palestinian in exile from his occupied homeland, going upstream from these assessments and considering the condition of exile, factual or symbolic, as definitive to being an intellectual. Al-e Ahmad could never imagine himself an outsider like a Palestinian, and thus took place his morally bankrupt journey to Palestine hosted by the Israeli government, where it did not even occur to him or his wife at least to go and visit a Palestinian community while visiting their occupied homeland. But that fact is tangential to the more serious issue that the structural transformation of the public/parapublic sphere under the Islamic republic has made it impossible for a figure like Al-e Ahmad ever to emerge under their tyranny. Such a radical transformation had not yet taken place under the Pahlavis, for the Pahlavis were authoritarian, while the Islamists are totalitarian.

In his own homeland and within his own public and parapublic spheres Al-e Ahmad could have been and he did become a public intellectual par excellence – and it is precisely the systematic erosion of those spheres that accounts for why his failed attempt at self-theorisation could not anticipate the calamity of the Islamic Republic that emerged almost a decade after his sudden and untimely death. The Islamist takeover of the Iranian revolution of 1977–9 ushered in a period of sectarianism inside and outside the country the major intellectual consequence of which was a calamity called 'Roshanfekr-e Dini' (the 'religious intellectual'), a catastrophe that combined with the fabricated Sunni–Shi'a hostility it exacerbated. It facilitated the Islamism of the region, and the total erasure of a para/public sphere upon which a public intellectual could appear led to the regional and global depravity of the public intellectual, except as an exile out of place, as Said would say, in search of a new organicity. Jalal Al-e Ahmad's *Services and Treasons* is the historic document of the failure to read his own time or anticipate ours.

When Ayatollah Khomeini launched his second putsch to topple the Pahlavi monarchy in the late 1970s, he did not call the uprising a 'Shi'i revolution', he insisted instead on calling it an 'Islamic Revolution', and from there he wished to establish an Islamic Republic. His hostilities with the Saudis or any other Arab leaders or regimes had nothing to do with their being Sunni or Shi'a. He was as much if not more hostile to the nominally Shi'a Saddam Hussein than he was against the Saudi leadership. That the revolution he led ultimately became a Shi'a revolution, or was branded as such, was a gradual process almost entirely contingent on outside forces. As Saddam Hussein's invasion of Iran in September 1980 and his pan-Arab propaganda turned the cosmopolitan character of the revolution in Iran into an 'Iranian' revolution, the CIA mobilisation of Sunni-inspired Wahhabism among the Mujahidin/Taliban in Afghanistan to fight the Russians and resist the spread of the revolution in Iran turned it into a 'Shi'a' revolution. Khomeini welcomed them both and used the occasion to destroy the cosmopolitan character of the political culture that had facilitated bringing him to power.

The revolutionary spirit that carried Khomeini to topple the Pahlavi monarchy and establish an Islamic Republic was entirely pluralistic, multifaceted and cosmopolitan; certainly including, but by no means limited to, Islam. Al-e Ahmad himself was the example *par excellence* of this political culture. Anticolonial nationalism and Third World socialism were as much, if not even more, integral to it. Khomeini took full advantage of that cosmopolitan political culture in the making of which Al-e Ahmad was a key force. In the Europhobia of the revolutionary uprising, Iranians were in the throes of a magnificent misunderstanding like the beginning of a love affair before the cold shower of reality hits in. The left and the liberals thought this was their evolution. The Islamists were determined to make it theirs. Two representatives of the left and the liberals wrote courageously against the alarmingly proto-fascist Islamism that was actively announcing itself: one was the towering poet Ahmad Shamlou (1925–2000) in the periodical he edited from London, *Iranshahr*, and the other Mustafa Rahimi (1926–2002) in a historic essay he published and called '*Chera ba Jomhuri-ye Islami Mokhalefam*' ('Why I Oppose the Islamic Republic') (1978). Scarce anyone paid any serious attention to them, and when they did it was too late. Both Shamlou and Rahimi, just like Al-e Ahmad, were towering public intellectuals of their time embedded in the multifaceted and pluralistic para/public sphere they personified.

Soon after the success of the Islamists in outmanoeuvring their ideological rivals, their intellectual functionaries led by Abdolkarim Soroush began to lead the cause of what they now called '*Roshanfekr-e Dini*' ('Religious Intellectuals'), by far the most intellectually calamitous consequence of the tyrannised space the Islamists had now radically militarised. Sectarian, closed-minded, fanatical, philistine in art and literature, and obsessed with what they called 'Islam', these religious intellectuals, now backed by the militant Islamists in power, began to claim the entirety of the Iranian intellectual scene for themselves, not by the force of any intellectual reason, but by the might of the Kalashnikov that had brought them to power. The most prominent intellectual of the Islamic Republic, Abdolkarim Soroush, was the metaphorical obituary of the long, cosmopolitan, and the worldly intellectual history of nineteenth- and twentieth-century Iran. Soroush was the antithesis of Al-e Ahmad, his bookend.

The systematic elimination of all its alterities and the establishment of an Islamic Republic were the beginning of the end of the pluralistic Iranian political culture and para/public sphere that included Islamic elements but was emphatically not limited to them. As best evident in the character of Jalal Al-e Ahmad, that political culture embraced militant Islamism within the bracing forces of anticolonial nationalism and Third World socialism. Although in his book on intellectuals he had failed to self-theorise, in reality Al-e Ahmad personified and epitomised these three traits in one confident, compelling and charismatic character. After him things began to degenerate first into the passionate Islamism of Ali Shari'ati, the erudite pedantries of Morteza Motahhari and a few other committed Muslim revolutionaries like Mehdi Bazargan and Mahmoud Taleqan, before Ayatollah Khomeini reasserted himself with tyrannical terror, taking full advantage of their groundwork and making a final push for power that destroyed the feeble Pahlavi regime, eliminating all its political and ideological alterities and with an iron fist and unrelenting fury establishing an Islamic Republic. Along the way the US plotted to once again topple an Iranian government, which led to the American Hostage Crisis of 1979–81, the US–Saudi instigated Saddam Hussein invasion of Iran, leading to the devastating Iran–Iraq war of 1980–8, as the Israeli invasion of Lebanon in 1982 led to the expansion of the ruling Iranian regime's sphere of influence into Lebanon, Syria and Palestine – all of which the ruling Islamist regime in Iran put to effective use to silence, crush, accommodate, or compromise all its ideological rivals.

'Nietzsche is Dead'

I left Iran in the mid-1970s with Jalal Al-e Ahmad as the towering intellectual of my youth, and I came to my own academic and intellectual self-consciousness in the US in the mid-1980s with Edward Said in my immediate moral and political vicinity at Columbia University, my academic home for the last thirty years. In between these two immanent events was my formative period of graduate studies in University of Pennsylvania under the shadow of arch conservative cultural theorist Philip Rieff (1922–2006). Neither Al-e

Ahmad nor Said had anything remotely comparable to the influence on my critical thinking that Philip Rieff wielded, and yet they were both politically poles apart from Philip Rieff. The pre-eminence of Philip Rieff in my academic youth was matched only by George Makdisi (1920–2002), the doyen of Islamic studies scholars with whom I was lucky to work for as many years as I did with Rieff. I came to intellectual maturity with Jalal Al-e Ahmad's politics, Edward Said's critical flair, Philip Rieff's hermeneutic exactitude and George Makdisi's scholarship. Their prose and politics echo through these four chambers of my mind.

One of the texts we read closely with Philip Rieff in one of his legendary seminars in the late 1970s early 1980s, when I was his chief graduate student and teaching and research assistant at Penn, was Nietzsche's *Die fröhliche Wissenschaft* (*The Gay Science*) (1882). During this seminar a few classmate friends and I formed a small reading group, getting together once a week after the seminar had met, with Rieff reading through Nietzsche one volume after another. Rieff's seminar was a memorable event and my friends and I thought we had to continue apace with the rest of Nietzsche's work. We would get together over cheap wine and a bit of palatable cheese and read Nietzsche – the German original on one side and the English translation on the other. At this time Walter Kauffmann's exquisite translations were out, and we were in his caring and capable hands. In North American philosophical scenes, Kauffmann had revolutionised the scholarship on Nietzsche – rescuing him from inadequate translations and abusive readings. I remember it was during this time we had learned about a joke that in a New York subway station graffiti someone had written: 'God is Dead – Nietzsche', under it someone had added: 'Nietzsche is Dead – God', someone else had added a third line: 'Some live posthumously – Nietzsche', and finally: 'Nietzsche is misspelled – Walter Kauffman!'

It was just about this time that David Farrell Krell's magnificent translation of Martin Heidegger's *Nietzsche* had also come out. On a trip to Munich I had procured for myself a complete set of Heidegger's and Nietzsche's German originals and for a period was preoccupied with both in the formative years of my thinking. I remember in an early passage, Heidegger writes on Nietzsche:

The task of our lecture course is to elucidate the fundamental position within which Nietzsche unfolds the guiding question of Western thought and responds to it. Such elucidation is needed in order to prepare a confrontation with Nietzsche. If in Nietzsche's thinking the prior tradition of Western thought is gathered and completed in a decisive respect, then the confrontation with Nietzsche becomes one with all Western thought hitherto.[47]

At the time I had not yet started writing my doctoral dissertation, which I had originally intended to be on the Iranian revolution of 1977–9. Because of the Hostage Crisis of 1979–81 I was not able to return to collect sources and be a witness to what was happening in my homeland, and perforce I had to change my subject and write my doctoral thesis on the charismatic authority of Prophet Muhammad, which subsequently became my first published book, *Authority in Islam* (1989). But soon after that, while I had my postdoctoral fellowship at Harvard, I began writing on the Iranian revolution and a major first chapter of what later became my *Theology of Discontent* (1993) was on Jalal Al-e Ahmad. In a way, as I can recollect now, that first chapter was influenced by this passage of Heidegger on Nietzsche for a 'confrontation' with Al-e Ahmad was a confrontation with the entirety of the course of militant Islamism. I began my book on the ideological foregrounding of the revolution with Al-e Ahmad for Al-e Ahmad was and remains the last Muslim intellectual bringing to conclusion a formative period of Muslim political thought. But in the passage immediately after that Heidegger says something even more important:

The confrontation with Nietzsche has not yet begun, nor has the prerequisite for it been established. For a long time, Nietzsche has been either celebrated and imitated or reviled and exploited. Nietzsche's thought and speech are still too contemporary for us. He and we have to yet be sufficiently separated in history; we lack the distance necessary for a sound appreciation of the thinker's strength.[48]

More than forty years after the Iranian revolution and its Islamist takeover, I believe the reading of Al-e Ahmad that placed him as a precursor of the 'Islamic ideology' has done its crucial service in helping us understand that historic event, and must now be actively reconsidered, very much on the model that Kauffmann helped us reread Nietzsche beyond the full disclosure of Heidegger's Nazism. Heidegger's phrase about Nietzsche, that he 'has been either celebrated and imitated or reviled and exploited', is very much applicable to the way Al-e Ahmad has been the subject of similar treatments by the ruling Islamist regime in Iran and its nemesis. We have, Al-e Ahmad and us, been sufficiently separated to rethink his significance for what is to come. The post-Islamist Muslim world will have to look back to be able to look forward. The Iranian revolution of 1977–9, which Al-e Ahmad in part anticipated, led to the calamitous takeover of an Islamist regime in which Al-e Ahmad himself would have had no place or peace. Reading him after the Islamic Republic is as liberating as reading Nietzsche after Nazism, and precisely in that liberating moment Heidegger's own Nazism places his reading of Nietzsche at the twilight zone of that philosophy of the future. In both my *Persophilia* (2015) and *The Emperor is Naked* (2020) I have had occasion to detail how German Romanticism (as Ernst Cassirer had also argued) was at the roots of German Nazism and (as I have shown) Iranian Islamism. This is the morning after, when we have woken up from the calamities of both Nazism and Islamism. The crucial question now is to see how the man whose Islam was not Islamist will configure in a post-Islamist liberation theology whose core and contour are still to happen in our future.

Once we strip both *Westoxication* and *Services and Treasons* of their superfluous fat we get down to a crucial essay on the condition of coloniality and of false consciousness that Al-e Ahmad had detected with uncommon intelligence. What is that core and what is it that Al-e Ahmad is telling us in these two central texts of his oeuvre? He is telling us that there is a global condition of coloniality, moral, political, imaginative and above all rooted in the economic domination of advanced capitalist societies over the globe, and we must resist and end that domination. He did not ever say 'Islam' was the condition of that resistance or fancy the delusion of any 'return to self'. He may have been, and he was, shortsighted regarding the ways in which 'Islam' could be a site of resistance to that cultural colonisation, or blindsided by the fact that Islam turned into Islamism would be the most degenerate form of cultural colonisation, but there can be little doubt that he was feeling his way, however blindly, towards the discovery of a postcolonial world.

Who then are the agents of this change? The figure of public intellectuals. But in his critical limitations the intellectuals were fragmented between the Westoxicated and the clerical. The two must come together, Al-e Ahmad thought, to lead the nation to resist such colonial domination. The first part of the argument in *Gharbzadegi* is cogent and crucial, the second part of the argument in *Services and Treasons* is weak and wobbly. As I have argued in my *Theology of Discontent*, the clergy itself, as well as the Islam they manufactured, were in fact the most Westoxicated part of resistance to colonialism. In the Islamism that the Shi'i clerics promoted Islam had become the agent of its own colonisation. Where Al-e Ahmad failed was in his detection of the morally and imaginatively weak public sphere upon which such a public intellectual could have arisen, to be able to see and show how Islam turned into Islamism (on the model of Judaism being turned into Zionism, or Hinduism into Hindu fundamentalism, etc.) was the greatest achievement of European colonialism.

What has historically exacerbated this blind spot of Al-e Ahmad is the critical milieu in which he was received and abused – friends and foes accusing him of 'nativism'. The critique of nativism levelled against Al-e Ahmad is fundamentally flawed and is rooted in the deeply and irretrievably colonised mind of those critics who think of anything non-European as 'native'. They have so fundamentally bought into the colonial project of European self-universalisation, and so uncritically and slavishly buy into what they call 'modernity' (without ever seeing its darkest colonial sites), that any Iranian, Arab, Indian, African or Latin American who resists such colonial occupation of critical thinking to them is a nativist. Al-e Ahmad is partially to blame for this falsehood because he was momentarily enamoured of a bizarre gestation of Third World Heideggerianism teaching at Tehran University, the university from which he had failed to obtain a doctoral degree. Al-e Ahmad's critique of colonial modernity is radically different from the Heideggerian critique of modernity at its heart. Heidegger's critique of European modernity placed him right in Hitler's bosom. But Hitler did to Europe what Europe had already done to the world. These are diametrically opposed reactions to the ravages of European as opposed to colonial modernity. Al-e Ahmad was blinded to the Heideggerian obscurantism of Fardid – insecure in his own lack of disciplined university education, enamoured of a professor of philosophy who manufactured a reputation for himself for knowing Heidegger among a milieu who had never heard of Heidegger: a one-eyed mystic became the king of the blind – and blinded Al-e Ahmad to his own insights. Al-e Ahmad had much more than just one dug well or two in his life, but his own fundamental flaws deluded him when he had chanced upon an utterly brilliant insight. Liberal intellectuals of far less critical intelligence than he have spent decades defending or dismissing him and thus falsely linking him to Fardid when there were no such links except for Al-e Ahmad's own insecurities.

Al-e Ahmad and other anticolonial thinkers of his time who were at work decolonising minds in Asia, Africa, Latin America and North America were not nativists – they were de-universalising the self-universalisation of Europe to which these Iranians were beholden. The generation of decolonising critical thinkers to which Al-e Ahmad belonged were discovering new universes, even if they did not fully see those universes, to which these Iranians to this day are blinded, indifferent, or hostile. What we have had in Iran and the rest of the imaginatively (as well as morally and materially) robbed and colonised world was not 'modernity' – it was colonial modernity and characters like Daryoush Ashuri are the finished products of that malady. What we have had was not 'reason' but revolutionary reason, not will to power but will to resist power, not delayed obedience as our Oedipal complex, but delayed defiance as the modus operandi of our revolts. Over the last two decades I have outlined in detail all the fundamental theoretical particulars of this de-universalising Europe, and yet in Iran and the colonised minds it has produced, that belated Euro-universalisation continues apace.

If in Al-e Ahmad I had read a precursor of the Iranian revolution of 1977–9 that in subsequent decades degenerated into an Islamic Republic, in Al-e Ahmad too I now read a precursor of a post-Islamist liberation theology that like a phoenix must rise from the ashes of that very Islamic Republic. So yes Al-e Ahmad is dead, but 'some live posthumously!'

From Governmentality to Coloniality

The problem with much of the criticism coming Al-e Ahmad's way about his *Gharbzadegi* and *Services and Treasons* was and remains the insularity of the critics' own entrapment inside 'the West and the Rest' binary.[49] For the life of them Iranian critics (or the whole spectrum of Iranists working in the field of 'Iranian Studies') coming to Al-e Ahmad's *Gharbzadegi* could not extract themselves from that binary opposition. It was just 'the West' and 'Iran'. The West was advanced and civilised, and Iran was backward and pathetic. Why could Iran not be just like the West? 'The West' was there, we and 'the Rest' were here. What should we do? There were those who hated 'the West' and loved Al-e Ahmad's book for all the wrong reasons, and there were those who loved and coveted 'the West' and thus hated Al-e Ahmad's book for another set of myopic reasons. The two sides of this binary kept exacerbating themselves and each other, and none could escape the trap and think of the larger context in which Al-e Ahmad's book should have, and could have been, and still has to be, read and placed to figure out its universal significance far beyond its limited objectives and flawed composition. We must take the most insightful part of *Gharbzadegi*, disregard the rest, and move forward with how to save Al-e Ahmad from the predicament of his own time and contemporaries, as well as the provincial (and at times decidedly sophomoric) scholarship that has come his way in order to rescue his project for what (following Asef Bayat's ground-breaking project)[50] I have called 'Post-Islamist liberation theology'. Bayat's project was and remains primarily sociological, but his insights are ground-breaking to enable the future of a liberation theology that could be far more enabling and historical than merely diagnostic. The headway out of the limitations imposed by Al-e Ahmad's immediate critics and towards that post-Islamic liberation theology is to be able to read his limited but crucial insights in his *Gharbzadegi* in a larger postcolonial context.

For the longest time in my work I have held that the condition of 'governmentality' as theorised by Michel Foucault translates into the condition of 'coloniality' for the rest of the world. The mind of the colonised person is colonised the same way that the mind of a European citizen of a modern liberal democracy is compromised by the conditions of governmentality. Foucault developed the idea of 'governmentality' in the late 1970s and early 1980s during his lectures at Collège de France. The concept, *gouvernementalité*, combines the two French words for *government* and *rationality/worldview/outlook*, when the mind and its reasoning in effect become governmentalised, conditioned for disciplinary formations and obedient mindset, through the instrumentalities of the technologies of power. The very logic and reason of the person become thus *governmentalised*, subject to obedience. Here is a key passage from Foucault's argument:

> The term itself, power, does no more than designate a [domain] of relations which are entirely still to be analysed, and what I have proposed to call governmentality, that is to say, the way in which one conducts the conduct of men, is no more than a proposed analytical grid for these relations of power . . . What I wanted to do – and this was what was at stake in the analysis – was to see the extent to which we could accept that the analysis of micro-powers, or of procedures of governmentality, is not confined by definition to a precise domain determined by a sector of the scale, but should be considered simply as a point of view, a method of decipherment which may be valid for the whole scale, whatever its size. In other words, the analysis of micro-powers is not a question of scale, and it is not a question of a sector, it is a question of a point of view. Good. This, if you like, was the methodological reason.[51]

It is precisely that methodological reason that promoted me to take Foucault's insight beyond his Eurocentric preoccupations and carry its logic to the condition of coloniality. Europe was the 'scale' of Foucault, even when his thought was not limited to any such scale. European modernity therefore was doing to itself what it had practised to perfection in its colonial territories. The varied scales of (what for the world at large was colonial) modernity extended from the European centres to their colonial peripheries. Thus, connected through coloniality as governmentality those centres and peripheries collapse into each other. I have made this proposal predicated on a sustained course of critical reflections by major postcolonial theorists from Frantz Fanon to Ashis Nandy to Albert Memmi and others – thinkers that must be brought together with Al-e Ahmad if we are to understand him beyond his own limitations and thus save him from his critics' nativism.

The condition of 'coloniality' (of being turned into a colonial subject via systematic acculturation, self-Orientalisation, de-subjection) for the world at the receiving end of European colonialism was, and remains, the condition Michel Foucault called and considered as 'governmentality'. The colonial condition of de-subjection as subjectivity infiltrates and occupies the colonised mind in the way that the condition of governmentality infiltrates and dominates the subject of European liberal democracies. You become the vehicle of your own de-humanisation. Whatever theoretical limitations *Gharbzadegi* has, and it has plenty, it was exacerbated by the pathological provincialism of its critics who brought nothing to the text except myopic nativism, ad homonym jealousies and categorical fixation with 'the West' as the universal measure of truth, making them thus unable to see beyond their own noses. Neither theoretically nor historically did Al-e Ahmad and his critics overcome the limited insights of *Gharbzadegi*, and see it in a larger postcolonial frame of reference. To overcome that limitation, we need to take Al-e Ahmad's *Gharbzadegi* and place it in the larger context of other colonised nations and how their critical thinkers have sought to liberate their mind. What the Kenyan novelist and postcolonial theorist Ngūgī wa Thiong'o argues in his collection of essays, *Decolonising the Mind: The Politics of Language in African Literature* (1986), about the role of language in literary and theoretical emancipation is at the roots of the problem of Al-e Ahmad studies, if we were to call it that. In this book Ngūgī wa Thiong'o argues for linguistic decolonisation, but the implications of his arguments are much wider. Al-e Ahmad had merely pointed to a problem of agency and subjectivity. Instead of theoretically enriching it, his critics sought to suffocate that budding criticism, while his friends sent him on the goose chase of reading and translating Ernst Jünger! In the process Al-e Ahmad's insights were thwarted into unrecognisable mutterings.

Where to start – to place Al-e Ahmad in the larger context where he belongs? We might go back to Aimé Césaire's seminal text *Discourse sur le colonialism* (*Discourse on Colonialism*) (1950) for one of the earliest accounts of how the condition of coloniality had occasioned a state of mind, a particular discourse of political power and cultural domination. Césaire saw through the fact that there was a structural link between abused labour internal to colonial powers and colonial domination stemming from the same fact. It was Frantz Fanon who in his *Peau noire, masques blancs* (*Black Skin, White Masks*) (1952) brought that condition of colonised mind and discourse of power to full psychopathological understanding. Soon after that Albert Memmi's *Portrait du colonisé: Précédé du portrait du colonisateur* (*The Coloniser and the Colonised*) (1957) paid closer attention to the dialectical condition of the relationship between a colonised mind that *Gharbzadegi* (1962) would call 'Westoxication'. Just a quick look at the dates of these texts shows that, contrary to Mahmoud Houman and Ahmad Farid's fundamentally flawed references to German sources, it was in fact to African and Latin American sources to which Al-e Ahmad's text was pointing – however weakly and insufficiently.

The story of course does not end there. When, in 1963, Malcolm X used and theorised the term 'House Negro', he too was extending a long history of the term going back to the eighteenth century in order to mark a deeply pathological state of master–slave relationship – where the slave totally identified with his master. When we look at the case of Malcolm X and other African American critical thinkers the presumed binary between centre and periphery begins to disappear. Decades later, Ashis Nandy's *The Intimate Enemy: Loss and Recovery of Self Under Colonialism* (1983) dealt much more fully with the psychological consequences of the condition of coloniality Al-e Ahmad had diagnosed in his *Gharbzadegi*. All of these insights, one might say, went back to 'the master–slave dialectic' that Hegel had articulated in his *Phenomenology of Spirit* (1807). Between Hegel and the postcolonial theorists stands the monumental figure of W. E. B. Du Bois who in his classic *The Souls of Black Folk* (1903) had outlined the contours of what he called the 'double consciousness' of African Americans. Here he too was marking precisely the same phenomenon of seeing oneself as one's self doubled with the imposition of a colonised consciousness. Based on all these insights decades after Fanon, I extended his arguments in *Black Skin White Masks* to my *Brown Skin White Masks* (2011), as Glen Sean Coulthard did a few years later in his *Red Skin White Masks* (2014). The phenomenon Al-e Ahmad had diagnosed and briefly articulated was integral to all these arguments long before and long after the publication of his *Gharbzadegi*. But the pathologically Eurocentric obsession of his contemporaries could not see any of these links.

The list is of course inexhaustible. But the point is not to be exhaustive. The point is to see the globality of the condition of coloniality to which Al-e Ahmad's *Gharbzadegi* (however clumsily) was pointing and yet his argument was almost entirely lost on his ardent critics, and wildly abused by his Islamist admirers. In mapping this globality we must keep in mind how as early Richard Wright's *Native Son* (1939), and certainly by the time James Baldwin had published his *Notes of a Native Son* (1955) or when Ralph Ellison published his *Invisible Man* (1952), the issue of conflicted and traumatised soul of the colonised, enslaved, abused and brutalised people was widely on the literary and critical map of racist white supremacy at the heart of European colonialism. The whole phenomenon of the *Négritude Movement* had decidedly scaled the globality of this condition of revolt against the colonial theft of character and culture. A multifaceted cultural and intellectual movement, Négritude was launched in the 1930s by leading intellectuals and artists from French colonies in Africa and the Caribbean. Almost simultaneous with it was the equally powerful Harlem Renaissance in the United States. These movements revolutionised colonised nations awareness and pride in who and what they were, and in the process, they crafted an entire alternative universe of being, of existence, of rebellious consciousness, of will to resist power, and certainty not opting for what the Iranian critics of Al-e Ahmad still call 'nativism'. The ignorance of such movements around the globe among these Iranians when attacking Al-e Ahmad is simply astounding. To be sure, even Al-e Ahmad himself was ignorant of the globality of the condition he had sensed in his own homeland, and wasted his time helping translate Ernst Jünger's *Crossing the Line* into Persian for the remote speculation suggested to him by Mahmoud Houman that he and the German nihilist had seen the same thing!

Almost at the same time that Al-e Ahmad was publishing his *Gharbzadegi* in piecemeal in Iran, in Latin America what would eventually be called the 'Philosophy of Liberation' was taking shape in the 1960s, with philosophers like Enrique Dussel, Rodolfo Kusch, Arturo Roig and Leopoldo Zea Aguilar leading the ground-breaking project, parting ways with the imperial domination of Eurocentric philosophy. By the time Walter Mignolo published his seminal book *The Darker Side of the Renaissance: Colonisation and the Discontinuity of the Classical Tradition* (1992) this critical strain of thinking had assumed global significance. Between the 1960s and the 1990s ground-breaking work was done in Latin America to expand our critical encounter with European coloniality. Al-e Ahmad himself and his nativist critics were entirely oblivious to this project. But, and there is the crucial point, Al-e Ahmad's *Gharbzadegi* shared the same critical consciousness of alerting the world that one soul at least in Iran was thinking in the same way.

Many of these developments, all of them entirely unfamiliar to Al-e Ahmad's Westoxicated critics, both predate and follow up the publication of *Gharbzadegi* in 1962. Five seminal publications are crucial in this regard: Talal Asad's *Anthropology and the Colonial Encounter* (1974), Edward Said's *Orientalism* (1978), Gayatri Chakravorty Spivak's 'Can the Subaltern Speak?' (1983), Y. V. Malimbe's *The Invention of Africa* (1988) and (to some extent) Achille Mbembe's *On the Postcolony* (2000). Predicated on the earlier classics, these texts advanced the field of postcolonial studies by leaps and bounds and crafted a global network of critical thinking, within which Al-e Ahmad's *Gharbzadegi* is now to make sense. Although they all postdate *Gharbzadegi* and Al-e Ahmad could not be faulted for not knowing them, the dismal condition of Al-e Ahmad studies today, particularly among the 'expat' scholars who work in English, is symptomatic of an enduring provincialism, which they paradoxically throw at Al-e Ahmad himself. It is unthinkable in the first quarter of the twenty-first century to see such poverty of critical thinking in what calls itself 'Iranian Studies'. The condition of coloniality as governmentality has by now deeply penetrated the epistemic backwardness of a barren and befuddled field.

It is crucial to keep in mind the fact of the epistemic violence at the heart of all anticolonial and postcolonial critical thoughts in which Al-e Ahmad's essay had a small place and must now be belatedly located. Al-e Ahmad was often criticised as he was neither a historian, nor a sociologist, nor an economist, and yet he was dabbling in all such fields. But the fact is that his prose was instrumental in crafting a new narratology of the nature and function of colonial domination, and by definition any such prose was perpetrating epistemic violence on all such fields in order to see through them a truth their disciplinary insights were concealing. This epistemic violence corresponded to the famous passage in Fanon's seminal text *Wretched of the Earth* (1961) where he had theorised violence at the roots of anticolonial insurrection – a violence that reads like a bookend to the diabolic violence of colonialism going back all the way back to the horrific passages in Bartolomé de las Casas' *A Short Account of the Destruction of the Indies* (1542–52). The condition of coloniality as governmentality demanded, and throughout the colonised world exacted, that violence in both physical and epistemic terms.

Let me conclude this chapter by pointing out yet another crucial way of reading Al-e Ahmad's *Westoxication* and *Services and Treasons* together, which is to see them as his inching towards a 'liberation theology' on the model of Latin American liberation theology, as it was being articulated by Gustavo Gutiérrez of Peru, Leonardo Boff of Brazil and Juan Luis Segundo of Uruguay, although, again Al-e Ahmad did not know this, for he was too busy catching up with the latest issue of *Les Temps modernes* from Paris to care about Buenos Aires or Mexico City or anywhere else in Latin America, Asia, or Africa. His critique of Westoxication in many ways was an auto-critique though again he did not know this. Strong elements of Westoxication were alive and well in his own mind and character: that is the reason he could diagnose the phenomenon so well. We might in fact read *Gharbzadegi* as the text in which its author is protesting too much. The people he did trust and admire, Mahmoud Houman, Ahmad Fardid and Khalil Maleki, were all even more Westoxicated than he was, entirely enamoured of and enmeshed in what passed for a knowledge of 'Heidegger' in that city of the blind where the one-eyed was the king.

This last link I propose between what Al-e Ahmad was doing in his most widely received and debated essays and the rise of liberation theology in Latin America is the crucial connection at the heart of my renewed attention to Al-e Ahmad to which all these chapters will lead at the end of this book. Working towards that objective, Al-e Ahmad's critical essays such as *Gharbzadegi* were instrumental in radically *de-familiarising*, to use Shklovsky's term, 'Western' colonial modernity for his contemporaries, making it strange, jarring and unnatural against the whole grain of Eurocentric power that had made it natural to a Hegelian force of history.

Notes

1. Jalal Al-e Ahmad, *Gharbzadegi* (*Westoxication*) (Tehran: Ravagh Publications, 1341/1962, the original publication): 25. There are many translations of this seminal text of Al-e Ahmad. One relatively reliable such translation is Jalal Al-e Ahmad: *Occidentosis: A Plague from the West*, translated by R. Campbell, annotations and introduction by Hamid Algar (Berkeley, CA: Mizan Press, 1984). In this chapter as indeed throughout this book I read the original Persian and do my own translations from the original.

2. The prime example of the nativist reading of Al-e Ahmad and other Iranian

intellectuals is Mehrzad Boroujerdi in his *Iranian Intellectuals and the West: The Tormented Triumph of Nativism* (Syracuse, NY: Syracuse University Press, 1996). This outlandish charge has now reached Iranian scholars writing in Persian too. See for example, Mohammad Taqi Qezelsofla and Negin Nourian Dehkordi, '*Naqd-e Bumi-gara'i dar Andisheh Jalal Al-e Ahmad*' ('Critique of Nativism in Al-e Ahmad's Thoughts') (*Fasl-nameh Tahqiqat-e Siyasi va Bin al-Melali*, Winter, 1989): 152–82. For these scholars anything that is not European is nativist! For alternative perspectives see the seminal text of Dipesh Chakrabarty, *Provincialising Europe: Postcolonial Thought and Historical Difference* (Princeton, NJ: Princeton University Press, 2007), and Hamid Dabashi *Can Non-Europeans Think?* (London: Zed, 2013), and for a complete overcoming of Europe as the epicentre of self-universalisation see Hamid Dabashi, *Europe and its Shadows: Coloniality after Empire* (London: Pluto, 2019).

3. My book, *Post-Orientalism: Knowledge and Power in Time of Terror* (New Brunswick, NJ: Transaction, 2008), was in part a product of this landmark conference.

4. Jalal Al-e Ahmad, *Gharbzadegi* (*Westoxication*) (Op. Cit.): 11–12. Al-e Ahmad cites this lyric under the title 'Instead of an Introduction', but the learned translator of the text into English that I just cited, *Occidentosis: A Plague from the West*, opts to disregard this Introduction. This is unfortunate and compromises the integrity of the text. In a note after the citation Al-e Ahmad writes, 'citing from a 33 – LP, Capital Records, US. I thank Betty Tavakkoli for having transcribed the lyrics for me.'

5. To watch an original performance of the song, go here: https://www.youtube.com/watch?v=TKnYN5C69RY.

6. The best study of Ahmad Fardid is by Ali Mirsepassi, *Transnationalism in Iranian Political Thought: The Life and Times of Ahmad Fardid* (Cambridge: Cambridge University Press, 2017).

7. Jalal Al-e Ahmad, *Gharbzadegi* (*Westoxication*) (Op. Cit.): 17–18.

8. Ibid: 21–35.

9. Ibid: 39–54.

10. Ibid: 78.

11. Ibid: 144.

12. Ibid: 136.

13. Ibid: 192.

14. Ibid: 225.

15. Ibid: 21.

16. Ibid: 21–2.
17. Daryoush Ashuri, *Ma va Modernity* (*We and Modernity*) (Tehran: Moassesseh Farhangi Sirat, 1997): 14.
18. Ibid: 22.
19. Ibid: 133–4.
20. Daryoush Ashuri came back to the same ideas yet again in 2016 in a conversation titled (again) *Ma va Moderniyyat* (*We and Modernity*) published by Tavana, an organisation established and funded by the US State Department to promote 'regime change' and military intervention against Iran. See Mehdi Jami, *Ma va Moderniyyat: Goftogu ba Daryoush Ashuri* (*We and Modernity: Conversation with Daryoush Ashuri*) (Online Publications: Tavana, 2016).
21. See Fereydun Adamiyyat, '*Ashoftegi dar Fekr-e Tarikhi*' (Confusion in Historical Thinking') (Tehran: No Publisher, 1981).
22. See the chapter on Malcolm X in Hamid Dabashi, *Islamic Liberation Theology: Resisting the Empire* (London: Routledge, 2008).
23. Jalal Al-e Ahmad, *Dar Khedmat va Khiyanat-e Roshanfekran* (*On the Services and Treasons of Intellectuals*) (Tehran: Khwarizmi Publications, 1357/1978), two volumes. Translation of Nima's poem is mine.
24. For an English translation see Julien Benda, *The Treason of the Intellectuals*, translated by Richard Aldington (New Brunswick, NJ: Transaction, 2007).
25. Jalal Al-e Ahmad, *Dar Khedmat va Khiyanat-e Roshanfekran* (*On the Services and Treasons of Intellectuals*) (Op. Cit.): I: 9–16.
26. Ibid: I: 17–49.
27. Ibid: I: 50–88.
28. Ibid: I: 89–109.
29. Ibid: I: 110–26.
30. Ibid: I: 127–88.
31. Ibid: I: 189–98.
32. Ibid: I: 199–206.
33. Ibid: I: 207–10.
34. Ibid: I: 210–11.
35. Ibid: I: 211.
36. Ibid: II: 9–80.
37. Ibid: II: 80–4.
38. Ibid: II: 84–91.
39. Ibid: II: 91–102.
40. Ibid: II: 103–60.

41. Ibid: II: 161–215.

42. Ibid: II: 216–31.

43. Ibid: II: 232–61.

44. Ibid: II: 262–73.

45. Ibid: II: 274–9.

46. See Chantal Mouffe, *Agonistics: Thinking the World Politically* (London and New York: Verso, 2013).

47. Martin Heidegger, *Nietzsche. Volume One: The Will to Power as Art*, translated from the German, with notes and and an analysis by David Farrell Krell (New York: Harper & Row, 1961/1979): I: 4.

48. Ibid.

49. Some have even extended this presumed antagonism towards 'the West' to other Iranian authors. See for example, Brad Hanson, 'The "Westoxication" of Iran: Depictions and Reactions of Behrangi, Al-e Ahmad, and Shariati' (*International Journal of Middle East Studies*, vol. 15, no. 1, 1983): 1–23.

50. See Asef Bayat, *Post-Islamism: The Changing Faces of Political Islam* (Oxford: Oxford University Press, 2013).

51. See Michel Foucault, *The Birth of Biopolitics: Lectures at the Collège de France, 1978–79*, edited by Michel Senellart (New York: Palgrave, 2008): 186.

6

Literary Interludes

Once upon a time there was a bald shepherd who had a flock of young goats. One day while he was fixing the cap he used to cover and protect his bald head from nasty flies, our Mr shepherd was attending to his goats near a sprawling city when he noticed quite a loud commotion. People had all come out of their city, gathered on this side of the ditch, raising flags and masts, all looking up to the heavens . . .[1]

Jalal Al-e Ahmad, *Nun wa al-Qalam* (*By the Pen*) (1961)

I concluded the last chapter by suggesting that Al-e Ahmad's turn to a renewed reading of Islam in *Gharbzadegi* and *On the Services and Treasons of Intellectuals* might be interpreted as his preliminary steps towards a kind of liberation theology, the full contours of which he could not see for he was unaware of similar events in Latin America led by theologian like Gustavo Gutiérrez and others. These ground-breaking events were happening almost simultaneously with the publication of Al-e Ahmad's *Gharbzadegi*. But his own mind being overly fixated on Europe, and his main interlocutors at Tehran University too Eurocentric even to be aware of such monumental developments, he never unpacked this crucial potential in his critical thinking. That aspect of Al-e Ahmad's project thus remained dormant until the Islamist takeover of his legacy would take it in a direction that would legitimise their tyranny and discredit Al-e Ahmad. A major task of this book is to retrieve that moment in Al-e Ahmad's thinking and push it in a direction he could not see or even anticipate.

What I wish to do in this chapter, as I turn to consider Al-e Ahmad's literary output, is to recall what in this and previous work I have called the 'cosmopolitan worldliness' of a Muslim intellectual. In the case of Al-e

Ahmad in particular that worldliness is embedded in the prose of his historicality, the sort of prose and politics he practised that put an open-ended literary twist to his rebellious politics. He electrified the classical Persian prose with his contemporary politics – no matter what genre he chose to exercise, from short essays to long travelogues, from short stories to novellas. Once placed next to his other work, his literary output is therefore the best place to locate his stylised prose, featuring his uncanny ability to make the foreign familiar by making the familiar foreign, through what the prominent Russian formalist Viktor Shklovsky has called *Ostranenie* and Brecht considered the *Verfremdungseffekt*, or today we call *Defamiliarisation* or *Enstrangement*.

Al-e Ahmad's decisively *literary* turn in his prose practices marks his signature diction as the politics of the Muslim cosmopolis – when a Muslim intellectual becomes worldly and cosmopolitan. This prose was and remains markedly political but with an expansive literary panache and verve. It staged the ability of a prose to be at once familiar and uncanny, foreign and homely. No one else commanded such versatility with a prose that made sense of a strangely senseless, self-alienating world. He both made the world sensible and turned it uniquely Persian in its dictions – precisely because he was ambidextrous and wrote both fact and fiction together. The rest of his contemporaries did not just seek to mimic his prose but in effect followed the politics it prescribed. How to read the literary project embedded in the tenacity of that project is where I propose Al-e Ahmad's prose extends his engaged politics to the liberating prospect of his posterity beyond the mishap of an Islamic Republic.

Al-e Ahmad: The Authorial Voice

About a decade ago I wrote a small book I called *Being a Muslim in the World* (2013).[2] In it I sought to recap the meaning of what it means to be a Muslim in this world, right now, today. By then I had already articulated the contours of a post-Western world where the colonial metaphor of 'the West' had lost its grip on the credulity of our historical consciousness, and thus Islam was released from its binary entanglement, to the detriment of its own robust historical memories. The making of that consciousness was contingent, I argued, on the formation of a *language* of critical conversation with the plurality of

Islamic intellectual history – from law and theology to philosophy and mysticism – and perforce with the place of Muslims in the contemporary world and its divergent and formative forces. The normative hegemony of 'the West' as a colonial allegory had lost its grip and had therefore liberated all the binaries it had manufactured to believe in and impose itself. The central task of that language is its ability to overcome Muslim self-alienation caused by the systematic colonial de-subjection. I tasked our current critical encounter with our faith and our world, with bringing the world to a renewed self-consciousness beyond our necessary but now outdated critical encounter with 'the West'. That language was and remains contrapuntal, works through alterity and not identity, both rooted in this world and yet able to speak to its tomorrow. The worldliness of that language obviously requires an authorial voice aware and confident of itself. But how can a postmodern world accommodate a postcolonial authorial voice? Isn't the 'crisis of the subject' universal, or is it perhaps just European?

In his famous essay ' La mort de l'auteur' ('The Death of the Author') (1967) the French literary theorist Roland Barthes (1915–80) put forward the idea of decoupling the literary text from the biographical context of its author.[3] This he thought delimits the interpretative apparatus of the text. The text would thus be freed to mean more than its author may have intended or implied. 'The removal of the Author', Barthes proposes, and one could talk here with Brecht of a veritable 'distancing', the Author diminishing like a figurine at the far end of the literary stage, 'is not merely an historical fact or an act of writing; it utterly transforms the modern text (or – which is the same thing – the text is henceforth made and read in such a way that at all its levels the author is absent).'[4] This sounds like a liberating gesture to set the text free, decoupling its open-ended prospects of signification from the vagaries of its author. 'We know now', Barthes further speculates, 'that a text is not a line of words releasing a single "theological meaning (the "message" of the Author–God) but a multi-dimensional space in which a variety of writings, none of them original, blend and clash.'[5] The very last presumption of 'the Author-God' reveals what sort of author Barthes wishes to dispense with and decouple from the text. But could that prospect of 'the Author-God' be anything other than the European author?

In the case of an author like Al-e Ahmad in fact precisely the opposite is true, for here it is not the death of the author but actually the birth of the author, of the authorial voice, that makes the voice of the author ventriloquise in order to make the familiar foreign, in order to make the foreign familiar. While in this essay Barthes was liberating the text from the authority of its author, on the postcolonial edges of the literary modernity, which he was pushing to its postmodern edges, we were doing precisely the opposite – not mourning the death of the author but in fact celebrating the birth of the author. For Barthes the death of the author followed up on Nietzsche's death of God, and therefore the 'Crisis of the European Subject'. We had no such crisis, for we had not plundered the globe and then turned around to slaughter six million Jews to realise something was wrong with the omnipotence and omniscience of the European all-knowing subject, or the philosophical death of its Christian God. The text that Barthes wanted to liberate from the author for us was the evidence of the author, the site of her birth and upbringing, for our author and our authorship had come to life with that text, and that text was its birth canal. While for Barthes and his Europe the death of the author was the unleashing of the text, for much of the rest of the world at the mercy of the European colonial desubjection of the postcolonial person the evidence of the text was the birth certificate of its author. While for Barthes it was an act of exegetical conservatism to hang the open-ended possibilities of the text on the authority of its author, for the postcolonial world it was an act of hermeneutical revolution to consider the evidence of the text the breathing space of its resurrected author. We had scarce come to life after a whole history of both thuggish and philosophical European denial of our agencies. As a Frenchman, Barthes was the inheritor of one global imperial project that had denied its colonies in Asia, Africa and Latin America any personhood, any agency, any authorial voice. His theorisation of 'the death of the author' could not be more alien to our ears.

Liberating the author as a ventriloquist to assert its authorial voice is indispensable if the Orientalised subjected is not to become a museum piece regurgitating its miseries in departments of 'Area Studies' or else self-anthropologising its communal identities, as ethnographic native informers, and instead to assume authorial agency to encounter and face the changing horizons of Europe or 'the West' at the centre of what Al-e Ahmad called 'Westoxication'.

The agential liberation of the author from its colonial desubjection was vital if the debate about Westoxication were not to remain stagnant and left to the limited devices of the 'Iranist gravediggers' (as Al-e Ahmad called them), for no one among them had bothered to check and see 'the West' that was at the centre of 'Westoxication' had not remained stable, stagnant and the same. It had moved and changed and altered. In the collection of his philosophical essays called *Postmetaphysical Thinking*, Jürgen Habermas writes not just about the fact that the horizons of modernity are changing but speculates about the rise of a metaphysics after Kant and identifies themes in a 'postmetaphysical' thinking. Here he identifies four seminal movements that have radically redefined the European modernity: analytic philosophy, phenomenology, Western Marxism and structuralism. 'The wave of restoration that has rolled over the Western world for a good decade', he believes, 'is also washing an issue up on shore that has accompanied modernity from the beginning: the imitation substantiality of a metaphysics renewed one more time'.[6] If European modernity can metaphysically renovate itself, who and how and where in the postcolonial world is to face up to this new hegemony if not the liberated postcolonial author and his and her ability to demystify 'the West' – and not to re-fetishise – it?[7]

The crisis of the subject in Europe, the epicentre of colonising modernity, is coterminous with the occasion when the postcolonial person finds her or his voice via contrapuntal dialectic with the hidden other of Europe, with, for example, the perennial European other, its Jewish other. By subjecting itself, the postcolonial author de-alienates itself from this colonial alienation. The necessary act of *defamiliarisation* becomes tantamount to de-alienation, to desubjection, to becoming a person with a voice, a pride of place, a dignity to his or her 'I'. But who, and there is the rub, would be Al-e Ahmad's European other with whom he would, or he could have if he only knew better, identify? Most certainly not with Ernst Jünger or *horribile dictu* Martin Heidegger. The prose of Al-e Ahmad's politics made the foreign familiar in a uniquely Persian diction, and to read that diction in Persian there were familiarities in some compelling comparable figures of moral and intellectual imagination. So yes – perhaps a German, but what German, and who else, and how and why?

Jalal Al-e Ahmad, Walter Benjamin and W. E. B. Du Bois

Al-e Ahmad's German counterpart was not Ernst Jünger or Martin Heidegger, but Walter Benjamin. This is not the false prophecy of yet another professor at Tehran University, but the carefully, consistently and painstakingly argued suggestion of a brilliant graduate student at Columbia University decades after Al-e Ahmad had rushed to meet his creator.

In 2013 one of my graduate students, Ajay Singh Chaudhary, wrote his doctoral dissertation with me at Columbia University and submitted his final draft as 'Religions of Doubt: Religion, Critique, and Modernity in Jalal Al-e Ahmad and Walter Benjamin'.[8] Based on my initial work on Al-e Ahmad in my *Theology of Discontent* (1993) and his own close and provocative readings of the Persian and German originals, Chaudhary had developed a comparative assessment of Al-e Ahmad and Benjamin and in the process advanced our understanding of both, particularly of Al-e Ahmad who at the time was still the subject of the most claustrophobic nativist reading by professional Iranists. Chaudhary had cast his arguments in the form of a comparative philosophy. As he put it in the abstract of his dissertation,

> I demonstrate that the perceived failure of utopian modern projects, particularly Marxism, led each of these twentieth-century thinkers to re-engage with religious questions and concerns in a simultaneous critique of the corrosive, reductive, and catastrophic nature of the modern condition and the idea of traditional religion – static, irrational, regressive – that modernist thought had conjured.

To do so Chaudhary argued that both Al-e Ahmad and Benjamin had to trespass the boundaries of genres, 'art, literature, science, technology, and ritual', to expand the limiting boundaries of 'philosophy' as it had been practised:

> I argue that reading these thinkers together allows a glimpse at ideas and modes in philosophical thought that were largely derailed by varying discourses of secularism, poststructuralism, naturalism, and fundamentalism. This reading suggests new synthetic possibilities for philosophy in the twenty-first century.

In the second chapter of his dissertation, 'How to Read *Gharbzadegi?*', Chaudhary completely and rightly dismisses the leading Iranists' over-reading of Al-e Ahmad's reference to Jünger and Heidegger and correctly identifies Marx as the key factor and force in both Al-e Ahmad and Benjamin's historiography. This chapter is the most exhaustive dismantling of the abusive reading of Al-e Ahmad in reference to Jünger or by extension Heidegger. Equally compelling is his dismissal of the reading of Al-e Ahmad (and an entire gamut of political leaders, critical thinkers and literary giants ranging from Yasir Arafat to Gabriel García Márquez!) as nativist by Boroujerdi and other Iranist scholars. Chaudhary also expands on my earlier critique of nativism in my *Post-Orientalism: Knowledge and Power in Time of Terror* (2008) as the binary manufacturing of 'the West and the Rest', of 'the native' not as a reality *sui generis* but as a manufactured colonial concoction. Chaudhary's project of bringing Al-e Ahmad to comparative sites with Benjamin leads him to exceptionally brilliant readings of Al-e Ahmad's *Gharbzadegi* that are otherwise implausible.

Although not of his immediate or particular interests in his doctoral dissertation, nevertheless Chaudhary's ground-breaking comparative reading of Al-e Ahmad and Benjamin opens up the sites of the postcolonial reconfiguration of authorial agency in unprecedent directions. At issue is not just the fact that a Jewish and a Muslim critical thinker take their respective Marxism to a critical encounter with their messianic Judaism or messianic Shi'ism – a subject Chaudhary explored brilliantly. That is indeed crucial enough a point of comparative religious studies project. At issue is also, and for me in this book more importantly, the dual marginalities of a colonised Iranian Muslim and an ostracised European Jew having hidden similarities that dismantle the allegory of 'the West' in liberating and unanticipated ways. It would be useful here if we were to add to these two a third figure, W. E. B. Du Bois, for then the three of them (from US, Europe and the Muslim world) guide us to the fundamental phenomenon of 'alienation' as Marx had originally articulated it and each one of these critical thinkers carried it to different domains. This comparative reading of Al-e Ahmad, Benjamin and Du Bois would be of immense importance as to how to read all their respective takes on the crucial gesture of *estrangement*, of *defamiliarisation*.

Let us begin upstream with Marx. Karl Marx's theory of 'alienation' inaugurated our understanding of *estrangement* of the labourer from the fruit of his or her labour, when commodity fetishism gives it a reality *sui generis*. This alienation from the whole self is a by-product of the incorporation of the labourer in the process of production, very much as we see in Charlie Chaplin's famous scene in his masterpiece *Modern Times* (1936), where he is literally swallowed by the machine.[9] Here is how Marx had defined *alienation* in his *Economic & Philosophic Manuscripts of 1844* (1844):

> This fact expresses merely that the object which labor produces – labor's product – confronts it as something alien, as a power independent of the producer. The product of labor is labor which has been embodied in an object, which has become material: it is the objectification of labor. Labor's realization is its objectification. Under these economic conditions this realization of labor appears as loss of realization for the workers, objectification as loss of the object and bondage to it; appropriation as estrangement, as alienation.[10]

This economically rooted alienation, embedded in the capitalist mode of production, becomes doubly effective in a colonial context and in the case of the pariahs and the underclass in the so-called advanced capitalist societies, thus the ostracised Jews and the enslaved Black become coterminous with the desubjected colonial subject. Consider when W. E. B. Du Bois describes what he calls 'double-consciousness' in *The Souls of Black Folk* (1903):

> It is a peculiar sensation, this double-consciousness, this sense of always looking at one's self through the eyes of others, of measuring one's soul by the tape of a world that looks on in amused contempt and pity. One ever feels his twoness, – an American, a Negro; two souls, two thoughts, two unreconciled strivings; two warring ideals in one dark body, whose dogged strength alone keeps it from being torn asunder.[11]

The state of this double-consciousness is the condition of alienation, of *Gharbzadegi*, as it were, of being stricken not with 'the West' but the witness of that 'West'. The Black Man looks at himself through the eyes of the White Man almost exactly the same way that the Iranian, the Muslim, the Orientalised, looks at himself/herself through the eye of 'the West': 'two souls, two thoughts, two unreconciled strivings; two warring ideals in one dark body, whose dogged strength alone keeps it from being torn asunder'. Except, in Al-e Ahmad's correct diagnosis, that battle had been lost and the Oriental body and soul, mind and mindset, had been conquered by 'the West'; and thus the overwhelming self-hatred and the violent reaction of characters like Daryoush Ashuri towards Al-e Ahmad's diagnosis.

In the case of Walter Benjamin, he knew how to self-theorise in universal terms: as he did in his iconic essay 'The Work of Art in the Age of Mechanical Reproduction' (1935):

> Mankind, which in Homer's time was an object of contemplation for the Olympian gods, now is one for itself. Its self-alienation has reached such a degree that it can experience its own destruction as an aesthetic pleasure of the first order. This is the situation of politics which Fascism is rendering aesthetic. Communism responds by politicizing art.[12]

It is not 'Mankind' that was one way in Homer's time and another in Benjamin's. It was the European kind, which here Benjamin as a European Jew could both see and not see he was self-theorising. Like all other Europeans, Benjamin saw Europe as the epicentre of the universe, and yet as a Jew he could also see the destructive self-degeneration of that Europe in the rise of fascism. As a European he could see fascism but could not see colonialism was the hidden side of the same coin. But as a European Jew, a self-alienated persona, and filtered through what Du Bois would call his 'double consciousness', he could see himself both as the European *self* and as the European *other*; thus perhaps one reason for his suicide.

It is now much easier to see how what Al-e Ahmad was arguing in his *Gharbzadegi* was precisely this process of self-alienation, and that insight enables us to see the *Verfremdungseffekt* of his literary turn. For in *Gharbzadegi* he had only too clumsily stated the ability of a far more literary prose to make the familiarity of the colonised mind uncanny, the foreign concept of resisting it homely, all through a prose that made sense of a senseless world in sensible terms, and all of that in a uniquely Persian diction. Al-e Ahmad had Marx, Du Bois and Benjamin about him but no one among his contemporaries could see that, least of all himself.

'By the pen and what it inscribes'

Let us now look at the body of Al-e Ahmad's literary wok. Al-e Ahmad was a prolific short story writer and novelist. My generation grew up with his *School Principle* and other works of fiction. I have enduring memories of my teenage years when I first began reading his short stories. Like all my classmates I was fascinated by his literary and critical output, and sometimes even tried to imitate his Persian prose. They turned out quite ridiculous and I soon abandoned the juvenile idiocy. For the purpose of writing this book I went back and read all his works afresh, including his works of fiction, to see if they have endured the test of time. They have not. Modern Persian fiction progressed and advanced by leaps and bounds during and after the time of Al-e Ahmad. Today the works of Sadegh Hedayat, Simin Daneshvar, Sadegh Chubak, Ebrahim Golestan, Mahmoud Dolatabadi, Shahrnoush Parsipour and Houshang Golshiri stand tall in a whole different category from Al-e Ahmad's fiction. But today we also read Al-e Ahmad's literary work for an entirely different sets of reasons.

Al-e Ahmad had literary aspirations, but his fiction was almost indistinguishable from his critical work, his dominant voice identical in both. You can hear Al-e Ahmad speak beyond the voice of his omniscient narrators. It is impossible to read his works of fiction without placing it in the context of his critical essays – and thus his signature prose roams from fact to fiction with identical ease and purpose. First and foremost, he was an essayist, in fact a master of the genre, and anything else he wrote drew from the same temperament. He could never check his critical mind at the door when he began writing fiction. No matter how good, mediocre or bad his works of fiction, they all extend from the critical social concerns – with tyranny, corruption, destitution and despair – dominant in his prose and politics. In this respect he was exactly the opposite of his wife Simin Daneshvar, who was primarily a novelist and short story writer of uncommon power, though occasionally she would indulge in writing short essays too, but even then, her storyteller voice would come out. When we place Al-e Ahmad's critical essays and works of fiction next to each other, as we should, a third kind of prose emerges in which the omniscient narrator is identically at home on both sides of the divide.

Al-e Ahmad began his literary career early with the stories that are placd together in the collection of short stories called *Did-o-Bazdid* (*Paying Visits*) (1945), then came *Az Ranji keh Mibarim* (*Our Suffering*) (1947), his second collection of short stories, followed by *Setar* (1948), yet another collection of short stories, and then *Zan-e Ziadi* (*The Redundant Wife*) (1952). It would be useful to consider Al-e Ahmad's literary work chronologically, though it can be approached any number of other ways. Considered chronologically, we can see better how his literary preoccupations were in fact an extension of his political state of mind – from social realism to existentialism to experimentations with folkloric prose. Considered in this light, we can also see better his lifetime oscillation between multiple genres and narratives in which he wrote. He would get bored or hit a cul-de-sac with one genre and run away to another, and when neither satisfied him he began packing his backpack and travelling – reading and writing the world anew.

In the title short story of *Paying Visits*, we read Al-e Ahmad's first experiment with plot, characterisation, but most memorably with dialogue. In this particular short story, however, there is not much of a plot. We enter a gathering in the presence of a prominent professor that consists of a politician, a journalist, a merchant and a few other characters, and the narrator reports to the readers what each believes and says in this gathering. Al-e Ahmad uses the occasion to ridicule their affected speech and useless exchanges. The rest of the story is the narrator following through visiting other gatherings and social types. Many of the other stories in this first volume depict war-torn Iran under Reza Shah, full of fear and anxiety, boredom and banality, such as the story in which a police officer vandalises candles in a mosque, or another story where we read about bombing near a women's public bath, where he shows his mastery of dialogue. Al-e Ahmad has a particular mastery of mimicking his female characters. Equally evident in these short stories are the coming-of-age stories of young men discovering the larger world, multiple social settings, varied characters. Though the stories are raw and even primitive, they are delivering Al-e Ahmad to his literary imagination, where he is discovering realities other than his own. Much of '*Ganj*' ('Treasure') is narrated by the auntie telling the story in a colloquial Tehrani accent. She smokes her waterpipe and tells the story of a treasure of precious coins being discovered in the neighbourhood.[13] Al-e Ahmad thrives in his ventriloquism of such female characters.

The collection of short stories in *Our Suffering* reveal Al-e Ahmad's penchant for socialist realism. In one story we read about the suppression of a labour unrest in a mine, in another story we read about those labour activists who are forced to leave their hometowns and families, in another story we encounter a labour activist being tortured by being forced to stand up in a prison cell. Booksellers, second-hand peddlers, photographers and a host of other characters are all under state surveillance in this story. There are moments of revealing psychological musings about the conditions of political prisoners in the short story '*Mohit-e Tang*' ('A Tight Place').[14] The interior monologue of the political prisoner remains on the surface of reminiscing about his comrades. By the end of the story when we realise the narrator, Rahman, is dying, the plot becomes threadbare and flat. But the collection of stories as a whole keeps us engaged with the world Al-e Ahmad has created, a world of fear and loathing, despair and struggle.

In *Setar* (1948) we see something of a distance from the socialist realism and enter the phase of existential angst, as in the story of a man who was petrified by the police and yet fascinated by their arms. In the story of 'Setar' he addresses the taboo issue of music amongst those whose religious fanaticism prohibits it. Here he is deeply critical of that fanaticism and identifies with the young musician protagonist and his music. The central character of the story is a young poor musician who loves to play the Setar and after much hardship buys his favourite instrument only to see it broken to pieces by a fanatical young man at the door of a mosque. We can feel the young Al-e Ahmad's fury and frustration with institutional and dogmatic religion in this short story.

In *Zan-e Ziadi* (*The Redundant Wife*) (1952), the opening scene of *Samanu-pazan* (a folk ritual cooking of a sweet paste, Samanu, made from germinated wheat) is a thoroughly authentic rendition of this ceremony, a clear indication that as a child he was privy to such scenes.[15] The eponymous story depicts the miseries of a woman from a poor family at the mercy of a charlatan husband. The interior monologue of this story is yet another superb example of Al-e Ahmad's ability to mimic elder women of his own class and acquaintances. Consistent throughout these short stories is Al-e Ahmad's palpable affinity and identification with the poorest women of his society.[16] He might be trapped inside certain clichés in his characterisations of these female characters, but they remain integral to his authorial voice.

Al-e Ahmad's most famous novella was *Modir-e Madreseh* (*School Principal*) (1958), perhaps his most widely read and debated literary piece. The story is entirely biographical and speaks of his own experiences as a public-school teacher, though the narrator of the story is the school principal. In this story we are smack in the middle of the petty politics of public schools in a country flooded with political corruption. At the end the school principal resigns, and in the nineteenth and final chapter of the book, he just strips all literary pretences and says he went home and wrote a report 'that despite its flaws could help a minister of education draft a seven-year programme for himself'.[17] This is the Al-e Ahmad we know well from his essays. The publication of his *Sargozasht-e Kandu-ha* (*The Story of Beehives*) (1958) in the same year shows his impatience with genres and literary schools. This is the story of a beekeeper and his beehives, in which he experimented with an allegorical prose. The story oscillates between Kamand Ali Beik the beekeeper and his bees, and the abuse of the bees by the beekeeper. What is evident here is how his exposure to various literary genres led him to literary experimentation in Persian.

His *Nun wa al-Qalam* (*By the Pen*) (1961), with its title a satirical pun on a Qur'anic verse, is a longer story in which he satirises political mobilisations and absolutist ideologies. This is perhaps his most politically robust work of fiction, evidently set in the Safavid period and deliberately cast in a fake old-fashioned narrative. The two characters of the story, Mirza Abd al-Zakki and Mirza Asadollah, represent the two-character types of intellectual, what Edward Said would later call an 'Aye-sayer' and the other a 'Nay-sayer'. Central to the character of Mirza Asadollah is his complete mistrust of all forms of government. It is the story of a useless revolt, and a circular rise of hope and onset of defeat. In describing these two central characters we see another autobiographical allusion, where we read that one of the two scribes does not have any children while the other has two, and this difference eventually deepens into major differences between the two scribes.[18]

Nefrin-e Zamin (*Curse of the Earth*) (1967) is set in the form of a novella but is in fact a thinly disguised critic of the Shah's White Revolution (1963) and land reform. It would be wrong to read it as a work of fiction, nor can we read it as an ethnography, nor indeed as travelogue. I would therefore place it in the context of his literary works only to show that all of his prose comprises really one and the same person thinking and writing – having mastered a unique prose that is ambidextrous and can serve both purposes. It is the story a teacher who goes to a small village to teach and Al-e Ahmad uses the occasion to discuss the dire circumstance of rural life in remote parts of the country. There is a bit of story here but the central theme is the poverty of life in rural areas.[19] The story calls for comparison with the work of the master of this genre, Al-e Ahmad's close friend, Gholamhossein Sa'edi (1936–85) who had elevated such stories to the sublime level of psychopathological despair. Al-e Ahmad's has nowhere near that level of psychological depth and complexity.[20]

His *Panj Dastan* (*Five Stories*) (1971), published posthumously, brought him back to his preferred genre of short stories. In the story of '*Jashn-e Farkhondeh*' ('The Auspicious Feast') he returns to the Reza Shah period and the question of unveiling, while in '*Shohar-e Emrika'i*' ('American Husband') we discover the original profession of a much-coveted American spouse was actually a gravedigger in Arlington Cemetery. The Iranian wife picks up her daughter and goes back to Iran, in a kind of reverse story of Betty Mahmoody's *Not Without My Daughter* (1987). What this posthumous volume clearly shows is Al-e Ahmad's sustained preoccupation with the short story genre, so much so that his literary persona and fictional prose had remained integral to his legacy from the first to the last moments of his career literature.

Put together alongside his critical essays, travelogues and translations these works of fiction add fuller dimensions and momentum to Al-e Ahmad's singularly precise and provocative Persian prose, which he had sharpened with the very tempo of his time. To be sure, Al-e Ahmad was not a sophisticated storyteller. He wrote fiction the way Sartre wrote philosophical novels. They are both to be read with a grain of salt as literary works but add crucial momentum to their author's respective ideas. Sartre's *Huis Clos* (*No Exit*) (1944) is fairly incomprehensible except as an extension of his philosophical existentialism. The same is the case with Al-e Ahmad. He had a critical project. He was no literary figure. He admired Sadegh Hedayat, but he was no Hedayat. He was married to Simin Daneshvar, but he was no Simin Daneshvar. He translated Camus but read him too critically to be able to learn from his artistry. Al-e Ahmad was no artist. He was and he remained, and he died, a critical thinker – too critical to be creative. He knew Ebrahim

Golestan well, was critical of his prose and politics, but was unable to see the artistry of Golestan's prose and distinguish it from his dubious politics.

That assessment raises the question: what are we to make of his fictional work? You might say Al-e Ahmad *impersonates* a writer of fiction, almost tongue in cheek. It is precisely that impersonation that is at stake here. His fact and fiction cannot be separated and should not be separated. They are porous and interchangeable. He wrote fiction with the same pen and penmanship that he wrote his critical essays. He was ambidextrous in his prose and politics. His prose had a political chutzpah, his politics had literary flair. His literary bent is where the familiar becomes foreign, the uncanny canny, the *Unheimlich Heimlich*, and all of them vice-versa, and thus the power of his prose to invoke *Verfremdungseffekt*, of making the alien acquainted. In my chapter on his essays I have already suggested how his prose mimicked orality, intimacy, conversational proximity – and it is precisely that mimicking of orality that works here in his work of fictions too. 'Experience', wrote Walter Benjamin in his exquisite essay, 'The Storyteller', 'which is passed on from mouth to mouth is the source from which all storytellers have drawn. And among those who have written down the tales, it is the great ones whose written version differs least from the speech of the many nameless storytellers.'[21] Following this insight of Benjamin we might say that what is attractive about Al-e Ahmad's works of fiction is not their literary prowess but precisely their ability to mimic orality, of his sitting there and talking to us or else telling us a story. In that metaphysics of presence, we find him irresistible. Let's pay closer attention to what Benjamin says about the difference between a storyteller and a novelist:

> The earliest symptom of a process whose end is the decline of storytelling is the rise of the novel at the beginning of modern times. What distinguishes the novel from the story (and from the epic in the narrower sense) is its essential dependence on the book. The dissemination of the novel became possible only with the invention of printing. What can be handed on orally, the wealth of the epic, is of a different kind from what constitutes the stock in trade of the novel. What differentiates the novel from all other forms of prose literature – the fairy tale, the legend, even the novella – is that it neither comes from oral tradition nor goes into it. This distinguishes it from

storytelling in particular. The storyteller takes what he tells from experience – his own or, that reported by others. And he in turn makes it the experience of those who are listening to his tale. The novelist has isolated himself. The birthplace of the novel is the solitary individual, who is no longer able to express himself by giving examples of his most important concerns, is himself uncounseled, and cannot counsel others. To write a novel means to carry the incommensurable to extremes in the representation of human life.[22]

Benjamin is too teleological here, unable to shed his Hegel off at the door of this otherwise crucial insight. Things do not move teleologically from storyteller to novelists, from premodernity to modernity. A little bit of attention to the rest of colonially ravaged world would have done Benjamin lots of good. On the colonial edges of Benjamin's modernity things mix and match, the storyteller in the novelist, the novelist remembering the storyteller. The book in Persian and Arabic and a host of other languages was coterminous with the storyteller. The *Shahnameh* is in both, at one and the same time. The invention of printing created and crafted the public sphere, but if the illustrated manuscripts of yore had the royal atelier to imagine their worlds, the *naqqal* (storyteller) had the frescoes of coffee houses on a much larger scale. The popularity of the storyteller and the insularity of the novelist are porous. It is sad, it is exhilarating, to see how much Benjamin is so one of us, a solitary Jewish voice in the wilderness of European modernity.

Recall how in my chapter on Al-e Ahmad's relations with his wife, chapter four, I discussed the final scene in his *Sangi bar Guri* (*A Tombstone*) when he goes to a cemetery and pays a visit to the gravesites of his mother and sister and also of an old storyteller aunt. That storyteller aunt is at the heart of all his works of fiction, a hidden storyteller in all his short stories and novellas, doubling the point I made about the contrapuntal and dialogical voice of his prose, at once masculine and feminine, one with his wife Simin Daneshvar as his main interlocutor and the other with that old storyteller aunt as his storyteller alter ego. His wife was a towering novelist, and that made him a storyteller, his aunt was a natural-born storyteller, and that made him a novelist. In the transgendered possibilities of that prose Al-e Ahmad staged the ability of a way of reading the world that turned its dialogical disposition

Figure 6.1 Jalal Al-e Ahmad, Simin Daneshvar, Ebrahim Golestan and his wife Fakhri Golestan on their way to Northern Iran, 1956. (Photo courtesy of Ali Dehbashi, from the *Bokhara Magazine* archive) Al-e Ahmad and Golestan had a strange friendship. They were very close and yet their relationship was fraught with rivalry and contentious belligerence. The body languages of the two in this picture are emblematic of who they were. Al-e Ahmad could never stand up like Golestan so self-absorbed, Golestan could never sit like that, so sedate and confident. Their respective spouses meanwhile could not be more aloof from the two men.

strangely familiar, its uncanny insights entirely plausible, its foreign prospects homely. The hidden versatilities of that prose continue to make sense of a strangely senseless world. We must learn how to read it afresh.

Prose as Device

The contrapuntal voice of Al-e Ahmad, at once masculine and feminine, novelist and storyteller, critical and creative, in his multiple proses brings us right to the door of a key passage in Viktor Shklovsky seminal essay 'Art as Device', where he writes:

> This is how life becomes nothing and disappears. Automatization eats things, clothes, furniture, your wife, and the fear of war. 'If the whole complex life of many people is lived unconsciously, it is as if this life had never been.' And so this thing we call art exists in order to restore the sensation of life, in order to make us feel things, in order to make a stone stony. The goal of art is to create the sensation of seeing, and not merely

recognizing, things; the device of art is the 'enstrangement' of things and the complication of the form, which increases the duration and complexity of perception, as the process of perception is, in art, an end in itself and must be prolonged. Art is the means to live through the making of a thing; what has been made does not matter in art.[23]

Life disappears in the face of routinisation and familiarisation – but not in a generic but a specific way. The condition of coloniality had become a metaphysical truth for much of the colonised world. They had to take it. They could not leave it except by picking up a gun and shooting back. But there was also the necessity of picking up the pen and thinking themselves back into their historical agency. Europe was there and we, the world, were here, and there was a Hegelian determinism to this automated disappearance of the colonial person. Al-e Ahmad's art was not in his fiction, or his essays, his travelogues, or translations. His art was somewhere else, somewhere porous, amorphous, mobile. His art was in his prose, the open-ended fluidity of his diction, his oscillations between fact and fiction, home and abroad, compositions and translations, being a stranger at home and at home in foreign lands. He made the world familiar by making it look strange and in the process he de-alienated us from our colonially alienated selves, by making us live through our familiar foreigners, being born into our postcoloniality.

Al-e Ahmad wrote in a variety of genres. But whatever he wrote he did so with a singular voice, and a distinct signature. Al-e Ahmad's inimitable prose, the manner and mode of his signature diction was and remains the single most important pathway to the politics of a cosmopolis that was uniquely Persian and identifiably Muslim – and yet all of these in a decidedly worldly way. Prose as the politics of a Muslim cosmopolis in the work of Al-e Ahmad was the manner in which we were de-alienated towards our own historical agencies. Al-e Ahmad's Persian prose was urban, urbane, politically potent and stylistically elegant. When we spoke politics, we spoke it with Al-e Ahmad's Persian prose. That prose was politically liberating. That prose was his art, whatever he wrote.

The idea of Al-e Ahmad's prose as the politics of the Muslim cosmopolis, as I detail it here, is an inroad towards a post-Islamist liberation theology where the thesis/antithesis of colonial modernity, an alienating contradiction in terms, results in a liberation as their synthesis. This synthesis is the blue-print of the Muslim cosmopolis as I envision it here – the manner in which the post-Islamist Muslim writes the Muslim back into a postcolonial history. Al-e Ahmad had a 'voice', a signature to his prose – often called 'telegraphic' because it was rushing to brevity. The texture of that voice in his prose was a fusion of Sa'di and Naser Khosrow, poetic and philosophical at one and the same time, all coming down to the simplification of nineteenth-century prose, which was facilitated by the introduction of the printing machine, a sustained course of translations, all reaching fruition in the Constitutional prose of the early twentieth century, the lyricism of poets and songwriters like Sheida and Aref. Al-e Ahmad practised that prose to perfection. In and with that prose he de-automatised the condition of our coloniality.

The crucial necessity of a close formal attention to Al-e Ahmad's prose, to *how* he wrote, not just to *what* he wrote, remains the singular manner in which we should understand the formal significance of his prose in his politics. Not a single critical thinker who came after Al-e Ahmad would come anywhere near the elegant urbanity, the cosmopolitan character and the worldly disposition of Al-e Ahmad's prose. The substance of what he wrote – some good, some mediocre, some negligible – all fades into the towering presence of his prose. Ali Shari'ati's prose was a fusion between sociological pretensions and revelatory spontaneity, almost mystical, passion-ate and mobilising. But he was no Jalal Al-e Ahmad. Morteza Motahhari's prose was a diligent attempt at simulating a neutral political purpose des-perately hiding his seminarian antiquarianism. Khomeini's prose oscillated between thriving in seminarian jurisprudence, embedded mysticism and Shi'a philosophy on the one hand, and pedantic populism on the other. After the revolution, Abdolkarim Soroush's prose thrived on hiding his affected hermeneutics in a concocted classicism. Soroush successfully faked an anti-quarian prose style, full of artificial showmanship in rhyme and rhythm to such a perfect pitch that the mannerism of the prose concealed the vacuity of the matter he sought to articulate. To see this, we need to compare his prose with a number of contemporaries among the self-same cadre of 'reli-gious intellectuals' – Mohammad Mojtahed Shabestari, Mostafa Malekian, Mohsen Kadivar, Akbar Ganji, Saeed Hjjarian, Hamidreza Jalalpur and so forth. These are all sincere attempts at a cogent and purposeful prose. But they have all categorically missed the pitch of agile and street-smart urbanity of Al-e Ahmad's prose that 'restored sensation to life'.

If we trace Al-e Ahmad's prose back to his own genealogy from Nasser Khosrow and Sa'di to the nineteenth- and twentieth-century master prose stylists, then we can see what exactly he did to that prose. He electrified the classical Persian prose into his contemporary politics. The singular character of Al-e Ahmad's prose is its telegraphic speed and urgent brevity, its happy, healthy, angry, playful, dropping of complete sentences in favour of short phrases, punctual speed, running away with a fleeting thought before dropping it altogether and turning to another topic punctuated with the Persian equivalent of 'Etc./Elkh.' He wrote like a jazz musician improvising. This is the reason why the best theoretical instrument we can take with us when we enter the long, winding, exciting sojourn with Al-e Ahmad's prose is Shklovsky's theory of *enstrangement* picked up by Brecht in his theory of *Verfremdung*.[24] With the guidance and aid of Shklovsky's formalism we can allow the potent prose of Al-e Ahmad to tell us how to read it. On the colonial edges of European modernity, we needed a prose that could expose the strange fact of this, for us, 'colonial modernity' (at once enabling and disabling and therefore alienating us from ourselves) in order for it to enable us to read it anew, and not to assimilate it and us backward to what we thought we knew. The condition of coloniality had made us strange to ourselves, unaccustomed to the critical tenor of our own voices. We needed to make colonial modernity strange in return in order to begin to trust our own voices. The fact of our colonial modernity was a reality *sui generis* generated not in and of itself, but in and out of ourselves. Its origin, the origin of the bizarre fact of our colonial modernity, was outside us and yet we were instrumentally implicated in it. Like a factory it used the raw material of our very existence to build a world that was above and beyond us. We were the raw material, the cheap labour and the fetishised commodity of European colonial modernity. As colonial subjects we were part of that world and yet alienated from it. Al-e Ahmad's uncanny prose brought that alienation home and made it unhomely, and thus made *Unheimlichkeit Heimlich*, by mimicking its alienation in a spectacular act of enstrangement.

The normalcy of the prose of our historicality, the way all other critical or normative thinkers wrote, further exacerbated the condition of our coloniality. Straightforward opposition to colonialism, or celebration of it by comprador intellectuals, exacerbated the condition of that coloniality, for it was merely substantive not formal. No prose could come close to or even copycat Al-e Ahmad's mimicry of orality. This mimicry of modernity and its alienating speed needed a prose that went into the colonial modality we lived, inhabited and owned it and began to speak and think and read and write it from that vertiginous space. With that prose Al-e Ahmad coordinated our critical prose with the condition of colonial modernity we lived but we did not know how to read. To be sure, in the poetry of the Nimaic tradition and those who followed him, in the fiction of Sadegh Hedayat and his followers, in the drama of Gholamhossein Saedi and Bahram Beizai, or cinema of Amir Naderi we had other shapes and shades of the prose Al-e Ahmad had mastered and unleashed. But the aesthetic and poetics of all those other genres were the mitigating force of their de-alienating gestures. Al-e Ahmad on the other hand had no such mitigating force. First and foremost, he was a prose stylist, an essayist in everything he wrote, even or particularly his work of fiction and travelogues. Thus, he restored 'the sensation of seeing, and not merely recognising, things'.

The perspective on Al-e Ahmad's prose I am proposing here requires we read all of his writings anew, to read all his work together, as an *hadeseh* (event), and all of his work not just for what he says but for *how* he says it. Here I have Alain Badiou in mind, where in his *Being and Event* he considers *the event* as that which does not exist (yet), does not make sense (yet), based on the rules of the situation, so it does not exist, except as a negation of that which is. There is not a single moment of affected prose in Al-e Ahmed's entire oeuvre. To read him is like listening to John Coltrane improvising. He writes from *within* when he writes *about* the condition of coloniality. Many have noted Al-e Ahmad's singular prose, but no one has ever thought of reading not the purpose but the panache of that prose. This inability to read the prose of Al-e Ahmed was integral to the condition of our coloniality. We were all drawn to his prose but did not know why. This inability to read the surface of his prose is rooted in the habitual mysticism of our classical literature. That mysticism emerged from the imperial confidence of our past and was nestled in the midst of its adjacent philosophical, juridical, literary and poetic discourses. In the course of our encounter with Europe and in the condition of our coloniality we had lost the depth of that confidence, and in Al-e Ahmad's prose, staged to make sense of a senseless, self-alienated world, we were now ready to face the surface mystery of our existential nudity.

'The Fourteenth Epistle' of Paul the Apostle

All of these theoretical speculations I make here find their concrete evidence in one of the strangest, most exhilarating pieces Al-e Ahmad ever wrote, a bizarre text that has no antecedent or consequence in his entire oeuvre. It appears out of nowhere, and nothing follows it. Some have read it as an allegory referring to his contemporary comprador intellectuals. But formally there is something revolutionary about this strange prose, beyond any contemporary purpose it may have had.

In the second edition of Al-e Ahmad's *Zan-e Ziadi* (*Redundant Wife*) his readers were pleasantly surprised by the appearance of a rather strange 'Introduction' provocatively titled, '*Risalah Polus-e Rasul beh Kateban*' ('The Epistle of Paul the Apostle to Writers'). You read this 'Epistle' forward and backward and it has absolutely nothing to do with the content of the book it is there to 'Introduce'. It is an entirely independent piece that could have appeared anywhere else or perhaps even on its own. But more importantly, this is a fake Epistle. There is no such Epistle of Saint Paul. Al-e Ahmad just made it up and used this stratagem as a literary device to make a crucial point.[25] If you recall, when I discussed his *Sangi bar Guri* (*A Tombstone*) I noted his use of an opening counterfeit Biblical citation; well, this was him carrying that simulated quote home to a whole epistolary level.

So Al-e Ahmad mimicked a Biblical prose for writing this 'epistle'. This mimicry in and of itself is crucial here for 'art as device' is precisely when art becomes instrumental in defamiliarising the facts by reading them with a jarring, strange and entirely mismatched and asymmetric prose. But let's first start with what the epistle actually says.

We might read Al-e Ahmad's '*Risalah Polus-e Rasul beh Kateban*', as others have, as his literary manifesto. The 'Epistle' appears 'as an Introduction' in the second edition of *The Redundant Wife*, while it has absolutely nothing to do with that collection of short stories, yet another disorienting gesture, and then begins by saying that there is a 'fourteenth epistle' of Saint Paul in addition to the thirteen canonical Pauline epistles in the New Testament.[26]

So how does he know about this hitherto unknown epistle? Al-e Ahmad tells us he has chanced upon this epistle through a Nestorian priest he knows. He is fully aware of the canonical thirteen epistles in the New Testament traditionally attributed to Paul the Apostle: *Romans, 1 Corinthians, 2 Corinthians, Philemon, Galatians, Philippians, 1 Thessalonians, 2 Thessalonians, Ephesians, Colossians, 1 Timothy, 2 Timothy* and *Titus*. Al-e Ahmad, now faking a pseudoscientific prose, even knows that there is a fourteenth Epistle called 'the Hebrews' that scholars do not believe to be authentic, but he uses that example as an indication that this particular epistle he has 'discovered' is also Paul's! Al-e Ahmad then speculates that it has been a conspiracy of the church fathers to have suppressed this epistle as they have the Gospel of Saint Barnabas, after which he proceeds to produce a Persian translation from the original Syriac which translation again he emphasises was done with the help of that Nestorian priest friend of his. This whole production, done with a straight face, as it were, mimicking a scholarly prose stages the theatrics of proceeding apace to 'translate' this 'Fourteenth Pauline Epistle'.

This is not just a fake epistle; this is ingenious literary craftmanship. We start reading the epistle with a sense of wonder, being made privy to a recent scholarly 'discovery' right in the beginning of a collection of short stories. The *Verfremdungseffekt* sucks in the reader and the writer and the text into a vortex where we escape reality and start seeing it through a liberating prose. We are in a twilight zone. Nothing is what it seems to be.

The epistle that follows has four chapters and each chapter has between 30 to 34 verses. So, what does this epistle tell us? 'This is the Epistle of Paul the Apostle, the Servant of our Father who is in heavens, to writers . . . to writers, reciters, copyists' scribes, secretaries, scholars, chroniclers, panegyrists, gibberish masters, historians, translators, modernists, traditionalists.' The rest of the first chapter is a praise of 'the Word' and how the word is the cause of imprisonment and crucifixion. Generation after generation words were put into books and books were written by historians at the service of power and distorting the truth while people were suffering, and their heroes were slaughtered. This is the first chapter (33 verses). We don't believe what we are reading. But we are reading, and what we are reading in a strange way makes sense.

The Word is then divided between East and West, and the writer was in jail in the West, but the light was rising from the East. The Word in the

East was old but unitary while the Word from the West was young and fragmented; this is the second chapter (30 verses). Then comes the third chapter
(34 verses), in which we read:

> So, who is the writer, and who is the poet, and who is the collector, and
> who is the one who writes the Word? Except for the inheritor of he who suf-
> fered in jail and did not deny the Word, and he who wrote the Word with
> his toes upon a pebble, and swore by it . . . Do not look into what others
> expect from you, look into what the heart asks from you . . . Beware, never
> pollute the Word with lies for you have sullied your own soul, beware, do
> not use the Word to spread hatred but love.[27]

Keep in mind this is a Shi'a Muslim putting these apocryphal words in
the mouth or on the pen of a Christian apostle. Why opt for a Christian
apostle, why not a Muslim saint, a Jewish prophet, a Hindu guru – you might
wonder? The answer is not religious but literary. Al-e Ahmad likes and invests
and thrives upon the existing translation prose of the Holy Bible. He mimics
and adapts it with uncanny power, feigning an amazing authenticity. He
preaches in this prose, like a priest from a pulpit, like a Christian apostle, and
in that prose, he praises the sanctity of the pen, the glory of the Word, the
sacred duties of a writer. And then in the fourth chapter (30 verses) we read:

> Your Word Oh Writer is like a flower, when it blossoms it smells beautiful
> and pleases the heart, and when it dies it scatters hundreds of seeds . . .
> Beware not to sell the Word for bread, or to put the soul in the service of
> the body, at no price, even the Treasure of Qarun, do not get yourself sold
> to another man, if you must sell the labour of your hand but the pen never,
> even your body do sell, but the Word never . . . Oh, writer give the good
> tiding of beauty, of goodness, of brotherhood, and of health, in the words
> be a solace to those who are mourning, a supporter of the weak, like a sword
> to the tyrant.[28]

This is a manifesto, a declaration, a 'sermon from the mount'. Through
this sudden moment of creative ingenuity coming as if out of nowhere,
Al-e Ahmad performed a literary manifesto where he owned a Christian
prose in his perfectly Muslim politics, thus making the foreign familiarity
of Christianity find a Muslim home via a Persian prose that now suddenly

performed an act of *enstrangement*. This decontextualising of Christianity and rendering of its sacred prose sensible in a Muslim prose suddenly allows the point of his politics of writing, a denunciation of comprador intellectuals, to find a homely habitat. By de-alienating a Christian diction in a Muslim habitat, Al-e Ahmad revived the Persian prose and restored in it a potent political contemporaneity.

Towards a Transcontinental Critical Theory

Al-e Ahmad's 'The Epistle of Paul the Apostle to Writers' is the culmination of his entire literary and intellectual career as a committed intellectual that is best read through the Russian formalist theorist Shklovsky:

> This method of seeing things outside their context led Tolstoy to the enstrangement of rites and dogmas in his late works, replacing the habitual religious terms with their usual meanings – the result was strange, monstrous; many sincerely regarded it as sacrilegious and were deeply offended. But it was the same method that Tolstoy used elsewhere to experience and show his surroundings. Tolstoy's perception unraveled his own faith, driving him toward things he had been long unwilling to approach.[29]

Tolstoy and Al-e Ahmad could not possibly be further apart regarding their respective projects and lifework. But as Shklovsky puts it, 'the device of enstrangement is not particular to Tolstoy. I described it using material from Tolstoy for purely practical reasons, because this material is familiar to everyone.'[30] 'Everyone' for Shklovsky of course was not and is not 'everyone' for the rest of the world. But Shklovsky's theoretical preoccupations remain deeply related to my proposal here about how to read Al-e Ahmad beyond the substance and through the formal force of his work – 'replacing the habitual' as he did with the unexpected. In the case of Al-e Ahmad this *enstrangement* came in the form of detecting a rampant state of *az-khod-biganegi* (self-alienation) that needed to be confronted and challenged in terms equally strange, unusual, unrepresented and uncertain. This *khod* (*self*) was not any metaphysical certainty for Al-e Ahmad, hidden somewhere to be retrieved. It was a historical agency incubated in a state of flux, of coming to terms with the world, but not 'the Western world', precisely the opposite, the world that accommodated agencies for the 'non-West' for 'the other than the West'.

To detect and articulate that world required staging the ability of a prose to be at once familiar but uncanny, foreign but homely in its registers. No one else commanded such versatility with a prose that made sense of a strangely senseless, self-alienated, estranged world. He both made the world sensible and turned it uniquely Persian in its diction, Muslim in its *weltanschauung*.

If we come to Al-e Ahmad with that lens of detecting his de-alienating prose, then we come to the threshold of my main proposal in this book, which has been for us to retrieve that world and reconsider Al-e Ahmad anew and re-examine his life and legacy during the decades of the first half of the twentieth century until his death in 1969: because in those critical decades the kind of Islamic (not Islamist) critical reflections he represented was integral to a larger transcontinental thinking that had hit the right creative balance between the forces of the colonisers and the resistance of the colonised. That is the world we need to retrieve, the world of Jalal Al-e Ahmad, Gamal Abdel Nasser, Frantz Fanon, Aimé Césaire, Léopold Sédar Senghor, Ernesto Che Guevara, Malcom X, James Baldwin, C. L. R. James and Fr Gustavo Gutiérrez, amongst others. That world and the critical thinking it had occasioned, enabled and delivered was the functional equivalent of the post-Holocaust environment that Theodor Adorno, Max Horkheimer, Herbert Marcuse and Hannah Arendt best represented. I therefore propose a structural affinity between these two worlds, one post-Holocaust, the other postcolonial, with the Holocaust and the colonial savageries of Europe on similar planes of affinities as traumas caused by European capitalist modernity.

In *The End of Progress: Decolonizing the Normative Foundations of Critical Theory* (2015), Amy Allen has brought to the attention of her readers how the central ideas of Eurocentric Reason and Progress have been meaningless for the colonially ravaged world.[31] She takes the legacy of the Frankfurt School to task, for in figures like Jürgen Habermas, Axel Honneth and Rainer Forst we still read such white mythologies. The task at hand, as Amy Allen demonstrates beautifully, is not to dispense with Critical Theory altogether, but to expand its logic to include the postcolonial world. Amy Allen's project is necessary but not sufficient. In a popular course I have been teaching at Columbia, *Critical Theory: A Global Perspective*, for years I have articulated a similar theme but from a different angle, for I trace the power of Adorno et al. not to the post-Soviet Marxist crisis but to the trauma of the Holocaust as best evident in the masterpiece document *The Dialectic of Enlightenment* (1944–7). That trauma was intensely productive in critical thinking for Adorno and Max Horkheimer and their colleagues, but they were entirely ignorant and decidedly oblivious to their non-European counterparts. The task is to begin a crucial conversation between these two modes of critical thinking stemming from the same terror of European colonial modernity – one internal to its imaginative geography, one external (a theme I will pick up in the next chapter as I turn to Al-e Ahmad's internal and external travels). That period embraced Walter Benjamin and Al-e Ahmad together, and that period I believe is the single most important phase of postcolonial thinking of our age, decidedly more important than the single-sided Islamism, socialism or nationalism put together. Think of Critical Theory and all its robust heritage writ large globally, with Al-e Ahmad as a key Muslim voice now added to its canon. That is the single most important reason for recalling the life and legacy of Al-e Ahmad as we move to think them through a post-Islamist liberation theology.

Notes

1. Jalal Al-e Ahmad, *Nun wa al-Qalam* (*By the Pen*) (Tehran: Gahbod Publishers, 1961/2004): 15. There is an excellent English translation of this novella. See Jalal Al-e Ahmad, *By the Pen*, translated by M. R. Ghanoonparvar (Austin, TX: University of Texas Press, 1989). As in all other cases I use the original Persian of all Al-e Ahmad's work and do my own translations.

2. See Hamid Dabashi, *Being a Muslim in the World* (New York: Palgrave MacMillan, 2013).

3. See Roland Barthes, 'The Death of the Author', in *Image Music, Text. Essays*, selected and translated by Stephen Heath (New York: Fontana Press, 1977): 142–8.

4. Ibid: 145.

5. Ibid: 146.

6. Jürgen Habermas, *Postmetaphysical Thinking: Philosophical Essays* (Cambridge, MA: The MIT Press, 1994): 9.

7. For one such act of de-mystification see my most recent book, *Europe and its Shadows: Coloniality after Empire* (London: Pluto, 2019).

8. Ajay Chaudhary's dissertation is not published in book form yet. Here is the

full citation of its original submission as his doctoral dissertation: Ajay Singh Chaudhary, 'Religions of Doubt: Religion, Critique, and Modernity in Jalal Al-e Ahmad and Walter Benjamin' (Submitted in partial fulfillment of the requirements for the degree of Doctor of Philosophy in the Graduate School of the Arts and Sciences, Columbia University, 2013). Like all other works of scholarship, Chaudhary's dissertation had benefited from other members of his dissertation committee, my Columbia colleagues Sudipta Kaviraj, Wayne Proudfoot, Andreas Huyssen and Timothy Mitchell. Chaudhary also worked closely with my other colleagues at Columbia, Marc Nichanian and Gil Anidjar. From outside Columbia, Chaudhary worked with Susan Buck-Morss, Diane Rubenstein, Jane Marie-Law, Shawkat Toorawa, Deborah Starr and Nigel Dodd. All these colleagues share the credit for guiding Chaudhary's ground-breaking doctoral work at Columbia.

9. The scene is available online and can be seen here: https://www.youtube.com/watch?v=GLeDdzGUTq0.

10. Karl Marx, *Economic & Philosophic Manuscripts of 1844*, translated by Martin Milligan (Moscow: Progress Publishers, 1959). Electronic version available online here: https://www.marxists.org/archive/marx/works/1844/manuscripts/preface.htm.

11. W. E. B. Du Bois: *Writings: The Suppression of the African Slave-Trade / The Souls of Black Folk / Dusk of Dawn / Essays and Articles* (Washington, DC: Library of America, 1987): 364.

12. Walter Benjamin, 'The Work of Art in the Age of Mechanical Reproduction', in *Illuminations: Essays and Reflections*, edited by Hannah Arendt, preface by Leon Wieseltier, translated by Harry Zohn (New York: Schocken Books, 1968): 242.

13. Jalal Al-e Ahmad, *Did-Bazdid* (*Paying Visits*) (Tehran: Amir kabir, 1970): 27–35.

14. Jalal Al-e Ahmad, *Az Ranji keh Mibarim* (*Our Suffering*) (Tehran: Amir Kabir, 1978): 49–56.

15. Jalal Al-e Ahmad, *Zan-e Ziadi* (*Redundant Wife*) (Tehran: Amir Kabir, 1371/1992): 22.

16. There are excellent critical studies of the position of female characters in Al-e Ahmad's fiction, studies that rarely make it to the bibliographical references of expat scholars working in English. For an example see an excellent essay, Simin Kazemi and Abd al-Reza Navvah, '*Barresi-ye Klisheh-ha-ye Jensiyyati dar Asar-e Dastani Jalal Al-e Ahmad*' ('An investigation of Gender Clichés in Al-e Ahmad's Fiction') (*Jame'eh Shenasi Honar va Adabiyat*, vol. 6, no. 1, Spring and Summer

1393/2014): 43–63. Available online here: https://jsal.ut.ac.ir/article_53609. html. I am grateful to my research Assistant Laila Hisham Fouad for her tireless work procuring me these sources.

17. Jalal Al-e Ahmad, *Modir Madreseh* (*The School Principal*) (Tehran: Parastu Publishers, 1345/1966): 170.

18. Jalal Al-e Ahmad, *Nun w al-Qalam* (*By the Pen*) (Tehran: Gahbod, 1383): 21–2.

19. For an excellent essay on this book in Persian see Elmira Dadvar, 'Barresi va Tahlil-e Roman-e Nefrin Zamin-e Al-e Ahmad' ('An Examination and Analysis of the Novel 'Curse of the Earth' of Al-e Ahmad'), *Nashriyyeh-e Daneshkadeh Adabiyat va Olum-e Ensani-e Tabriz University*, no. 190, 1383).

20. For a discussion of one such story, 'The Cow', turned into a masterpiece of Iranian cinema, see my *Masters and Masterpieces of Iranian Cinema* (Washington, DC: Mage Publications, 2007): 107–34.

21. Walter Benjamin, '*The Storyteller: Reflections on the Works of Nikolai Leskov*', in *Illuminations* (Op. Cit.): 84.

22. Ibid: 87.

23. See Viktor Shklovsky, 'Art as Device', translated and introduced by Alexandra Berlina (*Poetics Today*, vol. 36, no. 3, September, 2015): 162. Available online here: https://warwick.ac.uk/fac/arts/english/currentstudents/undergraduate/mo dules/fulllist/first/en122/lecturelist2017-18/art_as_device_2015.pdf.

24. For a thorough investigation of these links see Douglas Robinson, *Estrangement and the Somatics of Literature: Tolstoy, Shklovsky, Brecht* (Baltimore: Johns Hopkins University Press, 2008).

25. It is noteworthy that just one generation after Al-e Ahmad, literary historians in Iran had to write and publish detailed scholarly articles arguing that this 'Epistle' was fake and just a literary device he had used to make a point. A fact that my generation had taken for granted. See Mohammad Reza Movahhedi, 'Barresi-ye 'Nameh Polus Rasul beh Kateban' ('A Consideration of Saint Paul's Epistle to Writers (A Manifesto of Jalal Al-e Ahmad)') (*Fasl-nameh-ye Elmi-Pazhuheshi 'Pazhuhesh Zaban va Adabiyat Farsi'*, vol. 22: Fall 1390/2011): 95–112. In this article we read as prominent a major revolutionary figure as Seyyed Mahmoud Taleqani, who was even related to Al-e Ahmad, in his Qur'anic commentaries had failed to understand the fake nature of this Epistle and cites it as evidence of 'the Gospel of Barnabas!'

26. See Jalal Al-e Ahmad, *Zan-e Ziadi* (*Redundant Wife*): 11–21.

27. Ibid: 19–20.

28. Ibid: 21.
29. Ibid: 167.
30. Ibid: 167.
31. See Amy Allen, *The End of Progress: Decolonizing the Normative Foundations of Critical Theory* (New York: Columbia University Press, 2015).

7

Travelling In and Out of a Homeland

The roof of the heavens was over us, the stars were so close, and the sky you could almost touch, and the Scorpios were vividly visible ahead of us. The wind was howling. We were driving 80–100 kilometres per hour, the speed tossing and turning us about. I was responsible for looking after my uncle, who kept falling asleep and his head could have banged into the back of the front seat. I have never been as awake as I was that night, and so aware of sheer nothingness. Under the dome of that sky and that eternity, I kept reciting every single poem I knew by heart, just whispering them to myself. As closely as I knew how I stared into myself until dawn, and I realised I was just a speck of dust (*Khasi*) having come to the appointed desert (*Miqat*) not a person (*Kasi*) to a meeting place (*Mi'ad*), and there and then I realised that Time was now the Eternity, that is to say the ocean of Time, and *Miqat* was anywhere and anytime, and I was alone with myself, for *Mi'ad* is the place where you meet with someone else, but *Miqat* is the time of that same encounter though just with your own 'self'. Then I realised how beautifully did that Zindiq of Mihaneh'i or Bastami put it when he said to a pilgrim to Mecca at the gate of Nishabur: 'Give me your money and circumambulate around me and go back home.' There and then I realised travelling is just a means of getting to know 'your self', to measure yourself against the scale of different climes, in the midst of events and encounters and people, to figure out its contours, to see how limited it is, how insignificant, how absolutely nothing![1]

Jalal Al-e Ahmad, *Khasi dar Miqat (Dust in the Desert)* (1964)

There are two Persian terms (borrowed and slightly modified from Arabic) that are interrelated, they are binaries, they go together – *Safar* and *Hazar*. *Safar* means travelling, to be away on a journey, and *Hazar* means to be at home, or present. *Safar* is mobile, agile, transitory, *Hazar* is stationary, sedate, secure. *Hazar* is safe, *Safar* is fraught with danger. In *Hazar* one is protected, in *Safar* one is exposed. When we look at the etymological and textual references to these two interrelated terms, say in Dehkhoda's authoritative dictionary, we realise that *Hazar* also means city and urbanity and therefore to be in a city, your own city or hometown, where you are at home, say New York for me right now, and *Safar* means exactly the opposite of that, where you are not at home, you are in effect in wilderness, exposed, an alien. Dehkhoda brings examples from the poetry of Farrokhi Sistani (980–1038) that identify *Hazar* with a mountain, and *Safar* with the wind. *Safar* is exciting, *Hazar* is reassuring.

In the two terms *Safar* and *Hazar* we hear the echoes of the two Freudian ideas of the *Unheimlich* and *Heimlich*, unhomely and homely, strange and familiar, uncanny and common. *Safar* is like *Unheimlich*, *Hazar* is like *Heimlich*. The 'uncanny', the English translation used for the Freudian *Unheimlich*, means strangely familiar, meaning familiar but in a strange way, that would be our experience when we are in *Safar*, as opposed to 'homely' meaning familiar in a comforting way, which is the way we are, and things are, when we are in *Hazar*. As Freud argued in his seminal essay, '*Das Unheimliche*' ('The Uncanny') (1919), the uncanny is when the strangeness is detected in the ordinary, or we might reverse it and say when the familiar is made foreign. The central argument of Freud remains crucial to understanding how the dialectic between the homely and the unhomely works. Here is a crucial passage from Freud's essay:

> Among its different shades of meaning the word *heimlich* exhibits one which is identical with its opposite, *unheimlich*. What is *heimlich* thus comes to be *unheimlich* ... In general, we are reminded that the word *heimlich* is not unambiguous, but belongs to two sets of ideas, which, without being contradictory, are yet very different: on the one hand it means what is familiar and agreeable, and on the other, what is concealed and kept out of sight ... we notice that Schelling says something which throws quite a

new light on the concept of the *unheimlich*, for which we were certainly not prepared. According to him, everything is *unheimlich* that ought to have remained secret and hidden but has come to light.[2]

I wish to extend Freud's psychoanalytic reading of the two terms and propose *Heimlich* as 'homely' and therefore for a person to be at *Hazar*, to be at home, while *Unheimlich* is to be 'away from home' and therefore unfamiliar with things as in *Safar*, while travelling. There is a dialectic of reciprocity at work here – between travelling and being at home. When we combine *Hazar* and *Safar*, *Heimlich* and *Unheimlich*, the foreign becomes familiar, while the familiar foreign, both in a disconcerting, alerting way. The traveller abroad sees familiar things in an unfamiliar way, for there and then 'everything is *unheimlich* that ought to have remained secret and hidden but has come to light'. The traveller now sees things hitherto imagined in a foreign domain. The foreign familiarity of things to the travellers begins to render familiar things foreign. As the alien becomes de-alienated, the knowing subject overcomes the alienated de-subjection of who and what the person is. This is where Freud leads to Shklovsky and Brecht, where the interface between *Unheimlich* and *Heimlich*, or *Safar* and *Hazar* as I propose, leads to the condition of *enstrangement*, of *ostranenie*, where and when things begin to sing and dance to a whole different tune.

'One Must Travel Much'

Al-e Ahmad was a tireless traveller. Throughout his life, from his childhood to his untimely death, he was relentless in discovering new horizons. The legacy of a monumental body of travel narratives by Persian, Indian and Arab travellers was in the deep and immediate background of his travels. He travelled in and he travelled out of his homeland – and the two sets of travels must be read together. He literally walked the vast expanse of his homeland and narratively reclaimed it for his prose – his brilliant, bold, matchless, powerful prose, the prose that defines not just a generation but the whole tenor of how to write politics, poetics, aesthetics and truth. While travelling he wrote letters to his wife, he wrote letters to his friends and in between he took extensive notes of what he had done and what he had thought, some of which he published as travelogues, some of which his literary executors later published posthumously. There are still things he wrote while travelling that have not been published.

Al-e Ahmad was acutely aware and particularly conscious of and attentive to the work of the Persian philosopher, poet and traveller Naser Khosrow Qubadiani (1004–88). Naser Khosrow's *Safarnameh* (*Travelogue*) is a classic text of an Ismaili poet and philosopher who starts from Khurasan and travels all the way to Egypt to promote the Ismaili cause. But other legendary Muslim travellers like Ibn Battuta (1304–68) or geographer Yaqut al-Hamawi (1179–1229) could not have been far from his mind. For Al-e Ahmad these Iranian and Muslim travellers were the model of his moral and intellectual curiosity about the world. Closer to his own time there were scores of travellers from Iran, India and the rest of the Arab and Muslim world travelling around the globe and leaving detailed accounts of their observations. In my *Reversing the Colonial Gaze: Persian Travelers Abroad* (2020) I have studied a constellation of these nineteenth-century travellers.[3] Al-e Ahmad thought of his travel narratives in and out of his homeland in this larger and longer context.

This so far as the prose of Al-e Ahmadi's progeny as a traveller is concerned and the physical contours of his travelling soul. But the soul of no Iranian is ever too far from the poetic pantheon of his literary heritage. Three particular poets are more important for our purposes here to map out the poetic imagination and the emotive universe of Al-e Ahmad's prose: one is the avid traveller Sa'di Shirazi (1210–92) and another the notoriously sedentary Hafez (1315–90). If Sa'di was constantly in *Safar*, Hafez was adamantly in *Hazar*. If we add Rumi (1207–73) to them too we will arrive at a more complete picture of the poetic disposition of Al-e Ahmad's travelling consciousness. Sa'di was all over the world, Hafez never left Shiraz, Rumi undertook one massive journey from Khurasan to Anatolia and never returned to his homeland and lived a life of exile, scarcely learned Turkish and produced one of the masterpieces of world mysticism, the *Masnavi*, in his mother tongue. The three iconic poets put together project the paramount wisdom of travelling not just through *Afagh* (horizons) but also through *Anfos* (souls). The combined dialectic of *Afagh* and *Anfos* is the same as that of *Safar* and *Hazar*, of *Heimlich* and *Unheimlich*, whereby the traveller is liberated from habitual consciousness.

Al-e Ahmad's travel writings have been habitually divided into two cat-egories: ethnographies and travelogues. I wish to collapse them all into one category of travelogues, albeit all his observations when he travels have a strong ethnographic dimension. More importantly I propose a structural and cognitive link between the journeys he took inside his homeland, where he is *at home*, and those he took outside his homeland, where he is *abroad*. Being abroad and being at home are the two loci of *Safar* and *Hazar*, of the *uncanny* and the *ordinary*, of the *unheimlich* and *heimlich*. This dialectic was the most provocative act of de-alienating the knowing subject and placing it at the helm of reproducing the colonial space Al-e Ahmad and all other anticolonial thinkers of his generation shared. His earliest travels were with his parents as a child in Iran. These travels had enduring impacts and reper-cussion during his adult life. Al-e Ahmad's travels abroad began in 1942 when he went to Iraq and toured that country extensively. His father wanted him to go there to continue with his seminary studies. During this trip he visited Basra, Khanaqin, Samara, Karbala, Najaf and Kazimayn. For about a decade between 1948 and 1958, Al-e Ahmad travelled extensively inside Iran, and much of it on foot. Travelling in and out of his homeland was therefore integral to his personal and professional vocation as a writer. He travelled to write. If you took his pen and paper from him it would be like clipping his wings. He could no longer fly. We know from his travel notes that, when flying abroad, as soon as he boarded and sat in his seat he took out his pen and notebook and began writing.

Let us first take a quick look at the outline and itinerary of his travels in and out of Iran – before we turn to read them more closely. Among the first records of Al-e Ahmad's travels inside Iran is in his book *Ourazan* (1954). Ourazan is the name of Al-e Ahmad's own family village on which he wrote this detailed monograph. Were it written in English and by an anthropologist from a European or US university, it would be considered an 'ethnography'. But neither was Al-e Ahmad an anthropologist and nor would he be call-ing *Ourazan* an 'ethnography'. Therefore assimilating Al-e Ahmad into the colonial discipline of anthropology would not be entirely complimentary to him. I therefore place it in the context of Al-e Ahmad's travels inside Iran. *Ourazan* gives us detailed information about the habitat of people living in this village, their costumes, their wedding and mourning ceremonies, cuisine, dialect, proverbs and so forth. Soon after the publication of this book, during the summer of 1957 Al-e Ahmad travelled to Europe with his wife Simin Daneshvar, where they mostly spent their time in France and the UK. There is no travelogue from this European trip, but extensive notes.[4] This trafficking between his trips in and out of his homeland remains a constant with Al-e Ahmad. *'Besyar Safar Bayad'* ('One must travel much'), Sa'di says in a famous poem, *'Ta Pokhteh shaved Khami'* ('Till a Novice becomes Wise').

His second such journey into the heart of his homeland was recorded in his *Tat-Neshin-ha-ye Blok-e Zahra* (*The Tati Residents of Zahra District*) (1958), which is a travelogue concerning a community of Tats in Qazvin province, speaking an old Iranian language (dialect) called Tati.[5] The travelogue at times reads like an ethnographic monograph, but again only if we give primacy of genre to Western European and North American practice of anthropology, which we should not, for the whole world does not look at itself through that dehumanising colonial gaze. *The Tati Residents of Zahra District* is similar to *Ourazan* in its ethnographic details about the habitat of people living in small villages. Next comes *Jazireh-ye Kharg, Dorr-e Yatim Khalij* (*The Island of Kharg: The Pearl of the Gulf*) (1960), which is yet another travelogue 'ethnography' on the island of Kharg in the Persian Gulf. Here his prose oscillates between the wealth that is coming out of oil exploration in this island and his deep concern for the local customs and ways of lives that are disappearing.

Al-e Ahmad made multiple journeys outside Iran, the first of which was to Iraq and the last to the United States. In 1962 he travelled for a second time to Europe for four months, and this time he was alone (this is when he had his extramarital affair). During this trip, he visited Germany, France, Switzerland, Holland and the UK. There was an unfinished account of his travels to Europe on which he was working when he passed away from a sudden stroke. A volume of his notes has since been published as *Safar-e Farang* (*The Europe Journey*) (1997). In the autumn of the same year, Al-e Ahmad and his wife travelled to Palestine at the official invitation of the Israeli government. The trip took two weeks. The travelogue of this short trip, *Safar beh Velayat-e Ezrael* (*Journey to the Abode of the Angel of Death*) (1964/1967/1984), appeared in piecemeal, initially in 1964, and then in 1967, and the complete text only posthumously in 1984. This is his most 'controversial' journey: the Islamists take serious exception to it; the Zionists love it. In the first half, published before 1967, he seems to admire Israel, in the second half, published after the 1967 War, he unleashed his unconditional anger against the European settler colony. There are major stylistic and substantive differences between these two parts.

In the spring of 1964 Al-e Ahmad performed his Hajj pilgrimage, his reflections of which seminal event in his life he subsequently published in his *Khasi dar Miqat* (*Dust in the Desert*) (1966), by far his most significant travelogue and arguably his most important book, far more cogent and powerful than his famous *Gharbzadegi*. In the summer of the same year Al-e Ahmad travelled to Russia to participate in an ethnography conference in Moscow, and subsequently published a short travelogue on this journey, part of a much larger text which was published posthumously by his brother as *Safar-e Rus* (*The Russian Journey*) (1989). In the summer of the next year, in 1965 Al-e Ahmad travelled to the US with a brief visit to Canada. The visit was at the official invitation of Harvard University through a programme Henry Kissinger had initiated. His reflections on this occasion were also posthumously published as *Safar-e Emrika* (*The American Journey*) (2000). It was towards the end of this trip that Al-e Ahmad thought he wished to write a book with the possible title of 'Four Ka'bahs' – meaning Mecca, Jerusalem, Moscow and New York. He did not live to do as he had hoped.

This is the outline of his lifetime travels from his childhood to his premature death from a stroke at the age of forty-five, the sustained course of a dialectic of *Safar* and *Hazar*, a constant oscillation between homely and *Heimlich* or uncanny and *Unheimlich*, where the foreign and the familiar conflate and interpolate into each other. Through this critical and creative dialectic, upon which he crafted his prose, the colonial construction of *space* ('Iran' is here and 'the West' there, homeland here and abroad there) is dialectically fused into a tertiary space. When Freud proposed, 'Among its different shades of meaning the word *heimlich* exhibits one which is identical with its opposite, *unheimlich*', the idea brings that dialectic from his psychoanalytic to our literary domains. 'What is *heimlich* thus comes to be *unheimlich*', he proposed, or when in *Safar*, as I propose here, *Hazar* is heightened and enabled, and when in *Hazar* things become malleable and transformative. Al-e Ahmad carried his Persian prose with him when he travelled abroad, and he

Figure 7.1 Jalal Al-e Ahmad, Sar-e Pol-e Zahab, 1962. (Photo courtesy of Ali Dehbashi, from the *Bokhara Magazine* archive) His travels, mostly on foot, throughout Iran were as definitive to Al-e Ahmad's restless soul as those he made around the world. He was at home in his homeland, at ease with people of all walks of life, sympathised with them, was able to tease them into conversations about their daily lives. He was no ordinary Tehran-based intellectual. One could never imagine him to be an armchair intellectual. The piece of paper in his hand, the only evidence of his difference from others in this picture, is the solitary sign of his preoccupation with recording his mind and his life for his posterity.

wrote incessantly while travelling, and he brought that 'abroad', that 'West', back with him in his prose and politics when he came home and looked at things with fresh eyes and heightened sensibilities. The traffic had created a *third space* for his prose, neither homely or unhomely, both *Heimlich* and *Unheimlich*, where his prose began to dismantle the colonial boundaries that has savagely occupied the global space.

'Till a Novice becomes Wise'

Let us now look closer at the domestic journeys of Al-e Ahmad and see what he did during those sojourns of 'self-discovery'. How are we to read Al-e

Ahmad's domestic travels, regular trips he took from his childhood to rural, tribal and urban communities and wrote on them in detail? He travelled much more extensively domestically than he published on such journeys, though according to his brother and literary executor Shams Al-e Ahmad there are extensive unpublished notes of such systematic travels. To be sure, he was not the only one who engaged in such travels. His two prominent contemporaries, the literary scholar Iraj Afshar (1925–2011) and the eminent dramatist Gholamhossein Saedi (1936–85), did the same. Afshar travelled extensively and was an avid observer of Iranian domestic landscape. Sa'edi was a close and dear friend of Al-e Ahmad, and something of a disciple, and in such works as *Ilakhchi* (1963), *Khiav Ya Meshkin Shahr* (1965) and *Ahl-e Hava* (1966) he has left behind a similar body of work. All of these books were highly popular monographs with wide readership. It would be tempting to call them amateurish if we were to consider the Eurocentric discipline of anthropology as our measure. But we need not necessarily do so. Allow me to explain.

Al-e Ahmad was not a trained anthropologist. He was not a trained any-thing. He lacked disciplinary patience to finish his doctoral work at Tehran University and left it before getting any degree, his wife's serious objections notwithstanding. But as a widely read, fluently literate and deeply culti-vated, though mostly self-taught, person he represented a particular brand of Iranian literati. They read widely and deeply mostly for pleasure and that kind of literary cultivation gave them a certain flair about the world. Al-e Ahmad's writings about rural, tribal or urban communities was not informed by any disciplinary preoccupations with ethnography, anthropology and so on, but of a sort and category that was usually called '*Moshahedat*' ('observa-tions'). This term *Moshahedat* is quite useful in understanding what this body of work represents. But in terms of the literary origins of these observations we must go back and look at the field of Muslim geographical literature that is equally crucial in understanding the genre of his writings habitually called 'ethnography'. This vast and variegated field has a deep and varied genre in Islamic intellectual history. When Sa'di in the thirteenth century says a person must much travel much, he then immediately adds '*Ta Pokhteh shaved Khami*' ('Till a novice becomes wise'). The two words I translate as 'novice' and 'wise' in Persian are '*kham*' and '*pokhteh*', literally 'raw' and 'cooked'.

Such metaphors are rooted in a vast and pervasive travelling consciousness. Someone rooted in that tradition, as Al-e Ahmad was, does not need the colonial discipline of anthropology to teach them how to travel, observe or record their observations.

What I have in mind are classical texts such as *Kitab al- Masalik wa al-Mamalik* (*The Book of Highways and Kingdoms*) (*c.* 847) by Ibn Khordadbeh (*c.* 820–912), one of the earliest books on geography. When we read this book, we see Ibn Khordadbeh widely interested in more than geography as we understand it today, in the strict sense of the term, and there are passages that today we might rather call 'ethnography' or 'anthropology'. Definitive to these texts are their fluent coverage of landscapes, peoples and cultures without much attention to where the border of one 'country' or 'kingdom' ends, and others begin. The same is true of Abu Zayd Ahmed ibn Sahl al-Balkhi (flourished in the late ninth century), a Persian polymath geographer, physician and scientist whose famous book *Suwar al-Aqali* (*Depictions of Regions*) includes both maps and 'ethnographic' descriptions of regions, including their customs and traditions. The same is true of al-Mas'udi (*c.* 896–956), another seminal historian and geographer whose masterpiece *Muruj al-Dhahab wa Ma'din al-Jawhar* (*The Meadows of Gold and Mines of Gems*) is a fusion of history and geography, including what today we might call sociological and anthropological observations and biographical dictionary. One can also add Ibn Rustah al-Isfahani, the tenth-century geographer whose *Al-A'laq al-Nafisah* (*Book of Precious Records*) is the classic of the same genre. The list of these sources is almost endless. Consider another masterpiece of the genre, Hamdullah Mowstofi's (1281–1349) *Nuzhat al-Qulub*, or before that Alberuni's (*c.* 973–1050) *India*. These texts and the content of their rich and powerful geographical imagination have left for posterity a veritable heritage of which Al-e Ahmad was fully aware and even boastful.

If we now turn to Jalal Al-e Ahmad's *Ourazan*, we see ourselves on familiar ground.[6] At the very outset he confesses he is not a dialectician, anthropologist or economist. He then disarmingly adds there is nothing particular about this village he is observing. He has selected it because it is the village of his ancestors, and he knows it well by virtue of the frequency of his visits. He then says in plain prose he does not know what to call this book:

a travelogue, an investigation on the customs and traditions of its inhabitants, a discussion of their dialect . . . because when I was preparing these
notes, I had no intention of publishing them. it was just an avocation
during my free time, and for others the same thing, if not entirely useless
then perhaps for their free time.[7]

From here he then proceeds to discuss the physical location of the village, the
sources of its irrigations, agricultural products, local habitats, regional histories, their notable families and an extensive discussion of ritual mourning.[8]
From there on things follow apace with chapters on their cuisine, customs,
wedding ceremonies, then a whole chapter on local dialectic, followed by a
description of their children's games, and so on. Is this ethnography? Good
for ethnography. Is it not disciplinary enough for a department of anthropology at a North American university? *Ma'a leish*, as the Arabs say, so be
it. The point is not to dismiss an entire discipline that is trying its best to
overcome its colonial legacy.[9] The point is rather to understand the terms of
Al-e Ahmad's engagements with his subject matters in a parlance that made
sense to him, and should to us.

   We see a similar pattern in his next monograph, *Tat-Neshin-ha-ye Blok-e
Zahra* (*The Tati Residents of Zahra District*).[10] The book starts with a beautiful
recollection of Al-e Ahmad's childhood, and the story of one of his sisters
being married off to a young seminarian in this area he is now introducing
to the world at large, and Al-e Ahmad's father frequently travelling to this
region to help his daughter and young son-in-law settle down. Al-e Ahmad
tells us the story of his sister and brother-in-law, their children and grand-
children being the main source of his information about the region.[11] There
is no feigning anthropological or ethnographic distance, fake objectivity, disciplinary methodology. It is exactly the opposite of Bronisław Malinowski's
anthropology and ethnography, full of racist hatred for his subjects; Al-e
Ahmad's text is full of love.[12] So here there is no 'fieldwork' over a hurried
summer and then rushing to write a doctoral dissertation and publish it with
a university press and hope to get tenured and train the next generation of
anthropologists. For about twenty years Al-e Ahmad went to see his sister
and her family at regular intervals. When he was there visiting his sister and
her family, he was reading books, translating books he liked, planting a little

garden, fishing from a *qanat*.[13] That is a whole different mise en scène from the one Malinowski and his progeny project – treating their 'subject' with racist contempt. Al-e Ahmad's prose is autobiographical, self-reflective, character and plot-driven. From there he moves onto writing about the location of the village, the influence of Tati and Turkish languages on each other, the landscape of the village, and people's livelihoods.[14] He writes about agricultural circumstances, *qanat*, vineyards, exchange of goods for goods, household and livelihood, dress and costumes, children's games, common proverbs and storytelling, linguistics and so on. No grand Eurocentric theory of our species emerges from these studies. Neither Freud nor Durkheim could rely on Al-e Ahmad's studies to speculate about our primitive origins. But the humanity of the people he was writing on were not compromised either.

In the Introduction to his last monograph of this kind, *Kharg, Dorr-e Yatim Khalij* (*The Island of Kharg: The Pearl of the Gulf*), he tells us how in 1958 he was invited by the infamous Oil Consortium (which was formed after the CIA coup of 1953) to visit Kharg Island, and how this was facilitated by his old friend Ebrahim Golestan. He tells us the book is based on both personal observations and investigation into historical records.[15] He spends the first chapter investigating the name of the island in Muslim and Roman sources, as well as ancient Persian documents. He then moves to a reflection on the coexistence of tribal life and oil discovery – the oddity that keeps his prose engaged for the rest of the book. From there he moves to write about people's habitat, pearl diving and the physical landscape. He even writes a chapter on the archaeology of the region. This is followed by a review of the place Kharg Island holds in Islamic history, coming forward all the way to the discovery of oil. He writes about local culture and folklore, about the regional fauna and flora. He then concludes with a few appendices of the literature he had researched on the Kharg Island, including those by major Orientalists like Ernst Herzfeld and Roman Ghirshman. The book as always with Al-e Ahmad reads like a compendium of researched and observed material awaiting a final draft. Through his experimentations he arrives at a particular prose that resembles ethnography. However, he is effectively searching for something in the dark which, as he often said himself, he does not quite know.

In a key passage in his seminal essay, 'Representing the Colonized: Anthropology's Interlocutors' (1989), Edward Said writes:

Like my own field of comparative literature, anthropology, however, is predicated on the fact of otherness and difference, on the lively, formative thrust supplied to it by what is strange or foreign, 'deep-down freshness' in Gerard Manley Hopkins' phrase . . . Yet the most striking thing about 'otherness' and 'difference' is, as with all general terms, how profoundly conditioned they are by their historical and worldly context. To speak about 'the other' in today's United States is, for the contemporary anthropologist here, quite a different thing than say for an Indian or Venezuelan anthropologist . . . To practice anthropology in the United States is therefore not just to be doing scholarly work investigating 'otherness' and 'difference' in a large country; it is to be discussing them in an enormously influential and powerful state whose global role is that of a superpower.[16]

This is good enough for 1989 when Edward Said wrote it but is no longer good enough for us in 2020 when we stand on his shoulders. It is not sufficient any more just to point the finger and accuse the whole morally and epistemically bankrupt discipline. The fact of *otherness* and *difference* become the domain of 'the strange and foreign' from a position of violent power, indeed, as Said points out here, for they are there to tickle the fancies of 'deep-down freshness' at the expense of human beings at the mercy of the anthropologists' camcorders and pens. For an Indian or Venezuelan anthropologist, or even more so for an Iranian, Arab or African thinking and writing about her and his homeland in a prose that does not fit anthropology, the condition is far more liberating than merely doing reverse anthropology. The question is not just to dismantle that fraudulent project that was coterminous with European imperialism. The task is to see how that Venezuelan or Indian or Iranian or Arab or African goes beyond the very discipline of anthropology and through a provocative prose of his or her own (where Said's quick reference to Comparative Literature and Anthropology meet); how they turn that sense of 'strange and foreign' upside down both to dismantle the European project and think of a superior, more emancipatory, more humane prose of our historicity. That is where the prose of *enstrangement* turns the European project of Anthropology or Comparative Literature upside down, as the Al-e Ahmads of the world *cannibalise* the Eurocentric discipline to write their 'not-ethnographies' and 'not-World Literatures'.[17]

This is not to thumb your nose at the colonising underbelly of anthropology. This is to turn the sense of *ostranenie* into an epistemological weapon by which you, with the 'deep-down freshness' of the naked natives, grab the clothed anthropologists by the throat and take them to the nearest ritual cooking of the tribe.

Sufi Nashavad Safi/A Mystic will not Become Pure

Let us now take a closer look at the four major trips Al-e Ahmad took outside Iran and on which he had planned to write a book he intended to call *Four Ka'bahs* by which he meant Mecca, Jerusalem, Russia and the US, with Europe 'somewhere in between', as he once put it.

Throughout his travels, as I have proposed, Al-e Ahmad was weaving 'the inside' and 'the outside', the homely and the uncanny, together, casting them onto an uncharted tertiary space which was neither and yet both. That kind of reading of Al-e Ahmad's travelogues requires looking at his travels not just for where he went and what he did but also in their allegorical potency that would give their author the idea of writing a book with a title like *Four Ka'bahs*. Such an allegorical space takes us for example to the seminal work of the Shi'a philosopher Mulla Sadra Shirazi (1571–1640) which is also called *Asfar Arba'ah* (*The Four Journeys*), or more fully *Hikmat al-Muta'aliyah fi al-Asfar al- 'Aqliyyah al-Arba'ah* (*The Transcendent Philosophy of the Four Journeys of the Intellect*), a major work in Islamic philosophy where the preeminent Shi'i philosopher seeks to bring together *Kalam* (speculative theology), *Ishraqi* (Illuminationist philosophy) and *Mashsha'i* (Peripatetic philosophy) in line with the doctrinal dogmas of Shi'ism. While teaching in Shiraz, Mulla Sadra was subject to severe harassment by the Shi'i juridical dogmatists, because of which he soon went into seclusion in the small village of Kahak, near Qom where he worked on his magnum opus.[18] He lived in that seclusion for about five years, before emerging to resume his life between Qom and Isfahan and Shiraz. The four journeys Mulla Sadra theorises in his transcendental theosophy consist of (1) the journey from *Khalq* (created beings) to *Haq* (truth), (2) From *Haq* (truth) to *Haq* (truth) with *Haq* (truth), (3) from the *Haq* (truth) back to *Khalq* (created beings) with *Haq* (truth), and finally (4) from *Khalq* (created beings) to the *Khalq* (created beings) though this time with the *Haq* (truth). The oscillation between *solitude* and *society* evident in Mulla Sadra's philosophy and life is where his *Asfar Arba'ah* could very well have acted as a metaphor for Al-e Ahmad's idea of writing a book on *Four Ka'bahs*.

Be that as it may, Al-e Ahmad may or may not have been conscious of this seminal philosophical work in Shi'ism when he thought he should write a book with the title of *Four Ka'bahs*. More probably, however, he was conscious and aware of a major poem of his contemporary Mehdi Akhavan Sales (1929–90), whom he knew and admired, in which the metaphor of a journey becomes definitive to one's pursuit of (political) truth. Akhavan's poem, called '*Chavoshi*' ('Harbinger's Song'), begins this way:

Beh San-e Rahnavardani keh dar Afsaneh ha guyand . . .

Just like those travellers
We read about in mythologies:
Carrying their backpack on their shoulders,
Holding a bamboo cane in hand,
Now talkative then quiet,
Walking in their misty mythic roads:
We too begin our journey –

Three paths are open ahead of us:
Upon a stone carved their description –
The like of which you will never read anywhere else:

The first is the path of success, comfort and joy
Yes, a bit mixed with dishonour
But heading towards urbanity, greenery and prosperity –

The Second is the path of half-fame, half-ignominy –
If you raise objection, much calamity, if you keep quiet, plenty of peace –

The Third the path of no-return no-end.

Here I feel so lonesome,
Any melody I hear out of tune –
Come let us collect our backpack
Walk upon the path of no-return and see
If the sky everywhere is really the same colour.[19]

Figure 7.2 Jalal Al-e Ahmad at a Harvard International Seminar, summer 1965. (Photo courtesy of Ali Dehbashi, from the *Bokhara Magazine* archive) Al-e Ahmad is sitting on the first step to the right and on the same step to the left sits their host Henry Kissinger. Kissinger's intentions for this seminar and those of Al-e Ahmad were radically different. Kissinger wanted to bring together leading intellectuals of 'the Third World' to Americanise and ingratiate them – while collecting intelligence from their moral and political preoccupations. For Al-e Ahmad the gathering led to precisely the opposite conclusions. He was neither grateful nor ingratiated. But the seminar nonetheless had a lasting influence on his global perception of imperial, colonial and anticolonial sentiments.

Whether Mulla Sadra's *Four Journeys* or Akhavan Sales' 'Chavoshi/Harbinger's Song', or any number of other philosophical or poetic metaphors of journey, Al-e Ahmad's fascinations with travelling was something more than mere sightseeing tourism. His tireless, homeless, soul was restless. He was looking for something, but he did not know exactly what – and in the beguiling anonymity of that search dwelled a direction of 'prayer', an orientation towards one object of desire or another. Al-e Ahmad's 'Four Ka'bahs' were all inside him. He was chasing after his own tail, with alterity the very quintessence of his identity.

Mecca

The *Four Ka'bahs* begins with the first and metonymic Ka'bah, the real Ka'bah, with Al-e Ahmad's Hajj pilgrimage. The single most important of these trips outside Iran for him was Mecca. It was like a metaphysical journey, an existential sojourn, transformative in its spiritual causes and consequences. But his Islamist and anti-Islamist readers have abused it, framing it as his 'returning to Islam'. He never left Islam to return to it. If a Muslim stops praying or performing other ritual duties, that does not make the person a non-Muslim. She or he seeks and performs her or his Islam elsewhere, differently. Al-e Ahmad was and remained a Muslim to the bone of his moral and intellectual imagination. His brief turn to the Tudeh Party or his attraction to existentialism were not despite, but through, his being a Muslim. His Hajj pilgrimage was through his Marxism and existentialism, not in spite of them. The Hajj experience, however, was deeply transformative in his moral disposition, of tapping into the inner sanctum of his certainties.

Al-e Ahmad's Hajj pilgrimage took place from Friday, 10 April 1964 to Sunday, 3 May 1964, and he kept a daily record of his deeds and thoughts, sometimes two or three entries a day. His first thoughts are on the ironies that French- and Armenian-speaking flight attendants are taking his group of 'would be Hajis' to perform their Hajj pilgrimage and then he catches himself and asks who he is to judge. He just prayed in the airport after he had abandoned praying for years. Much of his first day is spent flying from Tehran to Jedda in Saudi Arabia and he writes in detail about the flight, about their residence, about the quick tour of Jedda he took upon arrival. He is with his sister, two of his brothers-in-law and the maternal uncle of his father. Their Hajj group leader is a former devotee of his father's. He is completely in his element.[20]

In Medina Al-e Ahmad complains of shoulder pain and fears his coughing would soon start and then he says, 'be quiet' to himself, 'you have come to Hajj to forget yourself.'[21] He writes of the rampant poverty he witnesses. He walks around the city, meets people, strikes up conversations with them, makes observations about the signs he reads. Here in Medina Al-e Ahmad he is at his poignant and precise best. Very little is happening in the first few pages in terms of any moment of self-reflection or discovery. You read and read page after page of mostly trivial observations about mundane things, insightful but not haunting, and then suddenly you hit a gem when one day he wakes up to do his morning prayers:

> My highest regret all these times I have not been praying is having missed the early morning hours, its particular aroma, the gentility of its cold air, the quick pace of people. When you wake up before the sunrise it is like waking up before the day of creation, and to be a witness every day to this circadian recreation, from darkness to light, from sleep to awakening, from stillness to motion. Today I felt like greeting everyone, and I had no sense of hypocrisy when I stood up to pray, or felt fake when doing my ablution. Up until yesterday and the day before yesterday I could not believe it was me just like everyone else doing my ritual prayers. I could remember all the prayers, and all the short and long Qur'anic verses I had memorised since my childhood. But the Arabic phrases were now bearing heavily on my mind, and on my tongue, and how heavily! I could no longer just say them fast and get them over with. Those days I used to recite them like a senseless formula and be done with them. But this morning I was conscious of the heavy burden they put on one's consciousness. This morning when I said '*Ya Ayyuha al-Nabi/* Oh Thou the Prophet' suddenly I shivered. The Prophet's mausoleum was right in front of me, people were circumambulating it . . . suddenly I burst into tears and ran away from the Prophet's mosque.[22]

You turn the page and you see he has switched back to his usual reportage. He is severely critical of the Saudis and believes Mecca and Medina must be liberated from their rule and made into international cities for all Muslims.[23] When he becomes too critical, he stops himself and says he is just continuing with his *Gharbzadegi*. He is completely open and honest when he sees a young Arab woman beggar and is sexually aroused by the encounter.[24] In a footnote we learn he had read the French translation of Malcolm X's autobiography.[25] Throughout the travelogue he combines sightseeing and ritual performances, sociological observations and political commentaries. At one point he complains of the bristle on his foot and then he says he is writing gibberish and must stop doing so for his booklet is running out of blank pages.[26] At one point he complains of severe diarrhoea.[27] During the part of the pilgrimage known as Sa'i he has another of those moments of epiphany.[28]

He recalls the Persian poet and philosopher Nasser Khosrow when he prays around the actual Ka'bah.[29] Politics is never too far away from his mind. At one point he becomes entangled in a political discussion and accuses Nasser of populism, for being preoccupied with Israel instead of focusing on capitalism.[30] The travelogue sometimes reads like a guide for Hajj. At the end he confesses in this journey he has been looking for his brother, not God for God is everywhere.[31]

The Hajj pilgrimage is a transformative experience not because he rediscovered his Islam or did something drastic afterwards. There is no reason to believe he continued to pray, or fast, or stopped enjoying his vodka, or so on, after this pilgrimage. The experience was transformative because he took the whole of himself along when he went to Hajj, and he returned with the whole of himself reforming the ritual duties of a Muslim. He was a Marxist, existentialist Muslim when he went to Hajj and he returned with all of those purified in his convictions. The rest of his life carried that wholeness of his soul with him.

Jerusalem

The second Ka'bah, in a figurative sense, is Jerusalem, mirroring Mecca. This second one is not to be confused with Israel or 'the Israeli–Palestinian conflict', as the journalists put it. This is a reference to the fact that Jerusalem for a short period during the time of the Prophet was indeed the *qibla*, the direction of prayers, towards which early Muslims prayed, and also is, as Muslims believe, the site of the Prophet's ascendance to heaven, the *Mi'raj*. The idea as a result has nothing to do with the Zionist occupation of Jerusalem or Al-e Ahmad's visiting Palestine at the official invitation of the Israelis. It is in this historical context that we must understand Al-e Ahmad's trip and the subsequent travelogue that became far more important for Zionists and Islamists for two opposing sets of reasons – the Zionists loved it because in it they found a leading Muslim intellectual somewhat sympathetic to their conquest of Palestine, and the Islamists hated it precisely because it seemed to legitimise Israel. The two opposing readings made the travelogue more important than it is. The travelogue, and indeed the trip itself, is nowhere near his Hajj pilgrimage in its enduring significance. Moreover, as a volume, the text of his travelogue has a very choppy and haphazard history. But precisely for these reasons I need to spend more time on this text than it would otherwise deserve, clearing the confounding abuses of Islamists and Zionists around it. All the while, we must remember that it was towards the end of his US visit, in his mature life, that Al-e Ahmad had thought of putting a book together with the title of *Four Ka'bahs*. We must return to this central idea after we clear the path from so much abusive noise generated around this text.

Let's first start with the original Persian text as we have it today. The first issue is the playful title of the book, *Safar beh Velayat-e Ezrael* (*Journey to the Abode of the Angel of Death*) where Al-e Ahmad is playing with the English pronunciational of 'Israel' (with 'Ayn for Alif and Zeh for Sin) which in Persian becomes 'Ezrael', which is the angel of death. In the book itself he refers to 'Israel' in its Persian transliteration, with Alef and Sin but in the title, he plays with the English pronunciation of the word and thus provokes its colonial origin, while also invoking the fear of the angel of death. That he uses the term '*Velayat-e Ezrael*' sarcastically and in jest is also verified by Mostafa Zamani-Nia, the eminent scholar of Al-e Ahmad in Persian.[32] Al-e Ahmad also uses the word '*Velayat*' both to avoid calling Israel a country (*Keshvar*) and (intentionally or not) because it sounds like '*Ayalat*', which is the Persian word we use for the US states. *Velayat-e Ezrael* thus doubly places the Israeli settler colony under erasure and points to the British and American fore-grounding of the place, while associating it with death and destruction. Al-e Ahmad always uses the term '*Velayat*' sarcastically, or satirically: sometimes he refers to the village of his father's origin as *Velayat*, sometime refers to Iran as *Velayat*. It all depends on the context. This is a common satirical phrase, that I might refer to someone form Khuzestan as '*ham-Velayati*', meaning someone from my own province, or might refer to someone from Iran as '*ham-Velayati*' etc. This unmissable satirical aspect of the title alas is almost completely lost to the English language literature around the text.

This satirical title of the book assumes a more serious tone early in the book, however, when Al-e Ahmad gives his own explanation as to what he means by '*Velayat*'. He says he prefers to use the term '*Velayat*' because what the Israelis have built there is the extension of their Biblical prophetic tradition and not a state in the modern sense of Palestinians ruling over Palestine,[33] which means he has completely bought into the Zionist narrative and forgotten the colonial history of the region. The second reason he uses the term 'Velayat', he tells us, is that Israel is not an ordinary country, and he daydreams that it will be part of Asia with Tel Aviv and Tokyo facing each other and opposing Eurocentric *Gharbzadegi*. Today it is of course hard not to laugh at the sheer inanity of this argument, where Israel has always been the very garrison state for European and US militarism, including in 1957, a decade before 1967, when Al-e Ahmad was alive and well and knew how the UK and France had put their newly created settler colony to military use when invading Egypt to prevent the nationalisation of the Suez Canal. But mesmerised by the socialism of the *kibbutzim*, built on the stolen lands and broken backs of Palestinians, Al-e Ahmad could not see this and bought into the Zionist narrative of his hosts.

That brings us to the context and the substance of the book. Al-e Ahmad and his wife Simin Daneshvar spent two weeks in February 1963 as the official guests of the Israeli government, facilitated by an Israeli cultural attaché in Tehran named Zvi Rafiah, whose mission was to draw Iranian artists and literati to the settler colony. Al-e Ahmad goes there after four months in Europe and his wife joins him from Iran despite the fact that she is angry with him because of his affair with 'Hilda'. We know from their correspondence Al-e Ahmad makes quite a scene in Tel Aviv airport welcoming his wife to apologise to her. The trip as a result has an important personal and private aspect to it where the couple made up for Al-e Ahmad's indiscretions while travelling alone in Europe.

Be that as it may, the more political and public context of this trip is the way Iranian socialists were drawn to the putative socialist experiments of the Israeli *kibbutzim*, as in the case of the very positive impressions of Khalil Maleki, Al-e Ahmad's guru, who had just left the Tudeh Party and was deeply drawn to alternative socialist experiments away from Soviet examples. Khalil Malaki's legitimate criticism of the Soviets' imperialism and their Tudeh Party puppets in Iran had degenerated into a blind, ill-informed and astonishingly reactionary reading of European colonialism and its flowering into Zionism. Maleki, who also travelled to Israel and wrote glowingly of the settler colony, and other friends of Al-e Ahmad were drawn to the *kibbutzim* experience because of their legitimate disdain for Stalinism, and also by reading Zionist propaganda in a bookstore in downtown Tehran. Al-e Ahmad also mentions reading Arthur Koestler's *Thieves in the Night* (1946) as a keystone event. As a leading intellectual to whom Al-e Ahmad was drawn, Khalil Maleki was the main culprit of the Iranian socialists' attraction to Zionism.[34] Maleki also encouraged and arranged for a free roundtrip ticket for Daryoush Ashuri who also went to Israel and came back and became a zealous Zionist, and wrote gloriously about the settler colony without the slightest regard for what had happened to Palestinians during their Nakbah. This is one of the most shameful chapters in the history of Iranian socialist intellectuals, akin to the period of Black Zionism in the United States. For Al-e Ahmad and his wife going to Israel by official invitation is one thing, but categorically disregarding the catastrophe that had befallen the Palestinians is just morally corrupt and intellectually damning.[35]

In the body of the text itself, Al-e Ahmad swears that what he is about to write is not in gratitude for the Israelis having hosted him and wined and dined him and his wife.[36] He protests too much. Of course, he was ingratiated by the magic of a free roundtrip ticket and all other expenses covered. He and his wife lived frugally. While in the US, he incessantly complained of high expenses and of his poverty. His Israeli hosts knew this and took full advantage of it. Be that as it may, Al-e Ahmad is fully aware, he tells us, that 'the West' is giving Israel to the Zionists in exchange for the slaughter of Jews in World War II – again collapsing Zionism and Judaism together – and whitewashing the murder of six million human beings with the price tag of a settler colony as a garrison state for their colonial interests. His quick reference to Palestinians is astonishingly racist, that they have become accustomed to being '*Tofeili*' ('unwanted guests') of other Arab nations.[37] He then turns the edge of his criticism towards Arab leaders, which is a platitudinous nonsense – covering up his cowardly complicity with his hosts. Of course, Arab leaders are corrupt, but what does that have anything to with the plight of Palestinians who are the victims of such corruption? Such desperate attempts to justify his moral cowardice and political indifference actually exacerbate his compromised immoral position as a guest of a settler colony. Meanwhile, he does not shy away from blatant anti-Semitism and can easily speak of 'this Jewish self-victimisation' ('*Shahid-nama'i*').[38] He begins his visit with Yad Vashem and is deeply saddened by what it commemorates, but dismisses the rabbi presiding over the event as '*Rozeh-khan*', a derogatory reference to Shi'a mullahs' recitation of the sufferings of Imam

Hussein. He then turns into a self-righteous nationalist and speaks of Esther and Mordechai and such. The whole production is an embarrassment.

So, what are the causes of Al-e Ahmad's attraction to Israel? First, he tells us, is his attraction to an alternative to Soviet socialism. He then unleashes his anti-Arab sentiments because they call Iranians 'Ajam' (a derogatory term for non-Arabs). He then falls into his own racist anti-Arab sentiments calling Arabs 'rootless' and concludes: '. . . and I who have suffered much from these rootless Arabs am very happy to see Israel in the East'.[39] In short, a pair of roundtrip tickets and a couple of weeks of official Israeli hospitality turn him into the most repulsive anti-Arab Iranian nationalist with an occasional socialist quip here and there. The result is unreadable gibberish. The Israeli Hasbara got what they paid for and then some. The next chapter details his excitement about learning some basics of Israeli society, about the Ashkenazim, the Sephardic and the Sabras. He does on one occasion have a political discussion and tells his hosts they may have an ancient claim on this land but now they have seized it violently and are not willing to share the land, and that the Palestinians live in desperate conditions.[40] The depth of his historical ignorance while in Palestine is mind-boggling. Of course, Jews have a historical claim on Palestine. They have always had that claim and that right – and they will always have that privilege, to be able to live with their non-Jewish neighbours in peace in their ancestral homeland. But what has that to do with the anti-Semitic European project of settler colonial Zionism?

Soon after his return to Iran, Al-e Ahmad began giving lectures and publishing shorter versions of his travelogue, first in late 1963 in a Tehran University venue devoted to ethnography and run by his friend Ehsan Naraqi. The text of that report is almost entirely anthropological.[41] Soon after that talk he began to sketch out the outline of his book.[42] If this outline is to be trusted – and that is a big 'if' because we have all of this from his notoriously Islamist younger brother, who was only too eager to exonerate and endear his brother to the ruling Islamists – its tenth chapter has the title of 'Aghaz-e Yek Nefrat' ('the Beginning of a Hatred'), which is exactly the title Al-e Ahmad uses later, after the 1967 War, when in disguise of a 'letter from a friend' he writes against Israel. To be sure, the outline of this chapter, based on these notes, is very different from the content of the 'letter' Al-e Ahmad later published under that title. But if we were to trust Shams Al-e Ahmad, some three years before that later denunciation, and soon after his return from Israel, Al-e Ahmad had intended to write critically about the settler colony, even *before* he had published his favourable essay on them.

Late in the winter of 1963 Al-e Ahmad wrote and early in 1964 he published the first part of his love letter to Zionism, initially in a periodical called *Andisheh va Honar* that his long-time friend Nasser Vosouqi edited, which is the part that famously disappointed many of his admirers including the future leader of the Islamic Republic Ali Khamenei, who came to Tehran and objected to it. It is not until the Six-Day Arab–Israeli war in 1967, what the Palestinians call their *Naksah*,[43] that Al-e Ahmad published the second part of the travelogue but, again according to his highly unreliable brother, camouflaged it under the title '*Nameh Yek Dust Irani-ye Farang Neshasteh*' ('The Letter of an Iranian Friend Living in Europe'). Let us take a close look at that 'letter'.

What is now the fifth and final chapter of the final version of the volume, with the title of '*Aghaz-e Yek Nefrat*' ('Beginning of a Hatred'), represents a scathing criticism of Israel and was written after Al-e Ahmad had left Palestine and the June 1967 War. This chapter is written in the form of a letter Al-e Ahmad says he has received, not composed himself, from a friend who lives in Paris, to which he says he has added 'things', then he says the good parts are his friends and the gibberish (*part-o-pala*, his usual way of referring to his own work) is his.[44] The letter begins with a beautiful passage from a famous poem by Nima:

> Right now I think
> In the blood of my brothers –
> Unjustly lurching in blood
> Innocently rolling in blood –
> My steely heart is coloured
> Differently –

This is the letter/chapter where the following famous passage can be found:

> Because Nazism, this flowering achievement of European bourgeois civili-
> sation slaughtered six million poor Jews in concentration camps, today 2–3

million Palestinian Arabs of Palestine, Gaza and the West Bank are to be killed to protect the capital of Wall Street and Rothschild Bank, and just because European intellectuals were complacent with Hitler now Arabs have to pay back so that the people of Algeria, Syria, Egypt and Iraq don't have the illusion of fighting back against colonialism and try to close the Suez Canal to civilised nations.[45]

Is this the same author who said as an Iranian he was happy to see Israel in 'the East?' It does not make sense. Somebody, somehow, had admonished and educated Al-e Ahmad and corrected his delusional gibberish in the first part of his travelogue.

I was and I remain suspicious that these two parts are from the same pen, and perhaps the actual title of the piece – implying that someone else from Paris had written this to Al-e Ahmad – should be heeded. Could it be that Al-e Ahmad meant what he said, and that this was indeed a letter one of his many Iranian friends in Europe had written to him, which he had amended? This 'letter' first appeared independently in 1967 in a periodical called 'Donya-ye Jadid', edited by Sirus Tahbaz, and the issue was evidently soon collected and banned by the Shah's secret police. Blaming SAVAK for such atrocities is of course an easy charge, but the assertion that Al-e Ahmad had opted to call this piece 'a letter from a friend in Paris' by way of fooling SAVAK coming from Shams Al-e Ahmad makes it quite suspicious, for this is the man who also believes, against all evidence, that SAVAK killed his brother. There is every reason to believe that after Al-e Ahmad published his weak and wobbly piece following his trip to Israel it was not just Ayatollah Khamenei who objected to it, but also Iranian intellectuals living in Iran or abroad, who, knowing more about Israel than Al-e Ahmad did, wrote him this letter which he revised and published by way of restoring his credibility. So, the piece was published as a letter from a friend and Al-e Ahmad said he had added some notes to it. This 'chapter' as a result certainly has Al-e Ahmad's blessing and perhaps some editorial emendations, but the source of it indeed might be a friend from Paris educating Al-e Ahmad about the face of Zionism he had failed to see while being wined and dined by the Israelis in Tel Aviv, as he was trying to ingratiate and make up with his wife whom he had just betrayed. Whether indeed by a friend, or by himself, or by some combination of the two, this 'letter' that is now the final chapter of the book sets the record straight on what Al-e Ahmad thought of the Israeli settler colony.[46]

The troubled history of the publication of the original text of Al-e Ahmad's travelogue to Israel is exacerbated and further abused in the opposite direction in the publication of its English translation by its Zionist interpreters. There is an English translation of this text that subjects it to even more egregious abuse, this time in turning him into more of a Zionist than he actually was, before he radically changed his mind.[47] The manipulation of the original begins with the very title of the book, which is rendered into English as *The Israeli Republic*! This is an entirely flawed if not fraudulent translation. Al-e Ahmad never wrote a book with that title. The original title says neither a 'Republic' nor 'Israel'. If the attempt has been to make 'Israeli Republic' rhyme or resonate with 'Islamic Republic', then the silly joke is doubly fraudulent. The original says '*Safar beh Velayat-e Ezrael*' ('Journey to the Abode of the Angel of Death'). Where in the world is 'Israeli Republic' there? Al-e Ahmad says '*Velayat*' not 'republic', and Al-e Ahmad says '*Ezrael*' not 'Israel'. As already discussed, in the original title Al-e Ahmad plays with the English pronunciation of the word 'Israel' that sounds like '*Ezrael*' in Persian, and thus he writes it with an 'Ayn and not with an Alif, with a Zeh and not a Sin. In the body of the text, to be sure, he writes 'Israel' in Persian transliteration with Alef and Sin, but not so in the title, and that sarcastic twist, completely lost to the English translator, is crucial in our reading of the text.

Then we come to the crucial term '*Velayat*', which again is alas lost to the English translator of the text, who takes '*Velayat*' in the title for 'Republic' and then in his Introduction speaks of it as a sign of Al-e Ahmad using it as 'Guardianship' and therefore concludes that Al-e Ahmad had seen Israel as a model for Islamic states – an utterly bizarre, unfounded and outlandish reading of the text. Al-e Ahmad would be turning in his grave! 'He calls Israel a *Velayat*, a term describing a model state shepherded by clerical guardians,' the translator tells his readers.[48] But Ayatollah Khomeini's deeply controversial theory of '*Velayat-e faqih*' was not formulated until almost a decade later, the year after Al-e Ahmad had died in 1969. Was Al-e Ahmad a theorist of '*Velayat-e faqih*' *avant la lettre*? Evidently Zionists like to think that way, facts be damned. The translator is aware of this fact but wishes to pull a fast one to get around it.[49] So he opts for the entirely baseless speculation that the doctrine 'was circulating among the Ayatollah's inner circle, and the two men met briefly before Khomeini's exile in 1964'.[50] This whole argument betrays an astonishing ignorance of Shi'i clerical culture and who could or could not have been in Khomeini's inner circle – or else sheer charlatanism. Whoever else may have been, Al-e Ahmad was not among the inner circles of Khomeini. Yes, the two met briefly indeed but there is no indication, and it would be a wild stretch of manipulative imagination to assume, that they discussed '*Velayat-e faqih*', a theory which Khomeini did not articulate and publish until almost a decade later.[51] Let me also add here that as I showed in my *Theology of Discontent*, even figures like Morteza Motahhari, who as a close disciple of Khomeini could seriously be considered to be part of Khomeini's inner circle, had a far different conception of '*Velayat*' from Khomeini.

The translator proceeds to say 'Al-e Ahmadi's description of Israel as *Velayat* is "provocative and electrifying"',[52] which indeed it would have been if it were only true, and the poor man had in fact ever said anything remotely like that, but he did not. From there the translator just slips into wayward delusion: 'Al-e Ahmad's discussion of Israel as the ideal Islamic state makes one extreme of a book that also passes through the opposite passion and remains in motion, never coming to rest.'[53] The latter part of that sentence is of course complete nonsense, and in the first part he simply confuses Al-e Ahmad referring to the putative foundation of Israel on the Jewish prophetic tradition (in Al-e Ahmad's false estimation) with the Shi'i doctrine of '*Velayat-e faqih*'. In his very first page of the original Al-e Ahmad clearly says 'the Jewish rule over Palestine is a kind of *Velayat* and not a state. The rule of the new guardians (*Awliya*) of Bani-Israel on the Promised Land, and not the rule of Palestinians over Palestine.' That is not on the model of Khomeini's '*Velayat-e faqih*'. If anything, Al-e Ahmad is even hinting at the alternative to this false Zionist claim on Palestine vis-à-vis a normal Palestinian state, by Palestinians over their homeland. Al-e Ahmad even emphasises it is not fair to compare Abraham, David, or Moses with Ben Gurion or Moshe Dayan. This whole section is based on Al-e Ahmad's rather frivolous reading of the Hebrew Bible and not on Khomeini's highly suspect theory of '*Velayat-e faqih*'. Al-e Ahmad never ever thought of Israel as a model of the Islamic state. Even in his weakest moments early in his travelogue, Al-e Ahmad never for a second thought of Israel as anything other than a European colonial settlement but was, in his delusional moments, speculating to see if there was a silver lining to this factual cloud.

In his rush to take Al-e Ahmad's brief and lapsed moment of sympathy with Zionism to an extreme and make him turn Israel into a model of Islamic states, mirroring Shams Al-e Ahmad's rush to exonerate Al-e Ahmad's embarrassing *faux pas*, plus his limited and shaky command of Persian and Arabic languages and Shi'i doctrinal history, the English translator has here confused '*Velayat*' as a place with '*Velayat*' as position or political institution. In the title of the book Al-e Ahmad uses the term as a designation of a place, an abode, a land not as a reference to a person, a position or a political institution. This might be an entirely innocent mistake on part of the translator caused by limited command of Persian and Arabic.[54] The translator takes '*Velayat*' as in the case of '*Velayat-e faqih*', which we have indeed translated as 'the guardianship' or 'authority' of the Jurisconsult.[55] But the '*Velayat*' in '*Velayat-e Ezrael*' is not the same '*Velayat*' – not everything round is a walnut as we say in Persian. This '*Velayat*' is a designation of a place not a person. '*Velayat*' as in '*Velayat-e faqih*' is derived from '*Vali*' meaning (among other things) 'Guardian' and has nothing to do with '*Velayat*' as a place, meaning an abode, a land and so on. To the degree that Al-e Ahmad (falsely) sees Israel as a fulfilment of the Jewish prophetic tradition; there is not a shred of evidence he connects that playful speculation to the Shi'i doctrinal anomaly of '*Velayat-e faqih*', to which towering Shi'i authorities have taken serious exception.[56] Iran is today ruled by '*Velayat-e faqih*'. But the country is not called *Velayat-e Iran*.

In a bizarre but perfectly understandable way, both Islamists and Zionists are fully aware of their respectively illegitimate projects and they use any opportunity, in this case to abuse the poor Al-e Ahmad's weak and vulnerable text to justify their unjustifiable propositions. The reason I have spent so long dwelling upon this flawed and abusive English translation is to show how this exceptionally crude Zionist reading of the text exacerbates the Islamist abuse of Al-e Ahmad by this time actually suggesting that he was theorising '*Velayat-e faqih*' even before Khomeini did, and that he did so not just for all Muslim states to follow, but in fact for Israel too, as the very model of such theocracies!

Moscow

The third Ka'bah, again in a figurative sense, is Moscow, mirroring Mecca though in a political and normative way. In my chapter on Al-e Ahmad's essays I wrote briefly on AL-e Ahmad's trip to the (then) Soviet Union to participate in a conference on ethnography. A much fuller account of his travelogue to Soviet Union was published posthumously by his brother Shams Al-e Ahmad.[57] Based on his brother's detailed account, Al-e Ahmad travelled to Russia in 1964. The trip lasted a month from 7 Mordad 1343/29 July 1964 to 7 Shahrivar 1343/29 August 1964. The international ethnography congress was for a week in Moscow, but Al-e Ahmad spent a whole month travelling around Soviet Union. Al-e Ahmad was not a trained or disciplined ethnographer, and in fact he was deeply suspicious of the discipline and quite rightly so. He wonders himself why was he invited to this conference. But we know by now a number of his detailed 'ethnographic' studies of a small Iranian village which in this chapter I read as travelogues, had been published. He went to Russia in the summer of 1964, just a few months after his return from his Hajj pilgrimage in the same year, a couple of years after his European tour that brought him to Israel, and less than a year after that he travelled to the US, thus the temptation to write about 'Four Ka'bahs'.

The Russian travelogue begins with a beautiful poem from Rumi in his *Masnavi*:

> *Har Kabutar miparad dar Mazhabi* . . .
>
> Every pigeon flies in a direction,
> But this pigeon towards no-direction . . .
> We are neither domesticated birds nor wild birds
> The seeds that feed us are no-seeds.[58]

His restless soul neither domesticated nor wild, Al-e Ahmad begins his travelogue while he is still in Iran from Bandar Pahlavi (now Bandar Anzali) on Wednesday, 7 Morad 1343/29 July 1964, and from there he sails to Baku and from there flies to Moscow. Very early in his trip he shares his view of what anthropology as a discipline is:

The first anthropologists came with Alexander, then after Christianity, then after Islam. In other words, anthropology has always been in the camp of world conquerors – the best of them was Alexander, the worst of them the machine, in other words the very discipline of anthropology or ethnology has to do with world conquerors in need of knowing the people they wanted to rule. The same is the story with the Russians and this congress in Moscow.[59]

With such attitudes he wonders why in the world he has been invited to go to this congress.[60] He spends some time touring Baku, and he eventually reaches Moscow, where he immediately remembers Andre Gidé's *Retour de l'U.R.S.S.* (*Return from the U.S.S.R.*) (1936), which he had translated into Persian.[61] While in Moscow, he soon begins to suffer from a feverish reaction to the smallpox vaccine he had to receive in Baku.[62] He writes of an incident at Moscow University when his hosts ask if he has a PhD. They give him a registration card with the title 'Dr' on it. He crosses it out.[63] He sees an anthropologist from India but does not understand a word of his discipline which is physical anthropology. Instead he wants to learn about the Vedas from him, but the conversation proves useless. Throughout his travels, Al-e Ahmad suffers from his limited command of English and French and laments the fact that he is trapped inside Persian. While in Moscow he attends the conference, does a good amount of sightseeing, reflects on what he sees and does. He confesses he had to write his speech in English, but it turned out poorly for the did not have a solid command of English.[64] But he finds an American who in exchange for a good lunch corrects his English and types his paper for him! It is something of a fly-by-night operation, flying, as it were, by the seat of his pants, making it up as he moves on. He is out of his element, he is not a scholar, not a proper anthropologist, in fact severely critical of the discipline, except for an insatiable curiosity he has about the world around him.

At one point Al-e Ahmad objects to his hosts and wonders how it is they have fourteen anthropologists from Israel but only him from Iran, and no one from Iraq, Afghanistan or Turkey.[65] Despite the fact that he has limited English or French, and even less Russian, he enthusiastically participates in many sessions, and takes copious notes. He visits the Kremlin, writing about everything he observes.[66] He finally leaves Moscow and goes to Leningrad (St Petersburg) doing mostly sightseeing. He returns to Moscow on 16 August, then he flies back to Baku, where he visits the University of Azerbaijan.[67] On 20 August he leaves for Tashkent, where he attends a concert of Ravel's *Boléro* (1928), objecting to the clarinet player.[68] He finally goes to Samarkand for a quick visit, returns to Tashkent, flies back to Moscow, on his way back to Iran. He ultimately considers himself a wolf in the animal skinners' market, meaning he does not really belong to an ethnography conference, to whose very purpose he seriously objects.[69] The travelogue ends with a full report of the sessions of the conference. In a way this whole travelogue reads like an 'ethnography' of an ethnographic congress – perhaps the only redeeming factor in having been posthumously published.

There are no serious moments of introspection or critical thinking in this travelogue. It is fairly banal and even boring. The reason for that is very simple.

Figure 7.3 Jalal Al-e Ahmad, Simin Daneshvar and their friend the prominent artist Bahman Mohassess, Rome, 1958. (Photo courtesy of Ali Dehbashi, from the *Bokhara Magazine* archive) Bahman Mohassess (1931–2010) was a highly successful painter, sculptor and translator. Born and raised in Northern Iran, he eventually moved to Rome where he came to artistic fruition. Al-e Ahmad had a deep affection for him and wrote enthusiastically on his art.

This volume is not a travelogue that Al-e Ahmad wrote for the purpose of publication. These are his notes while he was travelling, which just before his death and towards the end of his trip to the US he had intended to turn into a single volume called *Four Ka'bahs*. That volume, and the critical and creative thinking that would have gone into it, never materialised. Ordinarily these notes should be kept in an archive and entrusted to a university for scholarly research. But his brother Shams Al-e Ahmad chooses to publish these notes with sometime dubious results. Reading these notes as they are, one does notice, however, how Al-e Ahmad reverses the colonial gaze, as I argue in my *Reversing the Colonial Gaze: Persian Travelers Abroad* (2020), which is the best way of reading such posthumous travelogues. The ultimate importance of these volumes published posthumously is to have a glance at the material that would have gone into that projected volume on *Four Ka'bahs*.

New York

The fourth and final Ka'bah, again in a figurative sense, is New York, mirroring Al-e Ahmad's floating signifier of Mecca.[70] The occasion of travelling to the US and keeping detailed notes of his observations was an invitation to attend a summer seminar which Henry Kissinger, at the time a member of the faculty in the Department of Government, had organised at Harvard University. Kissinger was director of the Harvard Defense Studies Program between 1958 and 1971, as well as the director of the Harvard International Seminar between 1951 and 1971, to which Al-e Ahmad was invited. Al-e Ahmad was fully aware that these summer programmes at Harvard were to ingratiate the so-called 'Third World' intellectuals and make them sympathetic to American foreign policies. At the time Kissinger was an advisor to Nelson Rockefeller in his presidential bid but would soon join the Nixon administration as his National Security Advisor. Before he visited Harvard, Al-e Ahmad found out, a few other Iranians had participated in these seminars, including his wife Simin Daneshvar in 1963, and after her he was invited in 1965. The CIA coup of 1953 had made characters like Kissinger fully conscious of places like Iran and they wanted to place its critical thinkers and academics on their radar. The Harvard seminar was at least partially sponsored by the CIA.

The editor of the original Persian travelogue, Mustafa Zamani-Nia, believes Al-e Ahmad and his literary executors never even considered publishing his US 'travelogue' because of its severe criticism of the Pahlavi monarchy.[71] Al-e Ahmad's detailed notes begins on 5 Tir 1344/26 June 1965 and ends in 23 Shahrivar 1344/14 September 1965. As his editor notices in his own long introduction, throughout his travel Al-e Ahmad is angry, vindictive, extremely rude and impolite towards his hosts, while he suffers from lack of financial resources.[72] All of these are clear indications that Al-e Ahmad himself did not intend these notes for publications as a 'travelogue', the way his brother has now opted to do. Again, these notes should have been entrusted to a university or any other research institution for safekeeping for scholars to study. Be that as it may, it is here in these notes that Al-e Ahmad writes about his idea of writing a book he would call either *Four Ka'bahs* or *Pilgrimage to Four Ka'bahs*, by which he meant Mecca, Jerusalem, Moscow and New York, and then he adds, 'I can fit Europe somewhere there too.'[73] That volume did not materialise, and therefore we should read these notes published by his brother as a 'travelogue' as the raw material for that projected volume.

Al-e Ahmad began his notes while he was still in Paris, where he saw Jean-Paul Sartre in the street and was tempted to go and introduce himself but did not manage to collect his courage and changed his mind.[74] He spends his time in Paris going to see movies, calling on his friends, writing on the eroticism of the films he has seen.[75] He drinks cheap vodka, complains of his lack of money and keeps writing his blues away.[76] He writes letters to his wife, makes notes in his own diary, goes out and talks with his friends. He is a bundle of raw nerves and incessant critical thinking. He finally boards a ship for New York, strikes a conversation with a Nigerian young man whom he describes as 'black black'.[77] Some of the people who are heading to Harvard are on this ship and they start getting to know each other.[78] He is not as reflective as before in these early parts of his travel notes while on his way to the US. He is excited but in a kind of subdued way.

By 7 July 1965 he begins his programme at Harvard proper. He hears of a Teach-in on Harvard campus and dismisses it as a spectacle, and just a 'safety valve'.[79] This is the 1960s and university campuses are deeply agitated in both anti-war and civil rights movement. He is not impressed. The Iranian student community in the region know of his arrival and among those who come to visit him is Seyyed Hossein Nasr, who will later return to Iran as a Pahlavi court philosopher.[80] Al-e Ahmad is consistently speaking condescendingly of people he meets and at one point refers to a whole 'cattle of French women'.[81] Expressions such as '*Mardak-e Holandi*' (the Dutch Guy'), '*Mardak-e Johud*' 'The Jewish Fellow'), '*Hendi-e* ('the Indian Guy'), and so on, all of them using the condescending and belittling Persian suffix 'k' abound in these notes. His guard is down. He thought he was writing to himself. He did not know his brother would publish these notes after his death. When he cites the Gregorian calendar, for example, on 12 July 1965, he adds in 'arazel' (of these hoodlums, meaning the date according to Americans!) These are all indications that these were shorthand notes he was writing to himself and did not intend them for publication in this shape.

At one point Kissinger sits next to him in a seminar and we learn he chews on his nails.[82] We also learn Kissinger invites the seminar participants for dinner to his house.[83] Al-e Ahmad discusses Mark Twain's *Tom Sawyer* and *Adventures of Huckleberry Finn* as well as *The Invisible Man* of Ralph Ellison with his colleagues at the seminar. Eventually he collects his courage and starts to speak his mind publicly in their seminars, citing Sartre on committed literature.[84] At one point he shares with us how he is neither sad nor happy for his inability to engage people in English to be the main barrier. 'I have no spiritual contact with these people, and bodily contact has not been possible so far either'.[85] He means sex, a few years after he had profusely apologised to his wife for his extramarital affair. He is asked to talk about *Gharbzadegi*. He prepares a short text and has a friend, Majid Tehranian (1937–2012), translate it for him.[86] He is always at the mercy of friends or strangers to translate for him text he had written in Persian, the only language in which he was fully fluent. On 20 July 1965 it occurs to him to write a book with the title of *Four Ka'bahs*:

> It has occurred to me to put together a book made of these travel notes plus the ones I have written before, a book to be called '*Four Ka'bahs*' or '*Pilgrimage to Four Ka'bahs*', or some such title, meaning placing myself in front of four *Ka'bahs* (Mecca, Jerusalem, Moscow and New York) and of course a comparison among these *Ka'bahs*. I can place the European notes somewhere there too. It will be a long book, almost 1000 pages, and I think it should be quite good. Being disappointed from these four *Ka'bahs*

is of course summarised in just one poem of Attar, but publishing such an experience, from a person in the twentieth century should not be bad, in utter brevity of course, with hammer-like sentences more than ever, and healthy humane conclusions.[87]

On 8 August Al-e Ahmad travels to Montreal, comes back on 10 August and then on 14 August he and his friend Tehranian drive to New York. He is always suspicious of the intention of Kissinger and of this whole seminar.[88] He attacks the very idea of a Peace Corps.[89] He visits Syracuse, travels to Chicago and then to St Louis, from there to Washington, DC. He mentions Columbia University, my own home institution, and refers to my predecessor the late Professor Ehsan Yarshater (1920–2018) as 'Bar-e Qater' ('The Load on a Mule'), his favourite nickname for him, and adds, 'the son of a bitch' who is wasting thousands of dollars from Iran on his Chair teaching Persian.[90] In September he flies to Paris and on 14 September he heads back home to Tehran.

The travelogue ends with a couple of appendixes where we read a short essay based on these notes in which he writes his most memorable encounter in this trip was meeting Ralph Elision whom he places above Richard Wright and James Baldwin, but there is no indication he knows the work of either. He considers Ellison influenced by Faulkner. It is here that he tells Ellison the problem with Blacks are two-fold: Christianity and jazz. He is clueless that Ellison was a theorist of jazz.[91] Throughout these pages he is honest, angry, furious, at odds with the world. In the US, he is Alice in Wonderland, has some generic political position, but as he said so himself, his language barrier made him unable to understand where he had actually come and what monumental issues were agitating the very soul of the country he had come to visit.

Europe

What about Europe, where does 'Europe', as both political geography and metonymic allegory, stand in the midst of these *Four Ka'bahs*?[92] That Europe was the epicentre of Al-e Ahmad's critical imagination, the *Gharb* in his *Gharbzadegi*, the zest in his zealotry, the very measure and the focal point of those '*Four Ka'bahs*' in whose mirrors he sought to see himself. He said he would place it 'somewhere' in between but that somewhere is the imaginative centre of his universe. In all these four mirrors reflecting four directions of prayers and hope he was trying to muster the courage to go forward in that fateful moment and introduce himself to Jean-Paul Sartre: 'Bonjour Monsieur Sartre! Je sui Jalal Al-e Ahmad!' He died unable to utter that sentence in that fatal moment when all his courage and imagination was at stake.[93]

Al-e Ahmad's European 'travelogue' is yet another posthumous volume in the sense that he never wrote any book with that title but his brother and a scholar of Al-e Ahmad's work, Mostafa Zamani-Nia, put together a volume of his notes while travelling in Europe plus a few other texts and called it 'Safar-e Farang' (The Journey to Europe). Al-e Ahmad did of course travel to Europe and habitually took extensive notes, though he never put together a volume with that title. He was sent to Europe by a governmental grant ostensibly to study their high school textbook. His travel notes run from Friday, 6 Mehr 1341/28 September 1962 while flying with Air France over Turkey and continue apace until Wednesday, 16 Aban 1341/7 November 1962 in Geneva when he meets the father of modern Persian fiction Mohammad Ali Jamalzadeh (1892–1997). Al-e Ahmad writes in detail only for 40 days of his 120 days.[94] The notes from which this travelogue has been produced, according to the editor, are not conclusive, clear, or consistent and there are a lot of discrepancies the editor has noted.[95] This is so probably because Al-e Ahmad had his extramarital affair with 'Hilda' in this trip, though the editor and his brother always blame the Shah's secret police, the notorious SAVAK, for having stolen Al-e Ahmad's notes. SAVAK may or may not have stolen things, Al-e Ahmad for sure had an extramarital affair in this trip, but more importantly these notes were not intended for publication as they are especially with the fictional title of The European Journey. But the important issue in this volume is his account of the historic encounter with Mohammad Ali Jamalzadeh to apologise for a nasty letter he had sent him years earlier. The courage he lacked even to step forward to introduce himself to Sartre was overcompensated by the vindictive anger he had unleashed on Jamalzadeh and he had now come to apologise, effectively, not in so many words.

The substance of the 'travelogue' is the usual notes Al-e Ahmad habitually took while travelling, with no particular difference whether he is in Europe or the US or Russia. He starts taking notes when he boards Air France in Tehran and while he is flying over Turkey. He considers these full expense-covered trips as something of a payback 'Shetel'.[96] He resumes his notes in Paris, where his host is UNESCO and his task is to study educational texts necessary for the world at large. But his mind and soul are not on this mission. He slips in the Paris Métro and injures his foot.[97] He is his usual self, constantly complains about everything, criticises everything, nothing impresses him. He does however see a Japanese film that deeply impresses him.[98] It is Kaneto Shindo's *The Naked Island* (1960). He does the usual touristy things – Versailles, the Louvre and so forth. At one point he says all he had to write was written in the form of a letter to his wife and he did not feel like writing any more.[99] He is curious about the copies of books being sold and does a little research on the matter. He is what in Persian we call 'Rafiq Baz' – loves to hang out with his friends. He watches Ingmar Bergman's *Through a Glass Darkly* (1961) and writes a quick review.[100] He sees Fritz Lang's *M* and writes a quick review.[101] He does a bit of shopping for his wife.[102] He then gets ready to move to Geneva and writes this time he had no lasting desire for Paris.[103]

The first thing he does in Geneva is to get rid of his roommate, whom he identifies with the Persian letter 'Jim', for he is getting on his nerves.[104] The most memorable event in Geneva is his historic meeting with Mohammad Ali Jamalzadeh with whom he had a nasty history of correspondence.[105] Jamalzadeh had written a negative review of Al-e Ahmad's *School Principal*, in response to which he had written Jamalzadeh a scathing letter, to which Jamalzadeh had responded gently and caringly. They have a cordial and friendly encounter in Geneva, though they remember it slightly differently if one were to compare Al-e Ahmad's notes here and Jamalzadeh's letter to the editor of the volume years later.[106] After his meeting with Jamalzadeh he gets bored with Europe and altogether abandons his duties at UNESCO.[107] He then becomes quiet, for he was too busy with 'Hilda', and then with his trip to Israel. The rest of the book is a reprint of Jamalzadeh's review of Al-e Ahmad's *School Principal*, Al-e Ahmad's angry response, followed by a letter Jamalzadeh writes to the editor of the volume, Zamani-Nia.

In comparison with his other trips abroad, Al-e Ahmad feels more at home in Europe than he does in the US or in the Soviet Union. He is more relaxed, goes to the movies, writes reviews, hangs out with his friends, sits in cafes and chats, complains less about money. His European persona was the doppelgänger of the author of *Gharbzadegi*.

'Unless he drinks a cup of wine'

The two lines of Sa'di's longer poem I have been citing as subheading for this chapter conclude with the conditional phrase that the Sufi becomes pure, or truly a mystic, not just in name but in essence, only when drinking a cup of wine. That is the supreme irony, where the mystic traveller needs a catalyst to become what he or she is hoping and is meant to become. Put together, these travels and the notes Al-e Ahmad took while en route to and from foreign lands were external sojourns of his restless soul, with his remorseless prose and formidable politics seeking to claim and own the world beyond its colonial borders. He was in these notes, travelogues and his letters to his wife reclaiming the world beyond its colonial geographies, with his confident encounters with friends and foes effectively liberating and decolonising the voice with which he claimed the cosmopolis he had inherited. Even in Israel, where he had a momentary lapse in judgement, not dissimilar to his marital infidelity, he demystified the European colonial outpost and took its claims to socialist utopia to its extreme, untenable conclusions.

In his projected but never fulfilled volume, Mecca, Jerusalem, Moscow, and New York – and then 'Europe' – were the signposts of his critical agitations, his circular search for direction and purpose. His sustained critique of capitalism did not result in rushing to Soviet socialism, from which he in fact ran away. He was in a moment of lapsed idealism, of wondering if a lemonade can be made of the lemon of European colonialism, attracted to Zionism – as he was to socialism and precisely because of its false claim to social and economic justice – but the false alarm ran aground with the first colonial expansionism of the settler colony that followed his visit. Both Soviet socialism and Israeli Zionism deeply disappointed him. These were not the *qiblas* to which he could pray, his initial wishful thinking notwithstanding. In Mecca he is ostensibly searching for his lost brother, which here is really himself, or a lost version of himself, the Salaman to his Absal, the allegory that confirmed him as a metaphor of himself. His hidden ego, his alter ego, was buried like a brother in a foreign but familiar land, and so he was resurrected from that grave as his own brother from the dead, as an existentialist Muslim, through dying before his death and being born again through a second birth, a sole and solitary Muslim, the last Muslim, like Søren Kierkegaard would think of his Christ – that's where his *Safar* and his *Hazar* become unified, where 'everything . . . unheimlich that ought to have remained secret and hidden . . . has come to light'.

In both decolonising and demystifying the colonially spatialised domains he visited, weaving together the *inside* and the *outside*, the coloniser and the colonised, the Westoxicated and the West, Al-e Ahmad was producing a 'liberation geography', as I have elsewhere called the decolonisation of the global spaces where non-Europeans travel.[108] The long history of European colonialism worked through mental and physical occupation of urban spaces, political borders and rural landscapes, as Timothy Mitchell shows in his classic *Colonizing Egypt* (1988) where the European colonial conception of order, truth and domination all come together to occupy Egypt politically, morally and imaginatively. What Mitchell effectively does in this seminal study is to cast a critical look at the very idea of modernity from its colonial underbelly. Colonially dominating Egypt meant imposing a new spatial regime of power, a political order marking domination, thus re-inscribing its social spacing, manufacturing a new topography of almost metaphysical dominance, and above all conditioning the experience of the real. Mitchell's concern was with the space *internal* to Egypt, where he writes of an advisor in Cairo who

> was the friend and assistant of the English reformer Jeremy Bentham, who in turn was the inventor of the Panopticon, the institution in which the use of coercion and commands to control a population was replaced by the partitioning of space, the isolation of individuals, and their systematic yet unseen surveillance. Foucault has suggested that the geometry and discipline of the Panopticon can serve as an emblem of the micro-physical forms of power that have proliferated in the last two centuries and formed the experience of capitalist modernity.[109]

But what I am suggesting here is to expand Mitchell's insight from one colonised country to the spatial mapping of the globe, where the *inside* of the country mirrors and reverses its *outside*, where Al-e Ahmad's 'ethnographies' become travelogues, contrasting and collapsing the home and the world – now catapulted into the colonial concoctions of 'the Near East', 'the Middle East', 'the Far East', etc. Mitchell writes: 'The essence of this kind of order is to produce an effect I am going to call *enframing*. Enframing is a method of

dividing up and containing, as in the construction of barracks or the rebuild-
ing of villages, which operates by conjuring up a neutral surface or volume
called "space".'[110] The same is true of drawing colonial borders, enframing of
a different order, defining frontier fictions, geopolitically carving up regions
into their 'internal affairs', and 'foreign policies'. Mitchell proposes:

> What characterizes all these descriptions is a common attempt to construct
> order, which has come into being as an end in itself. As with the new
> streets of the city, physical space – even respirable air – has become a
> surface and volume that can be divided up and marked out into places
> where individuals are positioned. Such acts create order in the abstract,
> not only by marking divisions and determining where things are to be put,
> but by distributing according to intervals that are identically spaced and
> geometrically aligned.[111]

The order becomes so 'an end in itself' that there was no other way to decolonise that space than to trespass on its internal and external bifurcations, with
one person consciously performing that trespassing. Al-e Ahmad succeeded
in his travelogues in trespassing that bifurcation and thus decolonising the
binary spacing in a manner far more successful than he sought to decolonise
the consciousness of his people in *Gharbzadegi*. He was in his element in his
travelogues – quick, piercing, liberating, simple, precise in a manner he had
mostly failed at in his *Gharbzadegi* or in his *On the Services and Treasons of
Intellectuals*. In these seminal works he was too self-conscious, had too many
chips on his shoulders. In his travelogues he was free as a bird.

Al-e Ahmad's oeuvre might be in fact read as targeted towards decolonising time (history), space (travels), prose (literature), politics (essays),
consciousnesses (*Gharbzadegi*) and agency (*On the Services and Treasons of
Intellectuals*), thus seeking to liberate the postcolonial subject, entrapped as
it was inside a self-loathing, self-alienated persona and persona. His travels
effectively, if not consciously, decolonise the very category of internalised/
externalised spaces. In his *La Production de l'espace* (*The Production of Space*)
(1974), Henri Lefebvre has theorised the social production of space. In a
key passage he narrows in on state apparatus as the key violent force in
spatialisation and writes:

The state is consolidating on a world scale. It weighs down on society (on all societies) in full force; it plans and organises society 'rationally', with the help of knowledge and technology, imposing analogous, if not homologous, measures irrespective of political ideology, historical background, or the class origins of those in power. The state crushes time by reducing differences to repetitions or circularities . . . Space in its Hegelian form comes back into its own . . . As both the end and the meaning of history – just as Hegel had forecast – it flattens the social and 'cultural' spheres. It enforces a logic that puts an end to conflicts and contradictions. It neutralises whatever resists it by castration or crushing.[112]

Looking back at Al-e Ahmad's travels in and out of his homeland we can see how and why Lefebvre places much of his emphasis on the state. However, the colonial and postcolonial state, with their inherent anxieties and insecurities, have a sharper focus on this spatiality. As they claim the national territories and demarcate the size and colour of the passports they issue to define and police one and alienate and defamiliarise the other side of their borders, states consolidate the fictive boundaries of here and there, of the inside and the outside. When we read Al-e Ahmad's travels together, disregarding if they are inside Iran or outside Iran, the systematic colonisation of that imaginative geography collapses upon itself. The more Al-e Ahmad becomes allegorical the more real he becomes.

After Lefebvre, his close follower Edward Soja took the question of space further and updated Lefebvre's concept of the spatial triad with his own idea of 'spatial trialectics' which concludes in what calls a *thirdspace*, or spaces that are both real and imagined. Soja expanded the bicameral thinking into the making of a thirdspace at once real and imaginative.[113] Soja suggests Jorge Luis Borges' short story 'The Aleph' and polyphonic music as the way to read Lefebvre, upon which proposition Soja then proposes his idea of 'trialectics of spatiality', by which he means the ontological, epistemological and theoretical 'rebalancing of spatiality, historicality, and sociality'.[114]

These are indeed ground-breaking insights into how space is conceived. But specifically absent from Lefebvre and Soja and yet enabled by both their insightful works is any serious attention to the colonial production of space, which I have most recently explored in my *Reversing the Colonial Gaze: Persian*

Travelers Abroad (2020). The colonial construction of space is far more brutal and violent, as Mitchell's work reveals, than the social production of space the way Lefebvre and Soja have theorised it. The colonial construction of space begins with the ruthless carving and imposition of borders, the way the Sykes–Picot Agreement (1916) between the British and the French butchered the Ottoman Empire into pieces. The active transmutation of *Hazar* and *Safar,* as I have proposed them here, physically and imaginatively retailor the world, bringing the homely and unhomely, the *Heimlich* and the *Unheimlich*, into that third space where Al-e Ahmad imagined his unpublished volume on the *Four Ka'bahs*, where his wandering soul would fly, as he cited from Masnavi where Rumi had said:

> Every pigeon flies in a direction,
> But this pigeon towards no-direction . . .
> We are neither domesticated birds nor wild birds
> The seeds that feed us are no-seeds

This poem from Rumi is precisely where Al-e Ahmad is, in between his multiple *Ka'bahs*, a restless soul that belongs nowhere and yet is everywhere: from his homeland and preoccupied with Europe he travels to four *Ka'bahs* and he finds none of them completely his, and it is precisely in that floating geography that he lives and anticipates a post-Islamist liberation theology.

Notes

1. Jalal Al-e Ahmad, *Khasi dar Miqat (Dust in the Desert)* (Tehran: Jameh-daran Publishers, 1964/2008): 85–6. There is an English translation of this text. See Jalal Al-e Ahmad, *Lost in the Crowd*, translated by John Green and Ahmad Alizadeh, with an introduction by Michael Hillmann (Washington, DC: Three Continents Press, 1985). As in all other cases, however, I read and translate from the original Persian. 'Lost in the Crowd' is a perfectly good translation for 'Khasi dar Miqat', a beautiful poetic phrase almost impossible to translate, but I opt for 'Dust in the Desert'. The passage I have selected and translated afresh above should give a fairly clear idea of what the title means. *Khasi* rhymes with *Kasi* (a speck of *dust* versus a *person*), and *Miqat* with *Mi'ad* (the *time* of a meeting versus the *place* of that meeting). Al-e Ahmad had a panache for such poetic titles. *Zindiq* means 'infidel' or 'outcast', but I have kept it in its

original. The reference to that Mihaneh'i refers to Muhammad ibn Monawwar (1157–1202), the author of *Asrar al-Tawhid*, on the life and legacy of Abu Sa'id abi al-Khayr, while the reference to Bastami is to Bayezid Bastami (*d. c.* 849) to whom the phrase Al-e Ahmad cites is attributed among his *Shathiyat* (*Ecstatic Utterances*).

2. Sigmund Freud, 'The Uncanny', in *An Infantile Neurosis and other Works*. From: *The Standard Edition of the Complete Psychological Works of Sigmund Freud*, translated from the German under the general editorship of James Strachey, vol. XVIII (London: The Hogarth Press, 1964): 224–5.

3. See Hamid Dabashi, *Reversing the Colonial Gaze: Persian Travelers Aboard* (Cambridge: Cambridge University Press, 2020).

4. Al-e Ahmad's brother Shams Al-e Ahmad, who was his literary executor, has given a list of these travels abroad in his introduction to the final edition of Al-e Ahmad's *Safar beh Velayat-e Ezrael* (*Journey to the Abode of the Angel of Death*). With an Introduction by Shams Al-e Ahmad (Tehran: Majid Publications, 1384/2005)): 10–12.

5. For more on Tati language (dialect) and its derivatives see the entry under 'Eštehārdī' in *Encyclopedia Iranica*. Available online here: http://www.irani-caonline.org/articles/estehardi.

6. Jalal Al-e Ahmad's *Ourazan*, English translation of the introduction by Simin Daneshvar (Tehran: Ketab Zaman Publications, 1333/1954).

7. Ibid: 7.

8. Ibid: 29–34.

9. For a classical text examining the colonial disposition of the discipline of anthropology see Talal Asad (ed.), *Anthropology and the Colonial Encounter* (Ithaca, NY: Ithaca Press, 1973). Al-e Ahmad had no idea who Talal Asad was, nor was my dear friend and distinguished colleague Talal Asad aware of Al-e Ahmad's work when editing this classic volume.

10. See Jalal Al-e Ahmad, *Tat-Neshin-ha-ye Blok-e Zahra* (*The Tati Residents of Zahra District*) (Tehran: Amir Kabir, 1958).

11. Ibid: 10–12.

12. For the racist terror of the doyen of Eurocentric anthropology on full display see Bronisław Malinowski's *A Diary in the Strict Sense of the Term*, translated by Norbert Guterman (Stanford, CA: Stanford University Press, 1989). Published posthumously by his widow in 1969, the diary reveals the pathological hatred of Malinowski towards the people he was 'studying' during his fieldwork in New Guinea and the Trobriand Islands between 1914 and 1918. Good thing

Al-e Ahmad never knew of these people and what they did as anthropologists. His criticism of the discipline was utterly brilliant and precise because he had intuited what they were doing epistemically violating the people whom their Europe and later US was ruling.

13. Al-e Ahmad, *Tat-Neshin-ha-ye Blok-e Zahra* (*The Tati Residents of Zahra District*) (Op. Cit.): 13.

14. Ibid: 15–32.

15. See Jalal Al-e Ahmad, *Kharg, Dorr-e Yatim Khalij* (*The Island of Kharg: The Pearl of the Gulf*) (Tehran: Majid Publications, 1960/2007): 11.

16. See Edward W. Said, 'Representing the Colonized: Anthropology's Interlocutors' (*Critical Inquiry*, vol. 15, no. 2, Winter, 1989): 205–25.

17. I have also undertaken one such move in regard to the idea of 'World Literature' in my recent book, *The Shahnameh: Persian Epic as World Literature* (New York: Columbia University Press, 2019).

18. For more on Mulla Sadra's philosophy and the intellectual context of Isfahan at this time see my *Shi'ism: A Religion of Protest* (Cambridge, MA: Harvard University Press, 2012).

19. This widely popular poem of Mehdi Akhavan Sales appeared for the first time in his collection *Zemestan* (*Winter*) (Tehran: Zaman Publications, 1335/1956). The English translation is mine.

20. See Jalal Al-e Ahmad, *Khasi dar Miqat* (*Dust in the Desert*) (Op. Cit.): 14.

21. Ibid: 21.

22. Ibid: 34.

23. Ibid: 42.

24. Ibid: 53.

25. Ibid: 59. There is an excellent comparative study of Al-e Ahmad's Hajj travelogue along with *The Autobiography of Malcolm X* by my former student and now colleague Golnar Nikpour, 'Revolutionary Journeys, Revolutionary Practice: The Hajj Writings of Jalal Al-e Ahmad and Malcolm X' (*Comparative Studies of South Asia, Africa and the Middle East*, vol. 34, no. 1, 2014): 67–85. As in the case of Ajay Singh Chaudhary's doctoral dissertation, to which I referred in the previous chapter, these comparative studies are exceptionally important in detecting uncharted territories in understanding both Al-e Ahmad and Benjamin, in Chaudhary's case, or in this case Al-e Ahmad and Malcolm X. What they lose in historical precision or textual nuances they doubly gain in theoretical insights.

26. Jalal Al-e Ahmad, *Khasi dar Miqat* (*Dust in the Desert*) (Op. Cit.): 67.

27. Ibid: 83.

28. Ibid: 93.

29. Ibid: 98.

30. Ibid: 107.

31. Ibid: 183.

32. See Mostafa Zamani-Nia's Introduction to Jalal Al-e Ahmad, *Safar-e Emrika*, edited by Shams Al-e Ahmad and Mustafa Zamani-Nia (Tehran: Siyamak, 1378/1999): 3.

33. Al-e Ahmad, *Safar beh Velayat-e Ezrael* (*Journey to the Abode of the Angel of Death*) (Tehran: Majid Publications, 1384/2005): 47.

34. There is a comprehensive recent essay assessing these Iranian socialists' attraction to Zionism. See Eskandar Sadeghi-Boroujerdi and Yaacov Yadgar, 'Jalal's Angels of Deliverance and Destruction: Genealogies of Theo-politics, Sovereignty and Coloniality in Iran and Israel' (*Modern Intellectual History*, 2019): 1–25.

35. It is instructive to keep in mind that similar rifts divided the US left almost at the same time. For a study of this phenomenon see Michael R. Fischbach, *The Movement and the Middle East: How the Arab–Israeli Conflict Divided the American Left* (Stanford, CA: Stanford University Press, 2019).

36. Al-e Ahmad, *Safar beh Velayat-e Ezrael* (*Journey to the Abode of the Angel of Death*) (Op. Cit.): 50.

37. Ibid: 51.

38. Ibid: 52.

39. Ibid: 62.

40. Ibid: 79.

41. Ibid: 26–31. The text in these pages is the outline of that lecture at Tehran University based on his notes as reported by his brother Shams Al-e Ahmad, who was his literary executor. Unless and until Al-e Ahmad's personal notes are deposited in an independent archive his brother's reports remain not entirely reliable. Until then we have no choice but use them cautiously as he conveys them.

42. Ibid: 31–4.

43. There is an utterly magnificent book (in Arabic) by the brilliant Palestinian scholar Ismail Nashef, *Tofulah Hozayran* (*June Childhood*) (Ramallah: Moassesseh Li- al-Ta'lim al-Mujtama'i, 2016), covering the children's literature around that calamitous event in the history of Palestinian struggles for their liberation. To this day the depth of Iranian scholars' and intellectuals'

ignorance of the Palestinian cause remains deeply embarrassing. They have completely abandoned the cause of one of the most noble national liberation movements in the world to the abuse of their ruling state.

44. Ibid: 86.

45. Ibid: 90.

46. The most detailed examination of Al-e Ahmad's travelogue to Israel is in the distinguished Iranian literary critic Reza Barahani's 'Jalal Al-e Ahmad va Felestin' ('Jalal Al-e Ahmad and Palestine') in Reza Barahani, Safar-e Mesr va Jalal Al-e Ahmad va Felestin (Travel to Egypt and Jalal Al-e Ahmad and Palestine) (Tehran: Nashr-e Aval, 1363/1984): 151–223. In this crucial text Barahani repeatedly states that Al-e Ahmad was lucky he did not die before 1967, and therefore got to see the Israelis in action – writing the second part of the travelogue to exonerate himself. See Ibid: 158. This book is a clear indication that Al-e Ahmad's frivolous first part in his Israel travelogue had generated much criticism from his own immediate friends and comrades and not just by Ali Khamenei. This seminal testimony by a close friend and comrade of Al-e Ahmad elaborating in detail the contemporary reception of Al-e Ahmadi's travelogue to Israel is far more reliable than Shams Al-e Ahmad's accounts. But alas, scarcely anyone reads these secondary sources in Persian when writing learned essays in English!

47. See Jalal Al-e Ahmad, The Israeli Republic: An Iranian Revolutionary's Journey to the Jewish State, translated from the Persian and with an essay by Samuel Thrope. Correspondence with Simin Daneshvar. Introduction by Bernard Avishai (New York: Restless Books, 2017). In some editions of this book the subtitle appears as 'Jalal Al-e Ahmad, Islam, and the Jewish state'.

48. Ibid: 10.

49. Ibid: 30.

50. Ibid: 30.

51. In the essay I just cited, Eskandar Sadeghi-Boroujerdi and Yaacov Yadgar, 'Jalal's Angels of Deliverance and Destruction: Genealogies of Theo-politics, Sovereignty and Coloniality in Iran and Israel', we read a comprehensive assessment of the Iranian socialists' attraction to Zionism. The essay, however, takes the abusive interpretation of the English translation too seriously and goes on the wild goose chase of the link between Al-e Ahmad's casual reference early in the travelogue to the prophetic tradition in Judaism, for which he uses the term 'Awliya', and Khomeini's theory of 'Velayat-e faqih'. The learned authors of this

essay of course make it quite clear 'for several reasons . . . it would be mistaken to draw the conclusion that Khomeini's theory directly informed Al-e Ahmad's travelogue or that he [Al-e Ahmad] could have possibly envisioned the Islamic state and clerically led constitutional order that would, to nearly everyone's dismay, emerge in 1979'. The authors are serious scholars and do not have any ideological agenda and thus see the truth. They further add: 'The *Velayat* spoken of by Al-e Ahmad never receives a jurisprudential rationale or expression; rather it is a kind of generative power harboring sovereign potentialities capable of summoning new modes of life and being-together into existence. It was not a precursor to the Islamic Republic *in concreto*, but rather a call for a new political order beyond coloniality.' They are correct in principle, but under the false shadow of the English translator's abusive reading, which alas they read uncritically, they concede too much. Al-e Ahmad never saw Israel as anything but a settler colony, even in the first part of the chopped-up text and before he (or he and a friend) wrote the resounding denunciation of Zionism in the second part.

52. Jalal Al-e Ahmad, *The Israeli Republic: An Iranian Revolutionary's Journey to the Jewish State* (Op. Cit.): 32.

53. Ibid: 33.

54. I just give one example of the translator's shaky command of colloquial Persian. Early in chapter five, Al-e Ahmad writes in his habitual colloquialism, 'this text is a letter from a friend from Paris, to which I have added a few things. All its gibberish is mine, all the serious parts his.' For 'all its gibberish is mine', Al-e Ahmad uses a common colloquial expression, '*part-o-pala-ha-yash bikh-e rish-e man*' ('all its gibberish hangs from my beard') – meaning is a cause of embarrassment for me. In the English translation this turns to: 'The nonsense and beard-pulling is mine!' There is no 'beard-pulling' in the original. The learned translator just did not get the colloquialism. The same is true with the title of the travelogue, *Safar beh Velayat-e Ezrael*, where the satirical sarcasm is lost on the translator, eager as he is to twist the text to his purposes.

55. I have written extensively on the doctrine of '*Velayat-e faqih*' on multiple occasions, particularly in my chapter on Ayatollah Khomeini in my *Theology of Discontent: The Ideological Foundations of Islamic Revolution in Iran* (New Brunswick, NJ: Transaction, 1993), as well as in my *Shi'ism: A Religion of Protest* (Cambridge, MA: Harvard University Press, 2011).

56. For the most cogent philosophical objection to the very idea of '*Velayat-e faqih*'

see Mehdi Ha'eri Yazdi, *Hekmat va Hokumat* (*Philosophy and Governance*) (London: Shadi Publications, 1994).

57. See Jalal Al-e Ahmad, *Safar-e Rus* (*The Russian Journey*), edited with notes by Shams Al-e Ahmad (Tehran: Ferdows Publications, 1368/1989).

58. Ibid: 22.

59. Ibid: 29.

60. Ibid: 36.

61. Ibid: 52.

62. Ibid: 64.

63. Ibid: 64.

64. Ibid: 79.

65. Ibid: 86.

66. Ibid: 110.

67. Ibid: 167.

68. Ibid: 205.

69. Ibid: 275.

70. See Jalal Al-e Ahmad, *Safar-e Emrika* (*The US Journey*), edited by Shams Al-e Ahmad and Mustafa Zamani-Nia (Tehran: Siyamak, 1378/1999).

71. Ibid: 4.

72. Ibid: 10–14.

73. Ibid: 145. The note is dated 20 July 1965.

74. Ibid: 25.

75. Ibid: 32.

76. Ibid: 37.

77. Ibid: 45.

78. Ibid: 52.

79. Ibid: 70.

80. Ibid: 71.

81. Ibid: 72.

82. Ibid: 81.

83. Ibid: 142.

84. Ibid: 127.

85. Ibid: 135.

86. Ibid: 136. When I was a graduate student, I met Majid Tehranian, one of the earliest Iranian students who had become a prominent scholar in the US. He taught at the University of Hawaii.

87. Ibid: 148.

88. Ibid: 222.

89. Ibid: 229.

90. Ibid: 302.

91. Ibid: 323. In his classic book, *The Mantle of the Prophet: Religion and Politics in Iran* (New York: Pantheon Books, 1985: 318–23), Roy Mottahedeh covers the US trip of Al-e Ahmad in some detail. Mottahedeh verifies that some of the funding for Kissinger's seminar 'came through a CIA conduit' (320).

92. For my sustained course of reflections on 'Europe' as metonymic allegory see my *Europe and its Shadows: Coloniality after Empire* (London: Pluto, 2019).

93. Would Al-e Ahmad been as disappointed in that encounter as Edward Said was when he went to Paris following an invitation by Sartre and Simone de Beauvoir to meet with them at Michel Foucault's residence in 1979? For Edward Said's account of the encounter see Edward Said, 'An Encounter with J.-P. Sartre' (*London Review of Books*, vol. 22, no. 11, 1 June 2000).

94. Jalal Al-e Ahmad, *Safar-e Farang* (*The European Journey*), edited by Mostafa Zamani-Nia (Tehran: Ketab Siyamak Publications, 1376/1997): II.

95. Ibid: III.

96. Ibid: 18.

97. Ibid: 26.

98. Ibid: 32.

99. Ibid: 42.

100. Ibid: 58.

101. Ibid: 86.

102. Ibid: 106.

103. Ibid: 118.

104. Ibid: 123.

105. Ibid: 128.

106. Jamalzadeh had become something of an iconic talisman for Iranian intellectuals to visit when in Geneva. I also called and went and visited him in his apartment in Geneva in the early 1980s, by which time he was almost completely deaf, but still had a sharp memory and quick wit. I was interested in his recollections of his years in Berlin. But the conversation took him to a journey he had taken as a young man from Baghdad to Berlin on which path he had been an eyewitness to the Armenian genocide. The tape I had made of this conversation I subsequently gave to Columbia University's archive of the oral history of the Armenian genocide.

107. Ibid: 133.

108. I have detailed that term and its argument particularly in my *Arab Spring: The End of Postcolonialism* (London: Zed, 2012).
109. Timothy Mitchell, *Colonizing Egypt* (Cambridge: Cambridge University Press, 1988): ix–x.
110. Ibid: 44.
111. Ibid: 78.
112. Henri Lefebvre, *The Production of Space*, translated by Donald Nicholson-Smith (Oxford: Blackwell, 1991): 23.
113. See Edward W. Soja, *Thirdspace: Journeys to Los Angeles and Other Real-and-Imagined Places* (Oxford: Blackwell, 1996).
114. Ibid: 10.

8

Translating the World

Although I do not know Italian, I am familiar with an Italian expression
that says '*traduttore, traditore*', which means 'the translator is a traitor'.
This expression is particularly applicable to a person who wishes to
translate André Gide.[1]

> Jalal Al-e Ahmad's Introduction to his translation of André Gide's
> *Bazgasht-e az Shoravi* (*Retour de l'U.R.S.S.*) (1954)

Once upon a time, in the sixteenth century, in what is now Brazil, members
of the Tupinambà tribe devoured a Catholic priest. This act sent shudders
of horror through Portugal and Spain, representing as it did the ultimate
taboo for a European Christian. The very term 'cannibal' was associated
with the Americas; originally referring to a group of Caribs in the Antilles,
it entered the English language definitively in the *OED* of 1796 meaning
'an eater of human flesh' and subsequently passed into other European
languages. The name of a tribe and the name given to savage peoples who
ate human flesh fused into a single term.[2]

With that splendid paragraph that should give priests, anthropologists
and European colonialists everywhere a moment of fearful reflection
before they venture out to their next conquest or 'fieldwork', the editors of
a volume on postcolonial translation introduce the collection of essays they
have gathered in their book addressing issues at the heart of their scholarly
interests. The editors then proceed to tell us how:

> the eating of the priest was not an illogical act on the part of the Tupinambà,
> and may even be said to have been an act of homage. After all, one does

not eat people one does not respect, and in some societies the devouring of the strongest enemies or most worthy elders has been seen as a means of acquiring the powers they had wielded in life.

Lest the next generation of anthropologists and Orientalists start theorising Brazilian cuisine, the editors remind their readers the practice of eating what you love and admire was not peculiar or exclusive to tribes in Brazil. 'We need only think of Portia', they remind us, 'the noble Roman widow who drank her husband's ashes in a glass of wine, declaring her body to be his fittest resting place.' Moreover, and this is most intriguing for the issue of translation in this chapter, 'the priest was seeking to convert, Christianity rests on the symbolism of devouring the body and blood of Christ, the saviour . . .' For the miserable priest being boiled to perfection, the eucharist may have been just a Christian allegory or a mere metaphor. But his Brazilian flock in the tribe took the idea quite literally.

From this premise the editors of this volume proceed to argue that 'translation does not happen in a vacuum, but in a continuum; it is not an isolated act, it is part of an ongoing process of intercultural transfer', as in the case of moving from a mere metaphor to a priestly feast. 'Moreover', they add,

> translation is a highly manipulative activity that involves all kinds of stages in that process of transfer across linguistic and cultural boundaries. Translation is not an innocent, transparent activity but is highly charged with significance at every stage; it rarely, if ever, involves a relationship of equality between texts, authors or systems.

The poor priest may have gone on his mission with a copy of the Bible he thought he knew well, but the natives opted to translate and read the Holy Scripture slightly differently to what he was taught in his seminar. The editors' conclusion therefore brings us to the heart of the activity we know as 'translation':

> Recent work in translation studies have challenged the long-standing notion of the translation as inferior to the original. In this respect, translation studies research has followed a similar path to other radical movements within literary and cultural studies, calling into question the politics of canonization and moving resolutely away from ideas of universal literary

greatness. This is not to deny that some texts are valued more highly than others, but simply to affirm that systems of evaluation vary from time to time and from culture to culture and are not consistent.[3]

However 'systems of evaluation' may 'vary from time to time and from culture to culture', it is safe to say cooking up a priest and having him for a feast is an over-interpretation of the eucharist, as Umberto Eco might say.[4] As a Christian rite that is considered a sacrament in most churches, the eucharist (Holy Communion) is believed to have been instituted by Jesus Christ during the Last Supper when he gave his disciples bread and wine, telling them the bread stood for his body and the wine for his blood. By partaking of that bread and wine Christians symbolically identify with their saviour and remember how he sacrificed himself on the cross for their sins. Historically Monophsites have differed from Dyophysites in their respective Christological interpretations of Christ bodily humanity/divinity. But to the best of our knowledge they have never eaten their priests or theologians on such doctrinal differences. Through Freud's theory of the *Totem and Taboo* (1913) I have made a similar argument for the food Shi'i believers consume during the Ashura ceremonies. This comparison was not a translation of the Christian conception of the eucharist into Shi'ism, but a theoretical approximation facilitated trough Freud's theory of totem and taboo.[5] It was therefore a theoretical speculation based on the fact and phenomenon of Shi'a communal gatherings and their redemptive commemoration of their martyred saint. What the Tupinambà tribe did to that unfortunate priest was a more literal mis/translation of the eucharist.

The Foreign Familiarity of Translated Prose

It has always been a mystery to me why I cannot stand Al-e Ahmad's translations, any of his translations, not a bit. I find them quite unreadable. This is so not because now I have read most of his translations (except Dostoevsky's) in their originals but even before, when I was a happy prisoner in my mother tongue. Al-e Ahmad's translations are not any better or worse than any of the other Persian translations of foreign sources I read growing up in Iran. I have already written how works of translations actually enrich a literary culture and of how much can be gained through translations.[6] This is so, I believe, because when we read Al-e Ahmad's translations we cannot get him, the translator, out of the way to access the author he is translating. Mohammad Qazi (1913–98) was perhaps the most celebrated translator of my generation, and he translated works of monumental importance and completely disappeared into thin air between the original author and ourselves, the readers. Not so Al-e Ahmad. He was and he still stands right between you and the original author staring at you. This is so because Al-e Ahmad was not really a translator. He had a project, an intellectual project, in which works he opted to translate were integral. We need therefore to place his translations in the larger context of this intellectual project.

Translation makes the foreign familiar, and in so doing it also makes the familiar foreign. Translating the eucharist into cannibalism makes the alien Christian concept familiar to its tribal converts, while giving to cannibalism a renewed Christological interpretation. In a more common understanding of translation, word for word, not word for flesh, the experience of ventriloquism from one to another language gives the translator something of an 'indigestion', as it were. In the voluminous oeuvre of Al-e Ahmad we notice quite a number of important translations mostly from French and English into Persian. When we read these translations in Persian today, we see how Al-e Ahmad, like most other translators, loses the confidence and pride of his prose the minute he forces himself out to yield to the authority of an André Gide, an Albert Camus, or a Fyodor Dostoevsky. It is just like when he saw Sartre in a street in Paris and was too shy to go and introduce himself. In his translated prose, he looks like a man wearing a suit that does not fit him, for it belongs to someone else. That yielding of confidence, authority and elegance is an act of authorial sacrifice in the service of a higher theoretical purpose, when the translator becomes a mouthpiece, a ventriloquist, for a foreigner unfamiliar with the translator's mother tongue. The translator is bringing the world as she or he scantily knows it, to the world he knows far better. The dialectic is at once jarring and yet exciting. It is, again, uncanny/ *Unheimlich*.

The issue becomes even more complicated when the translation is not made from the original but from another translation. Here is an example. In 1948, Al-e Ahmad published his translation of Dostoevsky's *Gambler* (*Qomarbaz*) from Henri Mongault's French translation and not from Russian, which he did not know. Later Soroush Habibi, a professional translator with no other axe to grind, translated the same novel directly from Russian. That raises the question of cannibalisation as canonisation, and at least in this, but in many other cases, the intermediary function of French points to two facts: that the French language was the *lingua franca* of this generation of Iranian literary intellectuals, and that they followed the blueprint of French cannibalisation/canonisation of what they believed to be the best of Russian and by extension world literature. Al-e Ahmad, the author of *Gharbzadegi*, never questioned such categorial attractions to all things French and European, even when it came to an encounter with Russian literature. He never questioned the authority of the French literary taste, and thus the French lens on the Russian masterpiece is where he placed his own gaze to receive Dostoevsky's novel. He grew increasingly drawn to existentialism, as a literary and philosophical school, and if the French existentialists were drawn to Dostoevsky, so was he.

The year 1948, as Shams Al-e Ahmad writes in his introduction to this translation, is the year Al-e Ahmad parted ways with the Tudeh Party and had much free time on his hands.[7] Translation was also a new source of income for him. A combination of political and financial reasons therefore drew him to explore worlds beyond his immediate experiences. In the process, and since he could not translate directly from Russian, Al-e Ahmad's Persian translation of Dostoevsky's *The Gambler* (Игрокъ) (1866) became doubly removed from any sense of 'the original' and thus crafts a tertiary space for the Russian master novelist to reach his Francophone Persian readers. Al-e Ahmad's Persian prose here becomes three times self-alienated. He is mimicking in Persian a French mimicking a Russian prose. As the translator becomes the secondary doppelgänger of the author, devours him and his French translator and makes them both speak a broken Persian, the fusion of the author and his translators in this staged act of narrative cannibalism is where the Brechtian *Verfremdungseffekt* exposes the theatricality of the whole performance. Here is the key passage in Brecht's theory of the *Verfremdungseffekt* in Chinese theatre – that, read carefully, alerts us to the alienating effect of mimicking Russian in French and from there into Persian:

> Above all, the Chinese artist never acts as if there were a fourth wall besides the three surrounding him. He expresses his awareness of being watched.

This immediately removes one of the European stage's characteristic illusions. The audience can no longer have the illusion of being the unseen spectator at an event which is really taking place. A whole elaborate European stage technique, which helps to conceal the fact that the scenes are so arranged that the audience can view them in the easiest way, is thereby made unnecessary. The actors openly choose those positions which will best show them off to the audience, just as if they were acrobats . . . The artist's object is to appear strange and even surprising to the audience. He achieves this by looking strangely at himself and his work. As a result, everything put forward by him has a touch of the amazing . . . [8]

Just as the Chinese artist, here the Persian translator, they both know they are performing, that they are being watched, they are in effect watching themselves being watched, reading themselves being read. They are both totally aware of the performativity of the whole act of translation as acting. I have made a similar argument as Brecht's about Chinese theatre about the mimetic dissonance in the Persian passion play or *Ta'ziyeh*.[9] It is therefore through his repressed Shi'i subconscious, and not Brecht's theory of the *Verfremdungseffekt*, that Al-e Ahmad reaches for the doctrinal dissimulation at the heart of what I have called 'the Karbala Complex', where the split between fact and fantasy, between the foreign and the familiar, becomes critically creative, as here in translation where he resurrects that moment of creative alienation to expose the fourth wall, to stage his performativity. Art as device, to use Shklovsky's argument, becomes art as an overcoming of an alienating power of coloniality via mimicking coloniality.

Reading the Old World Anew

How do we make a distinction between an original Russian, French, German or English text and its Persian, Arabic, Swahili or Turkish translation? The politics of canonisation as cannibalisation surely includes who gets to be translated into what languages. What does a translation of Gide, Camus, or Dostoevsky, or Ernst Jünger into Persian actually mean? Not just for the language into which these texts are translated, but for the texts themselves thus interpreted? There is of course a politics to translation, but what exactly is that politics? Translating from Russian is one thing, but disproportionately translating from French is something else. In mid-twentieth-century Iran, as well as in the wider Arab world, the rest of Asia, Africa or Latin America, the allegory of 'Europe' carried power and authority, even for, or particularly for, those who sought to oppose and confront that hegemony. Today 'Europe' has lost that allegorical power, and Al-e Ahmad's fixation with the French cultural scene seems a bit banal and blasé – but certainly not so during his lifetime.[10]

Al-e Ahmad was a versatile and by and large competent translator, and his translations were an integral part of his literary and critical output. He had a tentative command of Arabic and French in addition to his native Persian. He was also familiar with English, but only scantily. The important point to keep in mind is that most of his translations were in collaboration with friends and colleagues who had a better grasp of those languages. His wife Simin Daneshvar, with whom he undertook a translation, had a solid command of English. Al-e Ahmad began translating at a young age and his very first translation was an essay by Seyyed Mohsen Amin Jabal 'Amili, a prominent Shi'i reformer, called *Al-Tanzih li-al-A'mal al-Shabih* (1930) which he translated from Arabic as *Azadari-ha-ye Na-Mashru'* (*Illegal Mourning*) and published in 1943. This essay was a critique of Shi'a ritual performances of self-flagellations as redemptive suffering, and as such an indication of Al-e Ahmad's early attention to the religious reformists among important clerical thinkers. We also know he had translated a critical text by a French Orientalist, Paul Casanova, called *Mohammed et la fin du monde: Étude critique sur l'Islam primitive* (*Mohammad and the End of the World: A Critical Study on Primitive Islam*) (1911), which in 1947 Al-e Ahmad had translated as *Muhammad-e Akhar-e Zaman* (*Muhammad the Prophet of the End of the World*), but he did not publish that book. This translation, again, points to Al-e Ahmad's early impatience with the current condition of Islam in his own time and homeland and his desire to introduce some serious Arab and European critical angles targeting his own ancestral faith. However, he seems to have opted not to continue along that path. There are evident signs in these translations of an impatient and inquisitive mind, feeling its way around the world through the decipherment of what other thinkers were thinking. He is far more interested in understanding than in making understood. He is publicly reading the world. He is a *naqqal*, performing other people's stories.

Reading is also translating. Encountering the changing world forces a sense of urgency to read it to comprehend it. 'When we read or hear any language-statement from the past, be it Leviticus or last year's best-seller', as George Steiner says in his classic work *After Babel*, 'we translate' – and then he continues:

> Reader, actor, editor are translators of language out of time. The schematic model of translation is one in which a message from a source-language passes into a receptor-language via a transformational process. The barrier is the obvious fact that one language differs from the other, that an interpretative transfer, sometimes, albeit misleadingly, described as encoding and decoding, must occur so that the message 'gets through'. Exactly the same model – and this is what is rarely stressed – is operative within a single language. But here the barrier or distance between source and receptor is time.[11]

All translations are out of the time and timbre with the 'original'. The bifurcation between a 'source-language' passes and a 'receptor-language' disappears at the end point, through the power and authority of a foreign name, a French name which carries its own signature of authority. The message never gets through, but an assumption of that message does. The barrier or distance 'between source and receptor' is entirely exegetical – though in more than one sense. The crucial point George Steiner makes here is this: 'Exactly the same model – and this is what is rarely stressed – is operative within a single language. But here the barrier or distance between source and receptor is time' – to which I might add that exactly the same model is operative within a single language when sung by an author and when tortured by a translator. The distance is not just temporal but also spatial, when within a single time frame the prose oscillates between its homeliness and its unhomeliness. The distance between Al-e Ahmad's own flawless and fluent prose and his back-broken Persian when he translates is precisely where the *Verfremdungseffekt* works, where the *Heimlich* becomes *Unheimlich* and vice versa.

After his translations from Arabic and French, mostly on Shi'a and Islamic issues, much of Al-e Ahmad's attention in subsequent decades of his mature engagements was drawn to Russian and European sources, most of them associated with literary and philosophical existentialism. These translations included: Fyodor Dostoevsky's *Gambler/Ghomarbaz* (1948), Albert Camus's *L'Étranger/The Stranger/Biganeh* (with Ali Asghar Khobrehzadeh, 1949), Albert Camus's *Le Malentendu/The Misunderstanding/Su'-Tafahom* (1950), Jean-Paul Sartre's *Les Mains sales/Dirty Hands/Dast-ha-ye Aludeh* (1952). Then followed in succession: André Gide's *Retour de l'U.R.S.S./Return from the U.S.S.R./Bazgasht-e az Shoravi* (1954), André Gide's *Les Nourritures terres-tres/Fruits of the Earth/Ma'edeh-ha-ye Zamini* (with Parviz Daryoush, 1955), Eugène Ionesco's *Rhinocéros/Rhinoceros/Kargadan* (1966), Eugène Ionesco's *La Soif et la faim/Hunger and Thirst/Teshnegi va Goshnegi* (with Manouchehr Hezarkhani (1966). All these translations from the late 1940s to the mid-1960s, mark Al-e Ahmad's decisive turn towards philosophical and literary existentialism, the typical turn of his generation of intellectuals disappointed with the Tudeh Party and in fact all other forms of organised and disciplined politics. In existentialism they found a personal solace, a literary abode, a philosophical justification for their political disillusions.

There have been so many reprints of Al-e Ahmad's work over the last few decades with tangential and prejudicial prefaces and annotations that it is rare these days to come across editions of Al-e Ahmad's translations with no intro-duction and with cold opening – but nevertheless in personal libraries we can find such editions.[12] Once we come across a text like that we remember how common this turn from Soviet socialism to mostly French existentialism was at this time when there was a common idiomaticity to the prose they wrote. Al-e Ahmad's turn away from the organised politics of the Tudeh Party, his disappointment with the whole project of Soviet socialism, dovetailed with similar events in Europe in which he now took part via a translation project that reveals his penchant for an existential angst ranging from Dostoevsky to Sartre, Camus to Ionesco. The move was both satisfying and creative for Al-e Ahmad, mainly evident in his works of translation but finding its way also to perhaps his single most enduring text, *Khasi dar Miqat* (*Dust in a Desert*), where he discovers what in effect is an existentialist Muslim in him.

Translation: From the Original to the Un/Original

The question of translation has attracted the close attention of leading hermen-euticians like Hans-Georg Gadamer who at one point speaks of 'interpretive paraphrase' as the modus operandi of translation. This is how he puts it:

The agony of translation consists ultimately in the fact that the original words seem to be inseparable from the things they refer to, so that to make a text intelligible one often has to give an interpretive paraphrase of it rather than translate it. The more sensitively our historical consciousness reacts, the more it seems to be aware of the untranslatability of the unfamiliar. But this makes the intimate unity of word and thing a hermeneutical scandal. How can we possibly understand anything written in a foreign language if we are thus imprisoned in our own?[13]

This 'untranslatability of the unfamiliar' is of course not limited to words but extends to the worlds these words project. Gadamer's concern here is between words and things, in one language as opposed to another, but the issue could be extended to the worlds and universes these words and things project. Gadamer is conscious of the overtones of the original that are lost in the course of translation. 'Every translation that takes its task seriously is at once clearer and flatter than the original. Even if it is a masterly re-creation, it must lack some of the overtones that vibrate in the original.'[14] As we flatten the words we translate, we also flatten the worlds these words carry with them. Gadamer also writes of the opening up of 'horizons of understanding' through the act of translation:

Everything written is, in fact, the paradigmatic object of hermeneutics. What we found in the extreme case of a foreign language and in the problems of translation is confirmed here by the autonomy of reading: understanding is not a psychic transposition. The horizon of understanding cannot be limited either by what the writer originally had in mind or by the horizon of the person to whom the text was originally addressed.[15]

Two horizons, one in the original text and the other in the horizon of the un/original here come together and get confounded. The two proses collide and collapse into each other to create a tertiary space which is neither here nor there but somewhere else.

But this collapse of horizons is not a democratic exercise performed on equal footing on a level field. Absent from all these hermeneutic considerations is the embedded power of a language as original and other as un/original – and by who and what and how this is decided. Al-e Ahmad and his wife Simin Daneshvar translated a book from English they called *Chehel Tuti* (*Forty Parrots*) (1972) from B. Hale Wortham's *Enchanted Parrot*, based on the original Sanskrit of Śukasaptati (*c.* twelfth century).[16] In the preface to their translation they say this is the Sanskrit original of Chehel Tuti he had prepared when he wanted to write his doctoral dissertation on the Indian and Persian origins of Arabian Nights. This translation is the exception where the couple feel free to improvise and imitate *Kelilah and Dimnah*.[17]

The original Sanskrit of Śukasaptati (*Seventy Tales*) is a collection of stories narrated by a parrot to a young woman in order to prevent her from going out and having affairs while her husband is away. Neither Al-e Ahmad nor Daneshvar knew any Sanskrit. So they got the story from a British Orientalist, B. Hale Wortham, who had prepared an English translation and called it *Enchanted Parrot*.[18] The irony of the whole production is that the Sanskrit original was first rendered into Persian centuries earlier as *Tuti-nameh* by Ziya' al-Din Nakhshabi (died 1350) a fourteenth-century Persian physician and Sufi living in India. From this Persian and its Turkish translation initially, a German rendition and other European translations had followed. That circulate of the original and the un/original had by Al-e Ahmad's time changed location. It was no longer from Sanskrit into Persian but from English to Persian. Nakhshabi's was at the time of the great Mughal emperor Akbar, Wortham's at the time of British Raj. Between these two imperial contexts the fate of translation from an original had shifted from Sanskrit to Persian and from Persian to English.

At the time of this translation in the 1960s, Persian was at the receiving end of English, French or German in literary and philosophical sources. These European languages were the original and Persian the un/original. That power imbalance, and the political calculus it entailed, had placed the translated prose at a disadvantage of the ideas it could generate. By and large the less a literary culture is anxious about European sources to translate, the more confidence and chutzpah it has to create, whilst the more anxious of the enormity and power of these foreign sources it is, the more stifled its own provocative prose becomes. The period of Al-e Ahmad had reached an optimum of awareness of non-Persian, mostly European, sources. A generation before Al-e Ahmad they were mostly oblivious of these European sources, whilst a generation later they became too much aware of them – to the

Figure 8.1 Jalal Al-e Ahmad and his wife Simin Daneshvar, planting a tree together, Ourazan, 1965. (Photo courtesy of Ali Dehbashi, from the *Bokhara Magazine* archive) Al-e Ahmad and Daneshvar's life together as a couple had its ups and downs, both were deeply in love with each other, and yet the fact that he could not father a child pulled them apart. His brief extramarital affair deeply offended and hurt Daneshvar, but he later sincerely regretted it and she readily forgave him.

point of paralysis. Al-e Ahmad's generation was right in the middle, aware of foreign sources but not too much to frighten its original prose into creative paralysis.

Translator as Ventriloquist

The transmutation of the original and the un/original brings the author, and the translator he chooses to render in his own tongue, to speak for each other, their voices morphing into one another. One of the major French sources Al-e Ahmad had opted to translate into Persian was André Gide's (1869–1951) travelogue to Soviet Union, because in it the towering French icon speaks of his initial fascination, and subsequent disillusion, with Soviet socialism.[19]

In these two books, *Retour de l'U.R.S.S.* (*Return from the U.S.S.R.*) (1936), which details Gide's disillusion with the Russian revolution of 1917, followed by *Retouches à mon retour de l'U.R.S.S.* (*Afterthoughts: A Sequel to* Return from the U.S.S.R.) (1937), Al-e Ahmad had found a voice with which he deeply identified and which vindicated his departure from the Tudeh Party. Al-e Ahmad's own initial fascination and subsequent disillusion with the Soviet-style Stalinist political parties institutionalised in the Tudeh Party of Iran had a similar tone to it, though in Gide he had found a major European public intellectual articulating similar thoughts. He thought himself both vindicated and liberated in Gide's voice.

The result of these translations is a kind of hidden autobiography of Al-e Ahmad and his parting of ways with the Tudeh Party. Every sentence of his Introduction is full of self-referential allusions. Here Al-e Ahmad puts this travelogue next to Gide's travelogues to Congo and Chad to conclude that Gide's parting from Soviet socialism had liberated his humanism.[20] He appreciates Gide's confession of disappointment that he was fooled by the initial promises of Soviet socialism, and his trip in 1936 destroyed that dream with an ice-cold bucket of dreadful reality. It is therefore not surprising that in the Introduction we learn that it was Khalil Maleki who had encouraged Al-e Ahmad to translate Gide's book.[21] From the Introduction, and the fact that he seems to be deeply familiar with Gide's work and is almost done with his translation of *Les Nourritures terrestres/ The Fruits of the Earth/ Ma'edeh-ha-ye Zamini*, we realise he is preoccupied by the towering French intellectual.[22]

The same fascination Al-e Ahmad had with Gide is also evident in his choice of a major Sartre play to translate, *Dast-ha-ye Aludeh/ Dirty Hands/Les Mains sales* (1948), this time because he identifies with its lead character. As Seyyed Ali Shahroudi writes in his short introduction to the translation, Al-e Ahmad's choice of this play is because he identifies with both Sartre and the protagonist of the play.[23] *Les Mains sales* (*Dirty Hands*) was first performed on 2 April 1948 at the Théâtre Antoine in Paris. In the play we encounter Hugo Barine, a young bourgeois intellectual who has joined the Communist faction of a political party under the name of Raskolnikov, the lead character from Dostoevsky's *Crime and Punishment*. Hugo Barine is an idealist and cast in opposition to Hoederer, who is a realist, thus raising the question of whether the legitimate ends justify the immoral means. Because of his relatively rich background, Hugo Barine is not totally trusted by his would-be comrades, and thus he sets upon himself the dangerous task of a political assassination. Al-e Ahmad's Persian translation was also staged in Tehran on 18–25 Esfand 1335 (9–16 March 1957) in the Tehran Theatre, with leading Iranian actors that included Fakhri Khorvash as Jessica, Hugo's nineteen-year-old wife, and Naser Malak-Moti'i as Hoederer.[24] Through Sartre's characters and his play Al-e Ahmad became the vehicle for bringing the post-Stalinist moral conundrum of the European intellectual scene to the Iran of the post-Tudeh Party era.

What soon becomes evident in these works of translation is the fact that they are also something of a fantasy world for Al-e Ahmad, in which he actively imagines himself as a European intellectual, a French dramatic character, a Russian tragic hero, etc. This dramatic state of self-projection became essential to Al-e Ahmad and his generation of public intellectuals. In the originals of these works to which Al-e Ahmad was drawn, we see these public intellectuals and dramatic characters actually living the life of their traumatic age. In casting them into Persian and performing them on the Iranian public sphere, Al-e Ahmad and his followers lived a vicarious life that soon became equally real in its own right. This world was neither European nor non-European. It was a postcolonial world, formally aware and trans-formally conversant with the condition of coloniality from which it was arising. In his seminal essay 'The Task of the Translator', Walter Benjamin writes:

> Translation is a form. To comprehend it as a form, one must go back to the original, for the laws governing the translation lie within the original, contained in the issue of its translatability. The question of whether a work is translatable has a dual meaning. Either: Will an adequate translator ever be found among the totality of its readers? Or, more pertinently: Does its nature lend itself to translation and, therefore, in view of the significance of this form call for it.[25]

There was no doubt a hegemony at work here for Al-e Ahmad, a relation of power he may have been loath to admit. The 'nature' of the originals Al-e Ahmad had selected to translate mostly from the French were as important to him for the substance of their content as they were for the power of their form. The original was French not just in language but also in the power of its hegemonic form, to which Al-e Ahmad was attracted as something more than just political self-vindication. What in effect he was coining in these translations was the very figure of the 'public intellectual', the dramatic persona, the tragic hero. Here 'the laws' Walter Benjamin thought governed the translation did not lie exclusively in the original. Benjamin fetishises 'the original' beyond its worldly existence, especially outside Europe – which he could scarcely fathom. However clumsily and self-consciously performed, once staged in Persian these works assumed a different aura, an aura with which more than anyone else Al-e Ahmad himself cross-identified, rendering their foreign familiarity uncannily attractive to its Persian readership, and in the process positing the figure of a tragic hero as a public intellectual in its Persian version and Iranian prototype dramatically evident and therefore historically viable.

When Cannibalism gives Indigestion

Perhaps the most important translation of Al-e Ahmad in this period is Ernst Jünger's *Ubur-e az Khat/ Über die Linie/Crossing the Line* (1346/1967), with Mahmoud Houman, from the original German of Ernst Jünger's *Über die Linie* (*Crossing the Line*) (1950) – a translation related to his seminal essay *Gharbzadegi* (*Westoxication*).[26] This translation was a shot in the dark by the Iranian Heideggerian professoriate Germanophiles, entirely irrelevant to the central argument of *Gharbzadegi*, covering up its serious connection to anti-colonial literature of the period around the globe, and equally importantly neglecting its connection to Walter Benjamin – if any German echoes were to be sought. The anti-establishment, anti-imperial and iconoclastic significance of a critical thinker like Benjamin was entirely lost on the Germanophiliac (even proto-Nazi) professoriate of the Ahmad Fardid variety. Ernst Jünger had his own highfaluting fascistic ideas and was too arrogant even to join the Nazi Party! Jünger's anti-modernism came from a kind of Germanic romantic fatalism. He is sometimes compared with Heinrich von Kleist and Friedrich Hebbel in their romantic fatalism. Hegel's teleological historicism, Oswald Spengler's gloom and doom, and what the dominant Germanic nihilism had made of Friedrich Nietzsche all came to meet in Jünger.

We now know Jünger's essay *Über die Linie* was first presented to Heidegger on the occasion of Heidegger's sixtieth birthday, and that subsequently Heidegger had responded to it on the occasion of Jünger's own sixtieth birthday. Here is how Vincent Blok, a scholar who has written on the occasion, describes the exchange:

> In Über *die Linie*, which was first published in a *liber amicorum* occasioned by the sixtieth birthday of Heidegger in 1949, Jünger discusses the question of whether we live in the age of fulfilled nihilism and, if so, whether we can overcome such nihilism. Jünger wants to cross the line of nihilism into a new era where '*eine neue Zuwendung des Seins*' takes place and puts an end to the age of fulfilled nihilism . . . Six years later, in 1955, in a *liber amicorum* occasioned on Jünger's own sixtieth birthday, Heidegger responded with an 'open letter': 'Über die Linie', later published as *Zur Seinsfrage*. In this essay, Heidegger insists on the prior question about the essence of nihilism. Contrary to Jünger's crossing the line, Heidegger's main concern is the line itself: 'In the title of your essay *Über die Linie*, the über means as much as: across, trans, meta. By contrast, the following remarks understand the über only in the sense of de, peri. They deal "with" the line itself, with the zone of self-consummating nihilism' . . . In the end, Heidegger argues against Jünger that nihilism cannot be overcome at all and that the question of nihilism must be brought back to the question of Being.[27]

This, as we see, is an entirely domestic exchange between two significant German philosophers far removed from Al-e Ahmad's world and concerns. Just like Ahmad Fardid, Mahmoud Houman had sent Al-e Ahmad on a goose chase, wasting their own and everybody else's time, particularly the time and attention of later scholars who have cited this translation as an indication of Al-e Ahmad's own attraction to the antimodernist sentiments of Ernst Jünger or to his nihilism, or else to Heidegger's critique of modernity. This whole production is a confounded comedy of errors – where the translators have not cannibalised the original but the original has given severe constipation to the translators. Add to this gobbledygook of misbegotten amphigory Dariush Ashuri's habitually boorish defence of 'Western modernity' in his diatribes against Al-e Ahmad, and you get a nauseous headache from the whole theatre of the absurd. Be that as it may, Al-e Ahmad's translation of Jünger's *Über die Linie* into Persian has become something of a misguided bellwether as to the wayward precarity of a critical thinker in the Iranian context where the very author of *Gharbzadegi* becomes the prime example of his own insights.

On the Politics of Untranslatability

In her timely text, *Against World Literature: On the Politics of Untranslatability*, Emily Apter puts forward the argument that we need to reconsider the whole proposition of 'comparative literature' for such an operation, as it works now, has categorically disregarded the issue or more precisely the politics of the 'untranslatability', bringing our attention back to words and ideas that are subject to abusive translations or else disregard.[28] In my own recent intervention in the matter, my book on *The Shahnameh: The Persian Epic as World Literature*, I have opted not to dwell on the issue of words but the much more urgent matter of the worlds that what calls itself 'World Literature' had camouflaged and disregarded.[29] The distance between *words* and *worlds* is where the question of untranslatability points to a far more vibrant politics of the original and the un/original, and the power dynamics of deciding one over the other. What happens if we were to consider the Persian as the original and any European language into which a Persian text is rendered as un/original?

Emily Apter's argument, and the distinction I propose between word and worlds, draws our attention to the manner in which Al-e Ahmad's own crucial text *Gharbzadegi* has been variously translated into English. In this case, the word '*Gharbzadegi*' and the world it represents in fact come actively together. What happens when we consider Al-e Ahmad's Persian as the original and in this case English as un/original? The neologism '*Gharbzadegi*', which Al-e Ahmad borrowed from Ahmad Fardid, we are told, and to which he gave a potent political force, has been variously translated as 'Westoxication', 'Weststrickenness', 'Occidentosis', or even 'Euromania'. Needless to say, none of these words suffice for understanding what Al-e Ahmad meant by '*Gharbzadegi*'. Even Al-e Ahmad himself had to resort to examples to convey what he meant. In one translation, perhaps the best, we read the first crucial paragraph of the original rendered as follows:

I speak of 'occidentosis' as of tuberculosis. But perhaps it more closely resembles an infestation of weevils. Have you seen how they attack wheat? From the inside. The bran remains intact, but it is just a shell, like a cocoon left behind on a tree. At any rate, I am speaking of a disease: an accident from without, spreading in an environment rendered susceptible to it. Let us seek a diagnosis for this complaint and its causes – and, if possible, its cure.[30]

In a note the translator then adds: 'I offer "occidentosis" as a translation for the problematic term *gharbzadagi*, the original title of the work. As the author makes clear here, the force of the metaphor is clinical and focuses on the coercive and invasive qualities of Western influence.'[31]

The fact is that, as evident in his own moral and intellectual life, Al-e Ahmad was not as concerned with 'the invasive qualities of Western influence' as he was with mapping out the contours of a condition of capitalist coloniality. To a large extent because of the difficulty or impossibility even of translating the word '*Gharbzadegi*', Al-e Ahmad has been falsely accused of being *Gharb-setiz* (Europhobic), and therefore 'anti-modern'. The principal ideological nemesis of Al-e Ahmad's, proposing this systematic defamation, is Daryoush Ashuri, whose own wide-eyed and uncritical love for what he calls 'the West' is today much appreciated by the expat enemies of the Islamic Republic. The ruling elite of the Islamic Republic, meanwhile, continue to abuse Al-e Ahmad's term '*Gharbzadeh*' as an insult against their ideological enemies. It is all a comedy of errors!

Al-e Ahmad was not anti-Western, and his kind of critical thinking cannot be reduced to anti-modernity. Western philosophy from Heidegger to Foucault to Baudrillard, and leading up to the whole movement known as 'postmodernity', involves an ongoing critique of the whole project of modernity. Habermas, meanwhile, has defended modernity against the whole postmodern criticism.[32] This European project has ramifications for postcolonial critical thinking, but the two are not identical. Al-e Ahmad and other anticolonial thinkers were at the receiving end of European capitalist modernity and thus were critical of it, as the post-Holocaust critics of Enlightenment modernity like Adorno and Horkheimer were also critical of that project. Like many other critical thinkers from the decolonised and postcolonial world, Al-e Ahmad was rightly critical of colonial modernity. Being critical of the colonial constitution of European modernity does not make one 'anti-modern'. There is an ahistorically backwards assimilation of Al-e

Ahmad to Ahmad Fardid or other Germanophile Heideggerians who falsely collapsed Al-e Ahmad backwards to Jünger, Jünger to Heidegger, Heidegger to Nazism, and Nazism to Islamism. This is a categorically flawed line of thinking. Al-e Ahmad was inadvertently a partner to that false assimilation because, as a public intellectual who had no advanced formal education, he had a chip on his shoulder and became excited when a university professor took him seriously. Today we are all past that flawed moment in Iranian intellectual history.

Much of this assimilation backward to anti-modernity thinking has to do primarily with an over-emphasis and a flawed rendition of the term 'Gharbzadegi', reading it out of Al-e Ahmad's literary and critical context and thus cannibalising it to feed an anti-modern narrative leading to the formation of an Islamic Republic that is simply not true and in fact inimical to Al-e Ahmad's critical character. There has been an over-emphasis on Gharbzadegi at the expense of not just the rest, but in fact the entirety of his work and output. If we were to shift the attention to the much larger frame of Al-e Ahmad's writings, something extraordinary happens. We are not just made aware of the polemical properties of that seminal essay, but far more importantly we are made conscious of the literary disposition of its author, all embedded in his unique, unprecedented and iconic prose. This is not to rob Gharbzadegi of its political potency but in fact to add to it. It is the instrumentality of Al-e Ahmad's iconic prose, and therefore the self-conscious playfulness of that prose, that reveals the unique panache and power of his thinking, a thinking and a prose at once informed by but irreducible to all the contrapuntal forces that had made it possible. Read in this light, the word 'Gharbzadegi' and the world it represents invites a moral and intellectual encounter, and therefore an epistemic overcoming, and not a phobia of the thing that calls itself 'the West', and that we hear echoed in 'Gharb' at the base of 'Gharbzadegi'.

Translation as cannibalism: the poor priest being eaten in Brazil as eucharist, is fair to say is a misreading of eucharist. All such translations are misreading, but they revitalise the allegory of Europe by making the familiar European once more foreign, and the foreign Persian familiar, for ultimately the Verfremdungseffekt is a double-edged sword, it cuts both ways. In the case of Chinese theatre and Ta'ziyeh it is not just the staged play that is de-alienated, but the audience also who are staged and fictionalised. In Al-e Ahmad's translations as well, both French and Persian are de-fetishised and thus de-familiarised and thereby the agency of the author is staged in the very self-conscious mechanism of reading Gide or Camus in Al-e Ahmad's Persian prose.

Notes

1. Jalal Al-e Ahmad's Introduction to his translation of André Gide's *Bazgasht-e az Shoravi* (*Retour de l'U.R.S.S.*) (Tehran: Amir Kabir Publications, 1333/1954): 7.
2. See Susan Bassnett and Harish Trivedi (eds), *Post-colonial Translation: Theory and Practice* (London and New York: Routledge, 1999): 1.
3. Ibid: 2.
4. See Umberto Eco, *The Limits of Interpretation* (Bloomington, IN: Indiana University Press, 1991).
5. See my *Shi'ism: A Religion of Protest* (Cambridge, MA: Harvard University Press, 2011): 9–14.
6. See Hamid Dabashi, 'Found in Translation' (*The New York Times*, The Stone Forum of Contemporary Philosophy, 28 July 2013). Available online here: https://opinionator.blogs.nytimes.com/2013/07/28/found-in-translation/?mtrref=www.google.com&gwh=712ADB03703C9DA77E410CF4E7E44F8D&gwt=pay&assetType=REGIWALL.
7. Jalal Al-e Ahmad's (Translator), *Dostoevsky's Qomarbaz/The Gambler/Игрокъ* (Tehran: Ferdows Publications, 1384): 5.
8. Bertolt Brecht, 'Alienation Effects in Chinese Acting', in John Willett (Edited and Translated), *Brecht on Theatre* (New York: Hill and Wang, 1964): 91–3.
9. Dabashi, *Shi'ism* (Op. Cit.): 213–17.
10. For a more detailed argument see chapter six, 'Europe: The Indefinite Jest', in my *Europe and its Shadows: Coloniality after Empire* (Op. Cit.).
11. See George Steiner, *After Babel: Aspects of Language and Translation* (Oxford: Oxford University Press, 1975): 28.
12. As in a copy I have of Jalal Al-e Ahmad and Manouchehr Hezarkhani (Translators), *Teshnegi va Goshnegi/La Soif et la faim/Hunger and Thirst*. (Tehran: Amir Kabir, 1351/1972).
13. See Hans-Georg Gadamer, *Truth and Method* (London: Continuum, 1975): 403.
14. Ibid: 388.

15. Ibid: 396.
16. Jalal Al-e Ahmad and Simin Daneshvar (Translators), *Chehel Tuti/Forty Parrots*, illustrated by Ardeshir Mohassess (Tehran: Mowj Publishers, 1351/1972).
17. Ibid: 10–11.
18. For that English version from which Al-e Ahmads and Daneshvar prepared their Persian translation see B. Hale Wortham (Translator), *The Enchanted Parrot: Being a Selection from the 'Suka Saptati', or, The Seventy Tales of Parrot* (London: Luzac & Co., 1911).
19. See Jalal Al-e Ahmad's Introduction to his translation of André Gide's *Bazgasht-e az Shoravi (Retour de l'U.R.S.S.)* (Tehran: Amir Kabir, 1351/1972, the original edition 1333/1954): 7–16. This volume is actually the translation of both *Retour de l'U.R.S.S. (Return from the U.S.S.R.)* (1936) and *Retouches à mon retour de l'U.R.S.S. (Afterthoughts: A Sequel to* Return from the U.S.S.R.) (1937).
20. Ibid: 8.
21. Ibid: 15–16.
22. Ibid: 16.
23. Jalal Al-e Ahmad (Translator), *Dast-ha-ye Aludeh/ Dirty Hands/Les Mains sales* (Tehran: Majid Publications, 1387): 10.
24. Ibid: 11.
25. See Walter Benjamin, 'The Task of the Translator', in Marcus Bullock and Michael W. Jennings (eds), *Selected Writings of Walter Benjamin*, volume 1, 1913–1926 (Cambridge, MA: Harvard University Press, 1996): 254.
26. See Jalal Al-e Ahmad and Mahmoud Houman (Translators), *Ernst Jünger's Ubur-e az Khat/ Über die Linie/Crossing the Line* (Tehran: Barg Publications, 1370/1991, originally published in 1346/1967).
27. Vincent Blok, 'An Indication of Being – Reflections on Heidegger's Engagement with Ernst Jünger' (*Journal of the British Society for Phenomenology*, vol. 42, no. 2, May 2011): 194.
28. See Emily Apter, *Against World Literature: On the Politics of Untranslatability* (London and New York: Verso, 2013).
29. See Hamid Dabashi, *The Shahnameh: The Persian Epic as World Literature* (New York: Columbia University Press, 2019).
30. See Jalal Al-e Ahmad, *Occidentosis: A Plague from the West*, translated by R. Campbell, annotations and introduction by Hamid Algar (Berkeley, CA: Mizan Press, 1984): 27.
31. Ibid: 138.

32. For a collection of critical essays on this issue see Maurizio Passerin d'Entrèves and Seyla Benhabib (eds) *Habermas and the Unfinished Project of Modernity: Critical Essays on The Philosophical Discourse of Modernity* (Cambridge, MA: The MIT Press, 1997).

9

From a Short Life to a Lasting Legacy: Towards a Post-Islamist Liberation Theology

One more thing: Consider it a confession, a protest, an apostasy, or whatever else you wish – in this pilgrimage I was mostly in search of my own brother, and of other brothers, rather than in search of God, for he who believes in God, He is everywhere.[1]

Jalal Al-e Ahmad, *Khasi dar Miqat* (*Dust in the Desert*) (1964)

Why should one bother to go back and re-examine the short life and enduring significance of a public intellectual if not to push his crucial but limited achievements forward and place them on a global stage? It is now time for me to bring all my previous chapters together in this final push to deliver on my main objective of suggesting Al-e Ahmad as a harbinger of a post-Islamist liberation theology.[2]

Al-e Ahmad is revered and reviled by his admirers and detractors at one and the same time – both for entirely wrong reasons. He is revered by some and reviled by others because he is thought as a founding figure of the Islamic Republic. He was no such thing. He died almost a decade before the Islamic Republic violently took over the multifaceted foregrounding of the Iranian revolution of 1977–9. The bizarre assumption that he thought of Israel as a model for Iran almost a decade before Khomeini had articulated his theory of '*Velayat-e Faqih*' is inane. There was a strong Islamic streak in his character and culture, but he was no Islamist. After his death, Ali Shari'ati took this Islamic streak and drove it fast to the edge of militant Islamism, before he too died and passed the baton in turn to the even more fanatically Islamist functionary Abdolkarim Soroush who began his career as an ideologue of the triumphant Islamic Republic, completely siding with the ruling power before he exhausted his usefulness to the ruling Islamists and was spat out of its system. We must, as I have stated in my *Theology of Discontent*, categorically distinguish between the preparatory ideological foregrounding of the Iranian revolution of 1977–9 and its violent takeover by militant Islamists following Khomeini's lead. In my *Theology of Discontent*, I mapped out the historical trajectory of one Muslim critical thinker leading to the next, but there was no inevitability in any one of such moves. Beginning with Al-e Ahmad, these thinkers were in *dialogue* with the world, which the ruling Islamists instead seek to rule. Al-e Ahmad died without anticipating Shari'ati, and Shari'ati died without anticipating Khomeini or Soroush. It is only in retrospect that this chain of diverse thinkers might be read in anticipation of the Iranian revolution but not in the violent takeover of the Islamic Republic. If we are, as I intend here, to think towards a post-Islamist liberation theology we must start by disbanding this group of affiliations we had put together when trying to understand the Islamic component of the Iranian revolution of 1977–9.

When placed in his own pre-revolutionary time and space, Al-e Ahmad can be seen as a product of a multifaceted and pluralistic environment and by far its most important intellectual representative. He was a deeply cultivated and engaged intellectual rather than a cleric like Khomeini, or a revolutionary ideologue like Shari'ati, or a power-hungry preacher like Soroush. His domain of significance was the public sphere in which he resided and placed himself, as opposed to the clerical order that had a tangential presence in that public sphere. But, and here is the main point, he was a *Muslim* intellectual for he never abandoned his moral, imaginative, political or revolutionary commitment to the Muslim world; he remained as a Muslim, and not in a meaningless category called 'secular'. His towering figure became particularly palpable only after he died and soon after that a cataclysmic revolution happened in which single-sited monological fanaticism took over. He had no presence in that violent takeover. He was dead at the young age of forty-five. The sins of the Islamic Republic, and there are many, cannot be written in his balance sheet. It is therefore important to retrieve the cosmopolitan character of a Muslim intellectual at the height of his literary and political prowess, as I have sought to do in this book, for the events of the Muslim world since his passing have radically altered the character and disposition of what it means to be a Muslim intellectual. The events in the Muslim world ever since the Iranian revolution of 1977–9 and the subsequent Islamist takeover of its political culture and the consolidation of an Islamic Republic have radically changed the world Al-e Ahmad helped create and left behind when he rushed to meet his creator.

Al-e Ahmad as Anticolonial Icon and Postcolonial Thinker

Throughout this book I have affirmed that my purpose in writing on a seminal Muslim intellectual is to argue our path toward the articulation of a post-Islamist liberation theology, a path that ipso facto will have to be a pre-Islamist liberation theology. It is now time for me to deliver on that promise. I make a categorical distinction between the two terms 'Islamic' and 'Islamist'. 'Islamic liberation theology' is deeply rooted in Islamic intellectual traditions but is widely conversant with the world. 'Islamism' on the other hand is the product of the Muslim encounter with European colonialism and has actively cannibalised Muslim intellectual traditions for the sake of a triumphalist encounter with 'the West'. For this reason, I equate 'Islamism' with 'Zionism', and regard them in fact, though both evidently at odds with each other, as identical ideological products of European colonialism.

Al-e Ahmad was a unique and seminal figure in the history of Muslim anticolonial thinking. He thought and wrote on a critical borderline between what before and after him was falsely divided between 'secular' and 'religious' thinking. I have always been drawn to him for he does not completely belong to either of these two camps, for he speaks a language that had subsumed and surpassed them both. He had defied them both to craft his own prose. This fact becomes most evident if we were to place him in the immediate context of the last forty years since the Iranian revolution of 1977–9 and how he enables and yet compromises the voices of those who have come after him. In this context we might say that Ali Shari'ati was the unanticipated consequence of Al-e Ahmad, as Morteza Motahhari was an unanticipated consequence of Ali Shari'ati, and Abdolkarim Soroush would lay claim on all their legacies from a position of political power. The fact is that there was a Shari'ati waiting to happen in Al-e Ahmad, as there was a Motahhari waiting to happen in Shari'ati, and perforce a Soroush was contingent on them all. None of them could possibly know what the full implication of their prose and politics would be – and above all they could not have possibly known they were in fact anticipating a Khomeini. How could they? But the ground zero of them all, what made them all possible, was Jalal Al-e Amad. There was no inevitability in this direction, but a powerful potentiality that indeed took place. That potentiality became an actuality only retroactively. I wish to reverse that retroactive direction and capture Al-e Ahmad at the moment when, in addition to Shari'ati et al., any number of other things were also possible in him. I have sought to reconnect with that polyphonic moment.

There was neither a teleology nor an inevitability to the movement from Al-e Ahmad to Shari'ati and from Shari'ati to Khomeini. But Abdolkarim Soroush was fully aware and in fact integral to the political machinery of the Islamist takeover of the Iranian revolution of 1977–9. By making such crucial distinctions in this book I have sought to trace our critical thinking back to that seminal moment when Jalal Al-e Ahmad appeared on the Iranian political and intellectual scene, before he was yanked into a direction of which he may or may not have approved. My contention here is not speculative intellectual history. My objective is rather to clear the air of suspicion and narrow in on the fact and phenomenon of Jalal Al-Ahmad himself before any and all such uses and abuses in the aftermath of the Islamist takeover of the Iranian revolution. I do so not for any antiquarian or nostalgic interests, of which I trust I am now cured, but for the fact that I believe such a retrieval, before it is forever lost, is crucial for our post-Islamist critical thinking. I call Al-e Ahmad 'the last Muslim intellectual' precisely because I wish to make a distinction between the possibility of a Muslim cosmopolitan thinking and an Islamist triumphalist ideologue like Shari'ati or a repentant preacher like Soroush. I do not consider either of them, Shari'ati or Soroush, an 'intellectual' in this open-minded, expansive and worldly sense.

What is certain is that Jalal Al-e Ahmad was the integral product of a radically different period of intellectual organicity when the critical thinker was deeply rooted in a dialogical thinking and a national consciousness, but still fully aware of the transnational public sphere upon which that dialogical disposition and that national consciousness was formed. With the theocratic success of the Islamic Republic upon the ruins of the intellectual effervescence of the Iranian revolution of 1977–9, a shallow conception and category of 'religious intellectuals' emerged that blocked and dismantled that cosmopolitan worldliness and began to look at the world outside its flawed self-conception from the alienated insecurity of an insurmountable nativism. What they called 'tradition' was of course a colonially fabricated conception of Islam – of which fact they were entirely clueless. What they dismissed, or later embraced, as 'secularism' or 'modernity' or 'the West' were none of those in truth, and were in fact aspects of the cosmopolitan worldliness they were too blind and prejudiced to see, too limited in their critical imagination to overcome.

Not so paradoxically, the Pahlavi authoritarianism of the 1930s to the 1960s was conducive to that cosmopolitism while the Islamic Republic that succeeded it ruled for the following forty years over a systematically single-sited, morally myopic, imaginatively broken and intellectually deprived world. Al-e Ahmad's Marxism, as that of most his other contemporaries, was patently messianic, or Mahdistic to be more precise, but before Shari'ati took that Marxism from Al-e Ahmad and ran it aground into a single-sited Shi'i eschatology, Al-e Ahmad was practising it on a much wider, much richer and far more enabling canvas that ranged from politics to poetics to aesthetics. His brief membership and subsequent dismissal of the Tudeh Party was a clear sign of this liberated critical thinking. Persian literary and poetic humanism was and remains a mighty force and one of which the Islamism of Ali Shari'ati and his followers remained clueless. As an iconoclastic and a maverick public intellectual, Al-e Ahmad was integral to that cosmopolitanism – in both its classical and contemporary compositions. It was precisely in being both a Marxist and a Shi'a Muslim, and reading and writing the world while drawn to philosophical existentialism, that those two concurrent and contradictory planes of Al-e Ahmad's legacy are instrumental in re-imagining the cosmopolitan worldliness of our post-Islamist political thinking. In my book *The Arab Spring: The End of Postcolonialism* (2012) I have already addressed an open-ended revolutionary momentum that had decoupled the colonial concoction of the 'nation' from the myth of its 'state' in understanding and theorising the larger contours of that national/transnational public sphere and consciousness.[3] In this book I have sought to retrieve that cosmopolitanism through perhaps its single most prominent intellectual figure.

A Potent Prose and a Liberating Politics

In the life, legacy and character of Al-e Ahmad we witness, as I trust I have managed to show in this book, the coming together of a potent prose and a liberating politics both informing the effervescent dawning of a Muslim cosmopolis that his time promised but his history failed to deliver. Al-e Ahmad wrote the literary prose and articulated the emancipatory politics of a Muslim cosmopolis that read and received the world in terms at once receptive and critical, embracing of its location, open-minded to its otherwise. That literary prose and that liberation politics of the Muslim cosmopolis were definitive to his critical thinking. The telegraphic power and the literary panache of that proverbial prose marked its potent presence in defining Iranian postcolonial polity. Al-e Ahmad's thinking was so embedded in that particular prose that an entire generation sought but failed to emulate. His prose was real, living, lively, potent, robust, healthy, quick, agile, responsive and probing all at the same time. This entire book, one might say, is my attempt at grasping the potency and promise of that prose and mapping it out for the posterity.

Al-e Ahmad died long before the Islamic Republic abused his memory, among the other memories it abused, to consolidate its power. When it took over the militant leadership of the Iranian revolution of 1977–9 and ascended to power, the ruling echelons of the Islamic Republic, particularly its propaganda machinery, sought to eradicate, cannibalise and overcome such memories. Over the last forty years, the Islamic Republic has systematically abused and wasted all the political prowess of Islam very much on the model that Israel and Zionism abused and dishonoured Judaism, or the Myanmar genocidal Buddhists did with Buddhism, or Hindu fundamentalists did with Hinduism, or Evangelical Zionists with Christianity. In this vein, militant Islamism, xenophobic Zionism, puritanical Hinduism and jingoistic Buddhism have all been the common dialectical outcomes of European colonialism. Al-e Ahmad is the last evidence of how Islam, and in his case Shi'ism in particular, was capable of producing worldly public intellectuals, actively conversant with the world. That particularly worldly cosmopolitanism has come to a crushing end with the combined calamities of Islamism, Zionism, Evangelical Christianity, Hindu fundamentalism and Buddhist genocidal militancy.

Within Islam in particular today, Shi'a sectarianism, emanating from Iran, and Wahhabi jihadism, headquartered in Saudi Arabia, are the combined fanatical calamities wreaking havoc in the region. Without a careful assessment of that bygone history, and reading Al-e Ahmad as one of its finest achievements, it is impossible to collect our courage to look beyond the current predicaments of Muslim and non-Muslim sectarianism. Al-e Ahmad was a Muslim and his Islam was wholesome, critical, complete, worldly and dialogically engaged with the world at large. The rapidity of events over the last forty years since the Iranian revolution of 1977–9 and the violent imposition of an Islamic Republic at its peak have made it impossible to catch our breath and figure out what has exactly happened and how we got here. But in catching our breath, my contention in this book has been how we have lost something far more crucial than just the collapse of one monarchical dynasty and the rise of a militant Islamist theocracy. But what exactly is it that we have lost? And what is it we are yet to gain? Asef Bayat's notion of 'post-Islamism' and my own idea of 'post-ideological' are among the indications that ever since the Green Movement in Iran (2008–10) and the Arab Spring in the larger Arab World (2010–12) we have entered a new era. I have done my share of thinking and writing about where I think we are. It is perhaps in my *Islamic Liberation Theology* (2008) that I have most consistently reflected on our historical whereabouts. But it was not until I began to think of this book on Al-e Ahmad that the enormity of this passage from pre- to post-Islamism began to dawn on me. To face that challenge, we must go to the epicentre of Al-e Ahmad's anxiety about 'the West', at the heart of his 'Westoxication' diagnosis, the presumed centre that for long now can no longer hold.

The foregrounding for a post-Islamist liberation theology must first overcome 'the West' as its most disorienting alterity, and then override its own manufactured sectarian tensions as an internalised subterfuge for the external binary of 'Islam and the West'. The heavily politicised Sunni–Shi'a sectarianism and the Arab-Persian ethno-nationalism are both the loaded legacies of the colonial dictum of *divide and rule* and as such the internalised binaries reflecting the external bipolarity posited between 'Islam and the West'. As 'the West' has now metaphorically imploded, and thus 'Islam and the West' disengaged, so must its internalised projections onto Sunni–Shi'a divide and Arab-Persian binary be overcome. The living legacy of Jalal Al-e Ahmad I have detailed in this book reveals in detail a creative cosmopolitan consciousness that unfolded upon a transnational public sphere with the piercing critical judgement of a postcolonial knowing subject. He was a thinker of uncommon versatility who asserted his moral imagination and intellectual autonomy as a pre-Islamist prototype that can best be reimagined for that post-Islamist eventuality. With that figure in mind, I therefore begin this final chapter with the collapse of the metaphor of 'the West', go on to dismantle the colonially manufactured sectarian binaries of Sunni (Arab) against Shi'a (Iranian), and then conclude with the reassertion of a post-Islamist critical consciousness befitting a Muslim knowing subject far beyond the colonial legacies of mere protest as destiny. At the moment of liberation from its colonial predicament, the post-Islamist liberation theology has a fateful moment of solidarity with similar liberation in its two other sister religions: post-Zionist Judaism and post-Evangelical Christianity.

The life of Al-e Ahmad has given way to a manufactured legacy by the ruling Islamic Republic in his homeland compatible with and at the service of their otherwise belligerent and fragile ideology. They have named highways and literary prizes after his name and printed stamps in his honour. That legacy has less to do with Al-e Ahmad and more with the ideological apparatus of the Islamic Republic itself. The writing of this biography of Al-e Ahmad has been a prelude for me, as I said at the outset, to retrieve his life for a markedly different legacy, the long and still unfolding drama of postcolonial liberation from the combined calamities of European colonialism and the reactionary, nativist and self-defeating responses it engendered. This legacy, the cosmopolitan worldliness of Al-e Ahmad, when Islam was *in* the world rather than *against* it, I have sought to retrieve and document chapter and verse and now wish to wed to a post-Islamist liberation theology – a theology that is missing from a more global and worldly struggle for liberation from the shadow of Europe and the condition of coloniality it has engendered. The collapse of the metaphor of 'the West' is coterminous with the urgent need for overcoming the sectarian binaries it had generated to divide the world in order to rule it better. As 'the last Muslim intellectual', Al-e Ahmad is the living memory of that fateful liberation, of finally decolonising the postcolonial mind, of overcoming Islamism by paving the way towards a post-Islamist liberation theology.

After Europe: When the 'Western' Centre cannot Hold

Quite early in his *After Europe* (2017), Ivan Krastev makes a very apt observation – that by never considering the possibility of European disintegration, the framers of the European Union have led themselves to believe its integration inevitable.[4] This avoidance I might add is a sign of a return of the repressed, for the Europeans to realise they stand on very thin allegorical ice. Reading Krastev's learned and passionate book, widely praised by Europeanists, two things immediately grab your attention, not because but in fact despite the author's witty attempts to claim otherwise: (1) The idea of the European Union is a cold and calculated economic project predicated on an allegorical delusion; and (2) the influx of a few thousand immigrants from former European colonies has triggered and exposed the racist foundations of that allegory. What Europeans call their 'refugee crisis' is a mere tiny fragment of the terror of globalisation coming home to roost. So long as the masses of racist Europeans (now storming into Neo-Nazi rallies) were the beneficiaries of their leaders' plundering the world, they had no problem with the predatory logic of capitalism. Now that the very same logic of globalisation is sending a mere fragment of those it has ravaged heading towards European borders, suddenly they fear for their own jobs and worry about 'their culture'. As a Bulgarian observer, Krastev both yearns for his share of 'Europe' and yet fears its destruction just decades after the collapse of the Eastern Bloc of the Soviet Union allowed Eastern Europeans feel a bit 'European' about themselves. As late arrivals, they protest too much. They have a particular hostility towards Muslim immigrants, reminding as they do the Western Europeans how Eastern Europeans are as much strangers to their 'Europe' as these Muslim 'caravans'.

As in the aftermath of Brexit and the simmering murmurs of any number of other centrifugal forces at work – from Greece to Spain – pushing away from the troubled delusion of 'Europe', and while Europeans thus caught in the midst of their own meandering metaphor wonder what to do with themselves, the rest of the world is busy with the real parable of where their own futures lie beyond the delusion of Europe giving them a binary imbalance about who they are. One can only imagine what Al-e Ahmad would have wondered; where the *Gharb* ('The West') in his *Gharbzadegi* ('Westoxication') would be today. The violent turn of sectarianism throughout the Muslim world maps the contours of a corresponding collusion of an identity politics that mirrors and exacerbates the colonial condition of divide-and-rule European imperialism had occasioned ever since their colonial occupation and theft in India. In the course of the European colonial domination of Muslim lands following the decline and fall of the Ottoman Empire, 'Islam itself' became a colonial concoction manufactured in the binary engineering of 'Islam and the West' where and when the mirror images began to exacerbate and corroborate each other – 'Islam' did for 'the West' what 'the West' did for 'Islam', imagining one in the mirror image of the other. That colonial conception of 'Islam Itself' then in turn began to dig deeper into its own postcolonial grave with the rise of a rampant sectarianism that was blinded to its own colonial origins. In the 1960s when Al-e Ahmad wrote his *Gharbzadegi* no such facts or insights were or could have been known to him.

With the identity crisis of 'Europe', and thus the collapse of 'the West' as a metaphysical metaphor, 'Islam' too has been liberated from this binary bondage to this 'West'. In what Asef Bayat has aptly diagnosed as the phenomenon of 'post-Islamism' lies the groundwork for the future of a theology that will one day liberate itself from the colonial conditioning of this 'Islam itself' and all its contingent sectarian identity politics.[5] The 'Islamist' in Bayat's 'post-Islamism', I venture to say, is the 'Islam' of the 'Islam and the West', the Islamism that Western colonialism had engineered and cross-essentialised (just like 'the West') in Muslim lands, the triumphalism Islamist that Muslims rushed to co-invent at the heavy price of their own multifaceted worldly religion. We would need to remember in detail how the colonially conditioned 'Islam' and its ideological Islamism resulted in postcolonial sectarianism. Through the same logic, at the heart of Emmanuel Levinas's 'Face of the Other' and Gianni Vattimo's 'Weak Christianity', we see glimmers of hope of a Judaism beyond the abuses of Zionism and a Christianity after the horrors of its colonial heritage. The mere possibility of a liberation theology of all these three world religions coinciding opens vastly different horizons for the liberating alterity of the postcolonial person. More specifically, and closer to the task at hand, is the need to navigate the path from within the postcolonial conditioning of Islamist sectarianism towards the open space of a post-Islamist liberation theology. In the cosmopolitan worldliness of

Al-e Ahmad's legacy, as I have outlined it in detail in this book, we have a solid evidence of what that liberation would look like: worldly, dialogical, conversant, playful, with an abiding alterity at the centre of its identity.

The Sunnis, the Shi'is and the Sushis

For any future theology, philosophy, or ethics of liberation, we need a categorical disengagement between Europe and its shadows, between 'the West and the Rest'.[6] A decoupling of Europe from the destructive hold it has had over its main nemesis – Islam and Muslims – is definitive to any emerging theology of post-Islamism. By dwelling on the inner dynamics of the thing Europe calls 'Islam' we must expand our critical understanding of how Muslims are now liberated from their fabricated binary opposition to Europe and 'the West', via a recognition of their identity and alterity – of who they are and who they are not, in terms domestic to their postcolonial provenance. Theorising that provenance is the most elementary step towards a post-Islamist liberation theology. But how can we even imagine such a future liberation theology when Muslims are so ferociously divided, so it seems, along presumed ethnic and sectarian divides – Persians and Arabs, Sunnis and Shi'is? Beyond the apparition of these divides, the case of Al-e Ahmad offers us a potent blueprint for a critical agency at the epicentre of a postcolonial subject reclaiming moral and intellectual authority to imagine and navigate the prospect of a post-Islamist liberation theology.

Thinking through the sectarian tensions within Islam, between the Sunnis and the Shi'is in particular, as they are politically perceived today, enables us to mark and dismantle that binary. The hostility presumed between Sunnis and Shi'is is an entirely colonial product – categorically at odds with the precolonial place of such pluralistic readings of Islam. The dialectic of orthodoxy and heterodoxy throughout Islamic history has actually been a condition of emotive and theological pluralism and not identarian politics as we understand it today. It was only during the fateful encounter of Muslims with European imperialism that they robbed their own religion of its cosmopolitan and pluralistic proportions and turned it into a singular site of ideological contestation against European imperialism. With that mission partially accomplished and mostly defeated, Muslims are now on the cusp of a new discovery of their worldliness – not in antiquarian but in an entirely renewed sense of worldly belonging. The aggressive hostilities between Iran and Saudi Arabia now seek to resuscitate a deeply colonial tension between Sunnis and Shi'is. However, the fact of that rivalry is far more predicated on regional rivalries than on factual theological differences. This shifting of attention away from Europe and deep into the Muslim lived-experience, both historical and contemporary, helps us actively decouple the central metaphor of 'Europe' from any relevance in the most potent polar preoccupation of one of its chief manufactured nemeses. We just finished reading Al-e Ahmad from beginning to end. He was a Shi'a, born and raised in a prominent Shi'a clerical family. But he never thought of himself as a sectarian Shi'a. He thought of himself, and he left a sustained record of his life, as a worldly Muslim.

With the rise of the self-appointed Islamic State (IS) (also known as ISIS or ISIL – Islamic State of Iraq and Sham, or Islamic State of Iraq and Levantine, respectively) in the Arab and Muslim world in the aftermath of the Arab revolutions of 2011, the increasingly complicated geopolitics of the region is systematically and consistently over-simplified by being often analysed along sectarian and ethnic lines: Sunnis versus Shi'is or Arabs versus Persians. Such false and falsifying binaries not only do not help us understand the nature of the conflicts across the world at large, but in fact camouflage them in deceptively simplified conceptual binaries. Presumed sectarian differences between Sunnis and Shi'is or between 'secular' and 'religious' convictions and sentiments, ideologies and their corresponding movements, serve as the main explanations for conflicts and wars in multiple Arab and Muslim countries. These are the result of specific political developments and propaganda machinations and must be understood in these terms and not assimilated backward into long historical developments in Islamic theological pluralism. The immediate urgencies of such events cut them off from their historical roots and enduring facts that contradict their abusive interpretations.

By critically reflecting on such false identity constructions and their significance, we need to look for very different and alternative interpretations of where we stand and where we are headed in a post-Western world that is losing 'the West' as its central hegemonic metaphor. We need to think through multiple starting points of our alternative narratives: from the cataclysmic events of 9/11, or from the Iran–Iraq war of 1980–8, or perhaps from the Iranian revolution of 1977–9 – each one of such events will give us a slightly different angle but ultimately a correcting lens for seeing the way the avalanche of events demands and exacts falsifying narratives. In either of those cases the geopolitics of the region will give us a much more realistic and immediate assessment of the current crisis than outdated and misplaced theological differences falsely presumed between one group of Muslims who followed one Muslim leader or another after the death of the Prophet more than 1400 years ago. Islam is a living organism and a changing universe and thus its most sacrosanct principles are always perceived in a state of flux. What has happened in Muslim history between the time of the Prophet and his immediate companions and today is a vertiginous spectrum of historical interpolations that refuse docile bifurcations.

As we have seen in specific details, Jalal Al-e Ahmad was the last Muslim intellectual of his generation who thought as a Muslim with his lived experiences as Muslim having metamorphosed into a global vision of what today we might consider a post-Islamist liberation theology. How are we to extend Al-e Ahmad's lived and thought-through experiences if we were to take the central metaphor of his critical thinking, 'the West', away from him and allow him to breathe more freely for our current realities and future emancipation?

Deep History

If we move back to examine a much deeper history that had informed and animated Jalal Al-e Ahmad we can see both Sunnis and Shi'is as having been integral to the worldly context of the Muslim moral imagination and imperial context, from the Umayyads and the Abbasids early in Islamic history more than a thousand years ago down to the Ottomans, the Safavids and the Mughals, when European colonial interests and imperial adventures began to infringe on these later Muslim empires. These prolonged integrations have been in a variety of theological, philosophical, mystic or altogether scholastic and humanist traditions. No one except scholars of these fields today has any patience left for these panoramic views of Muslim history and what they could mean. Suffice it to say that the juridical reasoning of the Islamic legal heritage at the roots of Sunni–Shi'i divide has been systematically, consistently and institutionally challenged and framed within a much larger pluralistic social setting by philosophical and mystical interpretations of Muslim scholastic heritage. It is a matter of historical fallacy to disregard that discursive context and cherry-pick only sectarian dimensions of the divide, and draw meaningful conclusion from them. Muslims like Al-e Ahmad were the contemporary outcome of such a deep-rooted historical imagination.

It is only under European colonial domination, both normative and imaginative, that Muslims have been instrumental in robbing themselves of that multifarious heritage and turning their own faith into a monolithic totality, and their heterodox effervescence degenerated into sectarian conflict. This dominant sectarianism I therefore suggest is a by-product of colonial contestation, when Muslims began aggressively transforming their own worldly religion into a singular site of ideological resistance against European imperialism, or what they called 'the West'. Al-e Ahmad's *Westoxication* is a product of this transmutation – and therefore its *pharmakon*. The early generation responsible for this fateful transformation, revolutionary activists like Jamal al-Din al-Afghani, Muhammad Abdu or Rashid Rida cannot be blamed (or exonerated) for having done this to Islamic intellectual history. They were facing a monumental military, political and intellectual assault. Be that as it may, what today passes for 'Sunnism' or 'Shi'ism' is in fact a complete distortion of Muslim historical experience and the continuation of an aggressive degeneration of Islamic moral, intellectual, imaginative and worldly pluralism under colonial duress – and as in fact performed by these leading revolutionary thinkers. While in his *Westoxication* Al-e Ahmad partook in that binary opposition, in the fuller body of his multifaceted work he had already overcome it.

If, as I suggest, the presumption that hostility between Sunnis and Shi'is is the root cause of the current crisis in the Arab and Muslim world is indeed fallacious, then how are we to understand these two major readings of Islam – and how would that understanding liberate Muslims from the binary trap of 'Islam and the West'? The initial conflict between the nascent communities of Muslims regarding the question of succession to Prophet Muhammad (who died in 632 CE) did not give rise to anything more significant than a mere family feud among the early Muslims. These feuds were eventually conflated with the internecine tribal rivalries among pre-Islamic Arabs and led to a number of fateful battles and civil wars among early Muslims. What was later theologically systematised and known as 'Sunnism' was and has ever since remained the confessional matrix of the overwhelming majority of Muslims

– and conversely what was much later systematised and termed 'Shi'ism' did not in any significant sense differ from the majority in terms of principled theological centrality of God, the sanctity of the Qur'an, or the significance of the Prophetic traditions as three pillars of Islamic law. As I have argued extensively in my previous works, *Authority in Islam* (1989) in particular, Sunnism and Shi'ism were in essence two different manners of coming to terms with the charismatic authority of the Prophet and the trauma of his death.[7] While the Sunnis opted to institutionalise his authority, the Shi'is transferred it to individual members of his family, from his daughter Fatima and his son-in-law Ali to eleven other male descendants in the main branch of Shi'ism.

There is much doctrinal articulation and communal ritual that stands between Al-e Ahmad's generation and these nascent events. But definitive to our current sociological reading of these early Islamic events remains the fact that Sunnism and Shi'ism emerged as two complementary takes, or two alternative readings, on the prophetic authority of Muhammad, and each has reflected and augmented the other. While Shi'ism preserved the Prophet's charismatic revolt, Sunnism reflected his proclivity for institution-building – so that one might even suggest Shi'ism celebrated his early Meccan period, while Sunnism his latter Medinan period. As I have repeatedly argued, all Muslims are Shi'is when they follow a charismatic leader and revolt against tyranny, and all Muslims are Sunnis when they seek to institutionalise the juridical terms of their endurance as Muslim communities. Neither have Sunnis been exempt from chronic uprisings against tyranny, nor have Shi'is hesitated from developing enduring intuitions of juridical and political authority. These elementary facts of Islamic doctrinal history have been systematically glossed over under the militant political duress of European colonial presence, in which Muslim intellectuals themselves have been instrumental in pushing their faith into the trap of 'Islam and the West'. The period we now call 'post-Islamist' is not the end of Islam. It is the emancipation of Muslims from this trap.

I offer this reading of the innate pluralism at the heart of the Muslim communal experience in order to safeguard Al-e Ahmad's Islam from the rampant sectarianism of the Islamism that succeeded his generation of public intellectuals and thus threatens to pigeonhole him somewhere where he does not belong. It is as a harbinger of that liberated Islam – vocal and ambi-dextrous with the world – that we can read Al-e Ahmad as evidence of a post-Islamist liberation theology.

From Theology to Demography

We have to place the theological argument I put forward here briefly (and have developed much more extensively in my other books)[8] next to a sociological, demographic and anthropological fact that Muslims (Sunnis and Shi'is) have lived and intermarried as Sunnis and Shi'is throughout their histories, and therefore the satirical term 'Sushi' (the magnificent offspring of Sunnis and Shi'is intermarrying) is in fact a perfect indicator of the reality of Muslim lives throughout the world. That crucial fact is completely camouflaged when we allow the fictive barriers manufactured between sects and sectarianism to degenerate the robust effervescence of Muslim intellectual life.

This reading of the Sunni and Shi'i divide should prevent any more undue emphasis on the manufactured sectarian rift and far more urgently draw our attention to the current scene of masses of millions of Muslims from war-torn areas leaving their homelands and some of them eventually finding their ways to Europe, facing two diametrically opposed receptions: (1) welcomed by some Europeans, and (2) conversely aggravating the xeno-phobic neurosis of many others. These refugees are the more intensified forms of labour migrations from poorer to richer countries and as such are a much more global phenomenon and not limited to Muslims coming to Christian countries to give them identity crises. But so far as these migrations are happening from Muslim countries, it is high time Europe came to face with two contradictory facts: (1) their own colonial histories, that Europeans crossed these borders into Muslim lands long before Muslims did; and (2) the Muslims' arrival in Europe is the return of the European repressed, some-thing in the making of the deeply forgotten European history. Since Tariq ibn Ziyad led the Islamic Umayyad conquest of Visigoth Hispania (711–18), since the Battle of Tours/Battle of Poitiers (October 732), since the Muslim conquest of Sicily (827–902), since the Fall of Constantinople (1453), and since the Christian European anxieties expressed in Dante's *Divine Comedy* (1308–20). In this larger historical context, Christian Europeans and Muslim Arabs are perhaps destined for a renewed formation of the Mediterranean civilisation. Al-e Ahmad was too close to the colonial conditioning of 'Islam and the West' to see this coming. But his manner of thinking can and should be revived to meet it.

The pluralistic and syncretic disposition of successive Muslim empires were paradoxically compromised in the course of Muslim encounters with European imperialism. It is now a rather strange historical destiny that perhaps also in Europe Sunnis and Shi'is will overcome their manufactured sectarian opposition to conceptualise a different cosmopolitan setting for themselves in conversation with their European interlocutors – thereby all such designations are critically overcome. The fact that in Iran there are Arab Shi'is as well as Iranian Sunnis points to a fundamental fact of post-colonial nation-building, which here I wish to mark and demarcate by way of pointing to a vision of the very idea of *the nation* far beyond its colonial limitations and postcolonial cul-de-sac.[9] People in Iran, the Arab world and the larger Muslim world are going through world historic changes with vital consequences. It is imperative for scholars and critical thinkers not to fall into a trap of religious sectarianism or ethnic nationalism that will in fact exacerbate the condition of coloniality by which we address this issue rather than overcoming it. Intellectual historians in particular should be aware of not assimilating figures like Al-e Ahmad forward to events happening after they had departed this world. The fact that the very 'West' at the root of his *Westoxication* has now become a location for a renewed reading of Islam means Muslims should cast a critical glance at his entire legacy – precisely in order to read him more fruitfully.

The collapse of the metaphor of 'the West' foretells the destruction of all its contingent conceptual categories – particularly Sunnis versus Shi'as, or Iranians versus Arabs. There is no better way to break the colonially manufactured binaries between Sunnis (Arabs) and Shi'as (Iranians) as mortal enemies than to reverse the proposition and think through the fact of Arab Shi'as and Iranian Sunnis. Dismantling such false binaries, the enduring legacy of the colonial dictum of *divide and rule*, is the crucial first step to thinking towards a post-Islamist liberation theology.

The mechanical solidarity that today is falsely assumed among all the Shi'as or all the Sunnis is sharply contested by the organic solidarity that nations (classed, gendered and racialised) forge by virtue of their sustained history of struggle against both domestic tyranny and colonial domination over the last three centuries. The rise of sectarian politics and ethnic nationalism which the whole category of Arab Shi'as or Sunni Iranians challenges is a sign of the fundamental failure of the nation-building project in a manner that secures the democratic rights for all its citizens in a democracy and protects them against colonial conquest and imperial domination. The same is true of an equally mechanical solidarity if it were to be assumed among all Arab nationals in multiple social contexts – particularly at a time in the late 2010s when Saudi Arabia, the richest Arab state, led a coalition of other Arab states against the poorest Arab nation, Yemen, pushing to the edges of genocide. Both postcolonial Arab nationalism and Arab nation-building projects and their constitutional formation of citizenship rights are today in pieces, scattered from one end of the Arab world to another precisely for having failed to overcome the periodic upsurgence of tribal, sectarian, gender, ethnic and class warfare within such nations. The chronic upsurgence of Sunni–Shi'i sectarianism and Persian–Arab ethnic bourgeois nationalisms as vacuous but dangerous political rhetoric are among the clearest indications of the fundamental failure of both Arab and Iranian nation-building projects on the received postcolonial models of the nation-state, where the most basic human rights and civil liberties are abandoned to be abused by the ideological forces pushing the US imperial and Israeli colonial projects in the region.[10] All these political pressures on the collective faith of Muslims of course have dire theological consequences that have hitherto been pushed under the radar.

It is now a common historical fallacy to trace the origin of this calamitous and abusive reading of Islamic history to the Ottoman–Safavid rivalries in the sixteenth century. Both the Ottomans and the Safavids, and to them one must add the Mughals in India for a more complete and correct picture, had deeply and pervasively cosmopolitan cultures in which Turkish, Arab, Iranian, Indian, Christian, Muslim, Jewish and many other communities lived and traded in commercial and cultural domains entirely traversing any ethnic or sectarian demarcations. Safavid Iran was the site for the rise of one of the most magnificent phases in Islamic philosophy, theology, mysticism, science, art, architecture and technology, the overwhelming majority of which was in fact performed in Arabic and not in Persian. There are more books in these fields produced in Arabic in Isfahan than in Baghdad, Damascus and Cairo from this time put together. This fact raises other crucial questions: who and what is an Arab – and who and what is a Persian? Are 'Arab' and 'Arabic', or 'Iranian' and 'Persian', ethnic and racial designations or linguistic and cultural markers? How can any Arab or Iranian intellectual or critical thinker dismiss the entirety of the Arabic intellectual spectrum simply because it was active in Isfahan and not in Baghdad, Damascus, Jerusalem, or Cairo, or conversely ignore the fact that much of the intellectual history of Iranians is found in Arabic?

The overwhelming evidence of these historical facts is at the root of lifting critical thinkers like Jalal Al-e Ahmad out of their sectarian pigeonholes and placing them at the epicentre of rethinking Islamic intellectual history and post-Islamist liberation theology.

False Binaries

In order to reach out for a legitimate post-Islamist liberation theology we must first overcome false binaries dividing to rule the Muslim world – and at the same time see in what entirely un-self-conscious ways critical thinkers like Al-e Ahmad have effectively trespassed such entrapments. The fact is that the manufactured binaries of 'Arab and Persian' as well as 'Sunni and Shi'a' are far more deeply interrelated and intersubjective than the fictive ethnic nationalism and sectarian hostilities on both sides are able to see. The lived experiences, collective fate and common memories of adjacent nations must be categorically severed from and set against the political machinations of their states and the insidious working of flawed ethnic nationalism of one sort or another to be able to breathe in a much healthier and more accurate social and intellectual environment. It is imperative to remember that the formation of the Safavid Empire (which is today trumpeted as a turning point of the political history of Shi'ism in the region) was in fact not the first instance of a Shi'i dynasty in history to abuse its legacy to mark a fictional divide between Arabs and Iranians. The formation of the Idrisids (780–985), the Fatimids (909–1171), the Rassids (893–970), the Qarmatians (900–1073), the Hamdanids (890–1004) and the Marwanids (990–1085), all in the heart of the Arab world, plus numerous other dynasties in India, all predate the formation of the Safavids in Iran. This historically flawed fixation on the Safavids even among Arab scholars and intellectuals is an astonishing sign of the success of the dominant political rhetoric of their ruling regimes. Even

Al-e Ahmad himself, when he wrote the first part of his travelogue to Israel, momentarily fell into this trap of a racist nationalism, before in the second part presumably correcting himself. Overcoming this false fixation is the first step towards decolonising our reading of Islamic history.

As for the specific case of the presumed Sunni–Shi'i divide or their sectarian hostility, this has been an almost entirely colonially exacerbated division that continues to plague the postcolonial nations. As I have argued and extensively demonstrated in my work elsewhere, Shi'ism has never been merely a sect, nor has Sunnism acted a hostile majority tormenting their own Muslim brothers and sisters. Sunnism and Shi'ism are two complementary readings of the Prophet's charismatic legacy: while what later emerged as Sunnism is generally the attempt to routinise and institutionalise the Prophet's charismatic authority, what later became known as Shi'ism was an attempt to preserve and perpetuate that charismatic authority into the lineage of his daughter's male descendants. What today we call Sunnism and Shi'ism are in effect two complementary spirits within the self-same normative, moral and imaginative body of Islam. Without seeing these two faces of Islam, its prophetic countenance will never become visible.

There has never been a Shi'i community devoid of institution-building proclivities of the Sunnis, nor has there ever been a Sunni community devoid of the Shi'i propensity to follow charismatic leaders in the spirit of their beloved Prophet. Sunnism and Shi'ism are therefore two organically linked readings of Muhammad's prophetic mission. The collapse of that fact of the doctrinal history of Sunnism and Shi'ism into sectarian hostility between two groups of Muslims has been almost entirely under colonial duress, which today retrograde, counterrevolutionary ruling regimes foment and exacerbate out of their identical fears of the liberating political language of the Arab revolutions picking up where the Iranian revolution of 1977–9 left off. Forgetting that fact, reducing the Iranian revolution of 1977–9 to its triumphalist clerical force, and considering the Arab revolutions as the cause of, and not the remedy for, such sectarianism is the most catastrophic misreading of history and a complete collapse into the political machinations of the ruling potentates in both Sunni- and Shi'i-majority countries – Saudi Arabi and Iran in particular. Actively remembering the cosmopolitan worldliness of Al-e Ahmad's world is one potent reason for me to have written this book.

It is in the aftermath of the fateful encounter with European colonialism and the eventual fragmentation of the three Muslim empires (the Ottomans, the Safavids and the Mughals) that the false fabrication of sectarian and ethnic boundaries began to foreground the calamitous conditions for the postcolonial formation of the nation-state. The postcolonial partition of India and the formation of Pakistan in 1947 and the establishment of the settler colony of Israel in 1948 are the hallmarks of two deeply sectarian state formations – an Islamic Republic and a Jewish state – that paved the way for the future sectarian strife in the region. Arab nations have been Sunni and Shi'a, as well as Christian, Jewish and agnostic, as have Iran, Turkey and India, among many other postcolonial national formations. There is nothing unusual or strange about that fact. These postcolonial nations still carry the social insignia of their last imperial pedigree in Ottoman, Safavid and Mughal territories. In figures like Al-e Ahmad (or Mohammad Iqbal from Pakistan before him or Nasr Hamed Abu Zaid from Egypt after him) we could still see the worldly confidence of Muslims remembering the height of their intellectual achievements at the depth of their colonial predicaments.

Might the fact of Arab Shi'as in Iran and elsewhere point to the proposition of Arab Shi'ism as a distinct phenomenon from Safavid Shi'ism? This is a highly dubious form of ethno-epistemology of Shi'ism that does not quite gel with either history or doctrine. The Safavids were a Turkic-Kurdish Sufi order that traced (falsely or correctly) their origin to the earliest Shi'a Imams. Under their reign, Iran became inhospitable to Persian literary humanism and a haven for Arab Shi'a scholars from Syria and Lebanon who could not even speak Persian. Under the Safavid rule Isfahan became a haven for Arab and Iranian Shi'a scholars, jurists, theologians, philosophers and mystics, as Iranian poets and literati migrated en masse to India which was far more welcoming to them. The constitution of a fictive 'Arab Shi'ism' cross-essentialises an equally fictive 'Safavid Shi'ism' and glosses over its internal dynamics and paradoxes, and thus neglects that the formation of a massive philosophical movement as 'the School of Isfahan' crosses over all such fictive binaries. Consider the fact that the leading Shi'i philosophers of the Safavid period – Mir Damad, Mir Fendereski, Shaykh Baha'i, Mohsen Faiz Kashani and above all Mulla Sadra – wrote the overwhelming majority of their work in Arabic, and not in Persian or Turkish. So how could this chimeric construction called 'Safavid Shi'ism' be in contradistinction to 'Arab Shi'ism' when its leading intellectual cadre were either Arab or wrote in Arabic? The constitution of Arab versus Safavid Shi'ism reproduces a nasty gestation of both the Sunni–Shi'a binary in conjunction with Arab–Iranian dualism and creates a master binary that in effect manufactures an ethno-epistemology to fit the current and dominant political bifurcations of the geopolitics of the region. Read two pages of Al-e Ahmad and you see the rich diversity of his cosmopolitan worldliness, dispelling any such false binaries.

The fact and phenomenon of postcolonial nations are not predicated on a single but in fact on multiple and plural identities, or even more accurately on a fusion of identities and alterities, a web of 'group affiliations' as Georg Simmel considered it.[11] Today that pluralist disposition of characters and cultures are threatened by the fearful phantasm of a dangerously atomised and one-dimensional person. In his classic book *One-Dimensional Man* (1964), Herbert Marcuse diagnosed the formation of a flattened and hapless persona that, consumed by the false needs of a late-capitalist society, is deprived of its own multi-dimensionalities. This person is robbed of critical thought and oppositional defiance that are contingent on the full recognition of humanity as the crosscurrent of multiple identities and alterities. It is the failure of the postcolonial nation-state in both Arab and Iranian (and in fact the larger postcolonial) contexts that their ideas of 'the nation' are falsely presumed to be deprived of such multi-dimensionalities. While Marcuse diagnosed the conditions of one-dimensionality at the heart of capitalist modernity, its colonial and postcolonial consequences are no less dire. When occasionally we come across a critical thinker like Al-e Ahmad who has consistently defied this postcolonial fate of one-dimensionality, we must seize upon that occasion and discover, as I hope I have in this book, what it was and how it remains possible.

From this vantage point we need to reconsider the entire social assignation of 'minorities' to ethnicised communities of Arab, Kurd, Azeri, Baluch, Lors or Turkmens, for their actual combination becomes the majority of postcolonial nations dismantling the racialised fiction of a 'Persian' or any other majority. Iranian Arabs are the proud inheritors of two cultural heritages, both Arab and Iranian. They speak Arabic and Persian with the ambidextrous joy and fluency of any other multicultural person thriving on more than one side of their characters and cultures. They are the living testimony of the fact that the divisive machinations of state prejudices have nothing to do with the rich heritage people inherit and inhabit. The lingering Islamist discourse of one-dimensional fanaticism fails them all – Arabs, Persians or otherwise.

Today the rise of sectarian and ethnic nationalism are decidedly counter-revolutionary mobilisations, extending the colonial logic of *divide and rule* into the domain of the US globalised empire, aided and abetted by retrograde Arab and Iranian regimes rightly fearful of the revolutionary potentials of these nations threatening their unjust and tyrannical regimes. Under these circumstances the task is not to corroborate these reactionary conceptualisations but in fact to historicise, analyse, theorise and therefore dismantle them towards liberating new horizons. In a predominately Islamic context, this liberation can also assume, though not exclusively, theological dimensions. Al-e Ahmad was neither a disciplined clergyman, nor an Islamophobic secular. He lived and thought through an existential livelihood of how to be a Muslim in the world.

On Parallax and Paradox

The manufactured binary between the Arab and the Persian, like that between the Sunni and the Shi'a, remains the most potent political force pre-empting the realisation of a post-Islamist liberation theology beyond such false premises. Today this debilitating binary is definitive of the Islamist militancy as best evidenced in the rise of the hateful counterrevolutionary gangs known as ISIS. This Islamism, as I have always emphasised, is the poisonous legacy of European cultural colonialism. If we are to reach for a post-Islamist liberation theology we must overcome this false binary between Sunnis and Shi'as, or between Arabs and Persians, which is a subterfuge for the overriding binary sustained between 'Islam and the West', an internalised and domesticated version of 'Islam and the West', whereby self-hatred has replaced a critical encounter with the ravages of European colonial modernity.

In his *Define and Rule: Native as Political Identity* (2012) Mahmood Mamdani uses the example of Sudan in order to draw attention to how during the nineteenth century a crisis of imperial domination initiated a significant change in British colonial statecraft, which in turn resulted in the introduction of a novel idea of governance through the articulation and administrative management of difference. Definitive for this politics of domination was the exacerbation of tribal differences, not just between the coloniser and the colonised but even more importantly among the colonised themselves. Rewarded by means of access to land and political power, this aggressive colonial tribalisation eventually emerged as the language of pluralism and difference. In an earlier study, *Castes of Mind: Colonialism and the Making of Modern India* (2001), Nicholas Dirks had also examined how in India the idea of 'caste' was used and abused in order to facilitate the British colonial domination. It is impossible to separate the history of European colonialism around the globe from its catalytic impact on the most innate aspects of the cultures they dominated. The racialised manufacturing of the 'Arab–Persian', or 'Sunni–Shi'i' divides in no uncertain terms is also the result of the same colonial legacy, except, through a classic case of Foucauldian governmentality, today's Arabs and Iranians, as well as Sunnis and Shi'is have become the carriers of these colonial traces in their political culture and critical judgements.

The question of Arab Shi'a and their relationship to citizenship and identity is today, in the aftermath of the US-led invasion of Iraq in March 2003 and subsequent occurrence of Arab revolutions in 2011, at the heart of a vastly transformative period in Arab and Islamic history. The position of Iranian Arab Shi'a is a perfect case study of the pluralistic political consciousness formed in the aftermath of exposure to colonial modernity conditioned by the onslaught of the European imperial adventurism and US military domination of the Islamic world. The postcolonial formation of the nation-state in much of this world has glossed over many subnational and transnational identities. It is imperative not exclusively to privilege the sectarian consciousness and place it adjacent to other equally critical divides along racialised, classed and gendered politics. The periodic upsurgence of sectarian politics in the Arab world – whether along Sunni–Shi'i, Muslim–Christian, Muslim–Jewish, Muslim–Hindu, religious–secular, or traditional–modern divides – must be examined along two parallax trajectories that enable a paradoxical understanding of the postcolonial syndrome of the nation-state. The case of Arab Shi'a in Iran shows how that parallax in effect enriches the national consciousness by a paradoxical dialectic between a *Gemeinschaft* and *Gesellschaft*. These interplay in the formation of an organic identity, always predicated on a transformative alterity. In much of his travel narratives inside and outside his homeland, Al-e Ahmad consistently traversed and brought together these bifurcations between *Gemeinschaft* and *Gesellschaft*, and thus crafted a tertiary space where the postcolonial subject was made creatively possible.

In an essay in the *Wall Street Journal*, a major institution of US imperial dispensations of the globalised capital, we read how 'Arab Shiites Are Caught in Iranian-Saudi Strife'.[12] The leading argument of this piece is how 'the interests and political outlook of many Shiite communities diverge from Iran's in crucial ways'. The piece first points out that:

> Stuck in the regional struggle between Saudi Arabia and Iran, the Shiite communities of the Arab world are often depicted – particularly in the Arab media – as little more than pawns of the Iranian theocracy. In reality, the interests of many of these Arab Shiites, their political outlook and even religious beliefs have long diverged from Iran's in many crucial aspects. Some of these Shiites, in fact, see little difference between Saudi Arabia and Iran, the two powers in whose battle for supremacy they are caught.[13]

Citing a Shiʻi Bahraini political activist (who was sentenced to a long prison term in absentia and had his Bahraini citizenship revoked for his role in the 2011 uprising against the Shiʻi-majority country's Sunni rulers), the piece further states:

> These two regimes are fighting, and I will not accept to be pulled into this fight in which they are using my identity and my sect to serve their own goals. I have my own goal: I want to be treated as a human in my country and in my region.

This act of defiance is done neither because or in spite of being a Shiʻa. The political staging of the revolutionary mobilisation against the ruling regime trumps any sectarian politics. But this decidedly post-Islamist revolutionary positioning still lacks any conscious theoretical or theological articulation.

The divisive issue of *Velayat-e Faqih*, the authority of the Jurist, and the fact that Shiʻis have the privilege of choosing alternative *Marjaʼ-e Taqlid*, or the source of exemplary conduct, closer to their own political beliefs, does not overwhelm other factors that are cited in this piece:

'The Shiites have always been diverse in their traditions, and this continues to be the case', said Seyed Ali Fadlullah, a leading Shiite cleric in Lebanon. 'Iran, as a state, seeks to solidify the leadership of *wilayat al faqih*. But *wilayat al faqih* is not endorsed by the majority of other *marja'a*s, not even within Iran and Iraq.'[14]

The increasing persecution of Shi'i communities in the Persian Gulf region and Saudi Arabia and the rise of Daesh (ISIS), have increased strategic alliances so that today 'most of these militias are under de facto Iranian control, thanks to funding and weapons supplied by Iran's Revolutionary Guards Corps. They are making their ideological allegiances clear by painting portraits of Mr. Khamenei on their banners and tanks.' The article warns that: 'Sectarian tensions that are reaching new heights in the Arab world may push its Shiite communities even further into Iran's embrace – long a strategic objective of the Iranian regime.'[15] Such pieces are quite typical of the manner

Figure 9.1 Al-e Ahmad on one of his legendary travels around Iran. Date unknown. (Photo courtesy of Ali Dehbashi, from the *Bokhara Magazine* archive) A restless soul, the more Al-e Ahmad travelled, wrote, published and did all of that all over again, the less he was satisfied. What was he looking for? Perhaps the soul of a soulless world, perhaps the place of his own people in the furious gathering of other nations.

in which the 'sectarian conflicts' throughout the Arab and Muslim world are portrayed and analysed. They are, however, fundamentally flawed and as such conceal a far more serious issue. How are we to imagine a Muslim world beyond its Islamist phase, beyond such obviated journalistic platitudes – not to ignore the facts to which they indeed allude but to read those facts with more liberating prose?

Flawed Categories

Such conceptual failures and categorical confusions are not limited to the dominant journalism of this sort and extend into the critical thinking of many Arab and Muslim scholars. The questions of social integration and identity formation in contemporary Arab and Muslim societies, and the related issues of the manufacturing of sectarian and ethnic minorities during the nation-building projects, are the enduring issues lingering from the earlier colonial encounters with European political modernity. Between colonial modernity and reactionary traditionalism there has always been a wide and widening space scarce considered. If we are to reach beyond the colonial consequences of that European modernity, and perforce the reactionary traditions it has caused to be cross-invented, the Muslim character and culture of the inhabitants of that future will need renewed hermeneutics.

Today the violent and divisive rise of sub-national, crypto-national or pre-national forms of identity-consciousness is a clear indication of the failure of postcolonial nation-building projects. While the US-led invasion and occupation of Afghanistan in 2001 and Iraq in 2003 might be considered a turning point in forcing the enduring formation of bona fide nation-states into divisive ethnic and sectarian constituent forces, the rise of the Green Movement in Iran in 2009 and the Arab Revolutions in 2011 mark precisely the opposite force of building on the shared memories of anticolonial and anti-tyrannical struggles towards a renewed and organic reconceptualisation of nations beyond the vagaries of the states that lay false claims on them.[16] It is factually and theoretically incorrect to think these two events – the US military interventions in the region and the rise of the revolutionary momentum in the Arab and Islamic world – as identically responsible for the rise of sectarian consciousness and violence in the region. They are in fact diametrically opposed. The US-led invasions occasioned and exacerbated such sectarianism, while the revolutionary mobilisations overcame them. The current counterrevolutionary mobilisations led by Iran and Saudi Arabia in fake hostility but effective collaboration with each other have renewed such shades of sectarianism – extending from Lebanon to Yemen.

The current rise of sectarian and ethnic consciousness in the Arab and Muslim world is a decidedly counterrevolutionary strategy systematically fomented and engineered by the ruling classes and against the very grain of the revolutionary momentum that has been brutally cracked down. Arab societies from Morocco to Syria down to Bahrain and Yemen were united around the emerging progressive ideas for their homeland during their revolutionary momentum and subsequently collapsed into sectarian and ethnicised consciousness by deliberate counterrevolutionary designs engineered by the ruling potentates endangered by these revolutions. The case of Iraq is quite important here, for it was denied the historic choice of joining the rest of the Arab world in defying the rule of Saddam Hussein's tyranny on its own terms and was instead subject to the US-led invasion and occupation, which then collapsed into sectarian and ethnic violence. The Arab revolutions placed the questions of citizenship, identity, integration and representative democracy at the heart of the new Arab consciousness, while both Saddam Hussein's tyranny and the US-led invasion deliberately destroyed any such liberating notions. In post-sectarian terms, as Muslims see through the fabricated hostilities of their ruling regimes, the question that faces them is a mode of post-Islamist liberation theology that will have exposed the fabricated nature of such sectarianism as it has abandoned 'the West' as the touchstone of any identity politics.

Arab Shi'is (whether located in Iran or any Arab country) relate to the wider political spheres in their home countries and their multifaceted Arab identities in no different ways than the Sunnis, Christians, Jews or self-proclaimed 'seculars' do. The fact of the political disenfranchisement of Shi'a communities in the Arab countries is not different from the Sunni, Christian or Jewish disenfranchisement in the same or in other countries. There is a fundamental failure of nation-building and the constitution of citizenship that underlie all such democratic deficits. The assumption of a regional or global Shi'i consciousness over and above all other factors is a decidedly retrograde, deceptive and misleading counterrevolutionary proposition. The

Shiʿas, Sunnis, Christians and Jews all rise to the occasion of a superior revolutionary consciousness when the historical moment arises. Both the ruling elite in Iran, and those in the Arab world who demonise Iran far more than it can actually influence the region, disregard and distort this fact. The Iranian revolution of 1977–9 was capable of exporting itself when it was a cosmopolitan proposition, and yet it ceased to have that appeal the instant Saddam Hussein's invasion of Iran turned it into a 'Persian' revolution, and the creation of the Sunni Taliban in Afghanistan turned it into a 'Shiʿi' revolution. The ruling Shiʿi clergy took full advantage of these adjacent developments to destroy its internal oppositions and turn the global appeal of the Iranian revolution to exactly its opposite: a model of reactionary politics. But Saddam Hussein's Arab nationalist anti-Persian rhetoric and the US–Pakistani–Saudi creation of the decidedly Sunni Taliban were equally instrumental in this degeneration of the Iranian revolutionary appeal. This early history of Iranian revolution is crucial to remember if we are to reach beyond its success and failure to fathom a post-Islamist theology.

The recent, entirely politically motivated, upsurgence of the Sunni–Shiʿa divide in the geopolitics of the region remains a deliberately manufactured rhetoric by the counterrevolutionary ruling elites of beleaguered states, and does not just disregard the theological foregrounding of various divisions within Islamic doctrinal history but in fact goes precisely against the very disposition of orthodoxy–heterodoxy dialectics in the lived historical experiences of Muslims. This dangerous development is not just against the very grain of Islamic intellectual history but by far the most successful triumph of the otherwise deeply shaken Arab and Iranian ruling elites that see their mutual survival in the incessant staging of the Sunni–Shiʿi divide. This counterrevolutionary mobilisation of a sectarian divide is the cornerstone of the survival of these postcolonial states beyond a shred of legitimacy at democratic representation.

Is there a 'Shiʿa Question?'

Dismantling this false consciousness of a Sunni–Shiʿa divide is of utmost significance here, if the constitution of a liberated postcolonial subject upon a healthy and robust transnational public sphere is to prepare the groundwork for a post-Islamist liberation theology. The very assumption of a 'Shiʿa

Question' is the enduring legacy of the failed project of postcolonial nation-state, a fact that must be read through the conflicting phases of revolutionary uprisings and counterrevolutionary mobilisation of one communal grouping or another. The rise of clerical Shi'ism in Iran or Wahhabism in Saudi Arabia and the rest of the Arab world must be read against the background of the rise of secular fanaticism of both Arab and Iranian 'secular modernism' projects that equally disenfranchised their own varied populations in Iran, Iraq, Syria or Palestine. The manufactured myth of a 'Shi'i crescent' has become a self-fulfilling prophecy, entirely negligent of the fact of not just intra-Shi'i dialectics of change and alterity, but of the varied national formations in the Arab and Muslim world that renders any assumption of a unified Shi'i position entirely untenable. Iran and Iraq, two ostensibly Shi'i countries, were engaged in a bloody eight-year war in which Shi'is were killing Shi'is under blatantly nationalistic rhetoric. Today the enduring support of the ruling Islamic Republic for the Palestinian cause, however politically motivated, is entirely contrary to any assumption of a Shi'i factor in the politics of this support. The reduction of nations to sects is as flawed as the expansion of sects to override nations. Within every current nation-state, Shi'i communities enjoy or suffer from varied degrees of integration, but the transnational forces of Arab nationalism or Third World socialism or militant Islamism are as important as the fact that the overriding history has forced the overcoming of even these factors towards a renewed national and transnational consciousness rather than a belated and retrograde resuscitation of sectarian identity politics. Without recognising this basic fact, the current sectarian trap will blind any further insight into the future of any post-Islamist theology.

It is imperative to remember the specific course of the 1979 Iranian revolution before the Shi'i Islamists violently and systemically appropriated it. It is flawed to think the course of this revolution alienated Shi'a Arabs from their home countries because they saw a Shi'i revolution in an Iranian homeland. The Iranian revolution of 1977–9 was widely popular among a whole slew of Arab and Muslim countries (Shi'a or non-Shi'a) by virtue of its multifaceted cosmopolitan character, in the making of which cosmopolitan character Al-e Ahmad was instrumental, and as such it was a very long time in the making – and therefore integral to the course of Third World revolutionary momentum.[17] The affinity of Mossaddegh's anticolonial nationalism with similar sentiments in the Arab and Muslim worlds, the structural link between Iranian guerrilla movements, and the armed struggle in the Palestinian national liberation movement are the prime examples and clear indications that the full body of the Iranian revolutionary momentum was deeply rooted in similar political forces as in the Arab and Muslim world. Presuming that the triumphalist component of the revolution, its Islamist Shi'ism, alienated Arab Shi'i communities, is to confuse it with the full-bodied disposition of the revolution. From Nehru's India to Mossaddegh's Iran to Nasser's Egypt to Houari Boumediene's Algeria to Kwame Nkrumah's Ghana to Fidel Castro's Cuba, we must remember that the vast and widely rooted global vision of anti-imperialism was anything but sectarian or ethnically national-ist in its revolutionary articulations. The cosmopolitan disposition of that revolution before its sectarian degeneration must be actively remembered as we imagine a post-Islamist future.

The failure of the postcolonial Arab and Iranian nation-states to over-come the subnational and/or transnational denominational affinities is in the nature of the colonial experience that left pan-Arabism (or pan-Persianism, pan-Turkism, etc.) critically unexamined, in fact exacerbating its problems instead of resolving them. Such ahistorical ethnic nationalism must begin by critically dismantling itself, incorporating non-Arab (from Kurdish to Amazigh) and intra-Arab (Jewish, Christian, Sunnis, Shi'is, Yazidis) elements and forces and expanding itself to the wider Muslim world (including Turkey, Iran, Central and South Asia) in order to overcome its colonial heritage of ethnicised bourgeois nationalism. It is this ahistorical, fetishised, absolutist metaphysics of Arabism, Arab nation, Arab nationalism (with its equally flawed counterparts in Persianism or Turkism) that is in fact the principal root of the problem and certainly not its solution. The wounded pride of Arab nations, the continued colonial thievery of Palestine, the fundamental failure of Arab nationalism to form enduring institutions of civil liberties and democratic principles might be considered chief among the reasons why this fetishised fixation with 'the Arab nation' continues to confuse the nature of the problem. The rise of such movements as the Sunni Muslim Brotherhood or Shi'i Dawa Party in Iraq must be seen also in the light of the ruling colo-nial conceptualisation of 'the secular' that has systematically disenfranchised certain subnational communities from political participation.

The mis-identification and re-definition of the Alawites in Syria or the Houthis in Yemen and their flawed mixture with the Twelver-Imami Shi'ism dominant in Iran is as much a success of the ruling rhetoric of the beleaguered states in the Arab world as it is attributable to the failure of Arab bourgeois nationalism to incorporate disenfranchised communities within its sphere of ideological influence. Precisely the same is true of Persian bourgeois and Turkish bourgeois nationalism – with Kurdish bourgeois nationalism as its primary victim. Today alas there seems to be an unfortunate fusion of the dominant counterrevolutionary rhetoric of the tyrannical Arab and Iranian regimes, the wounded pride of ethnic bourgeois nationalism, and the dominant ideologies informing a whole generation of flawed scholarship. It is easy to blame the ruling Islamic republic for problems domestic to the Arab world. The ruling elite in Iran certainly takes advantage of any possibility to become a more powerful regional player. But that political blame game will not address the enduring structural issues within both Iran and the Arab world. That emancipatory possibility requires a whole different language – the language of a liberated postcolonial agency.

To end this dangerous disease of sectarianism in the region and pave the way towards a renewed articulation of being a Muslim in the world, we need not just vigorous works of scholarship but also a serious reconsideration of the very concepts we choose. One cannot overcome dangerous sectarian trends by equally flawed ethnic nationalism or pan-Arabism, pan-Iranism or pan-Turkism. We must overcome this deadly colonial dictum of 'divide and rule' and begin to retrieve the lived experiences of nations beyond such outdated, distorting, fanatical and misplaced ideologies. The founding myths of ethnic nationalism are no less treacherous and distorting than the founding myths of Islamist sectarianism. As the condition of coloniality shifts both between and within postcolonial nation-states, so too have the dividing lines between coloniser and colonised, the hegemon and the hegemonised, and this historic shift requires a radically different reading of nations and their narrations, sects and sectarianism, people and their worldliness and in this particular case Muslims and their post-Islamist theology.

Rehistoricising Islamic History

In my *Being a Muslim in the World* (2013) I have already argued for the imperative of bringing the worlds in which Muslims live to self-consciousness beyond the self-alienating encounter with European colonial modernity.[18] In the aftermath of that exhausted encounter I have proposed *alterity*, not *identity*, as the defining moment of being a Muslim in the world. In a similar way, the post-Islamist liberation theology I propose here must be rooted in actively rehistoricising Islamic history in a manner that will recreate the cosmopolitan condition that was coterminous with the rise of a public intellectual like Al-Ahmad, though this time on a post-national scale, where the Muslim *self* is itself a worldly proposition beyond the false national or sectarian consciousness. To reach for that space we must rehistoricise our presence in the world. To understand the presence of Arabs in Iranian territories, we must remember the imperial context of the rise of Islam, which preceded even the rise of Muslim communities in the seventh century. Arab tribes were integral to the superpower rivalries between the Romans and the Sassanids. The rise of Islam and the Arab conquest of the Sassanid Empire carried both Arabs and their culture and their new religion deep into Iranian domains. Persian language and culture were and have remained deeply rooted in both Arabic language and cultures as well as Islam. Iranian territories were integral to the two successive Arab empires of the Umayyads and the Abbasids. The subsequent rise of the Turkic empires from the Ghaznavids to the Seljuqids included Arab, Iranian, Turkic and many other communities. The Islamic world was later divided into three major empires, ranging from the Mughals in India, the Safavids in Iran and the Ottomans in Central Asia, Asia Minor and deep into Europe and North Africa. Internal social and intellectual diversities of Islamic world, that included but were not limited to the Sunni–Shi'i components of Islam, covered Arab and Iranians and other Muslims equally. In the aftermath of the European imperial domination and colonial conquests of the Muslim world from North Africa to India, the rise of anticolonial movements ultimately resulted in the formation of postcolonial nation-states on the ruins of these last Muslim empires. While dominant ideologies of pan-Arabism, pan-Iranism or pan-Turkism sought to carve the postcolonial nation-states along their ideological parameters many subnational communities continued to agitate such broad claims on nationhood.

The postcolonial persona at the centre of the Muslim self-consciousness must become fully cognisant of these historical moments. Like the rest of Islam, Shi'ism emerged in an almost exclusively Arab context. Both Islam and all its internal variations expanded exponentially by the subsequent imperial conquest of non-Arab lands by Arab armies, from the seventh to the tenth centuries. With the rise of the Turkish and Mongol empires of the Ghaznavids, the Seljuqids and the Ilkhanids, non-Arab elements in Islamic societies began to expand exponentially, until the rise of the Ottomans, the Safavids and the Mughals as the very last Muslim empires which were all comprised of non-Arabs of Turkish, Iranian and Indian origins. The clash between these last Muslim empires and European colonialism ultimately resulted in the eventual rise of varied nation-states and the rise of ethnicised bourgeois nationalism of the Arab, Iranian, Turkish or Indian denominations. It is upon the ruins of the former Muslim empires and the formation of the postcolonial nation-states that a racialised, ethnicised and sectarian set of parameters began to afflict the region. The very formation of such flawed categories as 'Arab Shi'a' or 'Persian Sunni', are the symptomatic epitome of such false identity politics – all of them the result of a colonial identity politics.

Consider the fact that the political and doctrinal origin of Shi'ism is almost exclusively in what today we call the Arab world. Shi'ism emerged in Arabia among the earliest supporters of the Prophet's cousin and son-in-law Ali ibn Abi Talib who was an Arab (not an Iranian – it is quite ridiculous today we need to remember and remind these simple facts), and the Prophet's cousin and son-in-law. The movement assumed renewed significance at the battle of Karbala (680 CE) that was fought between two Arab factions early in the Umayyad period and had nothing to do with anything Iranian or Persian. All the subsequent divisions within Shi'ism, to generate the Zaydi or the Isma'ili branches of the faith, were almost entirely domestic to Arab history and territory. By the time Isma'ilism reached deep into the heartland of the Seljuqids, the movement was articulated in specifically doctrinal and theological terms and had nothing to do with ethnic origins of any faction. The establishment of the Safavid dynasty in the sixteenth century that is today ahistorically and inaccurately marked as threshold of Iranian ascendency in Shi'ism was in fact almost entirely contingent on massive Arab intellectual and scholarly migration from Lebanon and greater Syria into Isfahan. Throughout the early and middle Safavid period Arab scholars immigrated to the Safavid heartlands and gave momentum to a colossal rise in its intellectual history, as masses of Iranian poets and Persian literati moved east to India. You look today at the extraordinary achievements of Muslim scholars in Isfahan in theology, philosophy, mysticism and law, the overwhelming majority of it performed in Arabic and not in Persian, and you wonder what exactly Arab or Arabic could mean here.

The constitution of 'Arab' as an ethnic designation shows itself to be an entirely colonial construct when you consider the fact that precisely the Safavid period is one of the most glorious episodes of Arabic writing in the intellectual history of Muslims – rivalling if not surpassing the golden age of the Abbasids. From Mulla Sadra's *Asfar al-Araba'* in the sixteenth century to Tabataba'i's *Tafsir al-Mizan* in the twentieth, all of these seminal texts were done in Arabic and not in Persian. Who is then an Arab, and what is Arabic? Can Arab social and intellectual history really divorce itself from this extraordinary segment of its history that is squarely in the social and intellectual milieu of the current boundaries of Iran? The reverse of this fact is also true. From the earliest Persian poets of the Ghaznavid period to the masters of Persian poetry Rumi and Sa'di, all were Sunnis, proud and practising. It is ludicrous, and simply a sign of ignorance, to try to separate the history of nations along colonially manufactured fault lines entirely inimical to Muslim intellectual history. All we have to do is to imagine the wider Muslim world before (and after) the self-centralising metaphor of 'Europe' or 'the West' as the centre of universe, a centrality without any geographical or cultural demarcations and based almost exclusively on an imaginative geography of power. In the liberated geography of that imagination the post-Islamist horizon of Muslim societies will see its emerging theology of liberation.

The Crisis of the Postcolonial Subject

Today the singular task facing Arab and non-Arab, Muslim and non-Muslim critical thinkers is to overcome the fictive colonial borders manufactured to divide people in order to rule them better, and to detect the subterranean

sources of solidarity that are always pushed under the radars of the beleaguered and illegitimate ruling regimes. The phenomenon of colonialism has
evolved but the condition of coloniality continues. And it is right here that
the enduring legacy of Jalal Al-e Ahmad presents itself: a bona fide public
intellectual of enduring power and relevance. Siding with the hegemony
of one ruling regime against another is the classic example of the treason of
intellectuals, as Al-e Ahmad would put it, failing to perform their historic
task of clearing the air of distorting subterfuges to serve the interest of one
tyrannical regime against another. The ruling regimes in much of the Arab
and Muslim world are now integral to the imperial machinery of neoliberal
economic domination that still heavily banks on such fictive divisions as
Sunni versus Shi'i, or Arab versus Iranian. It is delusional to think that Arab
and Iranian, or the Sunni and Shi'i working class, women struggling for
equality, the youth frightened for their future, the disenfranchised migrant
labourer roaming around the region in hostile environments in search of
work, are all innately hostile to one another by virtue of an inherited identity
politics fomented by those who rule over them. The empowering paradox of
Shi'a Arabs or Sunni Iranians is precisely in this defiant disposition of who
and what they are: both Arab and Iranian, both Sunni and Shi'i, confounding
both the ruling Arab and Iranian regimes and the scholars and intellectuals
who keep perpetuating these myths instead of dismantling them. The Shi'a
Arabs and Sunni Iranians posit the paradox of complementary consciousness
that by confusing their colonial divides confound the dominant regimes of
knowledge that seek to separate to rule them both better. Arab scholars and
critical thinkers must cross these fictive borders, decolonise their minds and
produce emancipatory knowledge about Iran. Iranian scholars must cross
the very same fictive borders, decolonise their minds and produce liberating
knowledge about the Arab World. We must turn the lemon of our colonisers'
dictum of 'divide and rule' into the lemonade of cross-identification.

It is imperative to see the evolving Arab or Iranian or in fact any other
national consciousness in conjunction with the transnational habitat that
nations share beyond their fictive colonial divides – and vice versa the unfolding drama of Arab revolutions are taking place on a transnational public
sphere that includes Iran and all other nations as diversified polities. Reducing
Iran to its ruling regime, or Arabs to their beleaguered and failed states, is a

clear sign of theoretical failure to come to terms with the overriding politics of change in the entire region. In this historically syncretic consciousness, the *communal* (*Gemeinschaft*) identity of being a Shi'a or a Sunni dissolves into the more *societal* (*Gesellschaft*) configuration of being a Muslim, before it fades out into an even larger regional cosmopolitanism that includes non-Muslims from India to Asia Minor. The formation of postcolonial citizenship is perforce national, while the organic identity formations have always been plural and working towards all the existing and emerging alterities. Here all manners of subnational or crypto-national consciousness operate within a larger organicity of cosmopolitan self-awareness. This awareness places a major responsibility on the part of scholars and critical thinkers whose scholarship and critical thinking will have to be geared towards a retrieval of the unresolved problematic of our vanishing presence. I have written this book on a major Muslim public intellectual precisely in that spirit.

Organic solidarity is formed by the dialectic of primary relationship in a *Gemeinschaft* (community) and a secondary relationship in a *Gesellschaft* (society). It is that dialectic that has failed to condense into an organic force sufficient to sustain a mode of societal modernity to form an agential political subject – full-bodied, self-conscious and historically informed. The fragmentation of that political subject has pre-empted the formation of a self-conscious historical agency with full citizenship rights on an organic public sphere. The systematic thinning-out and disappearance of that public sphere and public domain into the political is the single most catastrophic consequence of the condition of *coloniality* as *governmentality* in which the question of 'Arab Shi'a' or 'Iranian Sunni' announces itself. Dismantling that governmentality as coloniality is the beginning of the end of 'the West' as the talismanic code of what I have called coloniality beyond empire.[19]

Here whether we believe there is a difference between Arab Shi'ism and Safavid Shi'ism (Iranian Shi'ism) depends on what sort of a sociological conception of 'religion' we have: a Weberian or a Durkheimian, a conception of religion based on ethical doctrines and metaphysical principles (Weber) or based on a *conscience collective* (Durkheim), which would be subject to historical vicissitudes. Neither of these two ideal types alone are singularly valid or sufficient. A critical combination of both will lead us to a much more balanced and organic reading of religion. The assumption that Safavid

Shi'ism is what is operative today in Iran is fundamentally flawed for it disregards the crucial Afsharid and Qajar interludes and the subsequent colonial interventions (the Russians, the French and the British) that resulted in the current resurrection of the clerical power. Neither internal nor indeed external factors could be ignored in understanding how a world religion like Islam or any rendition of it changes its doctrinal and institutional (or even its symbolic) registers.

Within postcolonial nation-states, separatist tendencies – such as those of the Azeris, the Kurds, the Arabs, or the Baluchis in Iran – have historically been exacerbated by the nasty racialised politics of centralised state apparatuses. This has mostly been the result of the fundamental failure of the postcolonial projects to produce a bona fide nation-state with the integrated idea of the pluralistic nation integral to the legitimacy of the ruling states. The Kurds in Iraq, Syria, Iran and Turkey, the Copts in Egypt, the Shi'as in Bahrain, Yemen, Lebanon, or Saudi Arabia, or the Amazigh across an expanded domain in Maghreb are chief among sub-nationalised communities that reflect the intersection of postcolonial nations and imperial debris from which they have emerged. This phenomenon is not peculiar to Arab or Muslim countries. The Scots, the Welsh and the Irish in the UK, the African Americans in the US, the secessionist movement in Newfoundland and Labrador or in Quebec in Canada, the Flemish Movement in the Flanders region of Belgium, the Basques and Catalans in Spain, and many more cases, all reflect similar phenomena in Western European and North American contexts. Two competing narratives wage one history against the other: the centripetal narrative of state authority versus the centrifugal tendencies of peripheral communities to break away from the nation-state that has failed to incorporate them. Against this background, the aggressive hostilities being fomented between the Sunnis and the Shi'as are entirely fixed on the colonially manufactured model of the Protestant and Catholics in Ireland, Muslims and Hindus in India, or Jews, Christians and Muslims in Palestine. Dismantling the fear and fascination associated with the metaphor of 'Europe', the 'West' in Al-e Ahmad's 'Westoxication', we need to overcome the psychological barricades and epistemological subterfuges the illusion of 'the West' has crafted against the world.

From Divisive Sectarianism to Organic Solidarity

The fictive feud between Arabs and Iranians, or between Sunnis and Shi'is, is a ruse, a colonial legacy pushed forward and backward into history. It is also a sustained quagmire of colonial heritage disfiguring the history of our presence. To combat this fictive hostility endangering the Muslim world, it is imperative to remember how the US invasion of Iraq immediately broke it up into three sections because of the centralised tyranny of Saddam Hussein. As the Arab Spring unified Arabs from Iraq to Morocco towards their common destiny, counterrevolutionary forces in the ruling Arab families pulled them back to ethnicised nationalism and sectarian politics. Saddam Hussein's slaughter of the Kurds in the North, mass murder of the Shi'is in the south, and the expulsion of tens of thousands of Iraqi-Iranians, or Iranian-Iraqis, were all brutal and vicious signs of his and his predecessors' delusional Arabism. Counterrevolutionary forces in the Arab world pulled the revolutionary momentum back to those pre-revolutionary regimes of *divide and rule*. As many millions of Arabs cried for a liberated future, the ruling elite ganged up together, under US and Israeli patronage, to push the clock backwards.

Bordering states like Iran and Iraq are enriched and enabled, and are thus threatened and endangered, by the factual evidence of cultures and commerce crossing their fictive colonial frontiers. Navigational routes are far more accurate barometers of historical consciousness. My generation grew up in a geography that had Shat al-Arab pour into the Persian Gulf into the Arabian Sea into the Indian Ocean – long before the current cycle of bourgeois ethnic nationalism began to pit Arabs and Iranians or Sunnis and Shi's against each other. From India to Africa, the Arab and Iranian communities in these regions of the globe have interacted commercially and culturally for millennia, long before or long after their colonial encounters with European and now US imperial designs. It is the cosmopolitan fact of successive waves of labour migrations that cures the xenophobic nativism which has afflicted many Arab and Iranian thinkers and leaders alike.

A healthy and robust national consciousness today also requires a much closer attention to the details of gender, class and racial politics to overcome them in terms that cut through those colonial constructs and postcolonial persistence. Bringing all these factors and forces together, the rise of Arab revolutions of the 2010s has occasioned a fundamental reconsideration of what it is exactly that we call a 'revolution'. Do all the revolutionaries come in one form, shape, or politics? When did these revolutions start? When Mohamed Bouazizi committed suicide on 4 January 2011 what exactly happened in the Arab world? When did it end? When General Sisi staged a military coup on 3 July 2013 did something come to an end? Do revolutions begin and end so abruptly? Arab and Muslim societies are going through world historic changes – of that there can be little doubt. The rise of what is rightly and justly called 'the Arab Spring' was the inaugural moment of a *longue durée* historic transformation of an entire world. On one side of the equation was, and remains, masses of millions of peaceful human beings who poured into the streets and squares of their cities demanding their civil liberties and the dignity of a democratic space in their homeland – articulated in entirely non-sectarian terms. On the other side were mobilised a massive counterrevolutionary force that extended from the dominant superpowers of the region and beyond and retrograde Arab ruling families, enabling a terrorising sectarian language, resulting in a monstrous apparition that calls itself 'the Islamic State'. All their protestations aside, the ruling elites in Iran and Saudi Arabia are integral to this counterrevolutionary mobilisation.

The result of this fateful encounter on the surface has been the ascendency of a military junta in Egypt and retrograde sectarian tribalism elsewhere. But neither of these vacuous surfacings of violent takeover of the civic space – manifested in the kidnapping, torture, murder, or else even open execution of those even suspected of destabilising the ruling regimes – is any indication of the final victory of the counterrevolutionaries. The entire region is going through fundamental structural changes – an 'open-ended revolution' as I called it in my book on the Arab Spring. Arab civil societies at large are enriched by far more enduring ideals and aspirations. The art scene is experimenting with vastly more liberating sentiments. The Internet has facilitated the revolutionary opening of borders beyond any possibility of police states to control. The fictive frontiers of states are fading away by the open exchange of ideas that liberate the citizens of any country from their ruling regimes. The beleaguered and illegitimate states in the overwhelming majority of Arab and Muslim countries are simply incapable of controlling such massive structural changes among nations. All these dysfunctional states can do is stage fake elections, fight phony wars against each other, target 'terrorists' more or less terrorising than themselves, gather in gaudy conference halls, issue pompous, useless and silly proclamations, once a year go to the UN General Assembly, deliver ludicrous speeches and pretend they are in charge of the world they are delusional enough to think they are running. The task of both responsible citizenship and critical thinking at this stage is not to take cues from the propaganda machinery of these failed states and wonder about the particularities of sectarian or ethnic differences between Sunnis and Shi'as or Iranians and Arabs. There are none that are significant enough to derail the course of these revolutionary changes.

The enduring categories of the coloniser and the colonised, the West and the Westernised, have been intertwined since their very inception. Even in their most critical moments the colonised can and do think in colonial terms. The master–slave relationship is ostensibly over, but not in the realm of ideas when postcolonial subjects are the carriers of their own enslavement inside colonial epistemic categories. In the heydays of colonialism and postcolonialism these false terms of liberation were ingrained in the colonised mind of Arabs and Muslims and they survive to this day. We need to understand the nature of the decolonised mind and the subjected agency of liberation in terms surfacing in a new regime of knowledge – far beyond the false categories of 'tradition and modernity'. The condition of decolonisation of the mind has already been evident in the course of anticolonial struggles but mostly in art and literature – where that spectrum is a far more accurate barometer of mental and intellectual decolonisation. Feeble minds trapped inside the 'good for Orientals' mental cubicle are alternatively siding with pathological tyranny at home or with neoliberal imperialism abroad and thus cannot see the emerging horizons of liberation and fall into the sectarian or ethnic nationalist traps of their ruling metaphors and become instrumental to the dictum of 'divide and rule'. The fate of nations, however, has an entirely different path to liberation. Frantz Fanon's seminal argument that 'Europe is literally the creation of the Third World' remains true in more than one sense today – but, and here is the rub, the colonial has always been embedded in the operation of capital, and capital rooted within its colonial consequences. If so, then as the condition of coloniality shifts so do the dividing lines between the coloniser and the colonised, and this shift, as it happens, requires a reappraisal of our understanding of the dominant and received conceptions of nation and nationalism, of fear and loathing rampant in xenophobia, and above all for Muslims the manufactured sectarianism that has camouflaged our reading of these emerging worlds.

Transcendent Forces of a Theology of Post-Islamism

Having overcome the central metaphor of 'the West' and its divisive reflections inside its own sectarian and ethnic nationalisms, the idea of a post-Islamist liberation ideology must then see its liberation in conjunction with its other sister-religions: post-Zionist Judaism and post-Evangelical Christianity. On a recent occasion when in 2018 the Jewish high holiday of Yom Kippur and the Muslim (Shi'a in particular) celebration of Ashura coincided, I had occasion to reflect in an essay on what such coincidences could mean and signify.[20] Moving in the opposite direction of sectarian tendencies among Muslims, Jews or Christians, in this piece I articulated an ecumenical position that transcended their corrosive polarisations into militant ideologies. Instead, I proposed a mode of critical thinking in decidedly Judeo-Islamic terms. The similarities, correspondences and affinities of such aspects of Islam and Judaism I proposed in this essay would appear as strange or bizarre only to those who have fallen into the trap of falsely projecting the Zionist colonial adventurism in Palestine backwards onto history and positing an entrenched hostility between Jews and Muslims. This was and remains entirely ahistorical. Like Christianity, we know for a fact that Islam is deeply rooted in Judaism and has an even stronger proximity to its theological monotheism. This is not a matter of opinion or ideological position. It is a matter of historical fact. How we had come to forget that fact was precisely the point of remembering alternative histories.

Much of the confusion and conflation of Judaism and Zionism, I proposed in this short essay, and particularly the false and pernicious extension of the charge of anti-Semitism against Muslims, shares the same roots as this forced approximation of both Jewish and Islamic calendars to the Gregorian calendar, where Jews and Muslims are forced to see each other in Christian terms and would see it as strange if a Muslim and a Jewish holiday were to coincide. Zionism, I suggested, is the condition of Jewish alienation from

Judaism, precisely in the same way militant Islamism is the condition of self-alienation for Muslims. Both Zionism and Islamism are the twin products of European colonialism. Contrary to 'the Judeo-Christian' concoction (contested and contradicted by a long history of Christian anti-Semitism), the idea of Judeo-Islamic tradition is not based on any political or ideological project but evident in the most robust period of Jewish and Islamic philosophies that is unrivalled in any other tradition. The crucial task at hand is to remember, perhaps even revive that tradition.

It is crucial to keep in mind that as a European colonial project, Zionism was formed in a decidedly Christian context and its endemic anti-Semitism – most violently evident in the course of the Crusades, of endless pogroms and, ultimately, the Holocaust. But before and beyond the Zionist abuse of Judaism (similar to the Islamist abuse of Islam in Iran, Saudi Arabia, or Egypt and beyond, or similarly of the colonial abuse of Christianity by Evangelical triumphalism in the US and beyond, or elsewhere the fundamentalist abuse of Hinduism in India, or the nationalist abuse of Buddhism in Myanmar), there is an enduring and historically grounded proximity to the Judeo-Islamic heritage which started even before the Golden era of Andalusia, which is now used proverbially. From Saadia Gaon (882–942) to Yehuda Halevi (1075–1141) to Maimonides (1135–1204), the leading luminaries of Jewish philosophy were in enduring conversation with their Muslim counterparts – Avicenna (980–1037), Abu Hamid al-Ghazali (1058–1111) and Averroes (1126–98) in particular. This Judeo-Islamic philosophical tradition was real and not created out of any political convenience or necessity – and it is precisely that tradition that now needs to be revived and reclaimed.

In my essay I proposed three complementary ideological fanaticisms being chiefly responsible for the sustained bifurcation manufactured today between Islam and Judaism – all of them handmade by European colonialism, all of them invested in denying and dismissing the legacies of the Judeo-Islamic tradition. Militant Islamism, fanatical Zionism and Evangelical imperialism are the triangulated foregrounding of fear and fanaticism that has wreaked havoc in our world and systematically and consistently distorted the clarity of our historical visions. Wahhabism in Saudi Arabia, militant Shi'ism in Iran and Zionism in Israel are today the identical ideological by-products of European colonialism. In opposition to European colonialism, militant Islamism (both the Sunni and Shi'a versions of it) stripped Islamic intellectual history of its factual pluralistic and cosmopolitan character, reducing it to a singular site of resistance to European colonialism. In the same vein, Zionism, extending the racist logic of European colonialism into the heart of the Arab and Muslim world, stripped Judaism of its equally worldly moral imagination. Walking in the opposite direction of pestiferous sectarianism within Islamism, the task today is to reconnect Islam to its Jewish roots and neighbourhood.

Fanatical Islamism, settler colonial Zionism and imperial Evangelicalism are chiefly responsible for this manufactured rift between Judaism and Islam against the historical grain of their proximities – and precisely for that reason, any legitimate criticism of Zionism as a racist colonial project that spills over into a racist attack on Judaism and Jews is falling fast into the Zionist trap and by definition is anti-Semitic. Of course, what has historically exacerbated the mutual impacts of Islamism and Zionism is the course of Evangelical imperialism. This brand of Evangelical imperialism now actively presides over and exacerbates both militant Islamism and fanatical Zionism. Transcending them all and robbing them all of their identical fanaticism requires not reforming any one of these world religions but in fact restoring to them their precolonial worldliness.

I made sure to point out that the idea of a once much-closer proximity between Islam and Judaism than now does not mean there has not historically been a relation of power between the two communities. From its very inception, Islam has been definitive to multiple and successive world empires, in which (from the Umayyads and the Abbasids down to the Safavids and the Ottomans) Zoroastrian, Jewish and Christian communities have lived under Muslim rule. There could not have possibly been any equality between the ruling elite of these powerful Muslim empires and these small minorities in their domains. That in these dynastic and imperial Muslim contexts there have been Judeo-Islamic theological, philosophical and mystical traditions unrivalled anywhere else in the world is a testimony to the presence of potent intellectual thrusts among Muslim and Jewish saints and philosophers alike responding to the mighty heritage of the Greek philosophical tradition they appropriated and shared. My purpose has always been to revive an interest on that tradition for a future theology of liberation that Judaism and Christianity could share.

The fates of Jews and Muslims, and therefore of Judaism and Islam, as I have pointed out before, have been pitted against each other in the context of European colonial conquests, giving almost simultaneous birth to militant Zionism and triumphalist Islamism. My point at the time of writing that essay was simply to mark this bankruptcy. But the implications of this premise for a post-Islamist, post-Zionist and post-Evangelical triumphalism are even more crucial to note.

The task at hand, I concluded, is how to save Islam, Judaism and Christianity – as three world religions and concurrent frames for our moral imagination – from the claws of so many decades of epistemic abuse. The concurrence of Yom Kippur and Ashura in that September in 2018 was a gentle reminder of a much different history than the one mandated in Palestine and beyond by European colonialism. There is nothing wrong, I pointed out, with Muslims celebrating a Jewish holiday while commemorating their own most sacrosanct days. The recognition will in fact be liberating for both Muslims and Jews. There is nothing wrong with Jews looking at a Muslim holiday and seeing the distant mirror of their own ancient beliefs in the act. If either of those two sentences sounds odd today, we need to overcome both fanatical Zionism and militant Islamism, upend Evangelical imperialism, so we can remember and retrieve a history of the world now hidden under the heavy smokescreen of fanaticism, ignorance and greed. I would now even go further and suggest the rise of what they call 'New Atheism' is in fact precisely the manner in which the secular rendition of the self-same Euro-American imperialism has targeted Judaism, Islam and Christianity alike.

Post-Islamist theology, as I propose it here, must be not just post-Islamist, by way of transcending the degenerate sectarianism it has occasioned, but it should be equally conducive to overcoming post- Zionist and post-Evangelical triumphalism – by overcoming itself it overcomes all its others. It is therefore post-Western, meaning it begins by transcending its own fixation with 'the West', for Islamism has historically devoured Islam and re-cast Islam as mere resistance to 'the West', to 'Europe', the same way that Zionism has sought to devour Judaism and Evangelical triumphalism Christianity. In the face of European material and moral domination, Islamism robbed Islam of its dialectics of totality and infinity, of history and divinity, and thus turned it into an ideological resistance to 'the West', which it dehistoricised and fetishised into an absolute evil other, and it is now precisely in those terms that it is further degenerating Islam into militant sectarianism.

Because ('Western') Christianity actively lent itself to globalised capitalism colonising the world, including Muslim lands, Muslims also gave a helping hand by colonising themselves into Islamism. Islamism is self-colonisation of Islam the same way that Zionism is self-colonisation of Judaism, and Evangelical triumphalism the globalisation of the very logic of European imperialism. To salvage itself beyond the European imperial history, Christianity recast itself as imperial Evangelicalism – telling the colonised people to turn their other cheek. As the primary ideological target of Euro-American Evangelical triumphalism now best represented by the proto-fascist ideology of militant Evangelicals like former US presidential advisor Steve Bannon, Muslims should be integral to that post-Islamist, post-Zionist, post-Evangelical triumphalism. Christian liberation theology of Latin America can best offer a model for post-Islamist, post-Zionist and post-Evangelical liberation theology. In my *Islamic Liberation Theology: Resisting the Empire* (2008) I took the first step towards such a prospect, but now I am convinced it must be in conjunction with post-Zionist Jewish and post-Evangelical Christian liberation theology. Looked at together, militant Islamism, Jewish and Evangelical Zionism are all categorically triumphalist – fixated with one final victory at all costs. In my *Islamic Liberation Theology*, I have already argued how such a theology must be predicated on a *theodicy* that holds the face of the other as the site of its critical consciousness. I now propose steps towards the post-Islamist theology that must be integral to a post-Zionist Judaism and a post-Evangelical Christianity. It is in that sense that we will have all entered a post-secular world in which Al-e Ahmad would be the last Muslim and the first post-Islamist intellectual: the sole and solitary existential Muslim at the dawn of a renewed dispensation of Being-a-Muslim-in-the-World.

Notes

1. Jalal Al-e Ahmad, *Khasi dar Miqat* (*Dust in the Desert*) (Op. Cit.): 173. My own translation.
2. I first began to think of the prospects of this *post-Islamist liberation theology* when I was invited to deliver a keynote at Vienna Institute for International Dialogue and Cooperation on 15 October 2015 in Vienna, Austria. I am grateful to

Magda Seewald and her colleagues for their kind invitation to Vienna. I subsequently expanded my argument during a talk I delivered at Arab Centre for
Research and Policy Studies in Doha, Qatar, on 27–8 February 2016. I am
grateful to Haider Said for his very kind invitation and for graciously including me in his timely conference on Shi'ism in the Arab world. I borrow the
term 'post-Islamism' from the brilliant work of my friend and colleague Asef
Bayt. See his edited volume *Post-Islamism: The Changing Faces of Political Islam*
(Oxford: Oxford University Press, 2013). All of these threads, however, came
together when I began writing this book on Al-e Ahmad.
3. I have now expanded that central argument in T*he Emperor is Naked: On the
Inevitable Demise of the Nation State* (London: Zed, 2020).
4. See Ivan Krastev *After Europe* (Philadelphia, PA: University of Pennsylvania
Press, 2017): 3.
5. See Asef Bayat (ed.), *Post-Islamism: The Changing Faces of Political Islam* (Oxford:
Oxford University Press, 2013).
6. I have made this argument in detail in my *Europe and its Shadows: Coloniality
after Empire* (Op. Cit.).
7. See Hamid Dabashi: *Authority in Islam: From the Rise of the Prophet to the
Establishment of the Umayyads* (New Brunswick, NJ: Transaction, 1989).
8. In two books in particular: Hamid Dabashi, *Shi'ism: A Religion of Protest*
(Cambridge, MA: Harvard University Press, 2011), and Hamid Dabashi,
Islamic Liberation Theology: Resisting the Empire (London: Routledge, 2008).
9. I have recently explored this theme in two books, *Iran: The Rebirth of a Nation*
(New York: Palgrave, 2016); and *Iran Without Borders: Towards a Critique of the
Postcolonial Nation* (New York: Verso, 2016).
10. I have discussed this breakdown of the very idea of the Nation State in detail in
The Emperor is Naked: On the Inevitable Demise of the Nation State (Op. Cit.).
11. See Georg Simmel, *Conflict / The Web of Group Affiliations* (New York: Free
Press, 1964): 125 ff.
12. See Yaroslav Trofimov, 'Arab Shiites Are Caught in Iranian-Saudi Strife' available online here: http://www.wsj.com/article_email/arab-shiites-are-caught-in-ir
anian-saudi-strife-1452162602-lMyQjAxMTI2MjA5NzEwNzcwWj. Accessed
5 February 2016.
13. Ibid.
14. Ibid.
15. Ibid.
16. See my two books on these two seminal events: Hamid Dabashi, *Iran, The*

Green Movement and the USA The Fox and the Paradox (London: Zed, 2011), and Hamid Dabashi, *The Arab Spring: The End of Postcolonialism* (London: Zed, 2102).

17. I have argued this cosmopolitan and transnational space in which social revolution happens in my *Iran without Borders* (London and New York: Verso, 2016).
18. See Hamid Dabashi, *Being a Muslim in the World* (New York: Palgrave, 2013).
19. This is detailed in my recent book, *Europe and its Shadows: Coloniality after Empire* (Op. Cit.).
20. I published these reflections in my regular column at *Aljazeera*, 'Yom Kippur and Ashura: Are Muslims Observing a Jewish Holiday?' (available online here: https://www.aljazeera.com/indepth/opinion/yum-kippur-ashura-muslims-celebrating-jewish-holiday-180919123152458.html).

Index